The History of

Britain's Military Training Aircraft

Foulis
Haynes

The History of Britain's Military Training Aircraft

Ray Sturtivant

Preceding pages: North American Harvards of the Harvard Formation Team. (via Anthony Hutton)

ISBN 0 85429 579 8

A **Foulis** Aviation Book

First published 1987

Published by:
Haynes Publishing Group
Sparkford, Nr. Yeovil, Somerset
BA22 7JJ, England.

Haynes Publications Inc.
861 Lawrence Drive, Newbury Park,
California 91320, USA.

British Library Cataloguing in Publication data

Sturtivant, Ray.
The history of Britain's military training aircraft.
1. Training planes — Great Britain — History
2. Airplanes, Military — Great Britain — History
I. Title
623.74'62'0941 UG1242.T6
ISBN 0-85429-579-8

Library of Congress catalog card number 87-82239

Editor: Mansur Darlington
Page layout: Chris Hull
Printed in England by: J.H. Haynes & Co. Ltd

Contents

Introduction

Innumerable books have been written about operational aircraft which have served over the years with the Royal Air Force and the Fleet Air Arm. Some have dealt with a particular type of aircraft, others with a group of aircraft designed to fulfil a particular function, generally fighters or bombers. Very few authors however have attempted to devote a whole book to a particular training type, and none have seen fit to devote a full length volume to the subject of training aircraft in general.

This apparent lack of interest amongst authors and their publishers has sadly been reflected in official quarters. The Public Record Office, for instance, holds many thousands of aviation files deposited over the years by various ministries, and these include much useful material pertaining to the origins, construction and testing of RAF aircraft. Where these were operational types, whether prototypes or production aircraft, sufficient material has generally been retained to preserve a fairly complete story for posterity. Training aircraft, unfortunately, seem to have been considered to be of limited interest, with the result that most relevant files have long since been sent for destruction. Added to this, the disappearance of all the older names in the British aviation industry has led to a similar loss of relevant company records.

This lack of interest in trainers is certainly not reflected amongst the many hundreds of thousands who attend air shows every summer. The Gnats and Hawks flown over the last quarter of a century by the Red Arrows are just as much welcomed by the air-minded public as were their pre-war predecessors, the aerobatic Tutors of the Central Flying School. Displays at Old Warden and elsewhere evoke a lively interest in surviving examples of such types as the Avro 504, Tutor, Magister, Tiger Moth and Harvard. Such aircraft bring back especial nostalgia to the many thousands of airmen who trained on them in years gone by, as well as the thousands more who worked on them as ground crew.

It is not possible in one book to do justice in detail to every type of training aircraft ever flown by the RAF and the other services, nor to the many hundreds of training units with which they were flown. The first section of this book is therefore devoted to a general outline of the development of training in this country, whilst the second section concentrates on a representative selection of 22 training types from the many flown over the three-quarters of a century which have elapsed since British military aviation commenced. The selection is purely the author's own choice, and all except the Harvard, Chipmunk, Gazelle and Tucano are of British origin, the reasons for the inclusion of these four being readily apparent from the text. Appendices summarise the official Specifications issued in respect of requirements for trainers, production details of all training aircraft and the main units with which each type served.

The text for each aircraft explains how it came to be built and also outlines, where relevant, any politicial, technical or economic factors affecting its adoption and construction. Of equal, or perhaps greater, importance, is its actual operation once it went into service. Viewpoints have therefore been sought from a variety of people who were involved as students, instructors or ground crew. From these have emerged a very clear picture of whether it was successful or unsuccessful, loved or hated, tame or a potential killer. Such types as the Avro 504 and Tiger Moth were well loved in their day, whilst their Prentice successor was regarded as a bad joke and the Meteor Trainer was feared by many. More recently, the Jet Provost has served faithfully for thirty years, and is only now being replaced in a reversion to propeller-driven initial training aircraft.

Many people have given of their time to help produce a good cross-section of the subject. In this respect my special thanks are due to both Don March and WO Paddy Porter, MBE, without whose invaluable efforts I would have been unable to provide such a wide coverage of personal recollections by both aircrew and ground crew. Also to Mike Keep for his magnificent cockpit drawings, prepared to his usual high standard, often from surviving source material of indifferent quality.

Sincere thanks are also due to the many other people and organisations who have generously provided me with material, photographs or recollections. I am particularly grateful to those who have spared the time to either write or tape-record reminiscences, many of which have been very candid. These have helped me to build up a picture of training as seen through their own eyes at the time, and from a variety of viewpoints. Such credits are due to: Chris Ashworth; Aviation News; Cdr Peter Bagley, RN (Rtd); Rick Barker (Keeper, RAF Museum); Bill Bateman; Lt Louis Beardsworth, RN; Harold Bennett; Flt Lt Peter A. Bouch, RAF; Chaz Bowyer; Cecil Bristow; British

Aerospace PLC; Sqn Ldr D. Brittain, RAF; Robin Brown; Mick Burrow; Sqn Ldr L.W. Collingridge, RAF (Rtd); Rupert Cooling; Sqn Ldr Allan H. Corkett, RAF (Retd); Ernie Cromie; Major (QM) J.R. Cross, AAC; Geoff Cruickshank; Ralph Dargue; Kev Darling; Allan Deacon; Verdun Edwards; Cdr Neville L. Featherstone, RN; Mick Fowen; Nevil Gardner; Sqn Ldr Stan Greenhow, RAF (Rtd); Mark Hanna; Ray Hanna; WO Jim Henderson, RAF; WO (Phot) S.R. Hobden, RN; Gordon Hodkinson; Harry Holmes; Les Howard (late Air Historical Branch, MoD); Tony Hughes; Paul Jackson; Wing Cdr C.G. Jefford, RAF (Retd); Richard Keefe; Flt Lt Rod King, RAF; Gordon Kinsey; Bob Lea; Les Leetham; Stuart Leslie; Roger Lindsay; Len Lovell (Librarian, FAA Museum); Brian Lowe; Don March; Ian McCubbrey; James McNamara; Peter Middlebrook; Eric Morgan; Flight Sergeant Sam Mullen; Eric Myall; Sqn Ldr Michael J. Neil, RAF; John Norris; Brian Pickering (Military Aircraft Photographs); Lt Cdr Don Pugh, RN (Retd); Peter Raeburn; Bill Reeks; Wing Cdr Robert Sage, OBE, AFC, RAF (Rtd); Eric Sharp; Harold Shear; Short Brothers PLC; Sqn Ldr Barrie Simmonds, RAF; Sqn Ldr Dick Smerdon, RAF (Retd); Cyril Smith; Sqn Ldr Mike Sparrow, RAF (Retd); Mike Stroud; Flt Lt Andy Thomas, RAF; Cdr Maurice Tibby, RN (Retd); Pat Tilley; Tom Twist; Sqn Ldr D.W. Warne, RAF (Rtd); David Watkins; Bill Williams.

Ray Sturtivant
St. Albans

Chapter 1
Early Days

The Royal Flying Corps, forerunner of the Royal Air Force, came into official existence on 13 April 1912, following recommendation made by a sub-committee of the Committee of Imperial Defence, chaired by Lord Haldane. It was to comprise both a Military Wing and a Naval Wing, both of whose foundations had already been laid. This was hardly before time, however, as by then Britain was one of the few major powers not to have recognised the potential of the flying machine for war purposes.

The British Army, which had already built up a significant amount of experience in flying airships, balloons and kites, was slowly beginning to recognise the advantages which heavier-than-air flight might bring. Some flying had been carried out at Larkhill, on Salisbury Plain, as early as 1909, and the following year the War Office encouraged the British and Colonial Aeroplane Company (later the Bristol Aeroplane Company) to establish a depot and later a flying school there. During the Army manoeuvres of September 1910, two Army officers attempted to demonstrate the advantages of aerial reconnaissance, using Bristol-built Farman-type biplanes, but bad weather did nothing to further their cause, and commanding officers thought that the noise would frighten the horses. Captain Bertram Dickson, one of the two officers concerned, then left the Army to help set up the school, but soon afterwards he was involved in the world's first air collision, at Milan in early October 1910, after which he never flew again, regrettably dying three years later, probably as a result of his injuries.

Bristol Boxkite being prepared for flight by Captain Bertram Dickson during the British Army manoeuvres at Larkhill in September 1910.
(Bristol Aeroplane Co. Ltd)

Despite the relatively slight impact of aeroplanes on these manoeuvres, their appearance set in train a series of events which led to an Army Order for a new Air Battalion of the Royal Engineers to be formed on 1 April 1911 at Farnborough. This was to be based on the existing Balloon School there and commanded by

Major Sir Alexander Bannerman, RE, whose personnel were to comprise a total of 13 officers, 23 NCOs and 155 men, not to mention 32 draught horses.

In addition to its headquarters, the Battalion would consist of No 1 (Airship and Kite) Company, similarly based at Farnborough, and No 2 (Aeroplane) Company based at Larkhill. The latter was equipped initially with a motley collection of contemporary types, which included a Bleriot Monoplane, and Wright, Henri Farman, Paulhan, and de Havilland Biplanes, all housed in sheds on Durrington Down. There was no provision for the personnel, however, and these had to be accommodated in nearby Bulford Camp.

In good old Army fashion, requirements were drawn up for officers applying for transfer to this new organisation. They had to be medically fit with good eyesight, they must have the ability to read maps and make field sketches, and a knowledge of foreign languages was also considered necessary. Preference would be given to volunteers under 30 years of age who weighed less than 11 stone 7 lbs.

Meanwhile the Royal Navy, whilst spending enormous sums on new warships, was taking little or no interest in these new-fangled machines, and its first hesitant venture into this field was entirely the result of a public-spirited offer by a private individual. Francis McClean, an early and wealthy British aviator, and a member of the committee of the Royal Aero Club, did his flying from Eastchurch in the Isle of Sheppey, south of the Thames Estuary. He was planning to join a Government expedition to the Fiji Islands, to view an eclipse of the sun, and in November 1910 very generously offered to place his Short S.27 machine at the disposal of the Admiralty during his absence. His proposal, which had the full backing of the Royal Aero Club, would allow his machine to be used to give a six-month flying course to four naval officers. Despite minimal cost to the public exchequer, this kindness received a lukewarm response from their Lordships, but they eventually accepted.

The terms to be offered to the 200 volunteers who put down their names were far from generous, though less stringent than those laid down for their Army counterparts. They would receive full pay during six months leave of absence, but only single officers could qualify, and these would be required to pay their own RAeC fees. They also had to undertake never to fly on a Sunday. The official machinery was slow to get under way, however, and it was not until 1 March 1911 that the first trainees arrived at Eastchurch, these first stalwarts being Lieutenants C.R. Samson, A.M. Longmore, R. Gregory and E.L. Gerrard, the last-named being a

Bristol-Prier Monoplane at Larkhill.
(J.M. Bruce/G.S. Leslie collection)

The Bristol Flying School at Larkhill around 1911, with Bristol Monoplanes and Boxkites.
(Author's collection)

Marine officer. Technical instruction was to be provided by Horace Short at his nearby works for the sum of twenty pounds, and George Cockburn, another pioneer aviator, volunteered to be their flying instructor.

This civilian-inspired initiative laid the foundation of British naval aviation training, and indeed of the present day Fleet Air Arm. The four pupils worked hard, learning to fly on the flimsy but reliable pusher biplanes, which were a mass of wires and struts, and by May 1911 all had gained their Aviators Certificates from the RAeC. By mid-summer they had progressed to making increasingly lengthy cross-country trips with compasses, to practice their navigational abilities. On these trips they would often take as passengers fellow officers from ships anchored at nearly Sheerness, invaluable lessons being learned on both sides, as well as giving the opportunity to pass on their new-found enthusiasm.

Lt Samson, who had been the first to gain his Aviators Certificate, was also the first to undertake such a trip, from Eastchurch to Brooklands. Departing on 22 June at 5 pm, he landed at Salfords, near Horley, not far from what is now Gatwick Airport. After spending the night sleeping under the wing of his machine, he departed again after daybreak, only to lose his bearings. Landing to enquire his whereabouts, he found he was at Hawthorn Hill, near Windsor, and taking to the air again soon reached Brooklands to much admiration from the local enthusiasts. The machine had performed faultlessly throughout, and it was later flown back to Eastchurch by Lt Longmore, who by now had also gained his certificate.

The six-month instruction period expired at the end of August, but the Admiralty had given no real thought as to what would happen next. Matters might well have rested there, but Samson and Longmore had other ideas. They had no intention of allowing the results of all their efforts to be wasted, and after bringing much pressure to bear in appropriate quarters, they gained permission in October for a naval flying school to be set up at Eastchurch, equipped with two Short machines bought from McClean. They had a greater reward than this meagre contribution, however, as McClean then very generously lent several other machines, so that in addition to being able to train four further officers, sufficient aircraft would thus be available for Samson and Longmore to undertake various trials.

By now it was becoming recognised that some better form of organisation was required for the new services, and the outcome of official deliberations was a reorganisation effective from 13 April 1912. The Military Wing of a new Royal Flying Corps was to comprise three squadrons, based as before at

Farnborough and Larkhill, whilst the Naval Flying School, as Eastchurch had become two months earlier, would form the nucleus for the new Naval Wing. In practice the title Naval Wing was never popular and the term Royal Naval Air Service came to be adopted.

Bleriot Monoplane 'No 4' during military trials at Larkhill in 1912.

(RAF Museum photo No P00903)

Under the reorganisation, basic flying instruction was for the first time recognised as an official responsibility, and on the same date that the RFC was formed, a Central Flying School was ordered to be set up to provide basic training for officers of both wings. Based at Upavon, it would be relatively near to the remainder of existing Army aviation. A new aerodrome was to be built on a hilltop above the village, until then used as Army training gallops, with seemingly no thought being given to the difficulties this would provide for the trainee pilots when they attempted to battle with the consequent air turbulence. The necessary buildings were quickly completed, and on 19 June 1912 the school officially opened, the first course commencing on 15 August.

The first Commandant of the CFS was Captain Godfrey Paine, RN, who had only recently been appointed commanding officer of the Eastchurch school. He was given a bare fortnight in which to gain his flying brevet, and Longmore found himself with the task, which he successfully performed, of ensuring that Paine did so. Samson then took over command at Eastchurch, and promptly set about his new duties with his customary zest, enlarging the facilities and forming his command into what was to prove a real fighting force when war eventually broke out. In true naval fashion, the aerodrome was given a ship's name, becoming HMS Pembroke II in 1913, under the parentage of HMS Pembroke at Chatham.

Despite having a sailor in charge, however, the

CFS never managed to take over its intended responsibilities for naval training. Their Lordships regarded aeroplanes as an extension of their warships, and therefore to be used to help win sea battles, and in this they were wholeheartedly supported by their First Lord, Winston Churchill. They also objected to the arrangement whereby naval personnel in the RFC would be paid and administered by the Admiralty, who would then have only shared responsibility with the War Office. Not deigning to become involved in inter-service argument they simply continued to use Eastchurch, their pilots then being primarily sailors, trained in a naval atmosphere, and liable to general naval service.

It was recognised in setting up the CFS that the establishment of a service training school could have a detrimental effect on the many civilian schools around the country, and it was therefore decided that service officers or civilians who wished to take commissions in the Royal Flying Corps would first have to learn the rudiments at one of the civilian schools. Once having gained an RAeC certificate, they could apply for admission to the CFS, and if accepted would be awarded £75 to help recompense the cost of their private tuition. They would then undergo a four-month course of military tuition, during which they would not only be given more advanced flying lessons, but would learn how to maintain their aircraft and engines, in addition to being instructed in navigation, meteorology, photography and signalling.

The original plan was for 146 pupils to pass through the CFS each year, in three successive courses, comprising 91 military, 40 naval and 15 civilian pilots. Orders were placed for 25 aircraft, and these would bear identification numbers in the series 401 – 600, which would distinguish them from those of the Military Wing (201 – 400) and the Naval Wing (1 – 200). The first machines to bear these numbers were an assorted collection which included the Short School Biplane, Bristol Boxkite, Avro Type E and Maurice Farman Longhorn, these being later supplemented by such types as the Henri Farman F.20, Deperdussin Monoplane and early B.E. variants. The Deperdussins were soon withdrawn, however, after a Military Wing machine of this type broke up in the air on 6 September, followed four days later by a fairly similar mishap to a Bristol monoplane, leading to a ban on all monoplanes for military purposes, a decision which was not overturned until February 1913.

By mid-March 1913, the RFC had 123 pilots, though only 45 of these had passed all the CFS tests, and between them they had aggregated 1,550 flying hours, roughly half of this being at the CFS. By contrast, the Naval wing by the end of the May had 57 pilots, flying B.E., Bristol, Caudron, Farman, Short, Sopwith and

Vickers Type VI monoplane 'No 3' during military trials at Larkhill in 1912.

(J.M. Bruce/G.S. Leslie collection)

Royal Aircraft Factory B.E.2 prototype, flown by No 3 Squadron at Larkhill during 1912. *(J.M. Bruce/G.S. Leslie collection)*

Vickers biplanes, and Bleriot, Borel, Bristol, Deperdussin and Nieuport monoplanes.

One of the most significant events of that year, however, was at that stage quite unconnected with the military. This was the introduction of the Avro 504, which made its first public appearance at Hendon for the Aerial Derby of 20 September 1913. The straightforward and pleasing design of this tractor biplane, powered by an 80 hp Gnome rotary engine, attracted much attention, not least by the RFC. The potential for service purposes of this workmanlike

Top:
Avro Type E (later Type 500) No 406 with 50 hp Gnome engine, of the Central Flying School at Upavon around 1913.

(A.V. Roe and Co. Ltd)

Bottom:
Short S.27 Biplane used by the RNAS at Eastchurch. Horace and Eustace Short are in the foreground, and Cecil Grace in the cockpit.

(J.M. Bruce/G.S. Leslie collection)

machine was readily apparent, and within six months an order had been placed for 12 machines for the Military Wing, the first of many thousands to be built for service flying. The Naval Wing also took an interest, and soon afterwards placed an order for 50 of the 504B variant, with various modifications.

The first fatal crash at the CFS occurred on 3 October, when Major Merrick, landing at Upavon in perfect weather conditions, made a gliding approach from 300 ft at a rather steep angle. It was afterwards conjectured that he slipped forward on to the control column, pushing it forward, as the machine went into a dive and then into a bunt on to its back, throwing him out. A safety belt might have saved his life, but fear of fire prevented many of the pilots of the day from using the belts which were then available, even though some were of a quick-release type. A second fatality at Upavon took place on 19 March 1914, when Lt Treeby took a Maurice Farman up for a twenty minute flight. He throttled back on approach from about 350 ft, but kept the nose too high and his machine stalled and dived in, crushing him beneath the engine.

The independent line adopted by the Admiralty was given formal approval on 1 July, when the RFC was officially split. The naval element now became the Royal Naval Air Service, a title which it had already adopted unofficially. It was to comprise an Air Department (Admiralty), a Central Air Office, Royal Naval Air Stations and the Royal Naval Flying School. All RNAS officers, of which there were then 95, would be naval officers, and these would be required to serve a spell at sea in a warship every year. The Admiralty drew the line, however, at permitting them actually to take charge of a ship.

Henceforth, the Navy would no longer have any interest in the CFS, which would in future be administered only by the War Office. From 1 January 1914 until the outbreak of war on 4 August, 23 fully trained pupils were turned out at Upavon, in addition to which a further 3 were trained at the Military Wing aerodrome at Netheravon, which was also used from time to time by a detached flight of the CFS.

Chapter 2
Put to the test

By the time Second World War broke out, the Military Wing had already expanded to seven squadrons, scattered around at Brooklands, Montrose, Netheravon, Eastchurch, Gosport and Farnborough. It was obvious that more would be necessary, and it quickly became equally apparent that the CFS would not have the resources to train the greatly increased number of pilots likely to be required, both for the new squadrons, and to make good wastage in action.

Several squadrons were rushed to France, but 6 Squadron at Farnborough was one of those that remained behind for a time, and shortly after hostilities commenced an element broke away to set up a Reserve Aeroplane Squadron there. The CFS was in no position to spare many instructors, so several military pilots were returned from France, and these were augmented by civilian pilots who volunteered their services. The RAS was equipped with about 10 aircraft, which included Morane and Bleriot monoplanes, Maurice Farman Shorthorn and Longhorn biplanes, and a B.E.2a biplane.

This was only a beginning, however, and further new schools would be required, as well as aerodromes to accommodate them. Fortunately some military aerodromes were now partially or wholly vacant following the departure of the active squadrons to France, and these were supplemented by requisitioning several civilian aerodromes. Work also commenced on building entirely new aerodromes in various parts of the country.

This policy helped to reduce overcrowding at established aerodromes in the south, but had the disadvantage of diluting meagre resources, so that a greater number of instructors became necessary than might otherwise have been the case. As partial

Caudron-type biplane built and used by the Ruffy-Baumann school from 1915 to teach RFC officer recruits.

(J.M. Bruce/G.S. Leslie collection)

compensation for this, however, aircraft could be delivered fairly locally from factories in various parts of the country, and the work of this comparatively new service would become visible to members of the rapidly expanding Army, who could then begin to learn something of its value to them.

The first civilian establishment to become incorporated was that at Brooklands, which on 12 November became No. 2 Reserve Aeroplane Squadron, the original Farnborough school then being restyled 1 RAS. This month also saw the decentralisation of the RFC, with the formation on 29 November of several Wings. These included the Administrative Wing, based at Farnborough, where it controlled the RFC depot, the Record Office and the Aircraft Park, as well as being administratively responsible for the Reserve Aeroplane Squadron organisation. The RASs, in addition to their training function, would also bear the responsibility for bringing into existence new active service squadrons.

The third RAS was formed at Netheravon on 21 January 1915 from the existing training element there, and eight days later 1 RAS gave birth at Farnborough to 4 RAS, which at the beginning of March moved to a new aerodrome at Northolt. This new school had its first offshoot when 18 Squadron formed at Northolt on 11 May, leaving on 16 August for Norwich where it undertook further training before going across to France in November. Further new schools now came thick and fast, and many well known aerodromes of later years had their origins in this phase. By the end of 1915 training aerodromes had been opened at such widespread locations as Castle Bromwich, Catterick, Norwich, Joyce Green, Dover, Lydd, Thetford, Beaulieu and Waddon (Croydon). By the end of the year there were 17 in operation, some stations being shared by two schools.

It had not been possible to introduce any form of standardisation of equipment, and the concept of an aircraft being designed specifically to meet the training needs of the RFC would at that stage have been considered a novel one. Schools consequently had a varied mixture of British and French designs, some of the latter being built under licence in the United Kingdom. In addition there were some Canadian-built Curtisses, and obsolescent first line machines were also pressed into service. Types in use included most of these already referred to, plus the Bleriot Parasol, Bristol Scout, Caudron G.3, Voisin Biplane, Martinsyde S.1, Vickers F.B.5 variants, Royal Aircraft Factory B.E.2c and Armstrong Whitworth F.K.3. The CFS had fairly similar equipment, augmented by a few other Royal Aircraft Factory-built machines, such as the R.E.5.

Expansion at this pace was again beginning to strain the organisation, and in August 1915 the Administrative Wing began to gradually relinquish most of its responsibilities for the RASs, which then started to come under the control of home-based numbered Wings of the RFC, largely organised on a geographical basis. Thus 7 RAS at Netheravon was transferred to the 4th Wing at that station, whilst 3 RAS at Shoreham and later 2 RAS at Brooklands came under the 5th Wing at Gosport. The 6th Wing at Dover had a heavy training commitment, with administrative responsibility for 9 RAS at Norwich and 10 RAS at Joyce Green, these being soon afterwards augmented by 12 RAS and 15 RAS at Thetford, 13 RAS at Dover, and 17 RAS at Waddon. With the departure to the Middle East in November of the 5th Wing, its training function was taken over by the 7th Wing, which later also added 4 RAS and 11 RAS at Northolt and 16 RAS at Beaulieu. The 8th Wing began to form at the end of the year at Catterick, and this then took over control of 14 RAS there, as well as 5 RAS at Castle Bromwich and 6 RAS at Montrose. By the end of 1915 this left only the locally-based 1 RAS beholden to the Administrative Wing at Farnborough.

The nomenclature of these units was unnecessarily clumsy, and on 16 January 1916 this was simplified by dropping the middle word, so that they became plain Reserve Squadrons. During the year most of the surviving older types of aircraft gradually expired or crashed, and newer designs began to appear on the scene, such as the De Havilland D.H.1, D.H.2 and D.H.5, Sopwith Pup and 1½ Strutter, and Royal Aircraft Factory B.E.2e, B.E.12, F.E.2b, F.E.2d and F.E.8.

The B.E.2c was proving to be one of the mainstays of these schools. Originally intended as a reconnaissance and artillery observation machine, it was now becoming obsolete for front line purposes, and instead being relegated to training use. It was by no means unsuited to this purpose, having been designed as a safe, stable and reliable aeroplane, though it could in certain conditions have a tendency to get into a spin if not controlled well. The real workhorses, however, were the two 70 hp Renault-powered Maurice Farman types, which were French machines manufactured under licence in some numbers. They were both pusher biplanes fitted with tail-booms, but otherwise differed radically in design. In front of the fuselage nacelle each had projecting skids, but these also differed, the long upturned skid of the S.7 causing it to be nicknamed the 'Longhorn', whilst the short skid of the S.11 gave rise to the appellation 'Shorthorn', though the term 'Rumpety' was also sometimes applied to this latter machine. They were both reasonably safe aircraft, capable of withstanding a fair amount of mishandling by pupil pilots, and both served in this capacity, though in decreasing numbers, throughout the war.

By the beginning of 1916, Zeppelin raids, especially those against the capital, were giving increasing cause for concern. A loose air defence organisation

Above:
Martinsyde S.1 2451 of No 2 Reserve Aeroplane Squadron on the flooded aerodrome at Brooklands in the spring of 1915.
(via H.F. Shear)

Below:
Maurice Farman Longhorn 307, nicknamed 'The Ticket Machine', with No 2 Reserve Aeroplane Squadron at Brooklands in 1915.
(via H.F. Shear)

Above:
Maurice Farman Longhorn 500 of No 2 Reserve Aeroplane Squadron flying in the snow at Brooklands early in 1915.
(via H.F. Shear)

Below:
Graham-White Type XV 8305, a Farman-type biplane, used at RN Air Station Chingford in 1915–16.
(Wing Cdr G.H. Lewis)

had consequently been set up, consisting of pairs of B.E.2c's stationed at aerodromes in the London area, namely Hounslow, Northolt, Hendon, Chingford, Hainault Farm, Suttons Farm (later renamed Hornchurch), Joyce Green, Farningham, Croydon and Wimbledon Common. As a stopgap measure, control of these was given on 1 February to the recently-formed 19 RS at Hounslow, commanded by Major T.C.R. Higgins. A new 18th Wing was formed on 25 March to control all RFC stations in the London area, and it was soon recognised that the home defence function was a distraction from that unit's primary task. On 15 April these elements were therefore removed from the responsibilities of 19 RS, being then grouped together as the Home Defence Squadron, soon becoming 39 Squadron.

This did not meet the needs of the remainder of the country, however, which was equally vulnerable to attack, and as a temporary measure three extra B.E.2c's were each allocated for home defence to 9 RS at Norwich, 12 RS at Thetford, 13 RS at Dover and 15 RS at Doncaster. As this number would be inadequate for the defence of Birmingham and Coventry, 6 RS at Castle Bromwich received six additional B.E.2c's. The schools soon lost this task, the 16th (Home Defence) Wing being set up on 25 June to take over all responsibility for such units throughout the United Kingdom, eventually expanding into a full Brigade with its own wings and squadrons.

The Reserve Squadron organisation, backed up by the CFS, served the needs of the RFC for the first year of war, but by the end of 1915 a more specialised and less wasteful approach was proving necessary. A School of Instruction was accordingly set up at Reading on 20 December, to give preparatory technical and other ground instructional training to officers, so that they would already have some awareness of these aspects before progressing to RSs, and could then concentrate mainly on their flying training. Non-airworthy airframes and engines were used, and as well as rudimentary engineering, pupils were instructed in aspects of rigging, signalling, reconnaissance and map reading. The Reading school became No. 1 School of Instruction when a second such unit was

Bristol Scout C 1250 seen here at RN Air Station Chingford was also used at Cranwell and Redcar.
(via Brian Lowe)

formed on 3 April 1916 at Christ Church, Oxford, both becoming Schools of Military Aeronautics on 27 October. No. 1 Training Centre was also set up in November 1915, at The Curragh in Ireland.

In addition to these, specialised armament instruction was available from 3 October 1915 at the Machine Gun School, initially at Dover until moving on 27 November to take advantage of better facilities at Hythe. Renamed the School of Aerial Gunnery on 13 September 1916, it gave instruction in operating the Lewis gun to officers and men temporarily detached from their squadrons. Wireless communication was now becoming more common, and a Wireless Experimental Flight formed in December 1915 at Brooklands to provide instruction for observers and wireless officers, being later renamed the Wireless School, and from 24 October 1916 the Wireless and Observers School. There was also a School for Wireless Operators at Farnborough, and a Wireless Testing Park at Biggin Hill.

The introduction of new and faster types of aircraft, and the development of more complex forms of aerial fighting, coupled with a high attrition rate amongst new pilots joining the squadrons in France, was beginning to give cause for concern by early 1916, and in March new qualification standards were introduced for pilot training. Before gaining his wings, a pupil would now have to complete 15 hours solo flying, make two 15 minute flights at 6,000 ft, and successfully land twice at night with the assistance of flares. Having achieved this, he was still not ready to be allowed overseas, but must have had as much further practise as possible in landing, bomb-dropping, aerial fighting, night flying and formation flying.

From May, a War Office order also authorised what was referred to as trick flying and the practising of flying manoeuvres. The qualification for pilots was again stepped up in December, when pilots were required to complete between 20 and 28 hours of solo flying, depending on the type of aircraft being flown. Training would also include gunnery, artillery observation, photography and bomb-dropping.

The organisation too was becoming more sophisticated. On 15 January 1916 the 6th Brigade was formed, becoming the Training Brigade on 20 July, responsible for all Reserve Squadrons. Mose of these then ceased to be all-through schools, some becoming responsible only for elementary training and the remainder for higher training. This distinction was to some extent reflected in their types of aircraft, but not in their titles.

A need was now seen for training facilities in support of the squadrons involved in fighting against Turkish forces in Egypt, Palestine and Mesopotamia. In April 1916, a nucleus for a new 21 RS was formed by 3 RS at Shoreham, and the components of this sailed for Egypt in stages from 18 May, to be established at Abbassia. It was soon followed by 22 RS and 23 RS at Aboukir (or Abu Qir), the tropical climate then being inficted on such types as the Maurice Farman, Avro 504A, BE.2c/e, Bristol Scout and Caudron G.3. In September these units became responsible to a new 20th (Reserve) Wing within the Middle East Brigade of the RFC, based at Aboukir. Technical knowledge was imparted at Aboukir from 21 August by a Technical Training Class, this becoming No 3 School of Military Aeronautics on 29 November.

At home the seemingly insatiable demands of the squadrons fighting on the Western Front were being met by a steadily increasing number of new Reserve Schools, and by the beginning of 1917 there were 42 of these, with two more being formed in Egypt. Even greater increases were being planned for 1917, a complement of 97 Reserve Schools being given approval in January, of which two were to specialise in night flying. The administration was therefore once more beginning to totter under the load, and further devolution was now overdue. Accordingly on 10 January the Training Brigade was decentralised.

Three geographically-based Group Commands were now set up, each subdivided further into three or four Reserve Wings. At Salisbury, the Southern Group Command became responsible for the 4th Wing at Netheravon, the 17th Wing at Gosport (later Beaulieu), the 21st Wing at Filton (later Cirencester) and the 25th Wing at Castle Bromwich. The Eastern Group Command, whose headquarters now took over the Holborn Viaduct Hotel in London, controlled the 6th Wing at Maidstone, the 7th Wing in Norwich, and the 18th Wing in London (Duke Street, St. James). Finally, the Northern Group Command at York looked after the 8th Wing in that city, the 19th Wing at Newcastle, the 23rd Wing at South Carlton and the 24th Wing at Wyton (later Spittlegate).

Further specialist training was now becoming increasingly necessary, if the RFC was to cope with the improved machines and tactics of their German opponents. No 1 (Auxiliary) School of Aerial Gunnery at Hythe had set up a detachment at Lympne, and it was now proposed to move the whole unit north to Loch Doon, but this plan was aborted when it was realised that the prevailing weather conditions at that location, and the proximity of the Rhinn of Kells, would seriously interrupt training. Instead No 2 School was formed at Turnberry in Ayrshire, where the infuence of the Gulf Stream, and the more open aspect of this seashore location, made conditions kinder. The Hythe school now concentrated on providing Lewis gun training for observers, while fighter pilots received gunnery instruction at its Scottish counterpart. Schools No 3 and 4 opened later in the year, respectively at New Romney and Marske, while a similar, but unnumbered, school formed in April at Aboukir.

With the advanced Bristol Fighter due to enter service shortly in the two-seater fighter-reconnaissance role, increased specialist training was becoming necessary for officers earmarked for observer duties. This was met by setting up in January 1917 a School of Photography, Maps and Reconnaissance, initially housed in Langham Place, London, but later at Farnborough, where the title was shortened to School of Photography. Further Schools of Military Aeronautics also appeared during 1917, No 5 being at Oxford (later Denham) and No 6 at Denham (later Bristol), whilst No 4 introduced a new element when it formed at Toronto on 1 July as the precursor of a planned Canadian training scheme.

The use of the word Reserve in this area was now becoming something of a misnomer, and on 31 May 1917 this was officially recognised when all the existing Reserve Squadrons were restyled Training Squadrons. Further such schools were to form during the year, 15 of these being Canadian units initially organised as nucleii within UK Training Squadrons before embarking for expansion to full strength in their home country.

Training aircraft for all these new units would still for the most part be the same old outmoded types, plus such few of the more modern service types as could be spared, though with one significant exception. For the first time a machine would become available which had been specifically designed for RFC training purposes. To meet this new demand, Geoffrey de Havilland had designed the Airco D.H.6, a two-seater biplane of simple construction, which was planned from the outset for easy maintenance and repair. The original engine was the 90 hp R.A.F.Ia, but the 90 hp Curtiss OX-5 and 80 hp Renault were also fitted in some numbers, depending largely on availability. Unfortunately production was slow to get under way, mainly because of official intransigence over providing suitable timber for the frames, but once it entered service in large numbers it was found to have few vices. More nicknames were probably bestowed on it, however, than any other type, its double open cockpit giving rise to 'The Flying Coffin' and 'The Clumsy Hearse', or 'The Dung Hunter' by Australians who likened it to one of their farm vehicles. Some of the more polite alternatives included 'The Crab', 'The Clockwork Mouse', 'The Sixty', 'The Sky Hook' and 'The Clutching Hand'.

The adoption of plans for night bombing tactics in France from early 1917 led to the introduction of a new type of training squadron. No 11 RS at Northolt, which had been responsible for all night training, moved to Rochford, becoming No 98 Depot Squadron in February. No 99 Depot Squadron formed alongside it in June, moving later in that month to East Retford, only to almost immediately become No 199 Depot Squadron, its senior counterpart becoming No 198 at the same time. This new numbering sequence was later extended by the formation of Nos 188 to 192 Depot Squadrons, the intervening allocations being taken by the Egyptian-based Nos 193 to 197 Training Squadrons. The titles of the Depot Squadrons were brought into line with their daytime counterparts on 21 December, when they were renamed (Night) Training Squadrons, two more of these coming into existence in April 1918, being Nos 186 and 187.

The most significant and far-reaching event of 1917, however, was undoubtedly the establishment at Gosport of the School of Special Flying. This came into existence on 2 August by amalgamating Nos 1, 27 and 55 Training Squadrons there. The guiding light for this unit was its commanding officer, Major R.R. Smith-Barry, an experienced scout pilot who had commanded No 1 TS, and prior to that 60 Squadron, a unit then fighting on the Western Front with French-built Moranes and Nieuports. He had given much thought to fighter tactics, learning both from his own experiences and those of his fellows. In particular, the discovery had gradually been made that a spin was not necessarily fatal, it being possible to recover if the nose of the aircraft was pushed downwards.

Trick flying was now part of the curriculum, and pupils at this new school were encouraged to undertake more adventurous forms of flying, to enable them to cope with all manner of difficult manoeuvres. They were taught how to cope with tricky wind conditions, especially during take-off and landing, and to recover control from various unaccustomed circumstances induced deliberately by their instructors. The principles painstakingly worked out by the school were in October 1917 embodied in an official pamphlet *General Methods of Teaching Scout Pilots,* which became a bible for this new style of flying, later copied extensively throughout the world's air forces.

Graduates from the school emerged confident of their own abilities, undertaking by instinct much of the manoeuvring necessary for survival, and consequently able to devote a much greater proportion of their attention to their opponents. One other new development at the school towards the end of the year, which also had far-reaching consequences, was the introduction of the 'Gosport tube', a primitive but effective intercommunications system which for the first time enabled verbal exchanges in flight between instructor and pupil.

Yet another important organisational development occurred in 1917. The rapid growth of training was taking too big a toll of agricultural land, and the scattering of aerodromes around the country was proving wasteful in both personnel and transport. Further new aerodromes were under construction, but to help minimise these problems they were formed into Training Depot Stations, combining the tasks formerly undertaken by several scattered Training Squadrons. The method of formation adopted was for three nucleus flights to be formed within existing Training Squadrons, and these soon moved to the new base to be

Martinsyde G.102 Elephant A3953 of No 22 Training Squadron at Aboukir, Egypt in 1917.
(J.M. Bruce/G.S. Leslie collection)

expanded into a TDS, which then became responsible for both basic and advanced training, a system which was to be continued and refined in the future. This system was standardised throughout in July 1918 when all surviving Training Squadrons were abolished, to become amalgamated as TDSs.

Specialisation was further enhanced towards the end of 1917. Two Schools of Aerial Fighting were set up in the United Kingdom based at Ayr and Eastburn (near Driffield), with a third in Egypt at Heliopolis, and an Artillery Observation School was formed at Almaza, near Cairo, by redesignating 197 TS. A second Wireless School opened at Penshurst, with an Egyptian counterpart by the New Year. The Wireless and Observers School at Hursley Park became the Artillery and Infantry Co-operation School, later moving to Worthy Down where it was later again restyled to become the RAF and Army Co-operation School.

Further thought had been given to training aircraft requirements, and in November 1917 an official Specification was issued for an elementary tractor

Airco D.H.6 A9611, flown by No 35 Training Depot Station at Duxford in 1918. In the background can be seen a hangar under construction.
(J.M. Bruce/G.S. Leslie collection)

B.E.2e B4429 of No 31 Training Depot Station at Fowlmere in 1918.
(RAF Museum Photo No P003688)

biplane, of similar configuration to the Avro 504 series, but powered by the new ABC Wasp engine. In the event, this failed to result in any new design entering service, though a prototype was eventually flown of the B.A.T. Baboon to meet this requirement. Instead the 504 soldiered on, alongside the newer D.H.6. The 504A and later the 504J variant had been built in large numbers, and a new 504K appeared during 1917, to become the standard elementary trainer for many years to come.

Meanwhile events had been moving towards drastic changes in the organisation of all the British flying services, and on 1 April 1918 this finally led to the formation of the Royal Air Force. Of necessity, this was built around the structure of the Royal Flying Corps, being by far the larger of the two air arms, which consequently had to absorb as best it could an assortment of RNAS flying training units, to no little resentment. The original naval training establishment at Eastchurch had in the meantime been supplemented by counterparts at Cranwell, Manston, Chingford, Fairlop, East Fortune, Lee-on-Solent (seaplane training), Calshot (flying boat training), Portholme Meadow (Oxford) and Vendome (France). All of these were now brought within the TDS structure, being given numbers in the sequence 201 to 213.

Specialist naval needs were catered for by two Marine Observers Schools, at Aldeburgh and

Bristol F.2b C4879 of No 33 Training Depot Station, in colourful chequered markings at Witney in 1918.
(via Brian Lowe)

Eastchurch, the first of these being originally known by its cumbersome wartime title of School for Anti-Submarine Inshore Patrol Observers. There was also a School for Marine Operational Pilots at Dover. 208 TDS at East Fortune was retitled the Grand Fleet School of Aerial Fighting and Gunnery, moving to Leuchars where the word 'Grand' was dropped. A Torpedo Aeroplane School equipped mainly with Sopwith Cuckoos was set up at East Fortune. Earlier in the year a School of Aerial Co-operation with Coastal Artillery had formed at Gosport.

The Schools of Military Aeronautics had their titles shortened to the now more suitable School of Aeronautics, further such schools being later formed at Bath and Cheltenham. Three Schools of Aerial Navigation and Bomb-dropping were formed in the United Kingdom, at Stonehenge, Andover and Thetford, and another at Almaza in Egypt, the word 'Aerial' being later omitted from the title. The various separate fighting and gunnery schools were reorganised in May to form three combined Schools of Fighting and Gunnery, later simplified to become simply Fighting Schools, these being based at Turnberry, Marske and Bircham Newton. Similar schools were later set up at Freiston, and in Egypt at Heliopolis. To augment the efforts of the Central Flying School, a number of Flying Instructors Schools were also set up, one within each of the new RAF Area Commands, these being based at Ayr, Redcar, Shoreham, Lilbourne and Gosport, with another in Ireland at The Curragh, and one in Egypt at El Khanka.

This then was essentially the position on Armistice Day, 11 November 1918, an event which left nearly all these units entirely surplus to any conceivable needs of the near future. Many of the newer units had barely begun to function, let alone provide trained fighting men to the operational squadrons. The main problem now was to organise an orderly rundown, yet retain sufficient hard won expertise to maintain the basic efficiency of this newly formed service which had not yet begun to think as one combined whole, with many officers and men still wearing the uniforms of their former services to which many of them, particularly those with naval backgrounds, felt, and would continue to feel, a continued allegiance.

Chapter 3
The Fallow Years

The beginning of 1919 saw the junior service with a motley assortment of training units, the majority of which would be gone by the end of that year. No longer would it be necessary to maintain a scattered series of Training Depot Stations around the country, and a start was soon made on running these down. Many were disbanded in the early part of the year, and the remaining dozen or so were reduced to Training Squadron status, though retaining their former TDS identity numbers. The only exception was 16 TDS at Abu Sueir in Egypt, which kept its TDS status, later moving to Heliopolis.

Quite a number of the specialist schools remained in existence at that stage, though consolidated and reorganised during the year, and the naval side was run down quite drastically. The various Observers' Schools were closed, as was the Fleet School of Aerial Fighting and Gunnery at Leuchars, but 209 TDS at Lee-on-Solent became the RAF and Naval Co-operation School and later the RAF Seaplane Establishment. At Gosport the Coastal Battery Co-operation School became the Coastal Battery Co-operation Flight.

A major reorganisation of both aircrew and ground crew training became effective from 23 December. The RAF and Army Co-operation School at Worthy Down became the School of Army Co-operation, based at Andover, the School of Air Pilotage became the Air Pilotage School, and the Electrical and Wireless School formed at Flower Down by renaming No 1 (Training) Wireless School. The Boys Training Depot at Halton became the School of Technical Training (Boys). The Cadet College, Cranwell was

Sopwith Snipe E6150 of No 1 Flying Training School at Netheravon in 1921.
(RAF Museum Photo No P008170)

Above:
De Havilland D.H.9A (Dual control) E797 of No 1 Flying Training School at Netheravon in 1921.
(RAF Museum Photo No P008173)

restyled the RAF (Cadet) College, the Central Flying School at Upavon became the Flying Instructors School, and the Photographic Park at Farnborough became the School of Photography. A portent for the future was the formation at Netheravon on 23 December of No 1 Flying Training School from the short-lived Netheravon Flying School.

One legacy of the wartime growth was that responsibility for training was spread across several area commands, and this situation continued for a time. In the South-Eastern Area, No 1 (Training) Group headquarters were initially in London, moving out to Croydon in August 1919, whilst No 2 (Training) Group headquarters was based in Southampton until it disbanded. In the Northern Area, No 3 (Training) Group was at Oxford until moving in mid-year to Uxbridge, reducing to a skeleton in December 1919, then disbanding on 15 March 1920. In the South Western Area, No 7 (Training) Group was based at Salisbury and later Andover, whilst No 8 (Training) Group at Cambridge moved to Norwich in July, then on 10 November to Spittlegate. No 7 Wing was based at Coal Aston and No 8 Wing at York and later Marske, both of these later going to Uxbridge.

This rationalisation continued into 1920, to complete the basic post-war training structure. The

Below:
Gloster Grebe IIIDC J7520 of the Central Flying School at Wittering, bearing Racing No 23 for the Kings Cup Air Race in July 1928. It won the following year's race.
(RAF Museum Photo No P008384)

Armstrong Whitworth Siskin IIIDC J9198 of 'B' Flight, RAF Training Base at Leuchars in 1929.
(RAF Museum Photo No P004294)

Aerial Navigation School formed in February at Calshot, soon being enlarged to become the School of Naval Co-operation and Aerial Navigation, moving in August to Lee-on-Solent. The Torpedo Training Squadron at Gosport became No 210 (Torpedo Training) Squadron in February. The School of Army Co-operation closed down at Worthy Down on 8 March, but immediately reopened at Stonehenge with a detachment at Worthy Down. The various schools of technical training were reorganised and renamed, to leave Nos 1 and 2 Schools of Technical Training (Boys) Home at Halton and Cranwell respectively and School of Technical Training (Men) Home at Eastchurch (later Manston).

No 2 (Training) Group disbanded in March, its remaining stations being transferred to No 1 Group, but this was followed by a more fundamental administrative change with the formation on 1 April of Inland Area, with headquarters at Hillingdon House, Uxbridge. This new organisation took over from the former Northern and Southern Area Commands, and at

a stroke the remnants of the labyrinthine wartime structure was dismantled to give a practical basis for peacetime air operations in the United Kingdom. It was given a wide range of responsibilities, which included control of Nos 1, 3 and 7 (Training) Groups, as well as Nos 7 and 8 Wings. For the first time, RAF home flying training was to be administered by a single body.

The first fruits of this were quickly seen, when on 26 April all the remaining Training Schools were redesignated to become Flying Training Schools. No 1 Flying Training School was already in existence within 7 Group at Netheravon. 3 Group now took over 2 FTS (formerly 31 TS) at Duxford (otherwise Royston), 3 FTS (formerly 59 TS) at Scopwick (renamed Digby) and 6 FTS (formerly 30 TS) at Spittlegate (later Manston). In 7 Wing, 4 TS at Shotwick (renamed Sealand) became 5 FTS, but there was no longer any justification for 8 and 9 Wings, and they consequently disbanded. No new types of aircraft were likely to be available for some time, so these units had to soldier on with wartime aircraft, many of them reconditioned, such as 504Ks, DH.9As, Bristol Fighters and Snipes, and also a few Vimys in the case of 6 FTS. The gap in this numbering sequence was accounted for by the Egypt-based 4 FTS, which formed the following year at Abu Sueir with fairly similar equipment, including Vimys. At Upavon, the Central Flying School reformed in No 7 Group, also with similar types of aircraft. A School of Aerial Gunnery and Bombing came into existence during the year at Eastchurch.

At that time, Britain still had a widespread Empire, and the RAF was soon being called upon to meet operational commitments in a number of places. Ireland was troubled, and there were problems in the Middle East and the Far East. Post-war economies left few resources, and the emphasis in both aircrew selection and training had of necessity to be on quality, within a framework suitable for rapid expansion should the necessity arise. Tasks were doubled up wherever possible, thus, for instance, the absence of special schools for advanced flying training was overcome by making the first-line squadrons responsible for training newly fledged pilots. Similarly, air gunners and observers were drawn from the better technical tradesmen, who could consequently perform a dual role. The pay bill was kept down by selecting suitable NCOs for flying training, these becoming sergeant pilots who later returned to their parent trades.

The School of Army Co-operation moved in 1921 to Old Sarum, and No 2 School of Technical Training (Boys) Home became the Boys Wing, Cranwell. At Gosport, an Observer Training Flight was formed, and at nearby Lee-on-Solent, the School of Naval Co-operation and Aerial Navigation became the Seaplane Training School. In India, a small RAF School was formed.

The controlling organisation was further reduced in 1921 when No 3 (Training) Group merged into No 1 Group, but this situation was reversed in February 1922 when No 11 Wing reformed at Spittlegate to take over all the units of the former No 3 Group, the situation moving full circle when this wing in turn became a new No 3 (Training) Group in May 1923. However, flying training needs had proved minimal, and both 3 FTS and 6 FTS disbanded in April 1922. Around the same time, the School of Aerial Gunnery and Bombing at Eastchurch was renamed the Armament and Gunnery School, equipped with Snipes, Bristol Fighters and DH.9As, and a small communications element for the RAF Staff College formed at Andover. A minor change later was the move of 2 FTS to Digby in June 1924.

Coastal training was still in a state of metamorphosis, and during 1923 an RAF Base formed at Calshot, to include both a Seaplane Training Flight and an Air Pilotage Flight, and at Lee-on-Solent the Seaplane Training School became the School of Naval Co-operation. Leuchars was reconstituted as an RAF Training Base in July 1925, responsible for training naval personnel. It then had three flights comprising 'A' (Fighter) Training Flight equipped with Flycatchers, 504Ks, and dual control Grebes and Siskins, 'B' (Spotter) Training Flight with Bisons and Blackburns, and 'C' (Reconnaissance) Training Flight flying Fairey IIIDs. 'D' (Torpedo Training) Flight formed at RAF Base Gosport at the same time, equipped with Darts.

A further rationalisation of flying training administration occurred on 12 April 1926. No 1 Group now became No 21 Group and ceased to have any training responsibility. No 3 Group was similarly redesignated, to become No 23 Group, which shortly moved out from Spittlegate to take up residence at St Vincents, Grantham. The new 23 Group continued to be

Blackburn B.2 G-ACEN of No 4 Elementary and Reserve Flying Training School at Brough.
(R.D. Cooling)

Right:
Fairey IIIF MkIIIB (DC) S1847 of RAF Training Base at Leuchars around 1934.
(MAP photo)

Below:
Avro Tutor K3248 '6' of No 5 Flying Training School at Sealand.
(RAF Museum Photo No P006304)

administered by Inland Area, which itself moved on 20 May to Bentley Priory, Stanmore, but it now took over responsibility for all home-based training establishments.

Training equipment was still much the same, with one significant exception, this being the receipt by the Central Flying School, soon to move to Wittering, of its first Avro 504N, or Lynx-Avro as it was generally known. Though no substitute for a new purpose-built trainer, the fitment of a Lynx engine and an oleo undercarriage gave the machine an extra lease of life, and over the course of the next two years this version gradually replaced the old wartime 504K in all the flying training units. At the CFS, wartime Snipe fighters were beginning to give way to Gamecocks and Grebes.

There were a few more changes among the training units. The Air Pilotage Flight at Calshot was renamed the Navigation School in 1926, new Southampton flying boats replacing the former Felixstowe F.5s. The RAF (Cadet) College changed its title in February 1929 to become simply the RAF College, being joined shortly afterwards at Cranwell by the Electrical and Wireless School.

By now, sufficient new pilot recruits were being accepted for the intake to overstrain the existing schools. In February 1928, therefore, RAF Base Leuchars took over initial training for naval officers, a task which had previously been performed by 1 FTS, and two months later 3 FTS reformed with 504Ns and Siskin fighters at RAF Grantham, this being the new name for Spittlegate. Further new types were at last beginning to reach these schools, with 5 FTS receiving Moths in 1929, whilst Tomtits were given to 3 FTS. The CFS replaced its Grebes with Bulldogs in February 1931, and the following month its D.H.9As gave way to Fairey IIIFs. The need for an additional FTS had by then passed, and 1 FTS was consequently disbanded, leaving an awkward gap at the beginning of the numbering system. The Seaplane Training Flight at Calshot was uprated in October to become the Seaplane Training Squadron, now flying Southampton flying boats and IIIF floatplanes.

Armament training, which had played a fairly minor role since the war, now began to assume a greater importance. At the beginning of 1932 the Armament and Gunnery School at Eastchurch became the Air Armament School, using Wapitis, IIIFs and Bulldogs. Three existing Practice Camps became Nos 1, 2 and 3 Armament Training Camps, formed respectively at Catfoss, North Coates Fitties and Sutton Bridge.

Output of qualified pilots from the Flying Training Schools by now amounted to around 300 each year. Permanent officers received their training at the RAF College, while the FTSs trained short service officers and airmen pilots.

During 1933 the Air Pilotage School formed at Andover, flying Victorias, Tutors and later Clouds. An element of the Armament and Gunnery School at Eastchurch broke away to become the Coastal Defence Training Flight at Gosport, with IIIFs, this soon being sub-divided to form Nos 1, 2 and 3 CDT Flights at Gosport, equipped respectively with IIIFs, Vildebeests and Harts. They re-amalgamated two years later, however, to become No 1 Coastal Defence Training Unit. 2 FTS disbanded in July 1933 at Digby, but reformed there just over a year later with Tutors, Harts and Furies.

By this time talk of expansion was in the air. It had been a basic presumption since 1919 that there would be no major war for ten years, and all forward planning had been based on this. Events in Europe now made this theory increasingly untenable, and on 23 March 1932, the Cabinet finally decided that this 'Ten Year Rule' should be abolished. It took some time to give practical effect to the decision, but the Annual Estimates of March 1934 authorised an increase in first line squadron strength, and this had inevitable consequences for the training organisation.

First of all, something fairly drastic had to be done to increase the flow of new recruits. Fortunately there was already in existence a nucleus which could be built upon for initial training, four civilian training schools for reservists having been set up as far back as 1923. The Director of Training now decided that the elementary training of all pupil pilots should be entrusted to such civilian schools. This would leave the FTSs free to concentrate on more advanced training, which in turn would relieve the training burden on the first line squadrons.

The new civilian schools were to be known as Elementary amd Reserve Flying Training Schools, and No 1 formed at Hatfield on 4 August 1935, with Gipsy Moths and later Tiger Moths, from the de Havilland-operated reserve school there, originally opened in May 1923 at Stag Lane. The next three, in numerical order, formed from the other reserve schools at Filton, Hamble and Brough, were operated respectively by the Bristol Aeroplane Company, Air Service Training Ltd and the North Sea Aerial and General Transport Company. The last-named was taken over the following year by Blackburn Aircraft, which then ran it with locally-built Blackburn B.2s.

Another source of partially-trained pilots was the three University Air Squadrons, those for Cambridge and Oxford having already been in existence since 1925, giving flying instruction from 1928 in 504Ns at Duxford and Abingdon respectively to pupils from those universities. New equipment in the shape of Tutors was now becoming available for these, and in October 1935 the two existing squadrons were joined by the similarly-equipped University of London Air Squadron based at Northolt, this having also a few Atlases.

A further nine reserve schools were now authorised, and the first two formed on 1 June, 5 E&RFTS with B.2s at Hanworth being initially run by Flying Training Ltd, until taken over by Blackburns, whilst Brooklands Aviation opened 6 E&RFTS at Sywell with the more usual Tiger Moths. Contract procedures could be lengthy, however, and only three more such schools materialised before the year end.

The slack in the service schools could now be put to good use. First the numerical gap was filled in April 1935 when RAF Base Leuchars was retitled to become 1 FTS, still for Fleet Air Arm officer training, by now on IIIFs, Seals and Harts. Simultaneously, 6 FTS reformed at Netheravon with Tutors and Harts, and six months later 11 FTS opened at Wittering with Harts, Audaxes and Tutors. At the end of the year 7 FTS opened at Peterborough with Harts and Tutors, and 10 FTS at Ternhill operating Harts, Audaxes and Tutors. All the FTSs were now reorganised so that pupils stayed with them for two terms, the first being devoted to flying training (or intermediate training as it was renamed in 1937), and the second to advanced training. Courses overlapped, with a new course being accepted every three months, each FTS being fed with pupils by specified E&RFTSs, for continuity.

A few other changes in 1935 included the renaming of the Air Pilotage School at Andover as the Air Navigation School, using Prefects, and the opening of a Temporary Armament Training Camp at Leuchars. The School of Technical Training (Men) at Manston became No 3 S of TT, and in September the Central Flying School returned to its traditional home at Upavon.

By 1936, with the political situation in Europe steadily worsening, the RAF was at last beginning to get some of the equipment it would need if it were to be able to carry out its duties effectively in a new-style war. Large and more modern types of aircraft were now coming into service, and except in the single-seaters the pilot could no longer be expected to be responsible also for navigation and in many instances bomb-dropping. It was therefore decreed that the crew of a bomber or two-seater fighter should be one pilot and one observer, plus a wireless operator and/or air gunner where necessary. In the case of coastal aircraft the crew would comprise one pilot plus a navigator who should also be a qualified pilot. Bombers would have two pilots wherever possible.

This immediately presented problems, as the specialist training schools had largely vanished in 1919, and modern counterparts would now have to be set up. The first of these was to be an Air Observers School, opened at North Coates Fitties in January 1936 with Gordons and Wallaces, this being quickly followed by combining the Air Navigation School at Andover with the Navigation School from Calshot to form a new School of Air Navigation at Manston equipped with Ansons, these latter aircraft being joined soon by the Saro Cloud flight of the Seaplane Training Squadron.

Further E&RFTSs appeared early in 1936, and by February the initial target of 13 such schools in operation had been achieved. In addition, 9 FTS formed at Thornaby in March with Harts, Furies and Tutors. The whole administrative structure, however, was by now beginning to creak from overloading. During the formative years of the RAF, most major functions had of necessity been retained by the Air Ministry, but devolution was now highly overdue.

Fortunately the lessons of the earlier conflict had not been lost, there being many senior officers still in service from that period, and it was decided to recreate a structure essentially similar to that which had been gradually dismantled in the early twenties. The Air Ministry would therefore in future be responsible only for policy-making, and its dictats would then be carried out through a chain starting with Commands and progressing downwards through Groups, Stations and Units. The existing Area Commands would cease to exist, to be superseded by specialised Bomber, Coastal, Fighter and Training Commands.

Accordingly, Inland Area was renamed Training Command on 1 May, and No 23 Group was then restyled No 23 (Training) Group. A further reorganisation took place in July, and the control of all technical training units then became the responsibility of a new No 24 (Training) Group at Halton. Bentley Priory was now needed for the new Fighter Command headquarters, which had to be near the centre of likely activities, and consequently Training Command headquarters moved out on 13 July to take up residence at Buntingsdale Hall, Market Drayton.

On paper, therefore, the RAF now had a training structure better able to see that this vital function was properly executed. In practice, however, as is so often the case, the new organisation was slow to settle down, and consequently it did not become properly effective until early 1938. Training Command, instead of being a brand new organisation with a closely defined objective, had taken over Inland Area virtually intact, including an assortment of scattered units having no conceivable bearing on flying training. Worse, far too few staff could be spared to run such a large new organisation. On the other hand it ought to have taken over a number of maritime training units operated by the new Coastal Command, but this task was to remain within that command, controlled by No 17 (Training) Group. The eventual solution to most of the problems was to hive off many of its duties to new Technical Training, Reserve and Maintenance Commands, but that took some time to plan and accomplish.

One of the components of Training Command was the Armament Group, which had formed in 1934 at Eastchurch to control the Air Armament School and the Armament Training Camps. The latter were steadily increased in number as newer and larger aircraft came into service, and by early 1938 there were seven in operation. In November 1937 the Air Armament School at Eastchurch was redesignated No 1 AAS, and a new No 2 AAS formed at North Coates Fitties, where it absorbed the units already based there, including the Air Observers School. The parent administration was brought within the numbering system in December 1937 when it changed its name from Armament Group to No 25 (Armament Training) Group.

A further 20 reserve schools had meanwhile been authorised, the first of these coming into operation in July 1937 at Castle Bromwich, Redhill and Shoreham. Advanced training had now been added to their curriculum, and the Tiger Moths, Magisters and other types were being augmented, mostly by Hart variants, but also later by some Battles and Ansons. The task of controlling this growing number of schools had until now been the responsibility of a Superintendent of Reserve and an Inspector of Civil Flying Training Schools, and their respective staffs, but these could not be expected to cope with such a rapidly increasing burden, and on 1 December a new No 26 (Training) Group was formed at Hendon to take over this responsibility.

There were a number of changes of location of Flying Training Schools around this time, but the only new one to appear was 12 FTS which formed at Grantham in December 1938 with Harvards, Harts and Ansons. 23 Group headquarters moved from St Vincents to Grantham (Spittlegate) aerodrome on 2 October.

The year of 1938 was to be one of great changes. In January the School of Naval Co-operation moved from Lee-on-Solent to the new aerodrome at Ford, by now using modern types of naval aircraft such as Sharks, Swordfishes and Walruses. A pressing need for air gunners and observers could not be properly met on inadequate resources, and proposals for a series of AOSs had therefore to be postponed, though it was possible to create No 1 Air Observers School at North Coates Fitties by retitling 2 AAS. Immediate needs were met by forming a temporary Air Observers School with Heyfords at Leconfield in June, this disbanding at the end of the year. A change of title in April saw Armament Training Camps restyled Armament Training Stations. A new 2 AAS formed at Eastchurch in July, and in August 1 AAS moved from Eastchurch to a new airfield at Manby. 7 ATS at Acklington became 2 AOS on 15 November. During 1939 further changes included the renaming of 2 ATS Acklington and 4 ATS West Freugh to become 2 AOS and 4 AOS respectively.

New specialist units formed in 1938. A School of General Reconnaissance opened at Thorney Island with Ansons, and a Floatplane Training School formed at Calshot. The RAF Staff College closed in September, and the Electrical and Wireless School became 1 E&WS in November to prepare the way for the formation in the New Year of 2 E&WS at Yatesbury with Dominies.

Many more new reserve schools also appeared during that year. In addition, those which had an Anson element for navigation training now had these break away to form separate Civil Air Navigation Schools, the first four being based respectively at Prestwick, Yatesbury, Desford and Ansty. 23 Group had by now grown too big to perform all its tasks effectively, and at

the end of the year a new No 21 (Training) Group formed at Cranwell to take over responsibility for RAF Cranwell, the RAF College, 1 E&WS, 5 FTS and later some of the other FTSs. A similar problem was affecting control of the reserve schools, and early in 1939 Reserve Command was formed, No 28 Group being retitled No 50 (Training) Group, and a new No 51 (Training) Group taking over responsibility for E& RFTSs in the Midlands and the North, with new E&RFTSs and CANSs continuing to be formed right up to the outbreak of war.

Three new Scottish-based regular schools also formed within 21 Group during the early part of 1939, being Nos 13, 14 and 15 respectively at Drem, Kinloss and Lossiemouth. The use of monoplanes at these establishments was becoming standard with the issue of Oxfords, and American-built Harvards.

To fill the gap between FTS and squadron, several Group Pools were set up in each of the operational commands to provide advanced training on modern aircraft for both pilots and crews. Coastal Command, however, lost all its responsibilites for naval training when this was taken over by the Admiralty on 24 May 1939, this reversing events of 21 years earlier.

The scene was now set for war, with a wide variety of training units in being, and others planned.

Chapter 4 The Onslaught of War

The outbreak of war immediately led to a hasty rationalisation of the training structure. The Reserve aspect of the E&RFTSs was dropped overnight, all those not actually in full operation were closed, and the remainder, drastically pruned in number, were brought within the mainstream RAF structure as Elementary Flying Training Schools, though continuing to be operated by civilian firms. Pupils would still carry on to the Flying Training Schools, but these now became Service Flying Training Schools, including 4 FTS in Egypt, which now moved to Iraq to become 4 SFTS at Habbaniya. Several of the other UK units moved, generally to make way for operational squadrons.

The south and east coast aerodromes would now be required for defensive and offensive operations by first line squadrons, and were in any event too vulnerable to be used for training purposes. The Seaplane Training Squadron went north from Calshot to Invergordon, and several of the armament schools left for safer locations, taking up war stations in Wales, Scotland, Ireland or the West Country. They were reorganised at the same time, so that all now became Air Observers Schools, providing navigation, bombing and gunnery training for observers, and also gunnery training for air gunners. In their new coastal locations they could carry out firing practice, generally over the Irish Sea and its environs, with a minimal fear of interruption by the enemy.

The standard of both navigation and air gunnery training left a lot to be desired at this time. To help remedy this, the pre-war civilian-operated CANSs were consequently transformed into Air Observer and Navigator Schools, and their instructors mobilised into the RAF. At the same time, the navigation training task was withdrawn from existing regular units, and several of the observer schools were then used as the basis for new Bombing and Gunnery Schools. In addition, a Central Gunnery School was set up at Warmwell to attempt to overcome the scarcity of gunnery leaders, which was causing considerable difficulty in the operational commands.

In Scotland, the aerodrome at Drem was now

Fairey Battle Trainer conversion.

(Official)

required for fighter operations over the North Sea, and therefore could no longer be occupied by 13 FTS. Instead of being moved this unit was disbanded and its resources spread among several similar units, of which there were now fourteen in operation in the United Kingdom. For similar, and even more cogent, reasons, the School of Air Navigation at Manston was also closed, its task being taken over by the Group Pools.

A significant proportion of Bomber Command's resources were now being devoted to training. Sixteen squadrons were under the control of No 6 (Training) Group, and soon after the outbreak of war these emulated the example already set by Fighter Command, by pairing into Group Pools, though squadrons still retained their separate identities within the pools. As their titles suggested, they acted as pools from which operational squadrons were able to draw replacement aircrew, and these could thus relinquish their own training role to concentrate entirely on their main purpose. The output from each pool was earmarked for a specific Group, and flew similar aircraft so that crews would already be experienced on these. This system was not entirely satisfactory, however, and in the spring of 1940 all existing Group Pools were redesignated Operational Training Units, those in Bomber Command ceasing to have component squadrons.

The success of the OTU system was sufficient to justify its extension overseas, and accordingly a Transit Unit Reserve Pool at Ismailia, in the Egyptian Canal Zone, was restyled 70 (Middle East) OTU at the end of 1940. This initially had both a bomber and fighter element, but the latter broke away in 1941 to form 71 OTU, and several more of these units later formed in the Eastern Mediterranean. The following year they were supplemented by a number of Middle East Training Schools, giving different types of specialised courses. OTUs were also formed in India.

At the beginning of 1940, plans were laid during the so-called 'Phoney War' period for several FTSs to be formed in France, to be located in the Vendome area, some distance south of Paris, though in the event this intention was overtaken by events. At home, there were sufficient refugee Pole volunteers for a Polish Training and Grading Flight to be set up at Kingstown. The number of Polish recruits later became sufficient to justify special facilities, and the following year the Nottingham area received both 25 (Polish) EFTS at Hucknall and 16 (Polish) SFTS at Newton. In addition a Polish Training Unit formed at Hucknall, later becoming 16 (Polish) OTU, and moving to Bramcote and then Finningley before being merged into 10 OTU towards the end of the war, by which time the supply of Polish recruits had dropped to much smaller numbers.

The nature of the SFTSs had begun to change by early 1940. Instead of being of a general nature, they were now categorised, those classified as Group I accepting only pupils earmarked as potential fighter pilots, whilst Group II schools took future bomber

Left:
Blackburn Botha I L6250 '1F' of No 3 School of General Reconnaissance at Squires Gate in 1942.
(MAP photo)

Below:
Armstrong Whitworth Whitley V N1503 'M' of No 19 Operational Training Unit at Kinloss in 1944.
(RAF Museum Photo No P017820)

Bristol Beaufort I N1113 'D1' of No 3 (Coastal) Operational Training Unit at Cranwell in 1942. (via A.S. Thomas)

pilots. They continued to use ageing Hart variants and Battles, as the newer Ansons and Oxfords would be required for shipment to the Dominions, where an Empire Air Training Scheme was beginning to get under way, which would take over many of the responsibilities for training both British and Dominion pilots and crews.

The rapid increase in training units was once more proving too great for the existing administrative structure, and on 27 May 1940 Training Command was split. In its place came Flying Training Command and Technical Training Command. The former comprised 21 and 23 Groups looking after advanced flying training, whilst 51 Group controlled the elementary training units and 54 Group was responsible for recruits.

The Central Flying School was now finding itself unable to cope with the vastly increased demands for qualified instructors, and this problem was met by setting up special Flying Instructors Schools. One of these, 2 FIS at Cranwell, was later designated No 2 Central Flying School, the original CFS at Upavon then becoming No 1 CFS.

From the late summer of 1940, several schools were shipped intact to one or other of the Dominions, to get the Empire Air Training Scheme, or British Commonwealth Air Training Plan to give it the official title, off the ground. Canada was particularly notable in this respect, but many schools were also set up in South Africa, Australia and Southern Rhodesia. These included not only EFTSs and SFTSs, but also such others as SANs, AOSs, B&GSs, OTUs and also Schools of General Reconnaissance. The departure of these units enabled the vacated aerodromes to become available either for operational purposes, or for operational training.

The B&GSs were phased out during 1941, and their places taken by more specialised Air Gunnery Schools, attached to which were special target towing flights. Around the same time, more attention was being given to radio communication and the use of new electronic devices. This led to the replacement of the Electrical and Wireless Schools by a series of new Signals Schools and Radio Schools.

Heavy losses being incurred in daylight operations by Bomber Command led to a switch to night raids. These brought their own hazards, particularly on return, and techniques therefore had to be developed to combat this. No 1 Blind Approach School was therefore set up in September 1940 at Watchfield and this was followed by a series of Blind Approach Training Flights attached to those advanced flying schools which were turning out bomber pilots. The use of radar beams by these units was later recognised in their titles, which in October 1941 were changed to

Beam Approach, being then renumbered in a new 1500-series of designations.

With the large numbers of aircraft now being received from the United States, plus those being turned out in quantity from UK production line factories, there was an increasing need for pilots capable of delivering these machines to the various theatres of war where they were needed. In October 1941, therefore, a Ferry Training Unit was formed at Honeybourne, the first of thirteen of these units, including one in Canada.

One new type of aerial warfare, dramatically used by the Germans in the invasion of Crete, was the use of gliders. The RAF was slow to adopt their use but, after some limited work at Ringway, several Glider Training Schools were set up during 1941 and 1942 in the Oxford area, equipped with Hotspur training gliders, these being towed initially by Hart variants, and later by a glider tug adaptation of the Miles Master pilot trainer. When the larger Horsa glider entered service in numbers the following year, the first of several Heavy Glider Conversion Units was set up.

The training of bomber crews by the OTUs was working satisfactorily by mid-1941, and in a number of cases it had been possible to send aircraft from these units on actual raids. A new complication then arose, however, with the impending introduction into service of large new bombers in the shape of twin-engined Manchesters and four-engined Halifaxes, Stirlings, Liberators and Lancasters. It was not considered practicable to issue these to Bomber OTUs and initially the squadrons found themselves reverting to the former situation of having to take responsibility for the final stages of training. They were able to ease the situation a little by forming separate conversion flights, sometimes detached to a satellite aerodrome to relieve congestion, but this was not entirely satisfactory, and in early 1941 the existing conversion flights were formed into quite separate Conversion Units.

By 1942 advance flying training and crew training was being largely provided by the Dominion schools. Whilst this relieved much of the burden on the home-based units, it provided a rather fluctuating supply of men who had carried out all their training in conditions vastly different from those they were soon to encounter. To help solve this problem, most of the surviving UK-based SFTSs were restyled as (Pilot) Advance Flying Units, with the primary task of getting pilots accustomed to the British terrain and rapidly changing weather conditions, as well as a busier airspace and the hazards of a total blackout. They could also be used as a pool of trainees, to act as a buffer between the uncertain intake, and the equally variable needs of the squadrons. It was envisaged originally that these units would also provide similar acclimatisation for observers, with a special four week course before joining their units. It was soon realised, however, that not only would the aircraft with which they were equipped have no suitable W/T equipment, but the units would lack the necessary trained and suitable pilots. Instead, therefore, several of the Air Observers Schools were reorganised as (Observer) Advanced Flying Units, manned by staff pilots, and with no ground training element in the course.

In March 1942 it was decided to economise in the use of bomber pilots, and the second pilot was dispensed with, but to compensate for this the standard of training for bomber pilots was raised at the same time. There was also concern about the general level of wastage from the schools, and in an attempt to reduce this the PNB (Pilot, Navigator, Air Bomber) Scheme was introduced, in which only good quality trainees would be selected, rather than continue to expend invaluable resources on a large number of recruits, many of whom would fall by the wayside during their courses.

Around the same time, the old title of Observer became obsolete, to be replaced by the Navigator, who would now no longer be concerned in the first instance with weapon training, but would concentrate purely on aircraft navigation. Having completed the basic course, he might then be given additional training to fit him for the particular role he was expected to fill. If he was likely to be posted to light or medium bombers, torpedo bombers or flying boats, he would have to go on to qualify as an Air Bomber, and if successful would become a Navigator (B). In similar fashion, a Navigator (R) would have taken an AI radar course to qualify him for night fighters, whilst W/T operator training would be required for a Navigator (W) on intruders, long-range fighters, torpedo patrol machines or photo-reconnaissance aircraft.

Another significant development at this time was the disbandment of the original Central Flying School, and the formation in its place of the Empire Central Flying School. The gradual dispersal of expertise to the many different flying training schools at home and abroad was giving rise to local variations in training methods, and this could be particularly dangerous with heavier and faster types of aircraft entering service. The new school, situated at Hullavington, would therefore co-ordinate training policy, so that the latest operational flying techniques could be taught uniformly.

The scope of Operational Training Units was increased in 1943 with the formation of the first Transport OTUs. These initially flew Wellingtons, but as the supply of American-built Dakotas built up, they switched over to that type, and crews were able to practise the kind of flying which would be required of them once they reached an airborne transport or glider towing squadron. These units were all eventually upgraded to Conversion Units specialising in different aspects of the transport role, later equipment including Halifax transports and Yorks.

Right:
Hawker Hurricane I Z4791 'H-33' of the Empire Central Flying School at Hullavington, accompanied by two Spitfire IIAs of the same unit, in September 1942.
(RAF Museum Photo No P1003601)

Below:
Supermarine Spitfire VC's JK926 '1' and MA681 '2' of No 73 Operational Training Unit at Fayid, in Egypt, 1945.
(MAP photo)

Bottom:
Vickers Wellington IA N2887 '5' of the Central Gunnery School at Sutton Bridge in fighter affiliation exercise with North American Mustang I in 1943.
(RAF Museum Photo No P009531)

Short Stirling III LK508 'U3' of the Central Navigation School at Shawbury in 1944.
(RAF Museum Photo No P015673)

Among other specialised units, the Staff Pilots Training Unit was formed in March 1942 at Cark to train pilots in day and night flying prior to their joining AOSs and (O)AFUs as staff pilots. At the end of that year No 1 Specialised Low Attack Instructors School formed at Milfield, to provide instruction on Hurricanes in the use of rocket projectiles and cannon, a form of warfare already being successfully practised in the Western Desert. This was followed by the introduction of the Fighter Leaders School at Aston Down, to provide potential fighter squadron commanders with specialised tactical training. This specialism was taken a stage further in October 1943, when several of the existing fighter OTUs were restyled Tactical Exercise Units, to provide practical combat training to fighter pilots.

The efforts of such units eventually culminated in October 1944 in the formation of the Central Fighter Establishment at Wittering. This combined the various miscellaneous elements of advanced training for fighter pilots with the development of fighter techniques. It was equipped with all the latest contemporary fighters, including Spitfire, Typhoon and Tempest day fighters and Beaufighter and Mosquito night fighters, as well as having three flying classrooms in the shape of AI-equipped Wellingtons.

By the beginning of 1944 the Commonwealth scheme had largely served its purpose, and was beginning to run down, and their duties returned to the UK. Consequently the (P) AFUs soon began to give way to new SFTSs and FTSs. With the prospect looming of victory in Europe, preparations began for continuing the war in the Far East. Particular emphasis was placed on tactical training, and as the number of bomber Heavy Conversion Units dwindled, their places were taken by various transport Conversion Units, ready for the battles which were thought to lie ahead in the Far East. All this proved unnecessary, however, with the dropping of the first atom bombs, and the capitulation of Japan.

Chapter 5 The Post-war Years

As in 1918/19, the end of the Second World War saw a massive rundown in the training organisation during 1945/46. The advent of modern aircraft, however, particularly jets, meant that even at a much reduced level, a more comprehensive training organisation would be necessary than had been required in the inter-war years. The difficulty was to determine exactly what form of structure would be required in the long term, and various formulae have been tried over the last four decades.

Many of the numerous specialist wartime training units would serve no useful purpose in a drastically reduced organisation. Their function was either totally unnecessary or could be incorporated more economically in the remit of other units, whose scope would then become more comprehensive.

There was the added problem of retaining sufficient trained personnel to run both first line and support units. By the end of the war most RAF personnel were members of the Volunteer Reserve, and as such were simply waiting for their demobilisation number to come up, so that they could return to civilian life and do their best to forget all about their wartime service. Some would be willing to remain in service, but they were not necessarily the ones the RAF would prefer to retain. If they were accepted, they would probably have to serve in a lower rank and lose the benefit of their temporarily acquired exalted wartime ranks. They would also have to be prepared to adapt to a level of peace-time pomp and discipline which was likely to come rather hard after the lengthy period when all that mattered was winning the war.

Living off the fat of retained wartime personnel would not suffice for long in any case. It would only be a matter of time before the supply of these began to dry up, and with newer types of aircraft coming along it

Vickers Wellington T.10 RP505 'FDBE' of No 1 (Pilots) Refresher Flying Unit at Finningley around 1949. (via Wing Cdr C.G. Jefford)

was preferable for the long term future to look to young new recruits, with no wartime habits to be discarded, and who would be experienced only in post-war aircraft.

The rundown of training units started immediately after VE-Day, and was accelerated when victory was later achieved in the Far East. A typical example, consequent on the rundown of the heavy bomber force and other reductions, was the disbandment of many of the dozens of Oxford-equipped Beam Approach Training Flights, the few remaining flights being either transformed or replaced within a few months by a small number of Radio Aids Training Flights. By early 1947, however, these too had disappeared, along with the Beam Approach School at Watchfield, their function being taken over by the Central Flying School, which used Harvards for this purpose.

The Central Flying School had been resurrected at Little Rissington in May 1946, by combining No 7 Flying Instructors School (Advanced) from Upavon and No 10 FIS (Elementary) from Woodley, by this time the only survivors of their genus. Despite the theoretical merger, the inherited tasks were too great for one aerodrome, and consequently the school divided between the Cotswolds aerodromes, CFS (Advanced Section) remaining with the headquarters at Little Rissington, whilst CFS (Elementary Section) used South Cerney.

The pilot training organisation was also drastically pruned and transformed. A few of the Elementary Flying Training Schools were disbanded, but the remainder were retained, some in fairly skeleton form, until the peacetime reserve organisation could be set up again. Then during the spring and summer of 1947 they all reverted to peacetime status, but instead of returning to their cumbersome pre-war titles, they now became Reserve Flying Schools. They mostly retained their wartime numbers so that, for instance, No 1 Elementary Flying Training School, which before the war had been No 1 Elementary and Reserve Flying Training School, became No 1 Reserve Flying School on 5 May 1947, having been civilian-run throughout by the de Havilland Aircraft Co. Ltd, first at Hatfield, then from 1943 at nearby Panshanger. The main equipment of these units continued for some time to be Tiger Moths, augmented in 1948 by small numbers of Anson T.1s, soon replaced by T.21s. From 1950 they gradually discarded their Tiger Moths for Chipmunks, or in some instances Prentices.

With the transformation of the EFTSs, the function of training service pupil pilots reverted to the Service Flying Training Schools. These too had been run down in numbers to some extent, and the wartime appellation would no longer be appropriate, so the survivors once more became all-through Flying Training Schools. Like the EFTSs, they largely retained their existing numbers, a typical example being No 3 Service Flying

Training School at Feltwell, which on 9 April 1947 once more became No 3 Flying Training School. Its main equipment of Harvards was augmented by a number of Tiger Moths, these latter giving way to Prentices towards the end of the following year.

The operational commands underwent a similar transformation. Whilst many of Operational Training Units and Conversion Units had disappeared by early 1946, several of each remained. In particular, Transport Command still had a need for trained crews for trooping purposes of various kinds, as well as airborne forces training, and therefore assorted CUs were necessary, equipped with such types as Dakotas, Halifaxes, Yorks and Liberators.

During the spring of 1947, two new series of units replaced the OTUs and CUs. These were given unit numbers in a new 200-series, with numbers 201 to 224 earmarked for Advanced Flying Schools, and those from 226 onwards reserved for Operational Conversion Units, although there was never any likelihood that either series would be fully taken up in peacetime conditions. Advanced Flying Schools, which were initially to have been called Crew Training Units, were formed from the remnants of the OTU organisation. Equipped initially with Wellingtons converted for crew training, 201 AFS at Swinderby and 202 AFS at Finningley were formed out of 21 and 17 OTUs respectively, though 202 soon closed down. Fighter training requirements were now to be met by 203 AFS, formed out of the Spitfire-equipped 61 OTU at Keevil, later moving to Chivenor. Finally, 16 OTU became 204 AFS, carrying out light bomber training on Mosquitoes at Cottesmore, then later at Driffield.

On completion of their relevant AFS course, crews would progress to an appropriate OCU. In Fighter Command, trainee fighter pilots who had survived the 203 AFS course would go on to 226 OCU, which had formed as early as August 1946 from 1335 CU at Molesworth before moving to Bentwaters, where its piston-engined machines gradually gave way to Vampires and then Meteors. AOP trainees were

Top:
Bristol Buckmaster T.1 RP246 'FCVE' of the Empire Flying School at Hullavington in 1947.
(Author's collection)

Centre:
Gloster Javelin T.3 XH443 'Z' of No 25 Squadron from Waterbeach in 1959.
(via Ray Hanna)

Bottom:
EEC Lightning T.5 XS452 of No 226 Operational Flying School from Coltishall, seen at Lakenheath in 1970.
(Roger Lindsay)

catered for by the Austers of 227 OCU, formed from 43 OTU at Andover, soon moving to Middle Wallop, to lay the foundations for the headquarters of Army aviation, still based there forty years on. The third such unit in this command was 228 OCU, which combined 13 and 54 OTUs at Leeming to provide tactical light bomber and night fighter training for pupils from 204 AFS, initially on Mosquitoes and a few radar-equipped Wellington trainers, but soon on Brigands.

In Bomber Command, heavy bomber crews went to 230 OCU, formed from No 1653 Heavy Conversion Unit at Lindholme, later moving to Scampton where Lincolns were received. Those destined for strategic light bomber units found their way to 231 OCU, formed from 16 OTU at Coningsby, flying in Mosquitoes. In Coastal Command, flying boats were still considered necessary for some years after the war, and the Sunderlands of 4 OTU at Calshot now became 235 OCU, whilst photographic reconnaissance trainees flew Mosquitoes and Spitfires at Benson with 237 OCU, which had previously been 8 OTU. The School of General Reconnaissance at Leuchars then became surplus and was disbanded. Finally, in Transport Command, No 1382 (Transport) CU at North Luffenham became 240 OCU, equipped with the ubiquitous Dakotas, soon augmented by Devons and Valettas. Crews for the heavier transports were catered for by 241 OCU, formed from No 1332 Heavy Transport CU at Dishforth, initially with Yorks and Halifaxes until the latter type gave way to the Hastings.

Specialised crew training also underwent some changes. The two surviving Air Gunnery Schools had closed down by the end of 1947, their function being absorbed in the Central Gunnery School at Leconfield. Several Air Navigation Schools remained, equipment being mainly Wellingtons and Ansons, but these were gradually rationalised and renumbered. By early 1948 only three remained, of which one was based in Southern Rhodesia using the specially designed Anson T.20, its home equivalents having the Anson T.21. The headquarters unit of this part of the organisation was the Empire Air Navigation School at Shawbury, which was renamed the Central Navigation School in July 1949, only to become the Central Navigation and Control School when it absorbed the School of Air Traffic Control in February 1950, equipment then being a motley assortment of Ansons, Wellingtons, Lancasters and Lincolns.

The RAF College at Cranwell had remained in existence throughout, but in April 1947 it absorbed the resident 19 FTS to reform its flying training element, which it had lost in the latter days of the war. In June 1949 an RAF Flying College was formed at Manby, soon absorbing the Empire Air Armament School there, as well as taking over most of the aircraft and functions of the Empire Flying School at Hullavington, apart from the Examining Wing which had already been transferred to CFS. The Empire Radio School at Debden had a similar transformation, becoming the Signals Division of the RAF Technical College in October 1949.

Thus, four years after an uneasy peace had broken out, the basic post-war structure was finally complete. This was to prove none too soon, as on 25 June 1950 North Korean forces crossed the 38th Parallel, the arbitrary post-war latitudinal border with South Korea, and another major conflagration was under way. For the RAF, the period of retrenchment and consolidation was suddenly at an end, and rapid expansion was to be the order of the day. New pilots would have to be quickly trained, as would new crews for the multi-seat aircraft which might be required to participate in this new war.

The existing intakes of pilot recruits had to suffice at first, but these would obviously be insufficient in the event of a prolonged and widespread war. The existing Flying Training Schools were operating all-through training, by now mainly on Prentices and Harvards, though 7 FTS at Cottesmore was due to get some Balliols. In early 1951, their *ab initio* element was augmented when No 1 Basic Flying Training School was formed at Booker, to be followed by four more of its kind, all civilian-operated and all equipped with Chipmunks. At Dalcross, No 8 Advanced Flying Training School formed with Oxfords, to cater specially for National Service pilots who had received their initial training at a BFTS, and three similar units were formed within the next few months.

These were supplemented by four Flying Refresher Schools performing the task suggested by their title, the first being 101 FRS formed from an existing unit at Finningley and catering for regulars. 102 FRS at North Luffenham and 103 FRS at Full Sutton trained non-regular recruits for fighters on Spitfires and Vampires, whilst 104 FRS at Lichfield took in bomber pilot recruits for training on Wellingtons and Oxfords. As the requirement for FRSs diminished, so the need for more Advanced Flying Schools increased, and by the late summer of 1952 there were 11 of these in existence, mostly equipped with Meteor or Vampire jets, the exception being 201 AFS at Swinderby, now re-equipped with Varsity crew trainers. In addition, two civilian-operated Basic Air Navigation Schools were formed, both equipped with Anson T.21s, and Ansons and Prentices formed the equipment of two new Air Signallers Schools.

There had been some changes in other units. In Fighter Command, the Vampire element of 226 OCU had broken away to form 229 OCU at Chivenor, a new Vampire-equipped 233 OCU was to form at Pembrey, whilst 227 OCU had been restyled the AOP School and later the Light Aircraft School. At Colerne, 238 OCU had formed for AI radar training with Brigand T.4s. In Bomber Command the original 231 OCU had disbanded, to be replaced later by a new unit with that title at

Bassingbourn, equipped with Canberra jet bombers, whilst at Marham the Washington Conversion Unit prepared bomber crews for these anglicised Boeing B-29s. In Transport Command, 240 and 241 OCUs combined at Dishforth in April 1951 as 242 OCU, flying Valettas and Hastings. Coastal Command saw a need for a new No 1 Marine Reconnaisance School, which formed with Lancaster GR.3s at St Mawgan in May 1951, and at Kinloss 236 OCU discarded this type for new Shackletons, later supplemented by Lockheed Neptunes which, like the Washingtons, were provided under a Mutual Defence Aid Pact.

In the event, no RAF squadrons served in Korea, the British air contribution being limited to Army-manned AOP squadrons and Fleet Air Arm squadrons operating from carriers. An Armistice was signed on 27 July 1953 at Panmunjom, near the 38th parallel, but by then the UK training organisation was already in the throes of a drastic cutback to something like its former strength.

All the fringe organisations were dismantled. The Rhodesian Air Training Wing ceased training activities and soon disbanded. The FRSs and some of the AFTSs had already gone, and they were now followed by the BANSs and BFTSs. Even the RFSs were at first cut back drastically in numbers, then within twelve months the remainder had disappeared altogether.

The AFS organisation had also gone within twelve months, but not all the schools were disbanded, a new use being found for their jet experience when several of them were transformed into new Flying Training Schools. 235 OCU became the Flying Boat Training Squadron for a time, but the days of the flying boat were now numbered, and within three years this had disbanded. A Sabre Conversion Unit had formed in April 1953 at Wildenrath in Germany, where squadrons of the 2nd Tactical Air force were beginning to operate this Canadian-built fighter supplied under MDAP arrangements.

Times were now changing in other ways, too, and one foretaste of this was the formation at Middle Wallop in March 1954 of a Helicopter (Development) Flight, soon to join CFS at South Cerney, where it operated Dragonflies and Sycamores. Middle Wallop also became the home of the Army Air Corps Centre when it came into existence on 1 September 1957, replacing the Light Aircraft School. It was initially divided into an Elementary Flight with Chipmunks, an Intermediate Flight and an Exercise Flight, both with Austers, and a Helicopter Flight with Skeeters.

Events now moved at a much slower pace, and relatively few changes in the surviving RAF training unit structure occurred in the remainder of the fifties. A Bomber Command Bombing School had formed at Lindholme in October 1952 with Lincolns and Varsities. At Leconfield, the Central Gunnery School took the more appropriate title Fighter Weapons School in January 1955, with Venoms and Hunters replacing some of the earlier types. In July of that year, 232 OCU formed at Gaydon to operate new V-bombers in the shape of Valiants and later Victors, and the following year 230 OCU reformed at Waddingtons with Vulcans. 236 OCU and 1 MRS combined at Kinloss in October 1956 to form the Marine Operational Training Unit, equipped with Shackletons. The Air Signallers School at Swanton Morley also modernised its title in April 1957, to become the Air Electronics School, with Ansons and Varsities.

By the end of the decade only six Flying Training Schools still existed, but equipment was changing rapidly. Piston Provosts had joined the FTSs just as the Korean War was ending, to produce a Provost/Harvard training sequence, quickly giving way to a Provost/ Vampire sequence as the Vampire T.11 became available. Within two years, however, the first Jet Provosts were to reach these units and herald a transformation in service training which has endured to the present day.

Events now proceeded to unfold at a similarly leisurely pace throughout the sixties. In November 1961, re-equipment within Transport Command brought a need for the formation of an Argosy Conversion Unit at Benson, this merging eighteen months later into 242 OCU, which already had Beverlys on strength, and was shortly to move south to Thorney Island. 228 OCU at Leeming, which had successively flown Meteor night fighters and Javelins, as well as Valettas and Canberra T.11s, disbanded in September 1961, Javelin conversion then becoming the responsibility of the Central Fighter Establishment at West Raynham, which had already absorbed the Fighter Weapons School in March 1958, the establishment moving to Binbrook in October 1962.

A Lightning Conversion Unit formed at Middleton St George in June 1962, becoming a new 226 OCU a year later, and in July 1962 the RAF Flying College at Manby became the College of Air Warfare. A reconstituted 228 OCU took over Javelin conversion training at Leuchars in June 1962, only to disband at the end of the following year. The rundown of the V-bomber force, and in particular the withdrawal of the Valiant due to fatigue problems, led to the closure of 232 OCU in July 1965, its remnants forming the Tanker Training Flight, which in turn itself became 232 OCU five years later. The next generation of aircraft began to appear when in February 1968 a further new 228 OCU formed at Coningsby with Phantoms. The demise of Bomber Command necessitated the Lindholme-based school becoming the Strike Command Bombing School in April 1968, now with Varsities and Hastings T.5s. Yet another major advance saw the formation at Wittering in January 1969 of the Harrier Conversion Unit, renamed 233 OCU in October 1970.

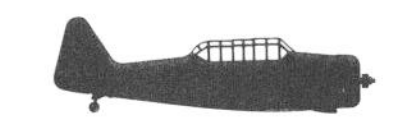

In the transport field, further new equipment led to the formation in January 1963 at Odiham of the Twin Pioneer Conversion Unit, and also at that station the Belvedere Conversion Unit, attached to 72 Squadron. Nineteen months later these formed the basis of the Short Range Conversion Unit, equipped with Twin Pioneers and Wessex transports, but only the latter type was used after it became the Helicopter Operational Conversion Flight in July 1967. An Andover Conversion Unit formed at Abingdon in July 1966, moving at the end of the decade to Thorney Island where it was absorbed into 242 OCU.

The Army Air Corps Centre at Middle Wallop was by now shifting its emphasis to helicopters, with a consequent change in structure. By 1965 the Chipmunk element had become the Basic Fixed Wing Flight, and was being operated by Bristow Helicopters Ltd, who were also responsible for the Basic Helicopter Flight equipped with civil-registered Hiller UH-12s. There was an Advanced Fixed Wing Flight operating Auster APO.9s and Beavers, and an Advanced Rotary Wing Flight initially using Skeeters until these could be replaced with Siouxs and Scouts.

Meanwhile, significant changes had taken place in the Flying Training Schools. The Jet Provost was now the standard trainer, but at Valley the Gnat had been introduced in November 1962, and 4 FTS then became the first advanced jet FTS, Hunters being also added to the strength in 1967. 2 FTS had ceased to exist for a short time, but in January 1970 it reformed at Church Fenton for naval *ab initio* flying training, from the Primary Flying School element of CFS, using Chipmunks until new Bulldogs arrived in 1973. This unit again lost its separate identity in November 1974, when it formed the RN EFTS within 3 FTS at Leeming.

Under a new system introduced in August 1960, pupil pilots destined for multi-engine piston aircraft undertook flying training on Varsities with 4 FTS at Valley. With the advent of Gnats, this became impracticable, and the task was transferred in 1962 to 5 FTS at Oakington. At the end of 1973 replacements in

Handley Page T.5 of the Strike Command Bombing School, running-up the starboard inner engine at Lindholme in 1971.

(Steve McAdam)

Hawker Siddeley HS.125 Dominie T.1 XS711 'L' of No 6 Flying Training School at Finningley.
(Paddy Porter collection)

the form of Jetstreams began to appear, but a change of policy led to the unit being disbanded in October 1974. The concept, however, was reintroduced in 1976, at 3 FTS Leeming, being transferred in 1979 to 5 FTS at Finningley. This latter unit had reformed there in May 1970 with Varsities, combining the functions of Nos 1 and 2 Air Navigation Schools and later also the Air Electronics and Air Engineers School, to become responsible for training all navigators, air engineers and air electronics operators. 7 FTS existed between March 1962 and November 1966 at Church Fenton, as a Jet Provost/Vampire T.11 school, being resurrected there in April 1979 with later versions of the Jet Provost.

Further changes had taken place at Middle Wallop by the mid-seventies. The Chipmunks soldiered on, giving basic training to both AAC and Marine pilots before converting to helicopters with the Basic Helicopter Flight, now flying civil-registered Westland-Bell 47G-4s. With the emphasis on helicopters, the Advanced Fixed Wing Flight disbanded in 1976, and around the same time the Advanced Rotary Wing Squadron, as it had now become, re-equipped with Gazelles.

A number of changes have taken place amongst OCUs in recent years. In July 1970, MOTU became a new Nimrod-equipped 236 OCU at St Mawgan, eventually moving to Kinloss in April 1982. 241 OCU reformed at Brize Norton in July 1970, relying on operational squadrons for its aircraft needs, which have included the BAe146, Tristar, Belfast, Britannia and VC-10. Buccaneer training is provided by 237 OCU, which reformed in March 1971 at Honington, moving to Lossiemouth in October 1984. The Helicopter Operational Conversion Flight at Odiham added Pumas when it became the Air Training Squadron in May 1971, and after yet a further metamorphosis in January 1972 to become a new 240 OCU, it has more recently received Chinooks. A Jaguar Conversion Unit, set up in May 1973 at Lossiemouth, became a new 226 OCU in October 1974. With the impending withdrawal of Vulcans (and without the insight necessary to foresee their vital use shortly afterwards in the South Atlantic),

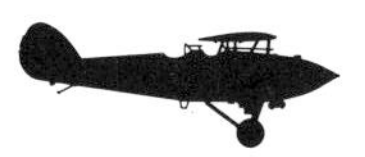

230 OCU closed at Scampton in August 1981, and more recently 232 OCU closed at Marham in April 1986. 229 OCU had moved to Brawdy in September, to become the Tactical Weapons Unit flying Hunters. Its number was not taken up again until a new 229 OCU formed at Coningsby in May 1985 for Tornado training.

A further step forward in pilot training occurred in 1976 with the introduction of the Hawk at 4 FTS Valley, where it replaced the Gnat. This type also later formed the equipment of the No 1 Tactical Weapons Unit at Brawdy, the reduced Hunter element of which became 2 TWU at Lossiemouth in August 1978. Other recent changes have included the move of the Central Flying School to Scampton in September 1984, after having spent some time at Cranwell and then Leeming. 237 OCU moved around the same time to Lossiemouth. 232 OCU disbanded at Marham in April 1986, and 228 OCU moved a year later to Leuchars.

Scottish Aviation Bulldog T.1 XX628 '04' of the University of Wales Air Squadron in 1985.
(MAP photo)

Chapter 6 The Navy Way

Supermarine Seafire IBs including NX809 'AC-C' of No 736 Squadron of the School of Air Combat Duties at St Merryn around 1943.

(RNAS Culdrose)

With the amalgamation of the Royal Flying Corps and the Royal Naval Air Service on April Fool's Day 1918, the separate naval training organisation also became merged. The original RN school at Eastchurch had by then been joined by a number of others around the country, and one in France, at Vendome. With the merger, these all became Training Depot Stations, numbered from 201 onwards to distinguish them from their RFC counterparts which were already numbered from 1 onwards.

By virtue of its different purpose, however, it was always necessary to maintain a naval training element of the RAF, and more specialised types of unit were soon set up, such as the Grand Fleet School of Aerial Fighting and Gunnery at East Fortune. This situation continued after the Armistice, with the emergence of such units as the RAF Training Bases at Gosport and Leuchars for training naval airmen, the Seaplane Training School at Calshot and the School of Naval

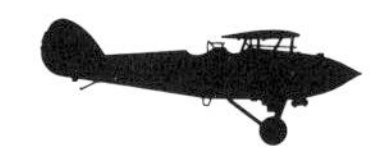

Co-operation at Lee-on-Solent. The naval element of the RAF became known as the Fleet Air Arm, and many of the officers of the carrier flights and squadrons carried dual RAF and RN ranking, though most gave the Navy their prime allegiance.

Their Lordships at the Admiralty were never happy with this situation, however, and fought for 20 years to reverse the merger. Shortly before the outbreak of the Second World War, they succeeded, and on 24 May 1939 the Fleet Air Arm became a separate entity, taking with it the responsibility for much of its own training. New pilot recruits still undertook primary and advanced flying training at RAF schools, but new units had to be formed to undertake most other forms of naval air training and support activities.

It was necessary to devise some system of titling for these second-line units and, contrary to RAF practice, they were given squadron status. It was not envisaged that more than 50 such units would exist at any one time, and therefore part of the 700-series, which was already reserved for catapult squadrons, was earmarked for this purpose. Accordingly, on the date of separation, squadrons numbered from 750 onwards were set up at those aerodromes coming under Admiralty control.

The RN Observers School at Ford then became 750, 751 and 752 Squadrons, grouped together as No 1 Observer School equipped with Ospreys, Sharks and Walruses, whilst the School of Naval Co-operation at Lee-on-Solent now formed No 2 Observer School consisting of 753 and 754 Squadrons with Seafoxes, Sharks and Walruses. 755, 756 and 757 Squadrons at Worthy Down made up No 1 Air Gunners School, training Telegraphist Air Gunners on Sharks, Ospreys and later Walruses. Another unit to be absorbed was the Floatplane Training Flight at Lee-on-Solent, which formed the basis of 765 Squadron, a Seaplane School and Pool with Walruses, Seafoxes and Swordfish seaplanes. First-line squadrons of HMS *Courageous* had for some time engaged in deck landing training, and these were now given formal second line status, becoming 767 and 769 Squadrons, shore based at Donibristle, although spending much of their time afloat, initially in HMS *Furious*.

As the war progressed, many other specialised training units emerged, all having numbers in the 700 series, though also having descriptive titles, and often grouped as a school. Bases were set up near naval shore establishments in such countries as Jamaica, Canada, South Africa, India, Ceylon and Australia. The advent of MAC-ships and escort carriers led to a decline in catapult flights, which in turn provided the opportunity to take up the earlier numbers in the 700-series, and by the end of the war the whole of this series had been used at one time or another for different second-line units.

Victory in Europe and then the Far East resulted in a rapid rundown of training facilities, and a reassessment of needs in the light of the post-war situation. The earlier stages of pilot training remained largely the responsibility of the RAF, with FAA units undertaking more specialised aspects. Most naval airmen were by this time RNVR volunteers, and those whom the Navy wished to retain were now given the option of permanent service.

It took some time for a real pattern to emerge, but by the beginning of 1951 a much reduced training strength was pointing the way to the future. 767 Squadron was the only one of the original units to have retained its identity, being now based at Yeovilton for Deck Landing Control Officer training, the term 'Clockwork Mouse' (once used on the D.H.6) being applied to the continual circuits and landings by its Fireflies, Seafires and Sea Furies. Also based there was 799 Squadron, giving refresher flying training on Harvards, Fireflies and Seafires. At Culdrose, the Naval Air Fighter School comprised 736 and 738 Squadrons with Seafires and Sea Furies and, as a sign of the times, 702 Squadron was giving jet evaluation and training on Meteor T.7s and Sea Vampire F.20s. Observer training was undertaken with 796 Squadron at St. Merryn, on Fireflies and ageing Barracudas, whilst 766 Squadron at Lossiemouth was now an Operational Flying School, using Fireflies and Seafires. Finally, the Naval Air Anti-Submarine School at Eglinton consisted of 719 and 737 Squadrons, both equipped with Fireflies. In addition, however, part of the task of 705 Squadron, the Helicopter Unit at Gosport, was to provide training for naval pilots and crewmen on Dragonflies, these having replaced the earlier pioneering Hoverflies.

At this time events on the other side of the world heralded a change of pace and emphasis. The Korean War had broken out a few months earlier, and the Royal Navy was becoming heavily involved. It was too early for naval jet aircraft to participate, but towards the end of that conflict British carriers were carrying their first helicopters.

Increased needs for fighter pilots led to the expansion of the Culdrose school. A new 759 Squadron took over most types of aircraft in use there, to leave both 736 and 738 Squadrons free to concentrate on training pilots to operate Sea Furies in Korean waters. At the end of the year, both the Yeovilton squadrons left that station, 799 going to the re-opened wartime base of Machrihanish, whilst 767 moved its 'mousing' activities to nearby Henstridge. At St. Merryn, the Barracuda element of 796 Squadron became 750 Squadron in April 1952, the latter unit surviving continuously until the present day at various locations.

A naval first-line squadron first received helicopters in late 1952, and a few months later 705 Squadron lost its other roles to become the Helicopter Training Squadron re-equipped with Hillers, Whirlwinds and a later version of the Dragonfly. Around the same time, 767 Squadron moved again, this time to Stretton, where it later operated Avengers, Attackers and Sea Hawks. In 1953 the Operational Flying School at Lossiemouth was split, 766 Squadron moving in October to Culdrose to concentrate on anti-submarine training with Fireflies. The fighter training element then became 764 Squadron, which moved at the same time to Yeovilton, where it re-equipped a few months later with Sea Hawks, and later Sea Venoms and Wyverns.

With the departure of the OFS, Lossiemouth became the new home for the NAFS where it was soon flying Attackers, Sea Vampires, Sea Hawks and Meteor T.7s, 759 Squadron being later disbanded. St. Merryn ceased to operate aircraft, and the Observer School then went to Culdrose, 750 Squadron having by now re-equipped with Sea Princes and Firefly T.7s. Only Eglinton maintained its status quo, though the first Gannets had arrived there by March 1955. In that year, operational flying training was transformed to take account of new equipment reaching the Fleet Air Arm. Both 764 and 766 Squadrons disbanded, and a new 766 Squadron formed at Yeovilton in October as an All Weather Fighter Pool equipped with Sea Venoms.

Below:
Hawker Sea Fury T.20 VZ370 '200/HF' of the Instrument Flying Flight of No 728 Squadron at Hal Far, Malta around 1954.
(via Brian Lowe)

Bottom:
Percival Sea Prince T.1 WP313 '568/CU' and others of No 750 Squadron lined up at Culdrose around 1975.
(RNAS Culdrose)

In 1956, Gosport, one of the oldest military aerodromes in the country, was closed down, and 705 Squadron moved to nearby Lee-on-Solent. At Brawdy, 727 Squadron reformed to give air experience to cadets from the Royal Naval College at Dartmouth, using Sea Balliols, Sea Princes and Sea Vampires. Both Brawdy and Ford were used for a time by 767 Squadron, until it disbanded in April 1957. 737 Squadron also disbanded in 1957, leaving only 719 Squadron in the Eglinton school. 796 Squadron re-equipped at Culdrose with Gannets and Sea Balliols, only to disband the following year.

Some retitling took place in 1959, to take account of changing functions and equipment. At Lossiemouth, 736 and 738 Squadrons, which had been known for a time as Jet Fighter Training Squadrons, became respectively the Day Fighter Operational Flying School and the All-Weather Fighter OFS, the former equipped with Scimitars, and the latter with Sea Hawks and Sea Venoms. 750 Squadron at Culdrose, which had expanded its title to Observer and Air Signal School, reverted to being plain Observer School before moving out to Malta to be based at Hal Far, where the climate was more conducive to training uninterrupted by weather conditions, some Sea Venoms being received the following year. At Yeovilton, 764 Squadron was now the Air Weapons Training Squadron with Scimitars and Hunter T.8s, whilst 766 Squadron had re-equipped with Sea Vixens, being termed an All Weather Fighter School.

There was by now an increasing emphasis in the Navy on the use of helicopters, particularly in the anti-submarine role. This led to the closure in 1959 of the fixed-wing school at Eglinton, and the reforming of 737 Squadron at Portland as a new Air Anti-Submarine School equipped with Whirlwinds. This was followed in 1961 by the formation of 771 Squadron at Portland for Helicopter Training and Trials, equipped not only with Whirlwinds, but also with the first Wasps, soon to become the standard aircraft for use on small ships.

Westland Sea King HAS.1 XV660 '595/CU' of No 706 Squadron at Culdrose air-lifting Hiller H.T.2 XS165 '543' of No 705 Squadron around 1972.

(RNAS Culdrose)

Hawker Hunter T.8M XL580 '719/VL' of No 899 Squadron at Yeovilton in company with British Aerospace Sea Harrier FRS.1 '711' and Harrier T.4N ZB605 '718' of the same unit.

(British Aerospace)

At Eglinton, meanwhile, 719 Squadron had reformed in May 1960 as the Joint Anti-Submarine School Flight, with Whirlwinds, being elevated to first-line status as 819 Squadron when it re-equipped the following year with Wessexes. 706 Squadron reformed with Wessexes at Culdrose in January 1962 as the Helicopter Advanced Flying Training Squadron, giving specialist training to helicopter pilots, as well as converting them to this new type. Wasps were added to the strength of this squadron in late 1964, for conversion training. In December 1964, 771 Squadron disbanded at Portland, but at the same time 707 Squadron reformed at Culdrose to undertake Advanced and Operational Flying Training for commando helicopter crews on Wessex HU.5s.

Fixed-wing flying was still very much an element of the Fleet Air Arm at this stage, however, and 759 Squadron formed at Brawdy in August 1963 as the Naval Advanced Flying Training Unit equipped with Hunter T.8s. Pupils graduated to either 738 for weapons training, or 849 Squadron for Airborne Early Warning training. At Lossiemouth 736 disbanded in 1965, but a new squadron formed there with that number as a Jet Strike Training Squadron equipped with Buccaneers. It was joined by 750 Squadron, returned from its spell in Malta. In January 1969, 767 reformed, this time with Phantoms at Yeovilton, where it converted both RN and RAF pilots to this aircraft. This was followed by the disbandment of first 759 then 738 Squadron, Brawdy being then handed over to the RAF.

At the end of 1970, 766 Squadron was also disbanded at Yeovilton, the Sea Vixen being phased out by that time. Similarly, the withdrawal of the Buccaneer for future use by the RAF led to the disbandment of 736 Squadron at Lossiemouth in February 1972. This was soon followed by the disbandment of 765 Squadron at Lossiemouth and 767 Squadron at Yeovilton. There was some reorganisation of responsibilities at the surviving stations, with Yeovilton becoming the home of the commando squadrons, and consequently 707 moved there from Culdrose, its strength including a Red Dragon Flight for a time, to give the Prince of Wales helicopter tuition. The vacant slot at Culdrose, was taken up by 771 Squadron, previously mainly a Fleet Requirements Unit at Portland, which now lost this task and began

EEC Canberra T.22 of the Fleet Requirement and Air Direction Unit at Yeovilton.

(RN photo)

Aircrewman Training. At the same station, 706 Squadron replaced its Wessexes with Sea Kings, whilst 750 Squadron discarded its Sea Venoms.

Changes since that time have been relatively few, but with the demise of the large carriers, the emphasis has been on helicopter training. The training element of 829 Squadron, which provided Wasp helicopters for small ships, became 703 Squadron early in 1972, taking over the Wasp element of 706 Squadron three years later to become responsible for all Wasp training. 705 Squadron at Culdrose began converting entirely to Gazelles in 1974. The gradual replacement of the Wasps led to the formation at Yeovilton in January 1978 of 702 Squadron as the Lynx headquarters and training squadron.

Towards the end of 1978, 750 Squadron started to re-equip with Jetstreams. In 1980 899 Squadron reformed as the Sea Harrier Headquarters Squadron, and as a part of its duties undertook training on this type, using four modified Harriers, designated T.4Ns. 706 Squadron disbanded back into 829 Squadron in January 1981, and at the same time the headquarters role of 702 Squadron broke away to become 815 Squadron. The following year 706 moved to Culdrose. Activities in the South Atlantic led in April 1982 to the hasty upgrading of 707 Squadron to operational status as 848 Squadron, but the task was still required, and within a month a new 707 Squadron had formed at Yeovilton, again with Wessexes, these giving way eighteen months later to Sea King HC.4s. This remains the naval training situation at the time of writing.

Training Aircraft Profiles

Avro 504

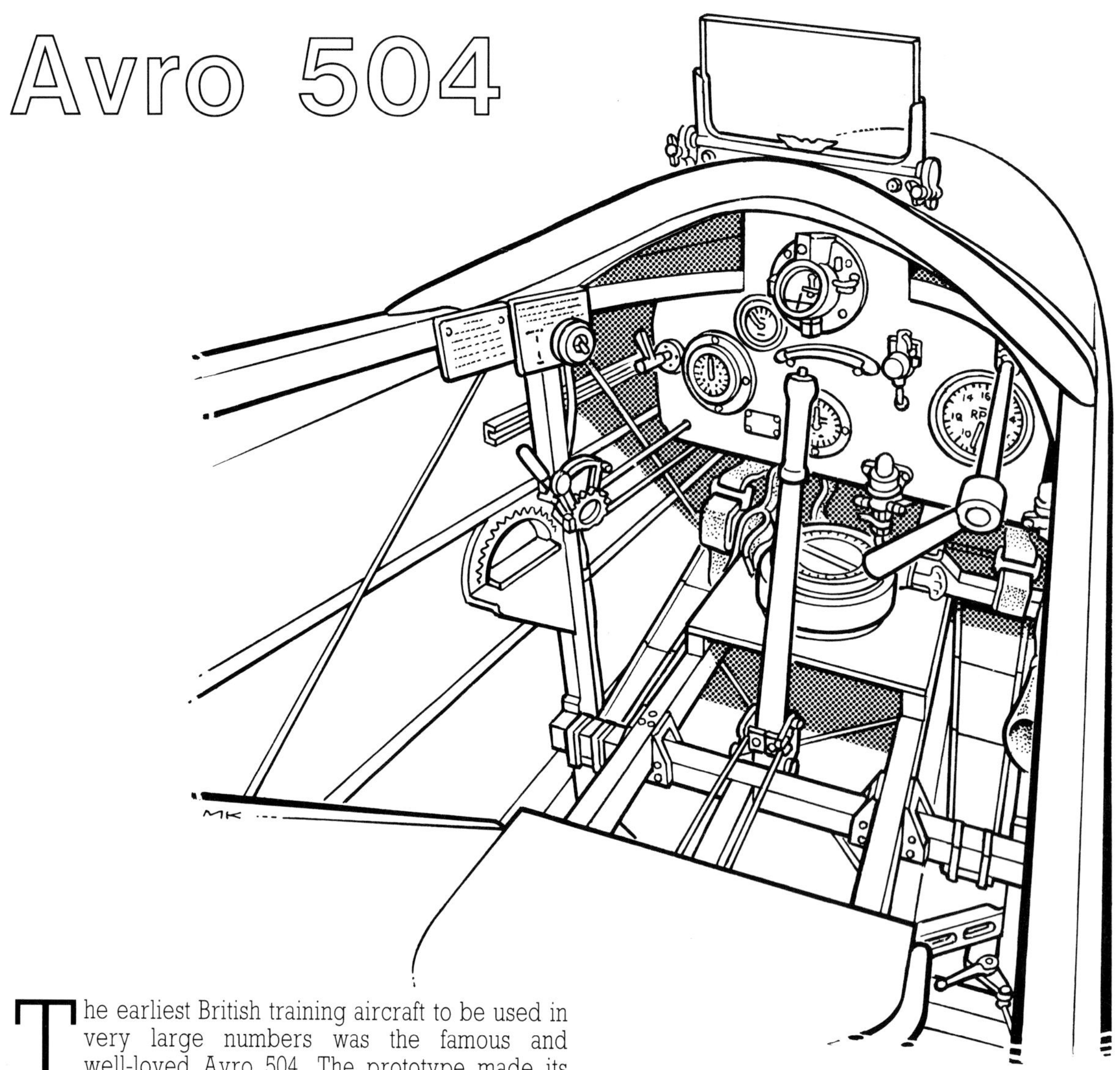

The earliest British training aircraft to be used in very large numbers was the famous and well-loved Avro 504. The prototype made its first flight at Brooklands on 18 September 1913, and its classical and simple lines were very advanced for that time. Shortly before the outbreak of the First World War it was adopted as a general purpose machine for use by both the RFC and the RNAS. Small numbers were used operationally by both services, a notable bombing raid being carried out in November 1914 by three naval machines on the Zeppelin sheds at Friedrichshafen, on the shores of Lake Constance.

Specification (504N)

Power plant:	*One 215 hp Armstrong-Siddeley Lynx IVC.*
Dimensions:	*Span 36 ft 0 in, length 28 ft 11 in, height 10 ft 5 in, wing area 320 sq ft.*
Weights:	*Empty 1,548 lb, loaded 2,240 lb.*
Performance:	*Maximum speed 100 mph at sea level, cruising speed 85 mph, initial climb 770 ft/min, range 255 miles, endurance 3 hrs, service ceiling 17,000 ft.*

Despite its advanced design, the 504 was not essentially a military machine, and consequently had its limitations for front-line use. The main problem was that the observer was situated in the front seat, where he was surrounded by wings, struts and wires, making his task difficult, and this was compounded when operational needs led to the installation of a gun. By 1915, therefore, the 504 was largely relegated to the training role, in which it was to prove the mainstay of the RFC and later RAF for nearly two decades.

Prior to the arrival of the first few trainers from the production line, the manufacturers provided a number of self-contained dual control conversion units for existing machines. Early versions of the 504 were mainly powered by the 80 hp Gnome engine, this being fitted to the 504A, the first true dual control training version. Built in quantity by both the parent company and a number of contractors, this appeared in 1915 and had shorter ailerons than the early 504s, broad-chord struts, and a tailskid attached to the bottom of the rudder. This version gave way in 1917 to the 504J, fitted with the rotary 100 hp Gnome Monosoupape, though difficulties in supply of this engine led to mixed production batches of 504As and 504Js. Various modifications were made in service, and it was not uncommon to see variations to the undercarriage, fuel system and cowling.

The subsequent fame of the 504, however, undoubtedly stemmed from the adoption in August 1917 of the 504J by Major R.R. Smith-Barry as the standard trainer at his new School of Special Flying at Gosport. With the more powerful engine he was able to introduce instructors to the art of recovery from the various manouevres likely to be encountered in aerial fighting, and they were then able to pass on this knowledge to their own pupils.

Above:
Avro 504A A5921, believed with No 55 Reserve Squadron at Yatesbury in 1917.
(J.M. Bruce/G.S. Leslie collection)

The success of the 504J led to its being ordered in quantity for the numerous training units by then in existence at home and overseas, but this only served to exacerbate the engine supply difficulties. In any event, the Monosoupape Gnome was regarded as obsolete by the end of 1917, and trials had already taken place at Gosport with a 130 hp Clerget. Avros were therefore asked to redesign the engine mounting so that a variety of rotary engines could be fitted. The new design had an overhung mounting consisting of two bearer plates, and allowed the fitment of a more streamlined open-fronted cowling.

In this form the machine became the 504K, and on its introduction numerous surplus 80 hp Le Rhône, 100 hp Le Rhône and 130 hp Clerget engines were recalled from RFC units for fitment in production machines. It was originally intended that the 504K would supplant the 504J on the production lines, but in practice there were never enough engines available, and therefore many of the initial batches comprised a mixture of the two versions, and sometimes also the 504A. By February 1918 the 504K had been adopted as the standard trainer aircraft, a role it was destined to fulfil for ten years with the Royal Air Force, which formed shortly afterwards. Planned production of 100 machines a week had almost been achieved by the time of the Armistice.

Despite having the same engine as aircraft at the front, the 504K was sufficiently docile for it to be handled easily by novice pilots. It highlighted the shortcomings of the less able pilots, but was capable of being flown at its best only by those of outstanding ability. Under the Smith-Barry system, pupils had control of the machine from the front seat, and could keep in touch with the instructor behind him, initially by waggling the control column, but later by the introduction of a 'Gosport' speaking tube, which in appearance and use was somewhat similar to those used by waiters to pass on orders to the kitchen. In its original form it was essentially a long flexible metal hose, to one end of which was fitted a triangular-shaped mouthpiece, this being secured to the

Avro 504J B3168 of 'A' Flight of the School of Special Flying at Gosport around 1918.
(J.M. Bruce/G.S. Leslie collection)

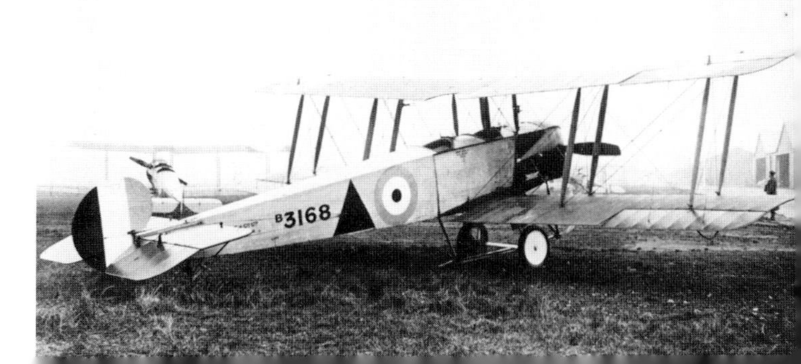

instructor's head by an elasticated strap. He passed the other end back to the pupil, who plugged it into a V-shaped earpiece on his helmet. It was strictly a one-way means of communication, and much was left to guesswork or hand signals. Use of the tube was rather hazardous in winter, as an instructor with a streaming cold could find his top lip stuck to the canvas bag.

A set routine of instruction was followed in the Smith-Barry system, comprising demonstration of controls, straight and level flying, turns, misuse of controls in a turn, then take-offs and landings. Manoeuvres would be analysed and commented on during flight, and after landing there would be a further discussion, during which the instructor would point out any bad habits which were developing. When the pupil was considered sufficiently advanced he would be sent up for his first solo flight.

The 504J was declared obsolete in September 1921, but the 504K remained in service after the war with the new Flying Training Schools, until it, too, gradually became outdated, though it was not until September 1926 that the last one left the Avro production line at Hamble. Meanwhile, Avros had been contracted to fit two machines (E9265 and E9266) experimentally with a 175 hp Siddeley Lynx, and in this Specification, redesignated 504N, they were flown to Croydon by their test pilot, Bert Hinkler, in May 1922, for demonstrations. The modification showed promise, and was developed with a new oleo-pneumatic undercarriage in place of the original skid type.

There were no resources available at that time for a completely new design of RAF trainer, but this modernisation of the 504 had produced an acceptable compromise. Production orders for the 504N were placed early in 1927, and later that year these began to enter service with the Flying Training Schools as well as many other units such as University Air Squadrons and reserve squadrons. Most service squadrons also had one or two on strength, for instrument and refresher flying, plus communications work. In addition, many of the surviving 504Ks were reconditioned from 1927 by the Home Aircraft Depot at Henlow and at the same time brought up to 504N standard. Fitting a more powerful engine was not the only modification distinguishing the new version from the 504K, other changes including the fitment of large twin 18-gallon fuel tanks just outside the upper centre section struts, and additional stringers making a more rounded fuselage. The wooden fuselages and tapered ailerons of the early production machines later gave way to welded steel fuselage construction and rectangular Frise ailerons. Various versions of the engine were fitted, final production aircraft having the 215 hp Lynx IVC.

An in-service modification was the fitment in 1931 of blind flying equipment on several aircraft of the Central Flying School at Wittering. This comprised a specially designed blind flying hood over the pupil's cockpit, Reid and Sigrist turn indicators and wings with slightly less dihedral to reduce inherent stability. In the early 1930s, crowds at the annual RAF Display at Hendon were treated as a star turn to an exhibition of so-called 'crazy flying' by experienced pilots flying 504Ns, but by then the type was nearing the end of its useful life. It was gradually withdrawn from 1933, to be largely superseded by the Avro Tutor, and later the de Havilland Tiger Moth.

Avro 504K rebuilds ER3546 and ER3545 of No 4 Flying Training School at Abu Sueir, Egypt.
(E.B. Morgan archives)

Commander Peter Bagley has provided some vivid recollections of its flying qualities from the viewpoint of a 'novice':

I cannot claim expertise in flying the 504 as my log book shows only one hour in this aircraft. This was at RAF Station Gosport on 25 August 1938 when I was appointed to do a torpedo dropping course – not in Avro 504Ns!

Avro 504N K1974 belonged to the Station Flight, whose Flight Commander was an RAF Flight Lieutenant. He briefed myself and a Sub Lieutenant aviator as my co-pilot, and threatened court martials if we broke the 504. His briefing seemed full of foreboding and tales of difficulties. However,

Avro 504N prototype conversion around 1922–23.
(Official)

he did not succeed in putting us off, so we climbed in and started the engine, a Lynx radial type.

The 504 was originally fitted with a fully rotary Gnome engine which required great skill in handling. In fact pilots were first taught engine handling before any flight manoeuvres because that type of engine had to be either shut off completely for landings or use made of a blip switch fitted on top of the stick – a solid wooden type like a walking stick. Apparently the engine was prone to coughing and to cutting out when throttled back, and could not be restarted until the fuel lever had been shut and a wait of eight seconds had gone by. Meanwhile pilots had to glide, so the blip switch was invented and pilots blipped their engine when approaching to land. I was grateful that K1974 had a different engine.

Taxiing out was when one first met vice number one. The aircraft delighted in weathercocking into wind, as the rudder was not very effective on the ground. Nor were there any brakes. Because of this tendency, both lower mainplanes were fitted with metal hoop skids to prevent the aircraft dropping one wing onto the ground and tearing the doped fabric covering. They also prevented the aircraft from turning right over if one wing had lifted badly during an uncontrolled ground loop – for which the aircraft was noted.

We were lucky that Gosport was a grass airfield with plenty of space, as during progress to the downwind hedge we continually went round in circles. On facing into wind I opened up the throttle fairly slowly only to find the aircraft swinging rapidly to port. Chopping the throttle and applying slight right rudder had an immediate effect, as the aircraft did a reverse swing to starboard. Not having lifted the tail or having to worry about other aircraft on the ground I just let it go, admittedly out of control, until it stopped facing 180 degrees from the original take-off direction.

On my second attempt at take-off, I opened the throttle rapidly and before the swing to port had really commenced I had rudder control with the rudder quickly up in flying position. I cannot claim a perfect straight take-off, but we got airborne in some 60 yards with 50 mph showing on the air speed indicator. I held the aircraft down until we had 55 mph showing, then started the climb out from the airfield.

The elevator was very sensitive, the ailerons the opposite, being very sloppy. Turning the aircraft resulted in bad skidding and/or a side-slip, shown by wind on the face from the direction of the side-slip or skid. A gyro effect giving nose rise took place on opening the throttle together with a left turn tendency. On closing the throttle the opposite occurred – a nose drop and turn right effect.

We climbed to 3,500 feet which took us some six minutes. We then did turns and generally got the feel of the aircraft including one stall. The nose dropped rapidly with its inherent tendency to turn to the right, but recovery was quick by use of throttle and stick.

When I felt happy, I shouted down the Gosport tube to Speedy Pollard, my co-pilot; had he any objection to my trying a loop? Getting an affirmative 'None', I took a good look round the sky for other aircraft, then dropped the nose and slowly opened up the engine. The Avro 504 took some time, and a loss of 750 feet before it had 115 mph showing on the ASI, shuddering considerably as though it disliked being dived. At that speed I started to gently pull round the loop, and much to my surprise the aircraft tightened up in a looping plane as the nose came over the horizon. The air speed had dropped alarmingly at the top of the loop to a mere 55 mph. Recovery was easy and we then decided to do our first landing. Mine to fly.

Avro 504N K1966 of the Cambridge University Air Squadron shown with the blind flying hood raised.
(RAF Museum)

As Gosport was that day on a right hand circuit I cheated by not doing a complete circuit, but by doing a curved approach over Fareham Creek to land over the Northern hedge. As we crossed the hedge I found the elevator control very touchy and light so tried not to hold the nose too high, for had I done so and dropped the tail skid onto the ground first, the aircraft would have done its famous kangaroo act. This it would perform in a series of ever ongoing bounces because the elastic bunjee cord rubber suspension of the undercarriage accentuated even a small bounce. Luckily we got the main wheels on first.

I then handed over to my co-pilot who made every mistake I had, but as this fine fellow has long since left us (for the unknown, as he failed to find his aircraft carrier in fog and with wireless silence imposed during the Norwegian Campaign in 1940), I must say no more. He cannot deny or confirm, and I respect the memory of him. I am sure he has told of the experience in the great hereafter about flying the Avro 504N. Quite an experience, I found.

A ground crew viewpoint is given by Cecil Bristow, who had some experience with 504s at Halton and later Manston:

I had three flights in a 504N whilst in the last stages of my apprenticeship at Halton in 1932, for air experience. We also had a 504K in the workshops for instructional purposes. I recall that when rigging a 504 from scratch one 'boxed' the mainplanes on the floor (top and bottom planes, struts and wire bracing into a rigid construction), then attached them to the fuselage as one unit. The fuel tanks were underneath the upper mainplanes near the root end. I lost some valuable marks in my final exams when I omitted to enumerate that the tanks should be drained before dismantling wings from the fuselage – our instructional airframes never had petrol in them, and it was an easily missed point!

At the end of 1933 I was loaned for a short time to Manston Station Flight, which then had two Moths, an Atlas and a 504N. The flight was housed in unsuitable premises. It was a building of three bays each with a set of folding doors, and had at one time been a Motor Transport shed. There were two lines of five brick pillars dividing the bays, and these supported the roof. I feel sure we only had part use of the building.

The 504 was always the last aircraft stowed away after the day's flying. It was an awkward job as its wing span was much greater than the width of the hangar doors. The procedure was to push the aircraft nose on to the first pillar with the tailskid on a special barrow, then with one wheel chocked the aircraft was pushed sideways so that the starboard mainplane swung into the hangar. By judicious use of the tail barrow, the wing tips were fed between the first and second brick pillars, some five or six feet, and the port wings were gradually brought inside the hangar enough to close the doors.

Aircraft ground handling was a knack not always learned by, and I heard a tale that when the 504 was due for a major periodic inspection early in 1933, it had to be housed out of the way at the rear end of the hangar. The wizard who achieved this juggling act was posted before the inspection was completed, and the story goes that it was three months later before it saw the light of day again! The aircraft had to be completely turned round three times in narrow confines, working wingtips through the various pillars, to get it to the rear. If it had been my problem, I think I might have removed a set of mainplanes to save a lot of damage and time.

I recall another handling mishap later when I was with 609 Auxiliary Squadron at Yeadon in 1938. Our Hinds were then housed in two very cramped Bessoneaux canvas hangars. We were getting the aircraft out for daily flying programme, when the Flight Sergeant called out to the port wing tip man (on his blind side) 'Clear, port wing?'. Back came the answer. 'Bags of room this side, Flight' – and the simultaneous sound of grinding metal. The said airman had forgotten that the upper mainplane extended some feet more than the one he was holding!'

de Havilland Tiger Moth

The ubiquitous Tiger Moth owed its origins to the famous de Havilland Moth, the first successful British private light aircraft. It was destined to remain in service for over 15 years, and to provide initial flying experience for most wartime RAF and Commonwealth pilots, who regarded it with great affection. Many machines are still flying in private hands, the number, happily increasing yearly.

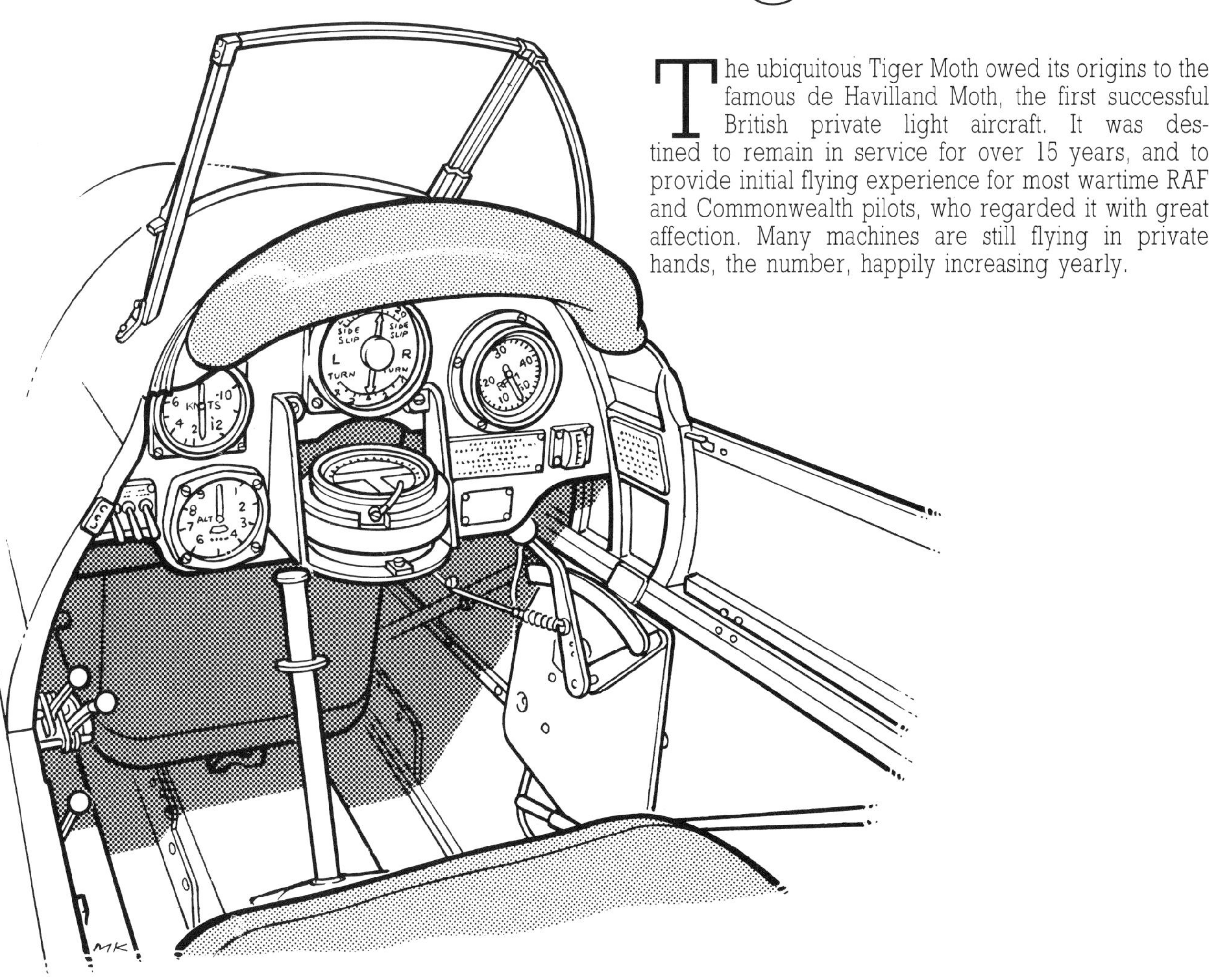

Specification (Tiger Moth II)

Power plant:	*One 130 hp de Havilland Gipsy Major I.*
Dimensions:	*span 29 ft 4 in, length 23 ft 11 in, height 8 ft 9½ in, wing area 239 sq ft.*
Weights:	*Empty 1,115 lb, loaded 1,825 lb.*
Performance:	*Maximum speed 109.5 mph at sea level, cruising speed 93 mph, initial climb 673 ft/min, range 302 miles, endurance 3 hrs, service ceiling 13,600 ft.*

By the late 1920s it was becoming apparent that a replacement would have to be found for the Avro 504N, but there were several possible options. Contemporary thinking centred round a metal-framed aircraft, since the number of woodworking tradesmen in the RAF was on the decline, and it was proposed that power be provided by an Armstrong-Siddeley Mongoose engine. Orders were consequently placed on this basis for a number of Hawker Tomtits and also Avro 621s, the latter being later re-engined with the more powerful Armstrong-Siddeley Lynx IVC and named the Tutor.

Although not powered by a Mongoose, the Moth had already been tried in RAF service with some success, and therefore had to be regarded as a serious contender. Initially powered by a 60 hp ADC Cirrus I engine when it first appeared in 1925, several hundred were eventually built with later Cirrus and Cirrus-Hermes engines and also the de Havilland Gipsy. The RAF received over 160 of these machines, the final deliveries consisting of the metal-framed Gipsy-engined version, designated the DH.60M or Metal Moth.

Developed from the latter was the DH.60T or Moth Trainer, of which a number were supplied to overseas air forces. The RAF showed an interest, and prototype E-3 was test flown at the Aeroplane and Armament Experimental Establishment at Martlesham Heath, being followed in August 1931 by a later machine, E-5 (afterwards G-ABNJ). Some modifications were made to the latter, including staggering the wings to make it easier to exit from the front cockpit with a parachute. This modification moved the C of G too far forward, which was rectified by giving the wings sweepback. The resulting report was particularly favourable as regards the ease of maintenance of the machine by service personnel. The only significant snag was that the wings were still not entirely satisfactory, the wingtips being likely to come too near the ground especially whilst landing in a cross-wind or if the tyres were not fully inflated. However, this was soon cured by increasing dihedral on the lower mainplane.

Comparison of the results of the trials of these three main contenders led to orders being placed for the Tutor and Moth Trainer. The Tomtit was dropped at this stage, and in the event only limited orders were placed for the Tutor, whose makers became preoccupied with production of the Anson and later the Manchester and Lancaster bombers. By this time the de Havilland machine had been modified to such an extent that it was redesignated DH.82 by the makers, and the RAF gave it the name Tiger Moth. Initial deliveries were 35 of the Mark I variant, powered by a Gipsy III, but this proved prone to overheating, especially when climbing with insufficient airspeed, and replacement with the slightly more powerful Gipsy Major produced the DH.82a or Mark II version, which was to become standard on the production lines. Another change on this version was the replacement of the doped fabric cover rear fuselage decking by a plywood decking.

Initial reaction to the Tiger Moth when it entered service in late 1931 and early 1932 was rather divided. It was not easy to fly, but this was no bad thing for a trainer. Problems of operating in a wind, the lack of brakes and fitment of a skid instead of a tailwheel caused unfavourable comment, but on the other hand it was easy and inexpensive to operate, and it soon wormed its way into the affections of the instructors and their pupils.

One of the first modifications to be carried out was the trial fitment of a mass balance to the ailerons. This had no effect on the handling characteristics, but reduced the risk of aileron flutter in a dive, a problem which had led to the loss of an Avro Cadet during trials. No major alterations were subsequently made, but some trouble was later experienced in recovering from spins, especially in Tiger Moths which had been fitted with bomb racks. Tests were carried out at Boscombe Down, and the trouble was found to be due to a number of reasons, including the effect of the bomb racks on the airflow over the tail surfaces, and added weight due to accumulated repainting and other factors. A cure was effected by removing the aileron mass balances, and fitting anti-spin strakes along the top rear fuselage, extending forward from the line of the tailplane, this becoming a standard modification.

De Havillands were fully engaged in Mosquito production by 1941, but Tiger Moths were still badly needed. The solution was to transfer production to Cowley, near Oxford, where Morris Motors soon brought to bear their great experience in assembly-line production, achieving a rate of nearly 40 machines a week at a peak. Eventual UK production of Tiger Moths totalled well over 4,000, nearly 3,500 of them by Morris Motors. Small numbers were also built of a radio-controlled pilotless target version, named the Queen Bee.

In addition nearly 3,000 machines were built in Australia, Canada and New Zealand for use under the Commonwealth Air Training Plan. Those made in Canada required some modification to suit local conditions. These included moving the undercarriage forward, fitting brakes and a tailwheel, and replacing the normal wooden interplane struts by steel ones. The harsh winter climate required the fitting of a perspex canopy and cockpit heating, and the unreliability of supplies of Gipsy Majors due to shipping losses led to the fitting of 125 hp Menasco Pirate engine, which had already been fitted in a trial installation. In this guise they were known as Menasco Moths, but suffered from having not only less power, but an engine which was also heavier.

The main users of the Tiger Moth were civilian-operated Elementary and Reserve Flying Training

Right:
De Havilland Tiger Moth II L6923 '20' of No 1 Elementary and Reserve Flying Training School around 1938.
(RAF Museum Photo No P016742)

Below:
De Havilland Tiger Moth K4242, the first production MkII in 1934.
(Official)

Schools, and later their wartime counterparts at home and overseas, the Elementary Flying Training Schools. Tiger Moths were also used to train instructors at Flying Instructors Schools, and after the war they also formed the main equipment of Reserve Flying Schools. When they were eventually replaced by Chipmunks and Prentices, they found a ready sale for civilian use, many being refurbished and sold in the mid-fifties by Rollasons, who at one stage had over 100 parked at Croydon.

Commander Peter Bagley has clear recollections of his experiences at one of the pre-war reserve schools:

Fifty years ago I first flew solo in a Tiger Moth at Prestwick, where Scottish Aviation Ltd had been assisted in setting up an *ab initio* flying training school by the Government of the day. I had joined Course No 2 together with 29 other pupils, some of whom had never flown at all, whilst others, like myself, had been airborne somewhere else. In my own case

I was lucky because the son of some friends had a Gipsy Moth and had taken me up twice, doing aerobatics each time.

Prestwick was then a small airfield, just outside the town, with one new hangar and adjoining administrative offices and class crewrooms. The Course lived in the Orangefield Hotel, which abutted the Western boundary of the airfield. Discipline was strict. We arose to do PT at 6.30 am on the tarmac under an instructor, then shaved, showered or bathed until breakfast at 7.45 am in the mess. At 8.30 we began either lectures or took flying lessons. We worked hard until 5.00 pm, then had to dine-in every night, wearing stiff shirts and black ties except on Friday, Saturday and Sunday.

The flying training was in Mark II Tiger Moths, painted a brilliant red. This Mark superseded the first design in 1934 by the late Captain (later Sir) Geoffrey de Havilland. It had a plywood fuselage instead of the earlier fabric cover. It was fitted with a 130 hp Gipsy Major engine driving a twin-bladed propeller made from wood, but with metal-clad leading edges. The fuselage had twin cockpits, in tandem and fitted with an instrument panel on which were mounted an air speed indicator, a turn and slip indicator, an altimeter, an engine revolution counter and an oil pressure gauge. The control column was wood, rather like a walking stick, but fitted at its base with a metal sheath which in turn fitted into a cup. The flying controls were wire operated.

In front of the control column, which was known as 'the stick' in those far-off days, was a magnetic compass, difficult to see when the seat was raised to its top height. By an adjustment, the length of leg to the rudder bar could be altered to suit different height pilots, and if you were to blind-fly with the hood over the cockpit for instrument flying practice you then had to lower the seat pan to be comfortable.

The cockpits were open so we wore Sidcot suits – a one piece overall of either rubberised cotton or Grenfell cloth. Such an overall had two large pockets in which to keep one's maps, notebook or other material whilst flying. A zip front closed the suit from the crutch up to the neck. A detachable fur collar was provided, and with the aid of flying boots and helmet one managed to retain some warmth in the freezing weather whilst flying.

For ten hours I was instructed by my flying instructor until I could take-off, do all types of turns, had recovered from a spin, could glide, judge distance and height and make reasonable landings. Flight Lieutenant Harry Comerford was one of the best, and through his patience, skill and sound teaching I owe my life for an incident many years later.

De Havilland Tiger Moth II R4922 of No 7 Elementary Flying Training School at Desford.
(Author's collection)

On 8 December 1936 I went solo, and my memory of that event now half a century away is as clear today as it was then; this is probably an occasion most pilots remember. The Chief Instructor, Squadron Leader McIntyre of Everest Flight fame, told me he would give me a flying test. After both of us had signed the flight authorisation book and the aircraft service documents we walked out to Tiger Moth G-ADWO and inspected the aircraft – a routine always practised. We then donned our parachutes and climbed into our respective cockpits, the instructor always in the front because it was difficult to bail out if need be, and the pupil in the rear because this was used for all solo flying.

He ordered me to start the engine, a procedure which required ground staff to hand swing the propeller, then when warmed up and run up to check for magneto drop or back firing, I taxied out. The Chief Instructor said down the Gosport tubing, which was then our means of communication in training aircraft, 'You take her off into wind please and when airborne I will tell you what to do'. We got airborne quite neatly for a Tiger Moth. They can hop, skip and jump if handled roughly during take-off. We climbed to 3,000 feet at 55 mph – yes, we used miles per hour on air speed indicators in those days, and if we wished could check our air speed by a primitive spring air-operated pendulum-type ASI on the starboard wing strut.

He then got me to perform everything I had been taught and finally said, OK take her down and do a good landing. I will not pretend this was perfect, but we got on the ground somehow. He then taxied the aircraft downwind to the far hedge and turned into wind. Suddenly his control column (stick) was thrown out and I knew I was to go solo.

The Chief Instructor did up his seat harness to stop it snagging the stick, checked around his front cockpit and then stood on the wing saying with a big grin, 'I want you to fly solo now. So take her off, fly twice round the airfield and then come in and do one landing. Look out for other aircraft and Good Luck', whereupon he jumped down off the lower wing and started walking back to the hangar with his parachute slung over his shoulder.

I remember thinking to myself 'you have her' and begin my take-off run. This was nice and straight, but when I had flying speed she seemed nose heavy so I had to apply a heavier stick force to climb out than I had ever experienced before. As I climbed ahead I thought I must make a turn so started to do so. Immediately I did this the nose went up in spite of my pressure on the stick forwards. I suddenly realised I had forgotten to adjust the 'cheese-cutter' trimmer at take-off and reached down with my left hand. This device was simply two elastic bunjees, like a catapult sling, which were attached to the bottom of the control column, and by tightening or loosening one or other bunjee it gave easier stick force for the prevailing flight condition. It was normal to set it half way along its quadrant for take-off, then reset it towards the back for landing.

The day was as cold as Scotland can be, fresh with hoar frost on the grass and with a pale blue sky with an odd white cumulus over the Highlands area to the North. I got so interested in looking at the sight I almost forgot what I was to do, but self-discipline took over. After flying twice around the circuit at 1,500 feet and about 65 mph I began my downwind procedure dropping gently down to 1,000 feet by reducing my speed and engine revolutions. At the turn across wind I knew exactly the place to be for I had flown this so often dual. Finally I turned into wind and took off speed and height to glide in to my landing – my first solo landing.

Without my realising it my throttle was not completely closed, so the Tiger Moth began dropping her tail when a few feet up, and when she hit Mother Earth she just creamed on without even a bounce. She eventually came to stop in a nice straight line, and I turned and taxied in and closed down when signalled to by ground staff making a throat cutting sign.

As I got out of the cockpit my instructor came round the tail grinning like a Cheshire Cat. 'Well', he said, 'if you can fly a Tiger Moth like that, one day you will fly many interesting aircraft'. This was indeed a compliment, and I never forgot him as a result, but I did let him down badly later.

We were doing forced landing practice on Ayr racecourse, with snow conditions on the ground. I was cold and could not fly well that day, so my rudder control work was ham-footed, like a man with heavy metal boots on his feet. Harry Comerford eventually landed and told me to get out. I thought 'He'd never make me walk back to Prestwick – or would he?' He told me to take off my flying boots, put them in the small locker behind the rear cockpit and get back in. My poor feet were nearly frozen, but I must confess the next two forced landing practices were less heavy on the rudder control. Finally he flew the aircraft back at low height – the first time I had experienced low flying, and I enjoyed it so much that I forgot my poor feet.

My instructor was an aerobatics buff, and he taught me the complete routine which I have always enjoyed. But he also taught me a far more important thing – recovery from an inverted spin. This type of spin is where the pilot is on the outside of the spinning aircraft, because the spin starts inverted, so he is flung outwards instead of being pushed inwards as in a normal spin. It is a frightening manoeuvre, but being taught it saved my life and got me out of a Meteor T.7 trainer which broke up over Cornwall many years later. I live to write this half a century later, thank God and Harry Comerford.

A rather different recollection comes from Les Leetham, who was sent to Sywell in 1943 for grading and his first solo:

We trainees were also used for airfield patrol – the field was covered with strings of old cars towed out after flying finished, and the station kept secure knowing that we were vigilantly guarding them with our non-firing rifles with their fixed bayonets. Our course must have been keener or thicker because very soon there was an enquiry as to how the Moths were being sabotaged despite hawk-eyed vigil, until a clued-up type noticed that it was only the undersides of the top mainplanes that were being slashed – by the bayonets on the rifles slung on our shoulders as we eagerly studied these wonderful machines that we were trying to master.

I soloed after 11.30 hrs for 35 minutes, and will never forget the one thing the instructor failed to mention and could never demonstrate – the amazing difference in performance without his weight aboard. It seemed like a rocket, and at the required height for a turn I was about over

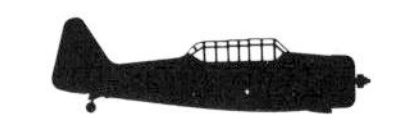

the boundary instead of well upwind, and this threw the whole circuit out with the approach just as different with the hold apparently never ending. I had talked to myself all the way – the patter had been drilled in for those hours and I was glad when the pilot waved me on to a second attempt as he had said might be needed. This did not surprise me, but I thought I was more prepared when I taxied back with a huge grin, only to finish by making a rather messier second landing.

De Havilland Canada DH82C Tiger Moth 4360, fitted with DH Gipsy Major IC engine, flown by No 20 Elementary Flying Training School at Oshawa, Ontario around 1941. Note the enclosed cockpit, metal interplane struts and the tail wheel of the Canadian spec version.

(via Chaz Bowyer)

Squadron Leader Dick Smerdon also flew the Tiger Moth:

The Tiger Moth was the aircraft on which I learned to fly, was trained as a Flying Instructor and in which I then instructed, in all a total of 500 hours. It is difficult not to become nostalgic, but the Tiger had endearing qualities. Though a simple aircraft to fly, it was not so easy to fly well, with ailerons on the lower mainplanes only. The rate of roll was moderate, but as I had not known the Stampe, ignorance was bliss – absolute bliss. It was very much more comfortable to fly from the front cockpit – less slipstream, better view and in the tropics more shaded from the sun. By the time I had totalled 300 hours, I could make that aircraft sit up and beg. I may be a poor self-analyser, but the Tiger was such a good trainer that I had little difficulty converting to the Harvard.

Squadron Leader Don Brittain writes:

I can't remember a great deal. I recall it did a tight spin – the nose seemed to stay in a small field whilst coming down. I also remember that no matter how tight you did up the old Sutton Harness – holes in three straps, a pin in the other to go in the holes, and then a retaining pin – it never seemed tight enough, and I always thought I was going to fall out when doing inverted aeros. (Isn't it funny the trivia you remember after 36 years?)

Cyril Smith was on duty one day at Thornhill in Southern Rhodesia when a couple of Tiger Moths happened to fly in:

At the time of departure I was instructed by the corporal in charge to see them off. 'I've never swung a Tiger Moth corp, what's the drill?' His reply went something like, 'The pilots will put you right. Remember legs apart, left behind the right, and bring the right leg back as you swing your right arm down – that way you don't walk into the prop'. I was bowled over somewhat by his apparent uncaring attitude and thought that at least he would lend a hand, being technically responsible for any accident that might occur. As things turned out it worked, but having since seen people with all sorts of problems I realise just how lucky I was.

Eric Sharp worked on the engine of a Tiger Moth of Cranwell HQ Flight in the early fifties:

Flying with one's work was considered normal, especially for engine fitters, and was expected if the aeroplane had more than one seat, to demonstrate a little faith and give

Top:
De Havilland Tiger Moth II T6026 'RUOD' of the Oxford University Air Squadron flying over Oxford in 1946 from its base at Shellingford.
(I. Faulconer)

Bottom:
De Havilland Tiger Moth II BB704 'FIWO' of No 21 Elementary Flying Training School at Booker in 1950. This aircraft was originally G-ADGF, but was impressed for the RAF on the outbreak of war.
(Author's collection)

De Havilland Tiger Moths of the Airwork-operated No 2 Grading Unit at Kirton-in-Lindsey in 1952.
(Paddy Porter collection)

confidence to the 'driver'. I flew in everything that I had the chance to, though I never really had any ambition to be aircrew. There was an enormous satisfaction in working on aeroplanes, such as our Tiger Moth, for instance. I could never decide whether I wanted to run the engine from the cockpit or swing the prop for somebody else – I'd have done both if I could! Refuelling was an art I enjoyed, which seems daft! Standing on the engine cowling with a 5 gallon jerry can pouring through a chamois leather draped over a funnel, desperately trying not to spill any, for it would run straight down the corrugations in the tank skin into the front cockpit.

I recall being told to get in a Tiger Moth on one occasion by the Air Traffic Officer, who flew often on the morning after a heavy night – it was said to clear his head! I remember quite vividly looking *up* at the spire of Ancaster church while the rest of the landscape rotated around it, all of me hanging on the Sutton harness, and trying like mad to keep my feet on the foot rails and not fall up and kick the stick. Inverted spins in fresh air probably did the trick for him!

Jim Henderson also recalls the Tiger Moth with affection:

It was a rigger's delight. One could rig it without trouble using a trestle table, a straight edge, a measuring tape and a lump of string. Covering it with fabric and doping over was a very satisfying task, though one could suffer from dope getting on one's chest.

One would run the aircraft out in the morning, and if it would not start the first time, it was a simple matter of hitting the impulse starter (part of the electrics) with a brick!

The Tiger Moth was fairly fragile, and riggers would wear plimsolls. It was quite common for them to need minor repairs. During refuelling, for instance, people would put a foot through the skin whilst climbing up to the centre section, and if they dropped the 5 gallon tanks which we used in those days these would go straight through, as the wings would not take the weight. So would a rigger if he forgot and gallantly stepped aside for someone. One also had to repair riblets quite often, as people used to squeeze and break them.

James McNamara remembers the Tiger Moth as his favourite little aeroplane, being the first biplane he was taught to rig, at a Civil Flying Club:

The aircraft had undergone a major overhaul and really looked like new. The Chief Rigger was showing me how it was done, and it was a most interesting experience – old Andy had helped to rig the Vimy of Alcock and Brown in Newfoundland, and really knew his stuff. We used to say that if one gave him a ball of wool and two needles, he would make you a Fair Isle H.P.42 or something!

The day for the initial air test came, and I went along as Observer, complete with clipboard and pencil. It was a great day for me, and the only snag was a slight starboard wing down condition. On return I asked Andy how to fix it as I wanted to be perfect. He told me to stick a four-inch piece of thick string on the top of the port upper wing trailing edge. This I did and it flew beautifully. I understood the reason for this, but asked how he knew it had to be four inches of string. His old eyes sparkled and he nodded his wise old head and said to me, pointing first at my head and then at my feet 'Up there for thinking – down there for dancing' . . . oh Golden Days . . .

Hawker Hart Trainer

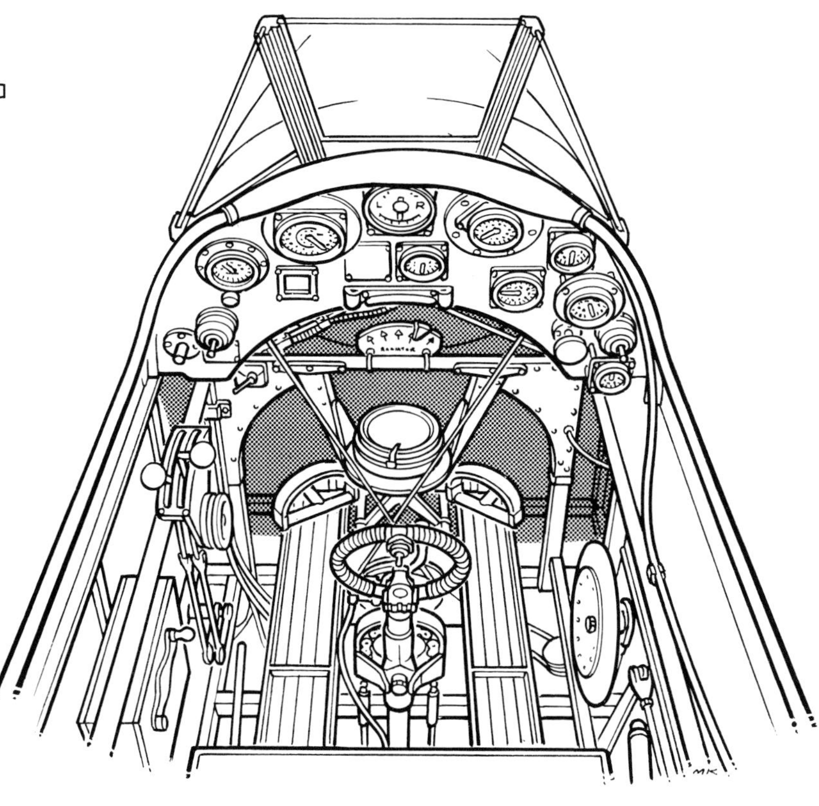

The Hawker Hart Trainer stemmed from a need to provide dual instruction for pilots who were to fly the basic Hart and its many planned variants. The concept of such a modification was by no means new, as the RAF had already flown dual versions of various aircraft, mainly at Flying Training Schools. Some were conversions of machines already in service, such as the Sopwith Snipe (dual). Others were specially built on the production line, such as the Armstrong Whitworth Siskin III (DC) and the Fairey IIID (T) and IIIF (DC).

The original Hart bomber first appeared in prototype form in 1928, and was most advanced for its time. The straightforward design for a single-engined bomber proved capable of adaptation, and from it came a long line of two-seat aircraft for various duties, including the Osprey, Demon, Audax, Hardy and Hind, as well as single engined fighters from the same stable. These were all powered by the Rolls-Royce Kestrel engine, which proved very reliable in service.

Designed by Sydney Camm, later responsible for such famous aircraft as the Hurricane, Typhoon and Tempest, the Hart was an immediate success on its introduction into service. It had been designed to a competitive 1926 specification requiring a top speed of 160 mph, which at that date was quite exceptional. To meet this demand, the Hawker design team worked closely with Rolls-Royce, the original proposal being to install a Falcon F.I engine.

Specification

Power plane	*One 535 hp Rolls-Royce Kestrel IB.*
Dimensions:	*Span 37 ft 3 in. Length 29 ft 4 in, height 10 ft 5 in, Wing area 348 sq ft.*
Weights:	*Empty 3,045 lb, loaded 4,100 lb.*
Performance	*Maximum speed 165 mph at 3,000 ft. cruising speed 145 mph, initial climb 1,500 ft/min, range 430 miles, endurance 2.9 hrs, service ceiling 22,800 ft.*

New construction techniques were necessary if the specification was to be met, and consequently the fuselage was built on the Warren tubular steel girder system, the nose having a pleasing and effective streamlined appearance. By the time of the first flight, the more powerful Rolls-Royce F.XIB engine had become available. It was lighter than the original engine, being cast in a single piece, and was later christened the Kestrel. The engine and fuel tank were completely enclosed with quick-release panels, and the honeycomb-type radiator could be retracted in flight.

There were two spacious and comfortable cockpits in the rear fuselage, which was fabric-covered and faired-in to retain the streamlining. The pilot had a .303 in Vickers Mk II gun in a trough on the port side of his cockpit, synchronised to fire safely through the propeller blades, whilst the observer had a movable .303 inch Lewis Mk III gun mounted on a Hawker-designed gun ring.

The unequal span single-bay wings were also of metal construction, the spars being of drawn steel strip and the ribs of duralumin. Differential ailerons of similar construction were fitted to the upper wings. Production machines had a conventional cross-axle undercarriage, although a divided-axle type had been tried on the prototype.

From the start, the aircraft had excellent flying qualities, the controls were reported as being light over the whole range of normal flight and very effective at the stall. Aerobatics presented no difficulties, and it would go into a spin easily, evenly and fast. In a dive it would remain steady, without any vibration.

Harts first entered service with 33 squadron in 1930, and in the Air Exercises of that year they outpaced the contemporary Siskin fighters. They were equally successful in the annual inter-squadron bombing competition, and no time was lost in placing further orders for this outstanding and versatile aircraft.

The advent of this fast new machine led to the need for an appropriate training syllabus, but existing slower types of dual control trainer were inadequate for the purpose. Official thinking was, therefore, that a new design was required. The simplest means of providing this would be to base it on the Hart, and in February 1932 Hawkers were asked to build such a

Hawker Hart Trainer prototype K1996, originally laid down as an Audax, soon after its first flight in April 1932. (British Aerospace)

machine for trials. Rather than build an entirely new machine, they decided to take a partially completed Hart variant off the production line, and consequently the second production Audax (K1996) was deleted from its contract and completed in the dual control trainer configuration.

Hawker Hart Trainer K3153 'R' of the RAF College, Cranwell, showing clearly the blind flying hood in the raised position.

(Ken Wixey collection)

K1996 made its first flight on 20 April 1932, only six weeks after receipt of the contract, and differed little from the early standard production Hart bombers. The main variations were removal of the gunner's ring in the rear cockpit, which was fitted with dual control, and duplication of the instruments and other equipment except for the fuel gauge, which could be a problem as it was not easy to read from the back seat. Maintenance facilities were excellent, with greatly improved access compared with the normal Hart, removable panels being fitted at each side aft of the cockpit, as well as each side under the tail and under the bottom of the rear cockpit. A modification introduced on later machines was a long Osprey-type exhaust extending under the lower starboard mainplane. A tailwheel was also fitted to later production aircraft, in place of the original tailskid.

Tests on K1996 found the controls to be effective and reasonably light, being somewhat lighter than those of the standard Hart. Both cockpits were comfortable, though they could become stifling in summer conditions at low altitude. The rear windscreen came in for some criticism, being so large as to make it impossible to look over or round it, which could cause problems if it became obscured by oil, and by deflecting the airflow it also had the effect of accentuating the summer overheating problem.

The test report considered the aircraft very suitable as a training type, being easy to fly and controllable at very low speeds. Its flying characteristics were very similar to those of the standard Hart, and aerobatics could be performed easily and cleanly. Several modifications were recommended, however, on the production version. Brakes should be controllable from both seats, the rear cockpit fitted with a duplicate petrol gauge, the windscreen size reduced and parachute grips provided. In addition the harness in both cockpits came in for criticism, and it was recommended that the leg straps be anchored further forward. Take off and initial climb proved to be quite good, and landing was slow and easy. There was, however some tendency to turn into wind whilst taxiing, especially when travelling across wind.

Two further test machines were completed, K2474 and K2745 having been laid down as Hart bombers, and these flew later in 1932 as Hart Trainers (Interim). The trials having proved the success of the concept, Specification 8/32 was issued, and initial production orders placed. Several of the early deliveries went to the RAF College at Cranwell, where they started to

replace Atlas Trainers from June 1933, and others went to the Central Flying School. Hart Trainers were also issued to No 25 and 43 Squadrons, replacing now-unsuitable dual Siskins in these Hawker Fury-equipped units, and others went to Hart-equipped auxiliary squadrons. Further large orders enabled the Flying Training Schools to replace their ageing Atlas and Bulldog Trainers, and eventually 473 machines were built, many being sub-contracted by Armstrong Whitworth and Vickers. In addition, a further 32 conversions were made by Glosters from Hart bombers.

Early Hart Trainers had the 535 hp Kestrel IB, but some were later fitted with the derated 510 hp Kestrel V(DR), this latter engine being replaced by the similarly rated Kestrel X(DR) in the Series 2 version, which was produced from 1934. Several of the later aircraft had tropical radiators fitted, and quite a number of Hart Trainers served overseas, including many with No 4 Flying Training School at Abu Sueir in the Egyptian Canal Zone. When first introduced into service, they were finished in the normal silver paint/aluminium overall. In 1935, however, they changed to the new all-yellow scheme adopted in that year for all RAF training aircraft. The Munich crisis of 1938 led to the upper surfaces being camouflaged in brown and green, this later replacing the yellow entirely.

By the outbreak of the Second World War, the Hart Trainers were obsolescent, being largely replaced by the Harvard and Master. Nevertheless, shortage of these types meant that many Hart Trainers continued in service until as late as the end of 1941. Quite a number ended their days as ground instructional airframes.

Some recollections of the Hart Trainer have been provided by Commander Peter Bagley, who flew them at both Wittering and Upavon:

My first impression of the Hart Trainer was one of being slightly awed by its size in comparison with Tiger Moths in which I had flown my *ab initio* flying training. However, the moment I began flying in this splendid aircraft I soon forgot this as it was easy to fly. I went solo in the type after about four hours dual.

The Hart was powered by a Rolls-Royce Kestrel, 12-cylinder in-line engine. It drove a two-bladed propeller through a reduction gearing mounted in front of the engine, which also powered the supercharger giving 6 lb per square inch at full throttle. This superb engine, the forerunner of the later Merlin series, was easy to handle and gave very good response even to ham-handed pilots. It was cooled by a radiator mounted below the engine, and between the main wheel struts. This was retractable and had to be in the retracted position for all aerobatics. When a pilot forgot to wind it in it fell in of its own accord with a loud thump, repeating this as the aircraft resumed level flight. Instructors and flight commanders extracted reparations in the form of pints of beer from those who perpetually forgot.

The cockpits were identical, and the pupils always flew the aircraft from the front seat, whether solo or dual. The

Hawker Hart Trainer K4752 '1', probably of No 2 Flying Training School at Brize Norton, seen in the snow. (RAF Museum Photo No P005034)

instrument layout included a turn and bank indicator, air speed indicator, engine revolution counter, radiator temperature gauge, oil temperature gauge, fuel gauge, plus a boost gauge. With fuel selector cock, engine priming pump and starting switch (energising a separate starting magneto until the engine fired) the starting drill was easy. When a Kestrel engine first fired it blew smoke and flames with oil from each side of its twelve exhaust stubs which were mounted at the top on each side. A finely polished metal cowling enclosed the engine, and every fitter tried to make his shinier than the others in the Flight. The throttle and mixture controls on the left side of the cockpit came to hand easily, and were tightened or slackened off by a friction knob.

The control column (stick) was of a spade grip type. It was hinged for aileron control, whilst for elevator control the whole stick moved fore and aft. Aerobatic flying was a delight in the Hart because this design of stick meant that it never engaged either of the pilot's legs unlike those in most other types of aircraft.

Rudder movement was from an adjustable rubber bar, which could be wound in or out by a foot-operated knurled wheel. This had a distinct advantage when flying 'under the hood', a canvas device with a safety pilot in the other cockpit. The pilot's seat had to be lowered to give headroom when under the hood, so instead of being cramped for legroom pilots merely pushed the rudder bar further away by operating the adjusting wheel. Toe brakes were fitted on the front of the rudder bar together with toe straps for foot restraint during aerobatics.

Taxiing was a delight in the Hart, as with both brakes and a fully castering tail wheel, and a good view over the nose, the pilot who handled the engine properly found it easy.

Taking off was also easy. First turning the aircraft into wind on the grass airfields of those far off days, the aircraft was allowed to move forward to straighten the tail wheel. A cockpit drill was followed and when everything had been correctly set the engine was slowly opened up. The Hart at full throttle bounced along the grass to begin with, but soon got up sufficient speed to stop this., With tail up in flying position, and the good view over the nose, it was easy to maintain a straight line take-off, first by a little brake use, then by rudder. The aircraft flew off at about 65 mph, and if held down until the ASI recorded 80 mph the climb could be commenced. Climbing turns in the Hart were easy to control.

When the required height had been reached, the full repertoire of aerobatics could be flown. Loops, slow rolls, rolls off the top of a loop, spins, aileron turns in the dive, stall turns and alternater side-slips. The inverted spin and the falling leaf were not permitted, although the former could be entered if a pilot made such a bog of a loop that the aircraft

Hawker Hart Trainer K5834 of No 7 Flying Training School at Peterborough. (RAF Museum Photo No P002580)

K 4907
K 4907
K5050
K 5050
K4917
K 4917
K5232
K 5232
K3120
K 3120

Facing page:
Hawker Hart Trainers and Audaxes (K3120 and K3123) lined up at No 4 Flying Training School, Abu Sueir, Egypt in 1936.
(RAF Museum Photo No P103061)

literally stalled upside down and he in panic applied rough rudder. The natural flying characteristics of the Hart – good lateral and longitudinal stability – usually prevented this, however, as the aircraft recovered well if the pilot temporarily lost control for some reason, usually insufficient air speed for a particular aerobatic manoeuvre.

When writing this fifty years on I am reminded of my instructor, a Sergeant Pilot Instructor with an 'A' class flying instructor category from the Central Flying School at Upavon, Wiltshire. He took me up one day to do advanced forced landings, and after some near copy book runs was so pleased he said 'Alright, I've got her, and flew the Hart a few miles, then did another copy book 'forced' landing alongside a pub – his favourite. Keeping the engine ticking over, the landlord came out with two pint tankards which we both drank with relish in our respective cockpits, holding a hand over the top of the beer to prevent the propeller slipstream from spilling the beer. I was 'instructed' by this fine fellow never to breathe a word of our exploit to anyone, and threatened with all sorts of dire and horrid things if I did so. However, I now look back on this incident with joy and amusement, and feel justified in breaking my silence.

Now let us land the Hart. Approaching on the downwind leg of No 11 FTS, RAF Station Wittering, Northants at regulation height of 1,000 feet, one first reduced air speed to

Below:
Armstrong Whitworth-built Hawker Hart Trainer K6528 of No 16 Elementary and Reserve Flying Training School at Shoreham in 1938.
(via F.C. Lynn)

Bottom:
Vickers-built Hawker Hart Trainer K4900 '4' of No 4 Service Flying Training School at Habbaniya, Iraq in 1941. In this aircraft the student occupies the front seat. Note also that navigation lights are now fitted.
(RAF Museum Photo No P013250)

80 mph. On turning crosswind at a reduced height of 750 – 800 feet the aircraft is flown into the position where it is judged that on turning on finals the aircraft would be correctly into the wind. A windsock always sited on the edge of the airfield gave pilots the near true direction of the wind and one read the wind strength by looking to see how straight out or drooping the windsock was. If fully horizontal the wind was over 30 mph.

As the aircraft passed over the downwind hedge (at Wittering so often the Great North Road hedge) pilots judged their distance and height so that they would hope to land far enough onto the grass airfield to avoid any turbulance at the hedge. Assuming all this had been done correctly and the height over the hedge was about 80 feet with an air speed of 70 – 75 mph, the nose was lifted sufficiently to get the aircraft into the three-point attitude. At about 60 mph the aircraft would kiss the grass, landing perfectly on both main and tail wheels. The landing run was easily controlled by careful use of the toe brakes and, if need be, a small amount of throttle. Only very ham-handed pilots ground-looped Harts, and then because they had stalled the aircraft too high and dropped onto Mother Earth.

In summary it can be said without any doubt that the Hawker Hart Trainer was a very fine training aircraft, and a great tribute to Sydney Camm (later Sir Sydney), its designer. I flew every variant of the Hart family – Audax, Osprey, Hind and Fury Mk I – and still think there was none better than the Hart. Was it the Rolls-Royce 12-cylinder Kestrel? Or was it that the variants had slightly different flying characteristics and parameters? Whatever it was, the smell of a Kestrel starting up will always be remembered.

Wing Commander Robert Sage flew Harts whilst training at Montrose:

My service training was on No 4 course at No 8 FTS Montrose, flying Harts and Audaxes, commencing in January 1937. One story is worth recounting. A pupil on No 2 course was despatched in exercise No 24, height test, which involved taking a Hart to about 8,000 feet carrying a passenger, in this case an apprentice armourer. The climb took the aircraft above cloud, and on descent the pilot was dismayed to find himself over the sea with no land in sight. For some reason he assumed he had drifted over the West coast, so he set an easterly course hoping to make a landfall. His confidence waned after some time and, seeing a fishing vessel below, he decided to attract the attention of the crew and get them to point their vessel in the direction of the nearest land.

To do this, he wrote messages on pieces of torn up maps which he attempted to drop, like leaflets, on the vessel as he made low passes. He also threw out his gloves with the same message. Having failed in his aim, and by now anxious about fuel, he instructed his passenger that he was going to fly the aircraft at very low level and minimum speed, and when he drew close to the vessel the passenger was to jump into the sea and make his way to the vessel and ask the crew to point the way to land. The manoeuvre commenced, and the passenger climbed out onto the wing, but before receiving orders to go, he fell off into the sea. The pilot was not prepared for the sudden change in the Centre of Gravity, and the Hart nose dived into the sea. Both crew members were rescued to recover from their injuries, and some years later the aircraft was dredged up by chance in a fishing trawl. It had crashed about 20 miles east of Aberdeen.

Hawker Hart Trainer K5861 '25' of No 7 Service Flying Training School at Peterborough around 1940.
(MAP photo)

Avro Anson

The Avro Anson, or 'Faithful Annie' as she was affectionately known to many thousands of wartime and post-war aircrew, was one of the most long-lived RAF aircraft, having served in various forms for 32 years when it was finally withdrawn in 1968.

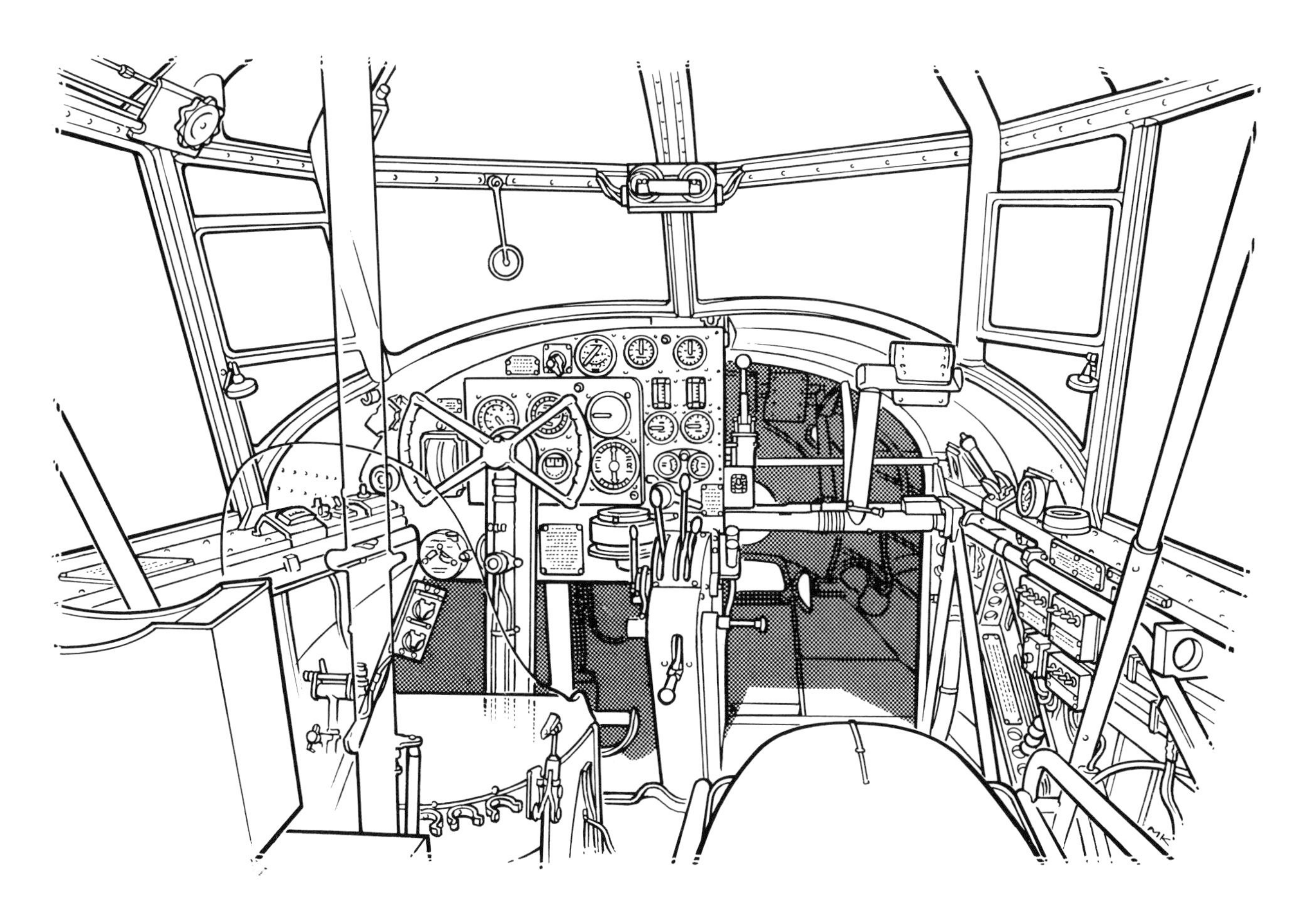

Specification (Mark I)

Power plant:	*Two 350 hp Armstrong Siddeley Cheetah IX.*
Dimensions:	*Span 56 ft 6 in, length 42 ft 3 in, height 13 ft 1 in, wing area 410 sq ft.*
Weights:	*Empty 5,512 lb, loaded 7,955 lb.*
Performance:	*Maximum speed 173 mph at 7,000 ft, cruising speed 140 mph, initial climb 750 ft/min range 700 miles, endurance 5 hrs, service ceiling 19,500 ft.*

The Anson owed its origin to the Avro 652 six-passenger commercial aircraft ordered in 1934 by Imperial Airways. At that time Germany was in the throes of re-arming, and as Britain woke up to the need to counter the growing threat, orders were placed for many new designs of aircraft. One pressing need was for a general reconnaissance land-based aircraft to combat the anticipated U-boat menace, and contracts were issued to both Avro and de Havilland, the requirements being later formed into Specification 18/35.

Each firm produced modifications of existing aircraft. The de Havilland entry was K4772, a military version of their semi-obsolescent Dragon Rapide biplane, designated D.H.89M. Avro, however, were able to take advantage of their 652 low-wing monoplane design to produce the 652A, serialled K4771. This made its first flight on 24 March 1935, and was basically similar to its predecessor, but had Armstrong Siddeley Cheetah VIs in place of Cheetah Vs, square windows instead of oval, and suitable military equipment including an Armstrong Whitworth manually-operated upper gun turret amidships.

Tests at Martlesham Heath were followed with comparative trials at Gosport by the Coast Defence Development Unit, the Anson being later involved in a Fleet Exercise in the North Sea, in which it was able to demonstrate its excellent range and endurance. The de Havilland design stood no real chance against its more advanced competitor, and in July 1935 the first of many orders was placed, for 174 aircraft, to be named the Anson.

The prototype had not been without its faults, however. When it was tested at Martlesham, criticism was made of its stability and the rudder control, and to counteract this it was fitted with longer tail surfaces, the fin was extended, and the horn balance was removed from the rudder. The Cheetah VI engines were also replaced by Mk.IXs, these being mounted 3 inches further forward. Following these and other modifications, it was possible to fly the aircraft for lengthy periods without attention. Difficulties with the Centre of Gravity were overcome, avoiding the need to make constant alterations to the trimming gear when passengers moved around. Quicker take-offs and slower landings were possible, and the aircraft could now also be side-slipped to some extent. As a result of all the improvements, it was considered possible for the average service pilot to fly the aircraft for lengthy periods without undue strain, and also to carry out cloud flying satisfactorily. This was to prove invaluable for the many roles in which it was destined to serve.

The first production machine, K6152, made its maiden flight at Woodford on 31 December 1935, and when the type entered squadron service three months later it became the first of the new service monoplanes to have a retractable undercarriage. Its row of single square windows had now been converted to a continuous rectangular series of windows on either side, to create what was virtually a glasshouse, giving outstanding visibility to the crew. Retractable wheels were new to the service, however, and several belly landings led to the fitting of a warning horn to remind forgetful pilots that they had failed to lower the undercarriage before closing the throttles. Lowering the landing gear was a tedious manual task on the Anson, requiring 144 turns on a handwheel by the pilot's seat, a task usually delegated to the navigator or wireless operator.

Despite its advanced design, the Anson was to be supplanted in the coastal role by Lockheed Hudsons, which had more powerful engines and a greater range. By the time these began to arrive from America, however, shortly before the outbreak of war, the Anson was already serving in what was to be its major role. The possibility of a trainer version had been mooted as early as 1935, and large orders were placed in 1939 for this purpose. In the meantime, though, quite a number of the early reconnaissance Ansons had been diverted to training units, pending the arrival of the Airspeed Oxford, which had been specifically designed as a trainer but was not yet available. Flying Training Schools started receiving Ansons for pilot training at the end of 1936, and many more reconnaissance Ansons were later to become trainers in a variety of roles.

The true trainer variant, unlike its predecessor, was fitted with wing flaps and also had modifications to the windscreen. It could be adapted for all types of crew training, and by the outbreak of war was being used at both service and reserve schools for instructing fledgling navigators, air gunners and wireless operators. Those used for gunnery training were equipped with a Bristol hydraulically operated upper turret, fairly similar in design to that of the Blenheim.

With the introduction of the British Commonwealth Air Training Plan at the end of 1939, further large orders were placed for machines to be shipped to Canada, Australia, New Zealand, South Africa and Southern Rhodesia. Large numbers were also built in Canada, where the RCAF used different versions of the machine. Canadian-built aircraft fitted with Jacobs engines were designated MkII, whilst MksIII and IV were British-built machines fitted respectively with Jacobs and Wright Whirlwind engines. Later came the Canadian-built MksV and VI, respectively for navigation and gunnery training, both fitted with Pratt and Whitney Wasp Juniors.

One major difficulty with Commonwealth training was that aircrew became accustomed to the clear skies prevalent for much of the year in several of the countries concerned, and had subsequent difficulty adjusting to the British climate, with mountains and high ground often obscured by bad weather. To reduce the consequent high casualty rate, several Advanced Flying Units were set up around the country, those for Observers all being equipped with Ansons, the type of aircraft to which they had already become accustomed while training.

Above:
Avro Anson I K8819 'S2' of the School of Air Navigation at St Athan around 1939–40.
(Author's collection)

Below:
Avro Anson I K8727 'H7' of No 10 Service Flying Training School at Ternhill in the autumn of 1940.
(via Eric Taylor)

Avro Anson I W2531 of No 8 Service Flying Training School at Moncton, New Brunswick in September 1941, wearing high-visibility markings.
(via Doug McPhaill)

The Anson was used widely by training units in both Bomber and Coastal Commands. A specially equipped version was also used by No 62 Operational Training Units to train radar operators in airborne interception, these being distinguished by an arrowhead-shaped aerial on the nose and a pair of vertical aerials on each wing leading edge.

Anson development continued with transport and communications variants, but it was not until after the war that three further modernised trainer versions were produced. All had metal wings and tailplanes, and were fitted with Cheetah XVs. The T.20 was built for use as a navigation trainer by the schools being set up in Southern Rhodesia, and was fitted with a transparent nose for bomb-aiming. When tested, however, it met with some criticism, as insufficient space and an inconvenient layout had been provided for trainee navigators, particularly where astro navigation was concerned, and in fact the aircraft was considered unsuitable as an astro or drift platform. Its equivalent for home use was the T.21, which was ordered in some quantity, whilst a few T.22s were built as radio trainers for air signallers. In all, over 9,000 Ansons were built by the parent company, in addition to nearly 3,000 constructed in Canada. The last trainer was delivered in 1952. Many surplus machines were civilianised and flown on charter work in the early post-war years.

Many aircrew have vivid memories of the Anson. Squadron Leader Dick Smerdon recalls:

The Anson was an extremely stable slow flying machine. I recall approaches at 40 mph. Its claim to fame was its being the first RAF type with retractable undercarriage. I well recall my first solo, all the 144 winds necessary to raise the undercarriage after take-off, and the necessary winding down again when flying downwind before landing. It would also carry a great number of persons and must have had a wide Centre of Gravity envelope, although expecting it to take off with a cricket team in Rhodesia, ground level 5,000 feet, was probably a bit too much! However, taking six to Cyprus from the Canal Zone was no problem.

Rupert Cooling flew quite a number of Ansons:

The sobriquet 'Old Annie' epitomised the motherly, nannie image attached to the Anson. It seemed so safe, so secure, viceless, forgiving. Paradoxically, this made it by extension a dangerous aircraft, as it was tediously boring. People did kill themselves in Ansons, usually by trying to fly under high tension cables, contour chasing round woods and copses, steep turns round chimney stacks of stately homes or showing off to the latest girl friend. Also, of course, by hitting hill tops hidden in cloud, but even then, the Anson could forgive. There are recorded cases of Ansons literally grinding to a halt while cruising in cloud, allowing its crew to step out, shaken but substantially uninjured, on to some upward sloping ground miles from their intended track. In

1942, one Flight Sergeant at an Air Observer School relieved the tedium of routine cross countries by teaching one of the navigator instructors to fly an Anson, including take-offs and landings.

I do not recall any units which used Anson for pilot training, although I believe there were some. No 1 Staff Pilots Training Unit at Cark was one at which I was based as an instructor, but that was a sort of OTU for Flying Training Command. A number of pilots were sent to Air Observer Schools in 1941/42 after getting their wings, primarily to allow them to gain more experience while being usefully employed. It was these chaps who were so vulnerable to the docility of the Anson for, with perhaps 500 hours in their log books, they felt they were pretty clued up. However, those who didn't die or suffer injury rapidly learned that the Annie was the exception and it was necessary to learn again to fly with due care and attention.

The Anson Mk I flew as if on rails. One could carry out a fighter type approach and landing, a power-off steep gliding turn to level out at fifty feet just short of touch down, without any qualms. It was a surprise, late in the war, to come to the Mk XII and, in the reactivated RAFVR, the T.21 with full hydraulics and constant speed airscrews which demanded the respect extended to real twin-engined aircraft. Perhaps this was the hidden danger in the Anson I as a pilot trainer. It engendered a false sense of competence and ability in those who came to fly it for any length of time before being switched to the heavier and more demanding aeroplanes closer to squadron service. The number of pilots posted from Anson units within Flying Training Command who were later to come to grief on higher performance aircraft appeared significant. It was too late to realise then how forgiving of casual handling the good old Annie had been.

There was one party trick probably unique to the Anson. Flying out of Prestwick in the winter of 1940/41, one met a good number of prodigious north-westerly gales. It was possible to climb to two or three thousand feet, to head into wind before manually lowering the undercarriage, throttle back, pump down the flaps then reduce airspeed until, at a little over fifty knots, the Annie would be partly hanging on its props. Mystified pupil navigators, lying prone on their bellies over the bombsight, would see the target drifting forward down the sighting wires, to disappear beyond the nose as the Anson moved steadily backward relative to the ground. Good old Annie, hard worked, much abused, but perhaps virtually indispensible.

Avro Anson I N5331 of No 10 Radio School at Carew Cheriton around 1943–44. This example appears to be a conversion from the flapless reconnaissance version. It is fitted with the Armstrong Whitworth AW.38 turret. (Author's collection)

Ralph Dargue, who served with training units in Canada, recalls one flight in an Anson, which left him with a vivid recollection of it being cold, draughty, noisy and enlivened only by the sight of an erk winding up the undercarriage and then minutes later, another poor devil wearing himself out winding it down! Ralph was well in the back row, but heard all about that experience.

Another ex Wireless Operator/Air Gunner was Ian McCubbrey, who flew in Ansons during the war at both Dumfries and Wigtown, and then post-war with No 11 Reserve Flying School at Scone:

My main recollection in these aircraft was of the poor trainee's job to wind up the undercarriage – 140-odd turns up on take-off, then another 140-odd down on landing. It was a good thing we were fit and able in our early days! The Mark Is were passable to fly in, but one did need Sidcot suit and furlined boots for comfort. Once airborne, I was mainly preoccupied with the operation of the complicated 1083 Receiver/Transmitter with its odd coils kept in the boxes beside it.

In 1949 I joined the RAFVR, and we did our flying in Anson T.21s and thoroughly enjoyed it as our seat was up forward beside the Airwork pilot, with a perfect frontal view of everything. This version had a hydraulic undercarriage, so we led a very comfortable existence! The W/T key was on the starboard window sill, and the receiver/transmitter behind the pilot.

Life was quite pleasant with two-week annual camps, visits to Jersey and back and also to other RAF stations. One incident I recall was on a flight to Gare Loch in April 1950. The pilot, Bill Hamilton, noticed a laid-up carrier there and said he would like to see if our Anson could make a landing on its deck! He then lowered his undercarriage and made an approach towards it in the normal manner. We saw naval boats shooting towards it, and red flares being fired off, then just as we neared the ship he revved up, did an overshoot and headed back to Scone.

Bill Williams spent a short time training as a Wireless Operator on Ansons at Dumfries during the summer of 1944:

During this time we carried out six day cross-country exercises and one night flight. The total day hours was 20 and the night 3 hours 10 minutes. I will never forget the night exercise, this being my very first taste of night flying. We flew over 10/10 cloud, with a full moon above, making it all look like cotton wool below. A magnificent sight and although I flew at night regularly afterwards, I cannot recall anything to touch that.

The Staff Pilots at 10 (0)AFU consisted of names like Karpinski, Cylwik and Rychlik, recorded in my Log Book.

There was one mid-air collision between two Ansons when we were there. One of the victims was a Scotsman, Sgt Rhodie, who was on our course at No 4 Radio School at Madley – a grand lad. I know for a fact that at least four of the hundred on this course were killed before they got to an operational squadron.

I also remember an occasion when the Anson I was flying in over the Irish Sea in thick fog only just avoided colliding with another Anson. The pilot decided that this was too dicey and returned to base!

One of the exercises was routed over my homeland – the Isle of Anglesey (now renamed Gwynedd). The instructor, a Warrant Officer, kindly took over the TR.1154/1155 radio and allowed me to view the island from above for the first time – he also gave me 98 per cent for the exercise! I was later able to fly over my home at about a hundred feet in a Lancaster.

Bill Bateman trained as a National Service navigator on Ansons at No 3 ANS Bishops Court, Northern Ireland in 1953, and later at CNCS Shawbury:

The Anson T.21s at 3 ANS were used for initial training exercises of about 2½ hours duration. They were a bit vulnerable to turbulence, and at times gave their crews a rough ride. There was no staff navigator aboard, so it was up to the pilot to monitor the work of the student navigators and find the way home when they got lost.

On completion of training I was posted to the Central Navigation and Control School at Shawbury. This was home to a swarm of Ansons and a squadron of Lincolns. The Lincolns were used as long range navigation trainers and the Ansons as guinea pigs for student air traffic controllers. Most of the officers on the Anson squadron were recalled reservists who had served during the war. They referred to themselves as the 'retreads', and a scruffy lot they were, still using their wartime uniforms as they flatly refused to buy anything new just for their eighteen months stint. The rest of the aircrew, apart from a couple of National Service navigators, consisted of what to us were hoary old NCO aircrew, signallers, gunners and the like. They were all great characters, and looked after us sprogs like Dutch uncles. The Flight Commander had flown various types of aircraft, and had spent some time as a prisoner-of-war, having been shot down in his Spitfire during an intruder sweep over France.

The long suffering aircraft and crews spent hours doing circuits and landings with the occasional emergency (real or simulated) thrown in to break the monotony. A rather more hairy variation on this was to act as guinea-pig for the student Ground Controlled Approach (GCA) operators, who had a caravan at Sleap, an otherwise deserted airfield some eight miles from Shawbury. This involved the pilot, flying on instruments, doing exactly as he was told, to see where he would finish up! Another crew member sitting beside him in the wireless operator's seat kept a lookout for other aircraft in the circuit doing the same thing, and monitored the aircraft's descent. The pilots were usually keen to co-operate with the students and would do a full approach, only breaking away at the last moment.

To save wear and tear on the hard-worked aircraft, the undercarriage was not raised or lowered on every circuit. This would have meant as much wear in one day as most aircraft would suffer in a month, so the undercarriage remained retracted. On two occasions the lookout's warning came too late to prevent the aircraft setting up the unofficial low-flying record. Two aircraft both managed to remove four inches from the blades of their propellers by touching the concrete runway with them. Fortunately the blades were

made of laminated wood, and the tips simply splintered so the aircraft were still able to climb away safely. Had the blades been made of metal, they would have bent, rendering them useless, and the aircraft would have flopped down and slid ignominously to a halt with disastrous consequences.

The Ansons were also used from time to time for communications flights and aerial searches. One day I undertook a trip to Chivenor which at that time was a Fighter Command OCU, using Vampires. The route had been planned to avoid an air-to-air firing range over the Bristol Channel, and on the return journey we were happily thinking that we were well clear of any excitement when suddenly from nowhere a bright yellow Tempest shot across in front of us at the same height and about 200 yards away, closely followed by a fluorescent green drogue, in turn closely followed by a Vampire banging away with red tracer. I have never known an Anson descend so fast, it dropped like a brick, the Polish pilot meantime cursing volubly in his native tongue. We crossed the Severn somewhere near Chepstow at a height of ten feet above the water, or so it seemed.

There was a big influx of Ansons into Shawbury during my stay, and for a while all the pilots were kept busy air testing the new arrivals. Some of the earlier marks, including some with wooden wings, soon disappeared, probably for scrap.

We had two mishaps during my sojourn on the squadron. W-Willie was reckoned to be our best aircraft, being 10 knots faster than any of the others, but one day it suffered an undercarriage malfunction. It would not lock down and couldn't be retracted again, so the aircraft was put down on the grass after a fast flat approach with flaps raised to minimise damage. It gently descended onto its belly and slithered through the boundary hedge, across the Shawbury-Grinshill road, coming to rest in a field. The crew lost no time getting out of it and retreating to a safe distance, and were still out of breath when the Flight Commander, who had followed the fire tender and ambulance to the scene, asked them to 'Go back and do it again, more slowly, as I missed it!'

On another occasion, Y-Yoke was taking part in an aerial search in South Wales, based on Pembrey, a Fighter Command OCU. When it arrived at Pembrey from Shawbury, Air Traffic Control informed the pilot of the runway in use and the surface wind. He realised that the crosswind was beyond the limitations of the aircraft, and told ATC so. The controller, presumably a fighter type, remarked condescendingly, 'What's the matter. Can't you fly that thing?' This was like a red rag to a bull, and the inevitable happened. The aircraft side-swiped its undercarriage from its fixings and slid on its belly, gently turning end for end as it want. The airmen down the back, who had been brought along as lookouts, sat open-mouthed at the sight of the navigator running back along the fuselage, kicking the door off its hinges and disappearing, closely followed by the pilot yelling at them to get out. He said afterwards that it looked as though they thought aeroplanes always landed that way! I believe both aircraft were subsequently repaired and saw further service, but I had left Shawbury by then and returned to humdrum civilian life.

On this same search, I was in another aircraft, which was being flown by the Flight Commander. We did the morning stint and Y-Yoke was to do the afternoon shift. There was quite a wind that day, and considerable turbulence round the Welsh mountains. We were only some 800-1,000 feet above the ground in order to get a close look at anything interesting. This was not really a good idea, as we found ourselves at one point descending rapidly even though the aircraft was in the climbing attitude, with full power on both engines. We had descended to some 200 feet and were looking for a reasonably flat area to drop into when we suddenly flew out of the downdraught and were able to climb away. We were both sweating a bit by then, though!

We had three Mk12s, in addition to the T.21s, these being used, amongst other things, for continuation training, and for the QFI to check out pilots. They were well suited for this, being fitted with dual controls, but they were something of a fire hazard. The manual priming pump used in the start-up procedure was mounted on the dashboard in front of the right-hand seat. It fell to me to work it, and these pumps always leaked, dripping 87 octane onto the legs of whoever occupied the seat. I still have my flying suit bearing the stains! If anything had gone wrong I would have made quite a blaze in my own right!

Wing Commander Robert Sage flew Ansons many times throughout his long career:

My first flight in an Anson was in December 1937 (K6301) and my last flight in April 1959. In the meantime I flew them in several different roles and theatres. During the late 1930s Ansons were being used for crew training in bomber squadrons which were being equipped with such things as Wellesleys and Hampdens, which could not be fitted with dual controls. I became a specialist in instrument flying (blind flying in those days) and beam approach techniques, and found myself on the strength of the Beam Approach Training and Development Unit at A&AEE Boscombe Down, equipped with Ansons. We reached a stage of proficiency enabling us to continue flying with a vertical visibility of just 50 feet. For that reason I suppose, in hindsight, one might question the value of that sort of training, because nothing like that proficiency was achieved with front-line aircraft.

I preferred the Anson to the Oxford, which I did not fly until 1947, though one had to concede the greater advantage of the hydraulic and electrical systems of the latter aircraft. There certainly were problems with the Standard Beam Approach equipment on the Ansons, with no generator to charge the battery, and receivers which were very sensitive to voltage changes. In winter this was aggravated by ice formation on the dipole and vertical aerials. The physical effort required for undercarriage operation and engine starting was of course legendary on the Anson.

Only twice during my many hours of Anson flying did I experience sudden failure of the Cheetah. Once was when an engine shed the valve gear from one cylinder, taking most of the cowling, fortunately near enough to a landing ground to be able to make gracefully the inevitable single-engined landing. When engines fell apart, of course, you could see it all happening. The second occasion was on take-off from the landing ground at Ventnor with a full load of passengers, when the starboard engine died completely with some sort of carburettor failure just at the point of unstick. I was able to re-land and was fortunate to over-run

the boundary into long grass which halted the aircraft without damage.

My blind approach experience was useful when the unit was renamed the Wireless Intelligence Development Unit in October 1940 to combat the German navigation and bombing beams. The ex-BAT&DU Ansons were used at first, after a special radio fit. I made many Anson sorties during the next two years, day and night in all weathers, sometimes several in one day. The work was very secret and not discussed outside our unit. This sometimes led to misunderstandings at the bases from which our detached flights operated. At bases with a day role anxious about night intruder attacks we were often expected to take off and land at night with no airfield lighting, using only SBA and our aircraft landing light. Some of our Ansons were lost to our own defences and some were in action with enemy bombers.

I myself, having taken off in fog from an East Anglian base when no other RAF aircraft were able to leave the ground, flew a mission to detect German beams deployed during a daylight attack on London. We were flying above a 10,000 feet cloud top when a He 111 appeared suddenly out of the cloud top below and in front of us. Having increased to full throttle, I made a diving attack with the Vickers gun. The He 111 returned fire and made back into cloud cover. An enemy aircraft later crashed in the area, but Fighter Command could not concede any credit, being unable to trace gunfire damage. On arrival back at base it was found that the battery voltage had dropped below the minimum required to operate the SBA system. I had inadvertently knocked on the landing light switch when cocking the Vickers. This meant a let-down through 8,000 feet of cloud with a 400 feet base and fog underneath with no aids, no hope. Fortunately my first sight of the ground was at a point which I recognised immediately, and we were able to hedge hop home. We were required to conduct these Anson operations at maximum possible height, above 13,000 feet, with no cabin heating and a primitive oxygen supply for emergency use.

Mike Sparrow recalls an unusual forced-landing of an Anson in Canada:

In the winter of 1942/43, the German U-Boat menace had spread its tentacles throughout the Northern Atlantic. Some adventurous commanders had even penetrated the St. Lawrence River.

No 1 General Reconnaissance School based on RCAF Summerside, Prince Edward Island, was equipped with Ansons Is, usually flying two and a half hour sorties covering areas of the Gulf of St. Lawrence. These training sorties were considered semi-operational and, should there be a known enemy intrusion into these waters, some aircraft would be armed with two 250 lb anti-submarine bombs.

One day in December 1942, a normal GR training exercise patrol was being flown over the Gulf to the north west of PEI; areas of the sea were solidly frozen over. When still some forty miles out from its base, an engine failure occurred. With its crew of four the Anson, at 2,000 feet, was unable to maintain height. While gently but persistently descending and transmitting 'Mayday' calls, it became patently obvious that the pilot was committed to ditching in the frozen waters – but with ice as far as he could see, a touchdown on that surface was inevitable. Question: was the aircraft going to smash through, or remain on the surface of the ice? With wheels retracted, the aircraft skidded to a halt on a relatively good surface.

In the meantime other aircraft had headed to the area of the forced landing and observed that the crew were all uninjured and waving. Radio communication with Summerside and Charlottetown informed these bases that all was well so far.

How about rescue? An air/sea rescue launch was out of the question; another Anson could not be considered. So it was that the captain of a small, individually-run airline volunteered to fly a light, high wing aircraft out, land and pick up the stranded survivors. Fortunately the weather was good and two or maybe three sorties successfuly made. The complete crew was recovered safely and the Anson left in solitary state.

For some weeks the aircraft could be seen floating on its slowly diminishing frozen island. Wagers were made on the possible date of its demise until it finally gave up to gravity and disappeared beneath the waters of the Gulf.

As a postcript, the crew suffered no ill effects from their temporary sojourn on the ice, merely some protracted hangovers from subsequent celebrations. Their rescuer deservedly received a civil award for gallantry.

Tom Twist was first involved with servicing Ansons at No 3 Air Observer and Navigator School at Bobbington, to where he was posted in the Spring of 1942:

On arrival there we found we were taking over from civilian contractors who had been doing the maintenance of all aircraft. We were told that subject only to the weather, flying would now be 24 hours a day, seven days a week and 365 days a year – and it was. The Ansons were worked hard and the ground crews very hard, as we always seemed to be short of manpower.

The unit consisted of several navigation flights and one bombing flight. Aircraft on navigation training used to be away about three hours, and were quite well equipped with wireless and Gee boxes. Bombing Flight aircraft were only

Facing page, top:
A late production Avro Anson I MG182 '4' of No 1 Air Gunnery School at Pembrey around 1943–44 fitted with the Bristol hydraulically-operated turret.
(via P.A. Tilley)

Centre:
Avro Anson I NK563 'FAGA' of the RAF College at Cranwell in 1948.
(Author)

Bottom:
Avro Anson I N4877 bearing the spurious marking 'VX-F' of No 206 Squadron with the Skyframe Aircraft Museum at Staverton in September 1965. It was restored to military markings after becoming G-AMDA.
(E.B. Morgan archives)

4
MG182
4

FA
GA
NK563

F
VX
N4877

away about one hour, and these had a bomb rack fitted under the fuselage for 25 lb practice bombs. We had to remove the pins from the bombs after the pilot had done his engine and ground checks, and hand them all to the trainee navigator who was going to drop the bombs.

The Ansons were well liked by the ground crews. I loved the years I was associated with them. The hand cranking of the engines to start could be hard work sometimes, though on the whole I think the Cheetah engine was good and reliable. One trouble we did have was cylinder retaining bolts breaking, causing engine failure, but as far as I can recollect we never had any losses caused by this.

One ground crew complaint was when you went up on air test and you had to wind up the undercarriage, the handle for this was behind the pilot's seat and it took nearly 150 turns to retract the wheels. Another poor thing was the fuel change-over cocks, which were low down on the starboard side of the cockpit. There was about 18 inches of movement on change-over and you had to be very careful as you could easily cut your hand.

I think we were lucky while I was at Bobbington as I recall very few accidents, despite the many flying hours put in. One I do remember was an Anson on take-off run down the runway when the starboard engine cut. Before the pilot could take action the plane veered off the runway and the starboard wing took the rudders off about five aircraft, but luckily no one was injured.

In the summer of 1943 I was posted to No 1 Air Gunnery School at Pembrey. At this time Blenheims were being phased out and Ansons brought in to replace them. We had to check the Ansons when they came in, and before they were allocated to flights. The flying pattern was much different at AGS as it was only done in daylight and they only flew out over the Bristol Channel doing air-to-air firing at drogues towed by Martinets. It was at Pembrey that I first worked with WAAF airframe and engine mechanics, and I think it showed how easy the Ansons were to maintain when we found it easy to teach WAAFs how to do Daily Inspection between flight inspection and refuelling, and they seem to have no trouble doing the work themselves afterwards.

The Anson could always carry a good weight of freight if need be. At Pembrey, soon after receiving Ansons, equipment was needed for use in servicing. One day the old Anson we used on Station Flight, with the pilot, navigator and myself, flew to Carew Cheriton to pick up some trestles and lifting jacks. We loaded up as much as we thought the plane could safely take, and then had to get to the end of the runway, hold her on the brakes and give the engines full power. We waited until the tail was trying to lift and then let off the brakes. As we lumbered down the runway our hearts were in our mouths, but the pilot just managed to clear the boundary hedges. There were no further problems, and we landed normally at Pembrey.

Another trip we had was when the CO from Pembrey, a Group Captain, was posted to Morpeth. We had to take him and all his kit, and he informed us that he would be doing the navigating. However, on our way over the Welsh mountains we ran into a thunderstorm, and as the Anson couldn't climb very high we were unable to get above it. We could not try

Avro Anson T.20 VS504 before being flown to Southern Rhodesia in 1948 for use by No 3 Air Navigation School at Thornhill.

(British Aerospace)

Avro Anson T.21 VV253 'RCT-1' of No 18 Reserve Flying School at Fair Oaks in 1950.
(MAP photo)

to get below the storm because of the mountains, and being a rather elderly machine it had no wireless equipment on board, so we had no means of communication. However, after flying for ages, the CO admitted he was lost anyway, and we eventually came out into clear weather, when we were able to identify landmarks. We were evidently now flying over Lancashire, as I recognised the area where my parents lived, and that made me sweat as I knew that many barrage balloons were protecting the various industries there. Our luck was in, though, as they were all on the ground at that time, and the rest of the journey was made in clear sunny skies.

I was posted to the 2nd Tactical Air Force in January 1944, so I left the Ansons behind, and it was not until November 1945 that I was reunited with them at No 84 Group Communications Squadron at Celle, Germany. These Ansons were much more modern, not as basic and bone shaking as the ones in Flying Training Command, being much warmer to fly in and having hydraulic undercarts. Working on these was much easier, things were not being rushed, though one thing that was hard was that all the petrol bowsers had to be refuelled from four gallon jerry cans.

Cyril Smith serviced Ansons soon after the war at Thornhill in Southern Rhodesia (now Zimbabwe):

A lot of the flying was carried out in fair weather, so life went on at a relaxed and most enjoyable pace. Normal working hours were 0600 – 1300 to avoid the heat of the afternoon sun, but with an increase in aircraft numbers the rules were changed to embrace afternoon and night flying. Ansons were the easiest aircraft in the world to keep flying, no serious problems ever being encountered. In fact we had more problems with the pilots. Certain characters were rather notorious at disobeying signals, and some of the luckless marshallers matured earlier than one would have wished. One visiting SRAF Anson pilot, independent of any ground crew signals, started up as an erk ducked under the wing, foolishly within the propellor arc, to advise the occupant that his door was still open and a trolley-acc was coming. He got away with it, but quite a heart-stopping lesson was learnt by everyone present that day.

One day I overheard a pilot tearing a strip off his two trainee navigators for getting hopelessly lost and not asking him where they were! I often pondered after this exchange whether the navigators were ever responsible for getting the aircraft back home.

It was a great relief to change over from MkIs to the Mk20s which did not need winding up. This involved getting tucked in between nacelle and fuselage, being blown backwards by the propellor just inches away, then ducking under the wing and repeating the performance on the other engine.

A recurring problem with the starboard engine on VM414 had resulted in several early returns. After further servicing I went along for the ride with one of our commissioned pilots on the called-for Air Test. Once airborne, amongst other checks was MAGDROP, first one off then the other and for 'complete satisfaction', as the man in the driving seat put it, both off together. There was an almighty bang, the aircraft lurched as power was restored behind a windmilling prop and he got away with it. The sequel to all this was the engine having to be completely stripped and broken valve parts replaced!

On the occasion of Navigators qualifying, it was the custom for the passing-out ceremony to be accompanied by

a flypast of six Ansons, which would fly over the hangars and dip in salute. This meant practice formation flying, and I went on two such flights leading up to the event. It was during one of these in the trailing 'vic' that we were nearly blown into the hangars when the leading vic dived too low in salute. I wouldn't like to hazard a guess as to which was the closest to us, the leader's tail above or the hangar roof below, but either way, there wasn't a lot in it. An immediate flat break guaranteed breathing space again. There were a few light-hearted recriminations afterwards, but practice made perfect.

There was a hiccup one day when an aircraft took-off with the luggage compartment door up. After a circuit it landed apparently none the worse, despite extra drag and possible handling problems. Fortunately these compartments were usually empty as in this instance.

One senior NCO we regarded as an ever-present hazard. He never seemed to have a good word for those on the flight-line, and invariably described us as 'Always scruffy, even on Sundays, and never eating on time', this last referring to the trouble we put the mess to as a result of flying commitments. One night, as we were despatching aircraft, this gentleman staggered along under alcoholic motivation and said he was going flying. Ignoring all resistance, he managed to board an Anson, but had not reckoned on the pilot being in charge. Engines were switched off and voices raised, before relative calm was established and reason, at least on our part, prevailed. The next day, sober in all respects, he came back to apologise. He was later permitted a flight, and we outwardly fussed over him, showing concern for his well-being and enjoyment. Afterwards there were definite signs of an improved relationship - although we never lost the 'scruffy' label.

John Norris was involved in 1957 in ground operation with Ansons at Chivenor:

I can recall no special problems in servicing the Anson, everything being pretty straightforward. Under the planned servicing scheme of that time, tradesmen were lettered by skill and ability as man A,B,C, and D. I was man 'D', and very much a sprog rigger. My daily job cards were of the 'clean undersurfaces of starboard mainplane and clear drainholes' variety. My only clear memories are of tripping over the low set tailplane while the aircraft was on the ground, and clouting my head on it when she was jacked up. That and manning the hydraulic hand pump for manual undercarriage retraction checks. From 'two greens' to 'lights out' was quite a slog, but the other way, undercarriage down, was not quite so bad. Four or five cycles of this and the bod on the pump took on a definite rosy glow.

I recall stripping fabric off the upper fuselage where a number of stringers were damaged. That lovely Anson whaleback took on the aspect of a rose trellis, and a 'chippy rigger' on the team (we still had one or two then) got busy with glue, tacks and timber. I opted out of a jolly on the air test, having seen what an Anson was really made of and been rather put off aviating in one.

Eric Sharp worked on Anson engines with the HQ Flight at Cranwell in the early fifties:

Anson exhaust systems were a non-stop battle, the support straps for the 'silencer' heat exchanger forever cracking. That Ansons never shed this large chunk of ironmongery all over the place I consider was just luck. The exhaust stub gaskets, too, were a pain. One checked every airframe for the tell-tale grey stain of blowing exhaust gas, and judged if it had to be fixed or let go until a collection made it worth the effort, for invariably large sections of the manifold had to be removed, if not all of it, to replace the offending gaskets. Each stub, too, held by two brass nuts on steel studs, would levy a toll in seized nuts and stripped or pulled studs. Looking back, I suppose it was what being an engine fitter was all about.

Looking at a picture of a bent Anson, I tend to think that at that time attitudes towards aircraft accidents and loss, and for that matter plain mortality, was very much a carry-over from wartime thinking. We had many accidents, mainly fatal, involving pupils and instructors, and these were shrugged off in a way completely unknown in later years.

This particular Anson had just been taken on charge following Major Inspection and was as good as new. Returning late one evening, the pilot taxied up the fairly steep apron in front of the hangar, cut the engines and free-wheeled in. The plan was to shut the doors and go, doing the refuel and an airframe B/F (before flight check) in the morning. Normally the Ansons were towed in backwards up the slope and pushed out in the morning, using a steering tiller on the tail wheel.

Come the morning it was a cold misty start with black ice on the pan. The kite with its rudder pointing the wrong way couldn't be pushed out with a tiller arm to guide it down the hill at speed. The tractor was hitched up to the tow arm, and with a National Service man on the brakes, my mate commenced to drive it off down the slope. Almost immediately the aircraft started to over-run the tractor. A shout for brakes locked the wheels, but the aircraft continued to jackknife on the tractor, skidding on the ice.

The tractor was the Fordson agricultural type, with big knobbly tyres, no mudguards and a sort of spring cast-iron seat between them. First the port elevator hit the tyres and rode up the treads, followed by the port tailplane. At this point my pal bailed out over the tractor's steering wheel and fuel tank. The whole lot came to a standstill with every one of the fuselage longerons broken in front of the fin. The station hierarchy, both technical and admin, led by the Camp Commandant, viewed the scene, shook their heads and said "Oh, an obvious accident!! Write a report". The two lads concerned did so, and heard nothing more of it. Times changed certainly.

Airspeed Oxford

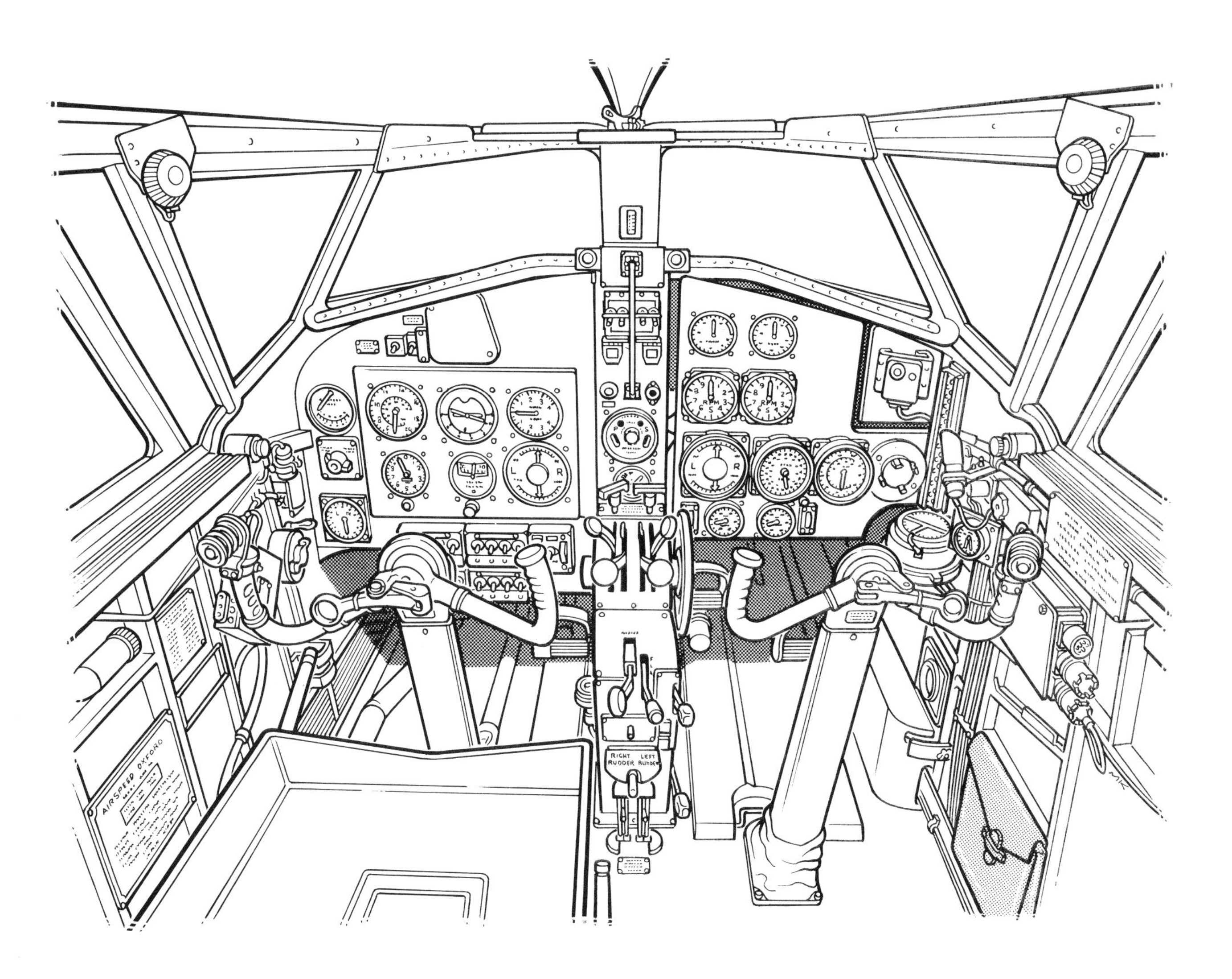

Specification (Mark 1)

Power plant:	*Two 375 hp Armstrong Siddeley Cheetah X.*
Dimensions:	*Span 53 ft 4 in, length 34 ft 6 in, height 11 ft 1 in, wing area 348 sq ft.*
Weights	*Empty 5,230 lb, loaded 7,300 lb.*
Performance:	*Maximum speed 184 mph at 7,500 ft, cruising speed 160 mph, initial climb 1,225 ft/min, range 960 miles, endurance 6 hrs, service ceiling 23,000 ft.*

Unlike its contemporary the Anson, the Airspeed Oxford was designed from the outset as a trainer, though it too had a civil predecessor, in this case the Envoy, which was well tried and tested, over 50 being built for successful use at home and overseas for feeder-liner and charter work. A development, the A.S.8 Viceroy had taken part in the 1936 air race to Johannesburg, and the South African Air Force had been supplied with several Convertible Envoys fitted with a removable upper gun turret, so that they could be quickly changed from passenger transport to a light bomber or reconnaissance aircraft.

During the expansion period of the mid-1930s, Airspeeds were handicapped in official eyes by a link with the Dutch firm of Fokker, founded by the young designer whose aircraft has been the scourge of the Royal Flying Corps in the First World War. Nevertheless, Airspeeds had already proved their ability to design and manufacture modern aircraft, and in late 1935 the Air Ministry made preliminary enquiries about the cost of converting the Envoy into a trainer. Some months later came an invitation to tender to Specification T.23/36 for a now urgently needed twin-engined advanced trainer. This had obviously been written around the Envoy design, no other manufacturer being invited to tender, and in the autumn of 1936, despite the frowned on Fokker connection, 136 machines were ordered straight from the drawing board.

Despite its origins, the machine which finally emerged was a virtual redesign, very little of the original Envoy having survived. The initial production aircraft, L4534, made its first flight in June 1937, powered by two Armstrong Siddeley Cheetah X engines. Fitted with retractable undercarriage, flaps, and other modern equipment, it was a versatile machine, which could be used for training in bombing, navigation, air gunnery, radio or aerial photography. L4534 was subjected to tests at Martlesham Heath, and the resulting report was generally favourable.

It was found to have a good field of view, the instrumentation was satisfactory, the engine controls were well placed, and the flap controls were convenient and easy to operate. The cockpit was also satisfactory, though space between the controls and the seats was limited, nor was there much elbow room in the left-hand seat. Headroom was normally ample, but difficulties could be encountered when the blind flying hood was in use, as the head of a tall pilot would touch it even when he had his seat fully down. The safety belt fitment also caused criticism, as it left the pilot

Airspeed Oxford I L4578 '27' in formation with other aircraft of No 3 Flying Training School at South Cerney in 1938.

(RAF Museum)

Airspeed Oxford Is of No 3 Flying Training School running up engines at South Cerney in 1938.
(RAF Museum)

vulnerable to head injuries in the event of a crash.

Its handling qualities were designed to match those of the larger aircraft which most pupils would go on to fly. There was a tendency to swing on take-off, and it became tail heavy with an increase in engine power, but for normal cruising conditions the change of trim could be easily held with the elevators, which were moderately light but effective and quick in response. When trimmed the aircraft could be flown feet-off at all speeds. On approach there was effective warning of stall by a marked vibration throughout the structure, but the stall could be easily controlled. In such conditions the wing which dropped suddenly, could be raised immediately by the ailerons alone, provided the control column was not brought further back, in which case the aircraft could develop a vicious stall, followed by a spin.

The design had a pleasing appearance, with a neatly streamlined fuselage, and engines mounted above the wings. The latter were in three sections, the centre of which was attached to the lower fuselage and accommodated both the engines and a retractable undercarriage. Four bolts and locking nuts were used to attach the outer sections to this. Split trailing-edge flaps were fitted inboard of the ailerons. For ease of construction, the wooden semi-monocoque fuselage was built in two sections, one including the cockpit and cabin, and the other the rear fuselage with its integrated fin. It had a cantilever tail unit, the wooden frame being plywood covered, apart from the movable surfaces, which had fabric covering. The tailwheel was of the fixed variety.

The fuselage was designed for a variety of training purposes. In addition to the pilot, it had provision for either a second pilot or a navigator. The third crew member could be a gunner, radio operator, camera operator or air bomber. The cabin, which was fitted with full dual control, had a full range of instruments, including a Sperry panel in the centre of the first pilot's dashboard, and for the second pilot a duplicate altimeter, airspeed indicator and turn and bank indicator. The height of the first pilot's seat was fully adjustable in flight, by use of a lever on his left, but the second pilot could only make such an adjustment on the ground, and was limited to three possible positions.

The Mark I, equipped with Cheetah Xs, was an all-purpose aircrew trainer fitted with an Armstrong Whitworth dorsal gun turret, a bomb bay and various ancillary equipment. The Mark II version, however,

being intended for navigation and radio training, had the turret omitted, but there were no other significant differences and very little change in the handling qualities. Both versions were built in large numbers, total production exceeding 8,500. Many were flown in Australia, Canada, New Zealand, South Africa and Southern Rhodesia. In practise, the crew training role largely fell to the Anson, and the Oxfords were mostly used for pilot training, the turrets being removed from MkIs. Many of the Oxfords used in Canada and Rhodesia had Pratt and Whitney Wasp Junior engines, and in this specification were designated MarkV. Neither the MkIII nor the MkIV versions had gone into production, these being fitted respectively with Cheetah XVs and experimental Gipsy Queen IVs.

Much of the production was sub-contracted to Percival and Standard, and a test report in April 1941 commented that one of the latter (V3868) compared favourably in performance and general handling qualities with those built by the parent firm. Much the same comment was made in October 1942 on the first production MkV (EB424), whose engines, cowling, exhaust ring and muff had been adapted from the equipment of the Vultee BT-13.

Colloquially known as the 'Ox-box', the Oxford entered service in late 1937, and was soon in use by the Central Flying School and the expanding number of Flying Training Schools. It continued to serve throughout the war, mostly with Service Flying Training Schools or their successors, the (Pilot) Advanced Flying Units.

Both aerobatics and spinning were prohibited, being a twin-engined machine, though it was not unknown for an Oxford to be rolled or looped. Recovery from an unintended spin was deemed not difficult, however, normal procedures in such a situation being effective, the inner motor being opened up to help rudder action. On occasion, however, an Oxford would spin unaccountably, and be difficult or impossible to recover, and consequently Flying Training Schools banned this manoeuvre. Investigation eventually found the aircraft susceptible to misalignment between the wing root fillets and the engine cowlings. Fitting a leather seal improved matters somewhat, but a hoped-for cure to the problem by fitting twin fins and rudders on N6327 proved unsuccessful.

The Oxford was much more demanding of the pilot than the Anson, and consequently those that survived their training course attained flying skills of a relatively high standard. On take-off extreme care was necessary with the throttles and controls, if the aircraft was not to swing smartly to starboard, resulting in either an S-shaped take-off or a ground loop. Single-engined flying could be tiring as the rudder proved inadequate in this situation despite its size. The good field of view was an asset in landing, which was not usually difficult,

Airspeed Oxford Is of No 14 Service Flying Training School at Cranfield in 1940. These are fitted with the Armstrong Whitworth gun turret.
(Author's collection)

except for attempts at three-pointers in cross-winds, when the rudder became blanketed, causing the aircraft to wander off-course.

In Canada, the Oxford was very prone to moisture problems. Having wooden wings, the damp climate affected the glue in the joints, which gradually filled up the drain holes. Consequently when the aircraft went in for repair or inspection, several gallons of water would pour out. It was not uncommon for dry-rot to develop in these conditions.

The wooden construction also gave trouble in the tropics. In humid conditions, the casein-based adhesive used in construction developed a fungoid growth, particularly in the joints. Experimentation led to production of a resin-based adhesive, and this was used for later production aircraft, entirely curing the problem.

As with the Anson, aircrew experienced difficulty adjusting to the normal British weather after learning to fly in clear overseas skies, and a number of (Pilot) Advanced Flying Units were set up, mainly equipped with Oxfords, to overcome this problem. In addition, several dozen Oxford-equipped Beam Approach Training Flights were set up, their aircraft being distinguished by large yellow triangles painted on the fuselage sides and under the wings. Attached to both Advanced Flying Units and Heavy Conversion Units, these units provided tuition in the Standard Beam Approach system for bringing in operational aircraft safely in conditions of poor visibility.

Production ended in July 1945, and the Oxford was largely superseded after the war, though a number were retained, mainly for communications duties, or attached to Fighter Command to help single-engine pilots to adjust to the Hornet and Meteor. They were also issued to re-formed reserve squadrons, some of which were equipped with Mosquitoes, being used for conversion and instrument training. When the Korean war and other factors led later to an expansion in flying training, many surviving Oxfords were brought out of storage and issued to Advanced Flying Training Schools, where they were used to train National Service pilots until the last of these closed in 1954. A number were also sold for civil use, some after being reworked as small airliners by Airspeed, in which

Airspeed Oxford I ED268 '12' of the Air Transport Auxiliary Training Unit at White Waltham in 1944.
(Author's collection)

P6823
24
N4640

guise they were rechristened Consuls.

Squadron Leader Dick Smerdon recalls:

The Oxford was distinctly British and provided the pilot with a good twin-engined trainer prior to his conversion to operational types. It introduced him to operating the (quadrant-mounted) throttles with his right hand, manipulating a 'spectacle' control column with his left hand, and flying from the left-hand seat. After the Tiger and the Harvard, the view from the flight deck was much improved.

Rupert Cooling trained on Oxfords with 15 SFTS at Lossiemouth, early in the war:

I found the Oxford a bit of a handful at first. True, my introduction to it was somewhat abrupt. It had been three months before that we reserve pilots, mobilised on the outbreak of war, had last flown. That had been on the graceful Hawker Harts, Hinds and Audaxes which sailed the seas of the air in partnership with their pilots in a harmony of pleasure and movement both effortless and natural. If that was flying, to wear one's wings seemed utterly logical.

Perhaps these regular airmen pilots who were to be the instructors at Lossiemouth felt that these callow youths needed to be shown that flight was a discipline, not a sporting pastime. They gave us ten minutes in the cockpit of an Oxford to describe the instruments and controls, then forty-five minutes dual to get the feel of the machine in the air; and finally two or three landings – well, arrivals. Then 'Off you go. Do at least four landings' the door slammed in the slipstream and you were on your own.

The Oxford was easy to taxi and visibility was excellent. It rode fairly roughly over the grass airfields for the undercarriage was robust – it had to be. Many aircraft were fitted with a turret aft of the port entrance door and, in early 1940, instrument layout was far from standard. The Blind Flying Panel was there, but ancillary instruments, switches and minor controls tended to be pretty variable.

Early take-offs were often crescent shaped until pilots got used to the swing, but once in the air the Oxford handled well. It was responsive to the controls and generally stable. Single-engine flying was hard work, but was largely a demonstration exercise, as the Cheetah was a very reliable power plant. Visibility was again excellent through an extensive clear vision canopy, and on approach, with flaps down, the impression was one of diving towards the ground. The change of attitude with flaps down was pronounced and, for some reason, power-off approaches were standard. Motoring in was discouraged and 'wheely' landings were not considered fair. The result was an almighty heave on the stick to flare out, for the change of attitude from power off glide to three point was substantial. The pirouettes of spring lambs were reminiscent of SFTS Oxfords as pilots put down the tailwheel first or dropped in from a foot or two, often on one wheel, but the aircraft seemed not to mind.

What was anathema to the Oxford was frost. Montrose had five accidents one January morning in 1940. Most were aircraft which failed to achieve flight and ground-looped or finished in the upwind hedge, but one had managed to get airborne before coming to rest on the local railway signal box, much to the dismay of the signalman. When night flying, pilots there carried torches to scan the leading edges of the wings for ice before each take-off.

The Oxfords were nice aeroplanes, good trainers, unexciting but quite capable of generating a bit of tension in the hands of pupil pilots.

Don March, a much-travelled wartime Air Training Corps cadet, later to become a very experienced pilot, scrounged about fifty Oxford flights with 15 (P)AFU at Ramsbury during 1943:

Very low flying with very steep turns was the order of the day, as were low-level cross-country flights. We did innumerable circuits and bumps, both by day and at night, as well as formation flights which I found particularly enjoyable. Day cross-countries lasting 1½ – 2 hours were complemented by similar night flights which were termed 'beacon bashing' as the turning points in the blackout conditions were marked by red identifying beacons.

From my personal experience and witnessing the Instructors' handling of the Oxford, I concluded it was a very manoeuvrable aircraft, eminently suitable for its purpose. When two Oxfords were being tested at the same time, it was a very good opportunity for a mock dogfight – I remember thinking at the time that it was a match for any Spitfire!

Gordon Kinsey was stationed at Lyneham during the winter of 1941/42:

When I joined No 14 SFTS at the Goatacre site, then known as RAF Lyneham, the resident Oxfords were painted in two schemes, one being all-over brown and green camouflage on all upper and side surfaces, trainer yellow undersides with black aircraft serial numbers. Serial numbers on sides were in yellow, equal width roundel colours and fin stripes and anti-gas diamond patches on rear fuselage and wing tip. The others carried the earlier style, camouflaged on top, but the fuselage was only brown and green to the centre stringer on the fuselage side, yellow below that. Aircraft serial in black on rear fuselage.

The unit had over 100 Oxfords at that time, these being

Airspeed Oxford I EB813 'LP-73' of No 237 Operational Conversion Unit at Benson in 1949.
(R.C.B. Ashworth)

used for cross-country and night flying by trainee Leading Aircraftsmen pilots, always flying in pairs. Lyneham was then a small grass aerodrome surrounded by the hangars of No 33 Maintenance Unit, a far cry from the great airfield of today. At night the pupils tended to get mixed up with the Tiger Moths from 29 EFTS Clyffe Pypard across the valley.

Operating at Lyneham from an often muddy grass airfield, the Oxford stood up remarkably well to the unkind conditions, and often rough handling both on the ground and in the air. An example of rough ground handling was that aircraft were picketed around the perimeter track, and after overnight rain they were usually semi-bogged down in soft mud. Quite often gangs of lads, summoned by shouts from chevroned NCOs of 'Two Six on this kite,' pushed and heaved on the leading edge of the tailplane and applied shoulders to the undercarriage legs, whilst the more timid among the gathering managed gently to lay their hands on the leading edge of the centre section, with the full knowlege that any exertions on that spot could lead to damage – hence the gentle approach.

More stringent methods were also manifest, and the most popular was to start the two Cheetahs, bring the oil temperature up, and then with gangs of chaps putting their shoulders up onto the undersurface, the motors were revved up and hopefully the 'Oxbox' moved on to firmer terrain. Bouncing was often resorted to, but this usually only resulted in extending the oleo legs. Precautions had to be taken when carrying out this procedure, the most important being to ensure that the locking struts, painted red and with a long

Airspeed Oxford I PH517 'FDCH' of No 1 (Pilot) Refresher Flying Unit at Finningley around 1949.
(via Wing Cdr C.G. Jefford)

red streamer, were in position locking the folding radius rods into the down position. This stiffened-up the undercarriage and prevented the locking pins from moving out of position should the hydraulic jack have crept up a bit.

Speaking of the locking struts, it was the groundcrews and the aircrews' duty to ensure that these were removed before the aircraft moved prior to flight. This also applied to the control locks, locking bar on the control column in the cockpit, and the slat locks on the ailerons, rudder and elevators.

A task always allotted to small numbers of the groundcrew was the fixing of the tailwheel towing tiller to the spools on the axle. These spools were on each side of the fork, and a spring-loaded claw engaged onto the spools. A lever at the handle end was attached to a wire which was connected to the claws, and when it was pulled it opened the claws and disengaged from the spools. One golden rule when using the tail tiller was to ensure that the 'bod in the office' kept the stick back to ensure that the elevators were up and out of the way of the tiller handle.

Airspeed Oxford Is including NJ382 'P-D' of No 9 Advanced Flying Training School at Wellesbourne Mountford around 1952.
(Official)

The Oxford was a comparatively easy aircraft to maintain and its all-wooden construction stood up remarkably well to being picketed out in all weathers. The only protection was engine covers and the cockpit cover, although every Flight Hut had what seemed like enormous piles of all-over mainplane and tailplane covers which were very rarely used. Shaped like a giant sleeve, they were made from canvas, and even when dry weighed a ton. When wet they were almost impossible to slide off, and if put on before a frost were impossible to shift. Wheel covers were always put on to prevent engine oil dripping onto the tyres. Picketing points were located outboard of the motors attached to the main spar, and a hole on the rear cone under the rudder was used at the stem. Quite often this aperture was covered with fabric, and doped over as it never seemed to be a really strong point, and the screw picket was more generally screwed into the ground near the tail strut and roped to it.

No two Oxfords seemed to have the same flight characteristics, and dropped either the port or starboard wing, the usual cure being to dope a length of electric flex on the trailing edge of the aileron. If an aileron needed to be depressed to lift that wing, the flex was put on top to push the surface down, and if the misalignment was severe the opposite remedy was also carried out on the other aileron, i.e. a strip was affixed underneath. The same remedy was

used for elevators and rudder, although of course the rudder was fitted with a bias setting gear, operated by a hand wheel in the cockpit. Trim tabs were also fitted to the elevators and operated by screw jacks in the fuselage, turning a screwed rod to push or pull a flexible rod to the horn on the tab.

It was the ideal trainer as it was unforgiving and had to be watched most of the time, especially when approaching the stall, as a wing dropped very quickly when it did occur.

Starting the Cheetahs was usually simple. One climbed up onto the centre section where a rubber mat gave a certain amount of grip on the wing surface. These rubber mats, one on each side of the engine nacelle, were a nuisance, and all manner of tricks were employed to hold them on. The official method was that they be laid with Black Bostik, but this did not always work and it was not unusual during an air test after a major overhaul to see a mat gradually peeling off from the wing and eventually slip back when it came adrift. One way out of the trouble was to screw thin dural strips round the edge.

A flap fitted with a Dzuz fastener was located on the inboard side of the engine nacelle, and the shaft with the starting dog on it was just inside. After the propeller had been turned over a few times, ensuring that the switches were off, signified by a thumbs-down from the man in the office, the Ki-gass engine priming pump was unscrewed and given three or four full strokes. The handle was then screwed down securely; this was most important, because if left loose would result in engine surging and possible cut-out. The starting handle was then inserted into the dogged shaft and turned. The Cheetah turned over and the wooden airscrew flicked slowly round in stuttering jumps, and if the man on the switches got it right, the engine burst into life, provided throttle settings and boost lever were in the correct position. Slow tick-over was the order of the day, because if the throttles were opened too far too soon, the Cheetah back-fired and cut out, then the process had to be started all over again. Needless to say, the ideal position at this time was in the cockpit, and this was qualified by rank or trade. In the main, the engine fitter was usually in the office and a rigger or flight mechanic on the handle.

Another problem was to prevent tyre wear caused by snatch on touch-down and a reward was available from the Air Ministry for a successful solution to this problem, although I never heard of it being awarded. The idea was to spin the wheel so that it was turning on impact, but unless the tyre surface speed and the runway speed were compatible the result was futile.

Airframe repairs were not too bad, the chippy riggers being able to cope with almost any damage. The usual method was to square the damage up, chamfer the edges at a fairly shallow angle, make a patch with the same profile, and attach it with casein glue, which had to be used within an hour of being mixed. The patch was then secured around its perimeter by strips of plywood and small nails, making sure no glue was touching either surface. After 24 hours the fixing strips were removed, the surface sanded, edges covered with serrated fabric strip, red doped, covered with madoplin (thin fabric) and then finished doped.

As designed, the Oxford was intended to be a complete crew trainer, but this in fact did not work out, and when new aircraft were received from Airspeeds at Portsmouth, de Havillands at Hatfield or Percivals at Luton, the Wireless Operators' and Navigators' positions were taken out and usually dumped. This left the interior clear with the top surface of the 'bomb bay' a clear area in the centre fuselage. When the Armstrong Whitworth manually-operated turret was removed, a bar was fitted with half a dozen or so weights pinned on it to compensate for the turret weight. In this area, a door, hinged at the bottom edge, lowered backwards into the rear fuselage and formed a working platform for any tasks which had to be carried out in that area. This was quite a little hideaway for both RAF and WAAF personnel – or both! There were also many stories of sleeping groundcrew being carried aloft in this position, but if anyone could sleep through the motors being run up, and the eventual taxiing, he must have been really tired!

When authorised passengers were carried they sat either on the front spar behind the two seats, or on the rear spar facing backwards. Passengers usually wore pilot type chutes which they sat on, but one had to be careful that the ripcord handle did not catch on anything and spill the chute all over the plane. This would cost two shillings when the chute was returned to the Parachute Section.

The Oxford was pleasant to fly in with its large perspex transparency over the cockpit, and four windows in the cabin. Down in the bomb-aimer's position the flat sighting window gave a good view of the scene forward and below. One modification we had to carry out on the cabin windows was to put a strut in them at mid position to prevent the perspex from buckling. A unique feature was the cabin door, which was attached by slip-latches, and if the emergency handle was pulled, a wire cable withdrew both pins and the door came away. When a kite went into hangar for a 'major', one of the first things to be carried out was to jettison the door and rip-away panel in the forward cabin roof, which was only held in position by doped fabric serrated strips!

In March the unit was moved to Ossington, in north Nottinghamshire, where it was to become 14 (P)AFU. The aircraft in which I was to be taken there took-off one rather misty afternoon and flew north, but navigation being a little hazy in the circumstances, the pilot put down at an aerodrome which turned out to be Spitalgate, near Grantham. Here he was advised to take off again, fly over the town, pick up the railway line crossing the River Trent, and finally look to port for the newly completed aerodrome. Our aircraft turned out to be the first to land on the then snow-covered airfield, but after accomplishing this successfully we then had the misfortune to drop the port undercarriage into a snow-filled ditch alongside the runway!'

Avro 504K 'H5199', originally a 504N which became G-ADEV, now with the Shuttleworth Collection at Old Warden, seen here in 1986. (Air Portraits)

De Havilland Tiger Moth II T6818, sold post-war as G-ANKT, but now restored to military markings with the Shuttleworth Collection at Old Warden, seen here in 1986. (Air Portraits)

Hawker Hart Trainer K4972 photographed at the CFS reunion at RAF Scampton in 1987. This machine was discovered some years ago in the loft of a barn near Wigton in Cumberland, after wartime service with the Air Training Corps, and later restored at RAF St Athan for display purposes. It is now on display in the RAF Museum at Hendon. (Author)

Avro Anson I being started at North Weald in 1942. (RAF Museum Photo No P100016)

Airspeed Oxford I N4633 of RAF Binbrook landing at South Cerney in October 1955. This machine had served with several wartime training units, and was one of the last of this type to survive, being scrapped only a few months later. *(M.J. Hooks)*

Airspeed Oxford I V3388 was civilianised as G-AHTW and used for many years by Boulton Paul as a company hack. It was later restored to its wartime markings, and is now exhibited in the Imperial War Museum collection at Duxford. *(Air Portraits)*

North American Harvard IIB FE992 was originally used by the Royal Canadian Air Force, then sold postwar to Sweden. It eventually became G-BDAM, and was then painted up with its original serial number, as seen here at Old Warden in 1986. *(Author)*

Distinctly battered Miles Master I of the Fleet Air Arm being refuelled, probably at RNAS Yeovilton.
(RAF Museum photo)

Miles Magister rebuild marked as P6382, though only the rear fuselage originated in that aircraft which later became G-AJRS. It was rebuilt for the Shuttleworth Collection and is seen here at Old Warden in 1986.
(Author)

Percival Prentice prototype TV163 during trials in May 1946. (RAF Museum Photo No P100499)

Boulton Paul Sea Balliol T.21 WP333 of the Aeroplane and Armament Experimental Establishment at Boscombe Down, visiting Culdrose around 1962. (A.E. Hughes)

Percival Provost prototype WE522, fitted with a Leonides engine, in May 1952.
(RAF Museum Photo No P100514)

De Havilland Chipmunk T.10 WD289 of the Liverpool University Air Squadron at Woodvale in 1970.
(Sally-Anne Steuart-Pownall)

De Havilland Chipmunk T.10 WD331 'A' of the Flying Selection Squadron at Swinderby in 1987.
(Flt Lt Peter Bouch)

Miles Magister

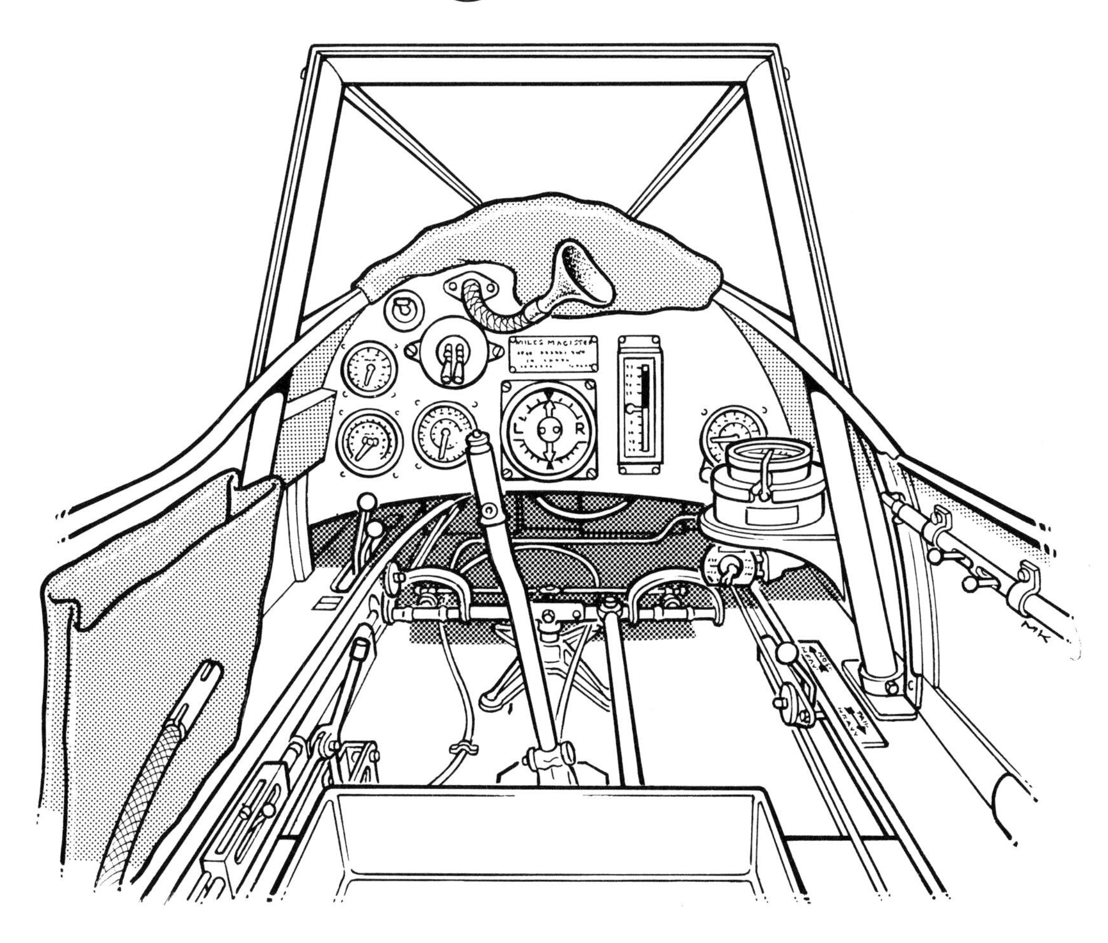

The Miles Magister, known to numerous trainee RAF pilots as the 'Maggie', was a product of the prolific design team led by George Miles. A contemporary of the Tiger Moth, it was the RAF's first monoplane trainer, but reversed the trend to metal construction by being all wood. It was faster than its biplane counterpart, but had a lower landing speed.

The Magister stemmed from the well-established M.2 Hawk series, the prototype of which (G-ACGH) had made its first flight on 29 March 1933 powered by a

Specification

Power plant:	*One 130 hp de Havilland Gipsy Major I.*
Dimensions:	*Span 33 ft 10 in, length 25 ft 3 in, height 6 ft 8 in, wing area 176 sq ft.*
Weights:	*Empty 1,260 lb, loaded 1,900 lb.*
Performance:	*Maximum speed 144 mph at 1,000 ft, cruising speed 124 mph, initial climb 850 ft/min range 380 miles, endurance 3 hrs, service ceiling 18,000 ft.*

95 hp Cirrus III engine, and this was an instant success. The design was steadily developed, and a 130 hp de Havilland Gipsy Major engine was fitted in 1934 to produce the Hawk Major, which attracted sufficient interest from the Air Ministry for a special machine (K8626) to be ordered in 1936 for evaluation at Farnborough. Another improved variant fitted with dual controls, full blind flying equipment and vacuum operated flaps was designated the Hawk Trainer. This formed the main equipment of No 7 Elementary and Reserve Flying Training School at Woodley, which opened in November 1936 and was operated by Phillips and Powis Ltd, the builders of Miles aircraft.

All these machines were given manufacturer's type numbers in the M.2 series, the first four Hawk Trainers being designated M.2W. The next nine machines were M.2Xs with a horn-balanced rudder of greater area, and the final twelve were M.2Ys with internal modifications. The type number M.14 was given, however, to the next development, designed to Specification T.40/36, which called for a low-wing monoplane elementary trainer to meet the need for instruction in this type of aircraft by pilots who would shortly be flying the new monoplane fighters and bombers being built under the expansion scheme. Civil machines reflected their origin by being known as Hawk Trainer IIIs, but the M.14A military version, which was essentially identical, was named the Magister.

In view of its already proven qualities, and successful completion of trials, no prototype was sought, and the design was ordered straight from the drawing board, an initial contract being placed for 90 aircraft. The main visible differences from the Hawk Major were larger cockpits equipped with blind flying equipment, and a spatted undercarriage. The first machine (L5912) was sent to Martlesham Heath on 14 June 1937 for testing, and trials were well advanced when it unfortunately crashed on 22 July.

Despite this, the subsequent official report was generally favourable, though it made quite a number of comments. The machine was reported to be stable at all speeds except at the stall, which arose quickly and with a slight tendency to vibration and a swing to the right. For most conditions it would fly straight with the feet off the rudder bar, and such slight swing as might develop was easily counteracted. In any event, it was thought that if rudder bias was fitted it would fly straight with feet off under all conditions.

The cockpits, which were connected with the usual Gosport tube with its faint smell of rubber, were ungenerous in size, though they offered no problems to the average or small pilot. A large pilot, however, would only just be able to achieve full aileron control if he sat in the rear cockpit, which was rather smaller than the contemporary Tiger Moth, and much smaller than the Avro Cadet being used by some of the pre-war Reserve Schools. If he sat in the front cockpit, his knees would foul the control column.

Aileron control was generally responsive and effective, except at the stall, when aileron drag would induce a spin, but it was suggested that this could be cured by increasing the differential action of the ailerons. The feel of the controls was not very good if a side-slip was attempted while coming in to land with the flaps down. The aircraft tended to swing against full rudder into the direction of the side-slip and the nose would drop, the rudder being insufficiently powerful to counteract this. Lowering the flaps made the aircraft nose heavy, and adversely affected manoeuvrability. The aircraft was lost when it crashed into the River Deben, near Felixstowe, and was considered to have been unable to recover from a spin.

The accident to the test machine was not the only one, and the Magister began to earn the unwanted name of 'The Yellow Peril' in the press as further accidents occurred. The company was mystified as they had experienced no similar problems with either the Magister or the Hawk Trainer. Finally, wind-tunnel tests at Farnborough identified the cause of the problem as being the enlarged cockpit openings fitted to the Magister, which tended to interfere with the airflow across the tail surfaces.

The lessons learned were applied to early production machines, and spinning trials were able to continue at Martlesham between 26 August and 2 October, using L5933, the twenty-second production

Right:
Miles Magister N3780 was delivered initially to No 15 Elementary Flying Training School at Redhill in 1939.
(Phillips and Powis)

Bottom right:
Miles Hawk Trainer III G-AFBS 'A' of No 8 Elementary and Reserve Flying Training School at Woodley. This machine was impressed during the war as BB661.
(via Chaz Bowyer)

aircraft. This had the tailplane raised six inches, flat top decking to the rear fuselage, flat fillets fitted at the rear end of the fuselage to merge into the leading edge of the tailplane, and a tail parachute anchored at the fin root. To the relief of the manufacturers, the combined effect of these modifications proved totally effective in curing the earlier problems, and the Magister went on to equip a number of the wartime Elementary Flying Training Schools.

Below:
Miles Magister L5933, an early production machine, being tested with the blind flying hood up at the Aeroplane and Armament Experimental Establishment at Martlesham Heath.
(MAP photo)

While L5933 was at Martlesham Heath it was also tested for ease of maintenance. In general it was found to be satisfactory, though there was some criticism of the control cable, which would be time-consuming to repair as it was necessary to make splices *in situ*. There was also poor access to the countershaft in the rear fuselage, and it was recommended that improvements be made to the elevator controls.

Experience in the schools led to further modifications to later machines. The effect of rough treatment on the solid-rubber tailwheel was too great in its original position, mounted on the fuselage sternpost. To overcome this, a stout ply bulkhead was fitted some inches further forward, to which the tailwheel was then fitted, and this in turn was later replaced by a pneumatic Dunlop type. The rather flimsy engine cowling also gave trouble, and the original two-piece version, hinged at the centre-top, gave way to a more rigid three-piece type. A larger curved windscreen also replaced the small angular one in the rear cockpit.

Once these difficulties had been overcome, production steadily increased, reaching a peak of 15 machines each week by 1941. The company was also busy with Master orders by this time, however, so much of the work was sub-contracted, final assembly

and test flying being at Woodley. They became standard *ab initio* training equipment at a number of the pre-war civilian-operated Elementary and Reserve Flying Training Schools, and subsequently with several wartime Elementary Flying Training Schools, the word 'Reserve' having been dropped on mobilisation. Numbers also served with the Central Flying School at Upavon. Many were used for communications, and they served in every RAF Command, both at home and overseas. A few machines of 8 EFTS were even fitted with bomb racks in June 1940, these 'Maggiebombers' carrying eight 25 lb bombs in underwing racks, dropped by pulling on a cockpit handle connected by Bowden cables to quick release pins.

The Magister had an unremarkable career in the elementary schools. Pupils flying one for the first time would be told by their instructor to start with a gentle take-off, then climb slowly at about 5 mph above the recommended speed. Once they had reached 3,000 feet or more they would be told to level off, by then having sufficient altitude to be able to recover from any manoeuvres they might attempt. When the time came for landing, they were to approach downwind, close the throttle, then readjust the trim and hold the speed at 65 mph. Checking round to ensure no other aircraft was approaching, the speed was increased to 70 mph, then a gliding turn brought the machine into wind. The flaps were then lowered for the final approach to the grass-covered airfield.

After the war, many surviving Magisters were sold, and in civilian guise as Hawk Trainer IIIs, were a familiar sight for many years. Despite the numbers which were around at one time, however, it does not appear to have imprinted itself so well on the memory as did many other trainers. A few recollections have been forthcoming, however.

Dick Smerdon flew in Magisters for only a short time:

It was a pleasant little aircraft, but perhaps of the few hours I flew in her, or perhaps because it was ordinary, it left no lasting impression. I do remember instrument flying under the hood, though, and how my examiner up front was covered in oil after an inverted spin recovery.

Wing Commander Robert Sage flew Magisters occasionally:

I first flew a Magister in January 1938 (L5983). They were established as Station Flight aircraft, and were used for continuation training and communications. I did not fly them a great deal, but I see from my log book that between 1938 and 1940 I flew seven different Magisters. I remember them best for the fact that they were the only light aircraft established at bomber stations providing an opportunity for more ebullient flying than was possible, or permitted, with the monoplane bombers introduced at that time. The only incident I recall relates to a Magister at Finningley when Percy Pickard, then a flying officer, was climbing into the cockpit for his first familiarisation flight and put his foot right through the floor!

Miles Magister R1853 of No 15 Elementary Flying Training School at Kingstown in 1940.
(Author's collection)

Rupert Cooling flew the Magister as a pre-war reservist at Brough, and his memories are still quite vivid:

In April 1938, the Magister was a novelty; it had entered service barely six months before. Three were issued to the Blackburn-operated No 4 Elementary and Reserve Flying Training School at Brough, being L6910, L6911, and L6912, and they were newer still. In lieu of the normal 130 hp Gipsy Major engine, they were fitted with the locally-produced Blackburn Cirrus Major power plant of 150 hp. Intended for use in the training of short service commission pilots, they were not normally available to the RAFVR pilots who flew Blackburn B.2s at the same school.

However, for one youth of eighteen and six foot seven tall, the B.2 was a bit cramped. Not noticeably so, but the CFI decided that things would be better in the Maggie. After five reasonably comfortable hours dual on the biplane, it was all change, start again on a sleek monoplane half as fast again, which had somehow acquired a sinister reputation as to its spinning characteristics. It did not help the pupil in that each instructor was keen to try out the Maggie. There seemed always to be a different silhouette in the front cockpit; a different voice down the Gosport tube.

These early Magisters differed from their later siblings. The flaps were operated mechanically by a large brake-style lever mounted on the starboard side of the cockpit, which had to be hauled up to bring down the flaps. This meant that on final approach, at about four hundred feet, it was necessary to switch hands from left on the throttle and right on the stick, to left on the stick and right on the flap lever. Another quick switch of the hands restored the pupil pilot to the established convention as he sought to stabilise the new glide angle and get the speed down (or up) to 65 knots. It was an added and unwelcome difficulty.

The Maggie had other tricks up its sleeve. If a pupil over-ruddered a turn, the outer wing would rise and the nose went down. The instinctive reaction was to haul back on the stick when the elevators, in a bank, accentuated the turn and the rudder became blanked by the skidding aircraft. The aircraft then encountered a sort of powered sideslip from which recovery was effected by centralising the controls and regaining normal attitude. It was disconcerting, not to say frightening, until the instructor, also somewhat foxed by the manoeuvre, decided to take over and sort things out.

On 16 June 1938, all Magisters were grounded. The previous afternoon a young New Zealander took off in L6910 from Brough to carry out circuits and landings. On his second approach, the aircraft suddenly flipped over into a spin and fell in to the Humber. When a boat reached him, he was dead, probably drowned while unconscious following the impact. It did not help the young reservist who, after going solo in L6912, suddenly found himself persistently under or overshooting on every approach. The CFI's check-out would determine his future; if he fluffed it, that would be the end of flying training.

Confidence was not enhanced when the instructor climbed to 4,000 ft and tried, wholly successfully, to induce a couple of spins off gliding turns. The sudden lurch, the rapid downward spiral, the delayed recovery did little to dispel apprehensions. The subsequent approach to the airfield above a yellow tail section bobbing in the water beneath as the wreck of L6910 was brought ashore was not conducive to a textbook landing. The week's reprieve offered was small comfort, but the next day there were no Magisters to fly. Forty minutes refresher on a B.2 was to begin sixteen years and four thousand hours of flying.

For the Maggie, it was back to the drawing board. It re-emerged with a taller fin and rudder, and pneumatically operated flaps. It was discovered that the pupil's head and the folded canvas hood for blind flying blanketed the airflow around the rudder, reducing effectiveness in pitch and yaw. Modified, the Magister was a trainer many remember with pleasure, even affection. It would have been nice to meet the gentler, more amenable younger brother, if only to prove to oneself that the tiger had been tamed.

Verdun Edwards, a wartime engine fitter, learned to fly a post-war civilianised Magister (Hawk Trainer III):

I had been used to flying the Auster, and I expected similar responses from the Magister. I thought, for instance, that in the stall the Magister would drop the port wing every time, as I had been used to, but it didn't. It was such a clean aeroplane that if there was a little bit of disturbance on the starboard wing when coming up to the stall, that one would drop. The first time I tried a stall in the Magister I was expecting the port wing to go down as usual, when suddenly the cockpit came round and hit me in the right ear. As I was going down I was thinking at first about the pain in my ear rather than recovering from the spin, but I quickly got out of it. I had been taught that 5,000 feet was the minimum height for practising a spin – and if you were not out of it by 2,500 feet you were to jump and use your parachute – but fortunately the Magister responded all right.

The thing one had to remember was that if, when spinning, the aircraft autorotated to the left, then you must use right rudder to stop the autorotation. As soon as the autorotation stopped, you pushed the stick forward, to take it off the stall, and then you had complete recovery, even without the engine. If you were going to do some other manoeuvre, such as a roll, you had to put some power on, but you didn't need the engine to recover flight attitude and control.

The ailerons on the Magister were very lively. On the Auster, if you put the stick over, the wing went over about two seconds later, but if you put it too far over on the Magister you were on your back in no time. That made it a good trainer, as a good trainer must have vices, and you must learn to react quickly. Some aircraft were far too docile to be of any real use as trainers, but the Magister really had to be flown. On one occasion I bent one a bit landing in a slight crosswind. There was a momentary gust and I pushed the throttle, but the rudder wasn't effective enough to check it, and the oleo leg was ripped. Nothing was said, however – it happened all the time, apparently.

Take-offs were very stable. You followed the usual procedure – throttle open, stick forward, and as soon as the tail was up the rudder became effective and you had complete control. You could then correct your direction up the runway, and it would leave the ground on its own at 65 mph and climb out. It was a beautiful aeroplane. You were

clean taking off, you didn't use any flap.

If you were going to do aerobatics, you had to make certain you removed the battery before taking off, as laid down in the Pilot's Notes. The battery was housed in a box to the pilot's left. It was very heavy, and was supported by a metal bracket screwed into the wooden frame of the aircraft. If it were left in the box during aerobatics it would be pulled out of its holdings and inflict structural damage on the wooden airframe. The Magister was therefore strictly non-aerobatic with the battery in, and only aerobatic with it out – you couldn't change your mind once you were in the air, as the g-forces on the battery would be quite heavy in a roll.

Miles Magister N3838 '3' of the Empire Central Flying School at Hullavington in October 1942.
(MAP photo)

Another stipulation was that you must have a parachute – though I found a cushion much more comfortable to sit on. With three of these I had a better view and I enjoyed it. At first I had a rather large instructor, and I wasn't getting on too well because from the back seat I couldn't see very much. I would tend to lean round him to see, and the wing would then go down. Then one day I had a new instructor who was much smaller. 'Jump in', he said to me, 'sit down, sit in position'. He looked at me, then said, 'You are too low. Jack your seat up,' so I pumped the seat up. 'That's better', he said, 'but you need a cushion underneath that suit', so he went and got me one and I got up, put it where the pack went and sat down. 'Fine,' he said. He then climbed in up front and said, 'Start up, and take off in your own time'. Whilst he was fiddling around putting his straps on, I was taxiing out, and I found I could now see the runway. I could see through both his windscreen and mine. What a difference! We were airborne, I did three approaches and he got out and said, 'There's nothing wrong with you'.

He was a very good instructor. He would talk to me; he would say – 50 knots – 70 knots, climb out – 500 feet, turn left 90 degrees – check for drift – look at the runway – 800 feet, throttle back – nose down. When I went solo I found his voice was still with me – 500 feet, turn left – check for drift (which means that you look at the runway, and if it is sliding away you are drifting, so you have to counteract it); 800 feet – nose down – throttle back (because you are accelerating a bit), level off, fly parallel to the runway, check your drift again so that you are not crabbing in or crabbing out, check the runway, go well past the runway, turn, 500 feet, finals, flaps down and halt. He was there, he was with me and I could hear him talking.

Verdun was also familiar with the Magister's engine:

The Gipsy Major engine on the Magister had four cylinders, inverted pushrod jobs on a common crankcase, so the rockers were underneath. The lids on the rocker-boxes were filled by hand from the ground. Every 30 hours you released a screw in the middle, pulled the box down and put oil in up to the arrowed level. It had a cork gasket, and you gently put this back and then turned the screw up with a screwdriver. You also checked the hot and cold clearances on the tappets. I used to do it cold, because if you did them when they were hot you invariably burned your fingers, and you were then not getting a proper feel, but cold clearances were no problem. The tappets only had a double lock nut, and a centre slot for the screwdriver and a spanner, so you loosened the lock nut just like a motor bike. You then put the feeler-gauge in, nipped it, locked, removed the screwdriver and rechecked the clearances with the feelers. They were very easy to work on.

Miles Master

Despite the obvious need for a high speed monoplane trainer, with the advent of fast fighters in this configuration, no attempt was made to order such a type at the time that the Hurricane and Spitfire were being conceived. Not everyone was convinced that such a machine was unnecessary, however, and George Miles used his powers of persuasion within the Phillips and Powis company to allow him to build just such a design as a private venture. The timing was fortunate, as in 1936 a substantial interest in the company had been acquired by Rolls-Royce, who gave the new project their full support.

The Rolls-Royce Merlin engine was by that time going into large-scale production, and consequently large numbers of the earlier Kestrel engines were likely to become surplus, but the design was still in full production. Miles therefore adopted this well-proven engine, and the firm's new backers produced a special version at no cost to Phillips and Powis, who themselves were restructured, with George Miles becoming their new managing director as well as chief designer. The clean new aircraft design emerged with a 745 hp Kestrel XVI, and the prototype machine was also given the name Kestrel. Although it was never fitted, the machine was also stressed to take the

Specification (Mark II)

Power plant:	*One 870 hp Bristol Mercury 20 or 30.*
Dimensions:	*Span 35 ft 8 in, length 29 ft 6 in, height 11 ft 6 in, wing area 209 sq ft.*
Weights:	*Empty 4,262 lb, loaded 5,673 lb.*
Performance:	*Maximum speed 243 mph at 7,500 ft, cruising speed 208 mph, initial climb 2,000 ft/min, range 450 miles, endurance 2 hrs, service ceiling 28,000 ft.*

1,030 hp Merlin, which if it had materialised would have given it an outstanding performance.

Carrying the manufacturers marking U5, the prototype had its maiden flight at Woodley piloted by its designer on the evening of 3 June 1937, and achieved a top speed of 296 mph, not very far short of that of the new fighters which the new breed of pilots would fly, and certainly faster than the previous generation of fighters. Being far in advance of anything previously produced, it was by no means perfect, one early fault being a nasty habit the undercarriage had of lowering itself again soon after being retracted. Nevertheless, despite its outstanding performance, with a top speed only a few miles per hour less than the Hurricane fighters then entering service, it was not initially considered as suitable for the RAF, the Air Ministry regarding it as premature and ahead of its time.

In the meantime Specification T.6/36 had been issued for an advanced low wing medium-powered monoplane pilot trainer for the RAF. The industry was by that time engaged in the expansion programme, and all the main manufacturers had full order books, but nevertheless Avro and de Havilland showed sufficient interest in this new concept to submit designs. Of these two, the Air Ministry preferred the D.H.93 design, and orders were placed straight from the drawing board for 250 machines of this type, to be named the Don. To save time, the first production machine (L2387), powered by a 525 hp de Havilland Gipsy King I engine, served as a prototype with manufacturer's marking E-3, making its first flight in early June 1937, the same month that the Miles Kestrel appeared. The specification, however, had turned out to be an impossible one to meet fully, and the Don was therefore inevitably a compromise.

The respective timings of the first flights soon gave an opportunity for comparison. Both machines were demonstrated at the 1937 RAF Display at Hendon on 26 June, and also on the following two days at that year's SBAC Display at Hatfield. The contrasting impressions given at these shows by the two machines, with their very different power and performance, led to a hasty official rethink, and a prototype Kestrel was ordered for testing.

Production of the Don was in the meantime cut back to only fifty machines, the majority of which saw only limited service. None of the Flying Training Schools for which they had been intended were ever equipped with them, most seeing service only as station hacks or ground instructional machines.

When the prototype service Kestrel (N3300) appeared in October 1938, it was fitted with a larger nose radiator, but this caused problems with weight distribution. A production order was placed on 11 June 1938 for 500 machines, and when these appeared they had the radiator positioned underneath the wing roots. A few other minor modifications were necessary on the production version, and the first deliveries of the Master I, as it had now become, were made in July 1939, shortly before the outbreak of war. The tailplane was raised fractionally, the fin and rudder had a greater area and the depth of the rear fuselage was increased. The power plant was now the derated 715 hp Kestrel XXX, becoming available from surplus supplies. This drop in power resulted in a much lower top speed, but this was still sufficient for the machine to be justifiably claimed as the fastest trainer in the world at that time. A second order was placed, for a further 400 Kestrel-powered machines, and these were distinguished by having a taller, improved windscreen, in which form they were designated the Master IA.

The Master reversed the trend towards stressed-skin metal structures, being of wooden construction, which was seen as having several advantages. Provided the design was kept simple, aircraft could be built more quickly in wood than in metal, and in the event of war, the country had plenty of skilled carpenters and ample supplies of raw material. Consequently there should be less competition for the scarce materials and labour which would be required for operational machines – though production of the de Havilland Mosquito and later of gliders would serve to reduce the validity of this argument. Wooden construction certainly enabled the machine to go quickly into production, the fuselage and wings being assembled independently, then joined on one of the two parallel production lines.

To make layout of the aircraft as near as possible to that of the first line machines to which the pupils would graduate, it was fitted with a tandem cockpit, which also helped performance. The Kestrel engine had already acquired a good reputation for extreme reliability, and it would provide experience of water-cooled engines. The design was as aerodynamically clean as any machine of its generation, but considerable thought had been given to ease of maintenance, most of the equipment being easily installed or removed. The canopy hinged on the starboard side, to open sideways.

The slightly-tapered wings had been made stiff and very thick, with the front spar continuing through the lower fuselage. The wings were constructed in three elements comprising two outboard panels and a centre-section, the latter having anhedral to give improved clearance for the propeller blades and to make a clean junction with the fuselage. The design of the fuselage was an oval semi-monocoque, comprising spruce frames and longerons skinned by stressed plywood. The tailwheel was positioned to aid easy recovery from a spin. The main retractable Lockheed undercarriage was situated in the deep wings, the wheels rotating through 90 degrees as they went up, to enable them to lie flat between the wing spars.

Above:
The ill-fated de Havilland Don was built to meet Specification T.6/36, but was ousted by the Miles Master. This is E-3, powered by the Gipsy King I.

Below:
The first production Miles Master Is being prepared for delivery. The nearest machine is N7411 which was taken over by the Admiralty in 1940 and used initially by No 759 Squadron at Eastleigh.
(Author's collection)

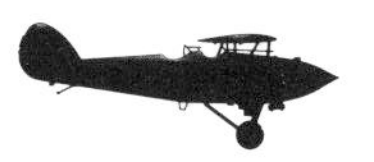

Miles Master IA taking off, its undercarriage twisting to fit into the wings as it retracts.

(Author's collection)

Although normally flown from the front seat, it was designed so that landings could be made by pupils in the back seat. They would commence their training from this position, then half way through the course would exchange places with the instructor. A retractable rear windscreen could be raised to give a better view over the front occupant when landing or taking off. The rear seat was capable of being raised twelve inches for this purpose, and the rudder-bar was adjusted at the same time. The canopy frame had a built in roll-bar between the two seats, to protect the crew should the machine overturn. The front windscreen incorporated an optical panel to provide undistorted reflector sight vision for gun-firing.

Despite the attention given to good all-round vision, it became apparent after the machine entered service that in practise the view was rather restricted. This was remedied by fitting a much taller windscreen, giving improved visibility to both the pupil and instructor, and with other modifications this version was restyled the Mark IA.

The success of the machine meant that stocks of surplus Kestrel engines, mainly available due to the obsolescence of the many pre-war Hawker biplane variants, would be insufficient for any further orders that might be placed, and due to their Merlin commitments no more would be produced by Rolls-Royce. After assurances that there were, however, ample stocks of Bristol Mercury radial engines available, since these were still in production for the Blenheim, the aircraft was redesigned to take this power plant, and N7422, which had been laid down as the fifteenth production Mk I, flew at Woodley in November 1939. Two months later this crashed while being test flown from Boscombe Down, but the tests were satisfactorily completed on N7447, the second such conversion, only for the manufacturers to be told that supplies of the Mercury would not after all be readily forthcoming, being required for other purposes.

Instead, the immediate substitution was required of the new American-built Pratt and Whitney Wasp Junior engine. Supplies were ordered from America and N7994, another Mk I conversion, flew with this early in 1940. In the event, both engines became available, and so each version was produced in some numbers. Ironically, each of these enforced changes of engine produced benefits. In the case of the Mk II, the additional power of the Mercury as compared with the Kestrel was more than ample to offset the effect of the greater frontal area. Pilots of the Mk III on the other hand, benefited from an improved view due to the smaller cowling diameter.

In production, the Mark II, fitted with either a Mercury XX or 30, differed from the prototype in having the wings shortened by over three feet, extended exhaust pipes and a larger airscrew spinner. The clipped wings, which were intended to reduce stress on the centre section of the gull-shaped wing, were also introduced on many of the Mark IIIs, both of these versions having sliding cockpit canopies which moved very easily. A proposed Mark IV was commenced, machine T8886 being intended to have a modified centre section and tailplane, and a redesigned rear cockpit giving improved all-round visibility for the instructor, but this was never completed. A projected Mark V with either Mercury or Wasp engine failed to materialise, and production came to a halt in 1942 after nearly 3,500 aircraft had been built, to be replaced by the Martinet target-tug, which employed many Master components.

The first thing that struck a trainee about the controls of the Mk II, as with the earlier versions, was that they were convenient and on the whole simple to operate. This was not a common feature at that time, and demonstrated the thought given to this aspect by the designers. There was one potential pitfall, however. The levers for flaps and undercarriage were nicely situated behind the pedestal, but were adjacent to each other. Although the undercarriage lever was longer and required more effort, it was far from unknown for a trainee pilot to lose his concentration sufficiently to select the wrong lever, to the detriment of both the aircraft and his own prospects of being allowed to finish his course.

Take-off could raise the flow of adrenalin in the trainee, as everything seemed to happen at once after he had opened the throttle and lifted the tail. The high power-weight ratio gave an exceptional acceleration, and as the aircraft rushed down the runway the pilot had to apply full left rudder to prevent it veering off-course. Once airborne it climbed rapidly, the high-pitched note of the Mercury engine being audible for some distance.

The Master had its limitations when performing aerobatics. This was particularly noticeable in a roll, which had to be started from a nose-up position, otherwise it was likely to end in a rather scrappy shallow dive. Landing was seldom a problem, as the large flaps enabled the aircraft to land in a very limited space, with minimal prospect of an overshoot. Its subsequent arrival for parking was accompanied by several squeals from the undercarriage.

From late 1941, over 400 Master IIs were shipped to South Africa for use by Air Schools for pilot training, but they were not a success. Bad packing for the voyage resulted in structural failure and shrinkage, and this combined with a lack of spares resulted in an alarmingly low serviceability rate of around 20 per cent. The problems steadily increased, and for a short time it was impossible to use them for front gun firing. By March 1942 it had been decided to replace them with Harvards, but not until the end of that year did this prove possible.

The MkIII differed very little from the MkII, apart from the engine, which although noisy had one advantage. When taxiing, and during take-off, the smaller diameter of the Pratt and Whitney compared with the Mercury gave a rather better view for the pilot. All three main versions saw service in numbers, and the Fleet Air Arm took over quite a few dozen MkIs and MkIIs for their various pilot training establishments around the country. The Master served for much of the war with RAF, mainly at (Pilot) Advanced Flying Units and Service Flying Training Schools, and also as a tug for Hotspur gliders with Glider Training Schools, but by the end of 1944 they were being rapidly replaced by Harvards.

Miles Master IA T8665 '11' of No 5 (Pilot) Advanced Flying Unit at Ternhill around 1943.
(via G.S. Leslie)

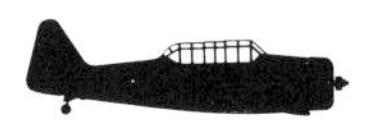

Miles Master I N7572 of No 5 Service Flying Training School at Sealand being refulled.
(R.D. Cooling)

Rupert Cooling flew various Masters:

The Master could be a bit of a bully boy. The Mark I, a handsome machine, looked fast, sleek and aggressive. It was reputed to shed its wings under circumstances which varied with the teller of the tale, however, and certainly it was much less in evidence after 1940. Its successors, the Marks II and III, were radial engined; less elegant, more bruisers than ballerinas.

No 516 (Combined Operations) Squadron held a Master II; its Mercury engine provided some compatibility with the unit's Blenheim IVs. It was intended as a trainer to convert twin-engine pilots to the Hurricanes, Mustang and even Lysanders with which the squadron was equipped. Most of those pilots, however, were sufficiently experienced to essay their first solo on type without the need of formal single-engine refresher flying, so the aircraft was little used. It was handy for visits to airfields, for taking and collecting people or for giving the Army and Navy grandstand views of exercises, but was not particularly sought after as a mount. The windscreen and side panels tended to become filmed with atomised oil from the engine, so the pilots perpetually peered at a landscape framed in mini-rainbows. The cockpit was comfortable and roomy; the controls positive and, rainbows and taxiing apart, visibility was above average.

The undercarriage gave a hard ride, particularly on the Somerfeldt tracking runway and PSP taxiways of RAF Dundonald. The tail came up almost as soon as the throttle was opened; lift off and climb were rapid. Noisy, it resented careless handling. It would spin off a steep turn if the stick were pulled too far back; similarly if too much rearward pressure were applied on going into a loop, the airframe would buffet as it approached the vertical. Simpler to pretend that, all along, it was a stall turn which had been intended, by applying rudder and closing the throttle. Like most Miles designs, the Master spun with enthusiasm and a margin of height for Mum and the family was a prudent provision when undertaking such manoeuvres.

There are few, if any, erstwhile pilots who go dreamy eyed at the mention of the Master, as do others when speaking of Spitfires, Hurricanes, Wellingtons, Lancasters, even Ansons. It was there to be flown, and flown it was. It did a job; taught many a tyro to treat aeroplanes with respect. It reminded those with experience that it was not to be trifled with.

Squadron Leader 'Colly' Collingridge, a former Battle of Britain Spitfire pilot, recalls:

I started flying Masters with the Central Flying School at Upavon in November 1941. The course ended in January 1942 and I was then posted to No 9 Service Flying Training School at Hullavington as an instructor until March 1942 when I was posted to No 5 SFTS Ternhill. The unit became an

Above:
Miles Master II W8691, fitted with the 870 hp Bristol Mercury engine, undergoing trials with the Aeroplane and Armament Experimental Establishment at Boscombe Down before being issued to the Central Flying School.
(Author's collection)

Below:
Miles Master III W8656 '7' in the company of another machine from No 5 Service Flying Training School at Ternhill in 1942, with a WAAF rigger as passenger. This photograph shows well the rear seat adjustment facility.
(Author's collection)

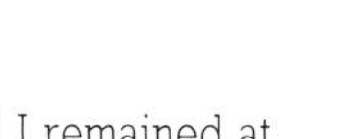

Advanced Flying Unit soon after I arrived, and I remained at Ternhill until August 1943 when I went out to Canada, again instructing.

We had some Mark Is at Hullavington, but did very little instruction on them. They were old machines, and therefore mainly used by the students for solo flying. The instructors used the limited number of IIs and IIIs, until the Is were gradually phased out. They were either broken up beyond repair or they ran out of time, and were slowly replaced by the IIs and IIIs.

One significant difference between the II and the III was that the prop went round the other way. I have seen it suggested that this must have been confusing, but I never found it so. One knew one was in a Mercury-engined Master II, and one simply expected the propeller to go round the opposite way from the Master III, and in any case would only notice this on take-off. The trims were a little bit different, but you knew this from the Pilots' Notes, so you would just check the trims and away you would go. There couldn't be any confusion between the two versions, because the Mercury engine had a massive cowling, so it was obvious which engine it was.

The Mark II was faster with the Mercury engine, which had plenty of power. Later they clipped off the tips of the wings to make it even faster. They were able to do this because the Master was a very strong machine, especially the wings, which had a very thick chord.

The view from the back seat was quite good, especially compared with Spitfires. It could be raised and lowered to give a better view during take-off and landing. You could see quite well at the side, but you couldn't see over the top of the pilot, though you could see enough for landing. One could peer round the pupil, of course, and I don't recall ever having any real difficulties.

One had the seat in the lower position for aerobatics and general flying, though the control column then seemed uncomfortably high. The normal position was with the control column low down between your legs, but there was a limiting speed for the rear hood of the Master to be open, and when you dropped your seat down after take off it didn't seem natural with the spade grip of the control column in front of your face.

On one or two occasions I have been out through the hood, usually during aerobatics with some ham student, mainly because the seat had a habit of not locking properly. If you didn't get it right into the notch, your seat would go up and you would hit the hood, even though you were still tightly in your straps. You would then get a nasty knock on the head and the hood would flip up. The hood was hinged in the corner, and after take off you would pull a handle on the top and it would come down in front of you.

The Mark I, being water-cooled, was prone to glycol leaks, especially the older machines, and you would get glycol coming out – usually from a head gasket. This then burnt, causing white smoke to be ejected through the exhaust stubs making it difficult to see for landing. The view in the Mark I was better, though, with its narrower in-line engine.

The Master undercarriage seemed to stand up very well to the treatment it received from pupils. It was well braced and very wide, which helped to make it stable. We preferred the Mark II for night flying, probably because of the extra power.

I was waiting to take off in a Master one day in January 1942 at Hullavington, while the runways were under construction. Things were not too well organised, and aircraft were taking off and landing on two different parts of the grass. Suddenly I saw a Master directly in the path of one taking off. The pilot of the former evidently saw the one taking off, and tried to accelerate out of the way, but failed to make it, and the other aircraft sliced his fuselage in half. It was lucky that there was no-one in the back seat, and after the remains came to rest he was able to stagger out of the front half, dazed but relatively unharmed.

North American Harvard

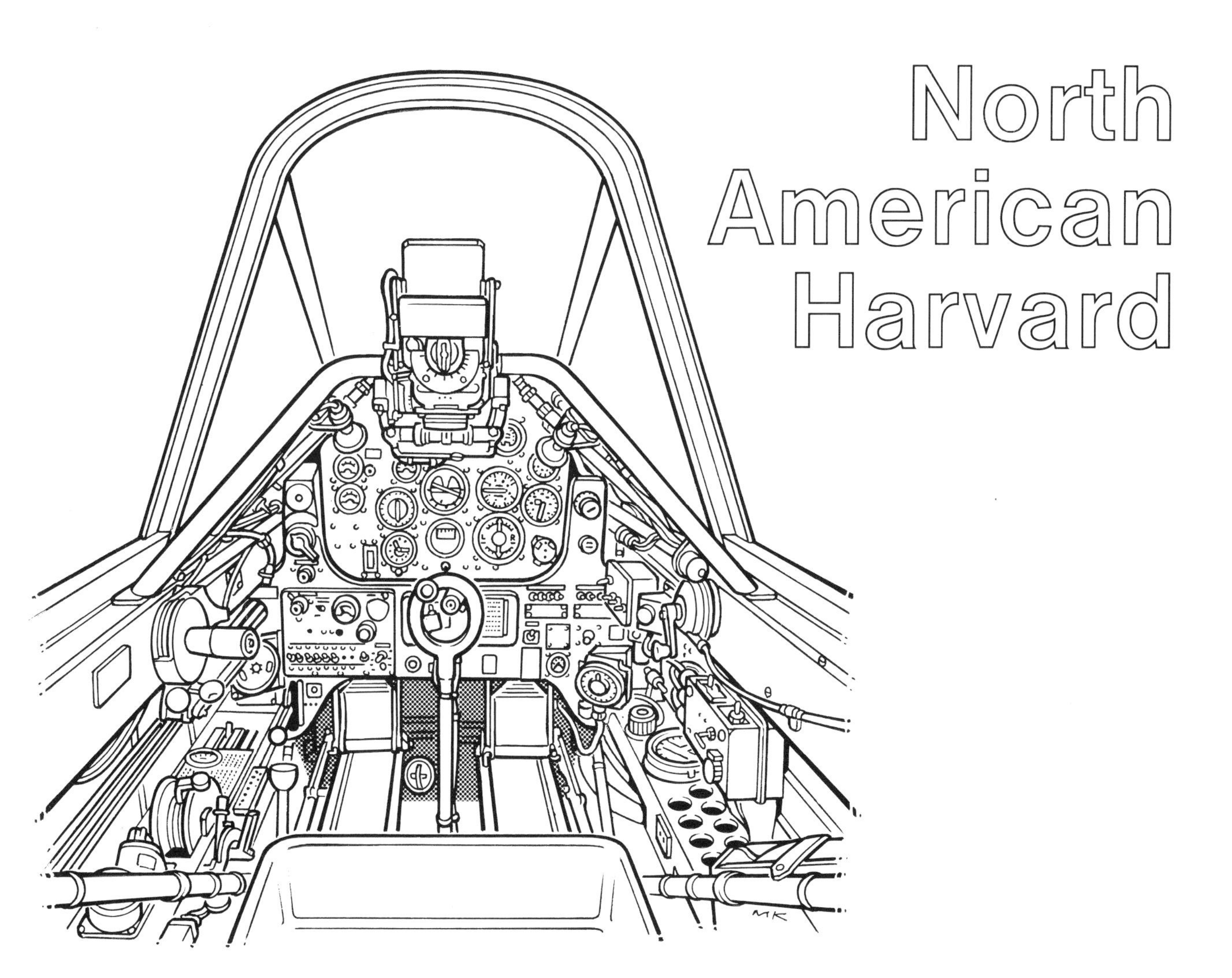

With war imminent, it was apparent that Britain would be unable to meet its own aircraft requirements, and home production would be largely concentrated on operational types. Accordingly orders were placed with American manufacturers to fill the gap. A pressing need was for a modern advanced trainer, and hopes had been pinned on the de Havilland Don, but this had turned out to be a failure. Its place would be taken by the Miles Kestrel, developed as the Master, but this was unlikely to be available for some time, and as a stop-gap an order was placed for an adaptation of the North American BC-1, a robust machine already supplied to the US Army Air Corps. Ironically, the Harvard as it became with the RAF, long outlasted the Master.

Specification (Mark IIB)

Power plant:	*One 600 hp Pratt and Whitney Wasp R-1340-AN-1.*
Dimension:	*Span 42 ft 0¼ in, length 28 ft 11 in, height 11 ft 8½ in, wing area 253 sq ft.*
Weights:	*Empty 3,995 lb, loaded 5,235 lb.*
Performance:	*Maximum speed 180 mph at 5,000 ft, cruising speed 140 mph, initial climb 1,300 ft/min, range 750 miles, endurance 3.9 hrs, service ceiling 22,400 ft.*

Powered by a Pratt and Whitney Wasp R-1340-S3H1 engine, the initial order was for 200 machines, and the deliveries commenced in December 1938. The first machine (N7000) was sent to Martlesham Heath for testing, but was lost when it dived into the ground at Eyke, Suffolk on 16 February 1939. Testing continued with N7001 and N7013, however, and a report was made at the end of the year.

The report made two main criticisms. Visibility forward from the front seat was below average, a severe handicap for a training aircraft, especially for taxiing, take-off and landing. It was even worse from the rear seat due to the strong-point between the seats. The view in other directions was good, however. A lever fitted on later aircraft enabled the front seat to be raised, which helped the pupil, but it increased the problems of the instructor in the back seat, who now had to lean sideways to get much of a view.

The other problem was noise. An electric intercom was fitted, but this only proved satisfactory at low speed as the microphones picked up considerable external noise, and it was impossible to hear properly while taking off or climbing, or when flying at high cruising speeds or above. The raucous sound of the Harvard was very noticeable externally. It was easily distinguishable from other aircraft, this feature being diagnosed as due to the high tip speed of the direct-drive airscrew, the pitch of the resulting note, rather than its volume, being instinctively seized by the ear. This noise reached its peak in the plane of the aircraft, and the problem was never eliminated, as can be readily heard on surviving Harvards.

Following the initial delivery, a further 200 Mark Is were ordered, many of which served in Southern Rhodesia. These were followed by the Mark II, based on the AT-6 for the USAAF, with squared off wing tips and a triangular fin and rudder, these features being retained on subsequent versions. The rear fuselage was of a light alloy monocoque, in place of the earlier fabric covered steel tubing. Some Mark IIs also went to Rhodesia, but the majority were retained in Canada for schools set up under the British Commonwealth Air Training Plan.

One of the few Mark IIs to reach the United Kingdom was BD134, which in January 1941 took part in comparative tests with the Mark I at the Aeroplane and Armament Experimental Establishment at Boscombe Down. Its handling characteristics were found to be similar to those of the MkI. It behaved satisfactorily in a dive, and recovery from a spin was certain. Behaviour in the stall was essentially the same, though there had been no improvement in the large height loss which occurred in this manoeuvre. During climb, both the cylinder and oil inlet temperatures were within permissible limits for tropical summer conditions, but the oil tended to run hot in level flight. this did not matter in normal English summer conditions, but was likely to cause difficulties in Rhodesia.

The next version to appear was the AT-6C, which became the Harvard IIA in RAF parlance, this having a plywood rear fuselage. The Wasp R-1340-S3H1 of the earlier marks was replaced by the Wasp R-1340-AN1, having only a short exhaust stub on the starboard side, as opposed to the long one of the MkII. A batch of 747 of these went mainly to the Middle East, Rhodesia and New Zealand. They were followed by the Mark IIB, the equivalent of the American AT-6A, built in large numbers under licence in Canada by the Noorduyn company, and used not only by the RAF but by all Commonwealth countries participating in the training plan. The final RAF version was the Mark III, corresponding to the AT-6D, all these American versions being known as Texans in the USAAF. Total production for the RAF and BCATP was 4905 machines.

The Harvard was a very strong machine, but could be dangerous if not properly handled. Pupils graduating from elementary machines could have great difficulty controlling it initially. It could flick suddenly, without warning, and would flick stall if looped too fast. Landings could be disastrous if the tail was held too high, and pupils were instructed not to throttle back until both main wheels were firmly on the ground. Even when the tail had come down it was not safe to relax, as the aircraft was prone to ground looping.

Don March graduated to Harvards from Prentices:

We Prentice pilots regarded the Harvard as a hot ship, and looked forward to flying them. Senior courses would fill us with stories about them swinging wildly off the runway during the landing run, and the very real probability of catching a wingtip. Some of us succeeded in getting those 'Wingtrips' to our shame, as Harvards needed some controlling during crosswind landings. I have heard a very experienced wartime Canadian pilot say that if you could fly a Harvard you could fly anything.

Obviously the rate of climb was better than that of the Prentice, but more power would have been welcome. During aerobatics, one preserved height, not wishing to lose too much, as one had to climb up again to above 3,000 ft to be able to continue, which took time and one wanted not to waste any time at all during a 45 minute flight.

Harvards enjoyed the privilege of landing and taking off from the runway, whilst the Prentices had to land on the grass area to the left of the runway. Consequently there were mixed circuits, with Harvards and Prentices at different speeds, a practice which would be considered undesirable today and probably would not be allowed.

Flaps and undercarriage levers were immediately next to each other, thus presenting the distinct danger of selecting flap instead of undercarriage and vice versa. To avoid this, whenever one moved the undercarriage lever, IT WAS ALWAYS WITH A CLENCHED FIST, but when handling the flap selector lever, one grasped it. So you had the clenched fist and grasping syndrome, which definitely helped to avoid wrong selection.

However, one of our chaps on a senior course, near to

getting his wings, was on a night cross-country solo at about 2,000 ft cruising level and flying along quite happily in the pitch dark when his engine started failing. He did the right thing, undid his straps and started leaving the cockpit to bale out, as you cannot do a forced landing at night in open country with much chance of success. He was just about to leap out when the engine picked up, so he got back in again, which turned out to be a mistake. He had just strapped in again when the engine again started to fail. He again went to bale out, and the engine once more picked up. All the time he was getting in and out, however, he was losing valuable height. In the end, the engine failed completely, by which time he was too low to bale out, so he was committed to making a forced landing at night – wheels up, of course. As it was very dark he could not see where to land, so did not know whether he was above woods or other obstacles.

On another occasion a pilot had engine failure immediately after take off on a night solo. He managed to land in a field with the aid of the Harvard's landing lights, but was chastened to discover in the morning daylight that he had flown under telegraph wires without hitting them, totally unaware they were there.

North American Harvard I N7021 was one of several early machines delivered to the Central Flying School at Upavon in the spring of 1939. This version had the fabric covered rear fuselage, and rounded rudder which gave way to a more angular shape on later models.

(Author's collection)

This is where the clenched fist should have come in. He did not have time to do up his shoulder straps as he was too low, only the lap strap, which was very unfortunate. In the heat of the moment he then forgot about the clenched fist, and selected undercarriage down and flaps up for forced landing. This was a disastrous mistake, but understandable in the circumstances – there but for the grace of God go I. From thereon the landing was doomed, and it was a helluva prang, the aircraft not being found for hours. The pilot, who was a damned good one, was not killed, but he was so badly injured as to be on crutches for the rest of his life.

Another of our chaps had an overspeeding prop on take-off during his first solo. It made a hell of a noise – Harvards props were normally pretty noisy anyway – with the prop tips exceeding the speed of sound. He made it round the circuit and landed, but I think we on the ground were more concerned due to the appalling noise being made.

The smallest chap on our course had to have the seat up to its fullest extent to be able to see out of the cockpit – the Harvard cockpit was quite roomy and deep. After completing his first solo night circuit his seat collapsed right

North American Harvard II BD136 was one of the few examples of this variant to reach the United Kingdom, being used in tests at the Aeroplane and Armament Experimental Establishment at Boscombe Down before being handed over to the USAAF at Bovingdon in September 1942.

(Author's collection)

down into the bottomless pit, and he was unable to see anything except the cockpit walls, but somehow managed to land successfully. That caused us quite a laugh.

For simulated instrument flying training one had to wear blue goggles and put up amber shields round the cockpit windows, so that you were unable to see out and had to rely entirely on the illuminated instruments. What made this difficult, however, was the condensation inside the goggles, which blurred the appearance of the instruments. This was very undesirable during an instrument take-off as it was very hard to see the Direction Indicator compass, which was essential for keeping straight. We bore this with fortitude, as we thought it bad form to blame our 'tools' when we careered all over the place. When I told my Instructor about this forty years later, however, his reply was 'Now you tell me!' They did a modification eventually, consisting of a tube from the goggles to outside air, through a hole in the cockpit wall, which helped.

One personal recollection is of an occasion when I was landing solo at night, thinking that I was becoming a pretty hot pilot. To my chagrin I shot off the runway on to the grass. Fortunately the only damage was to my ego – an ace pilot should not do that. Mustering all my self-control I called over the R/T, as coolly and calmly as I could, 'Clear runway', hoping nobody had noticed, or if they had they thought I had turned off intentionally. Unfortunately my Instructor was in the Control Tower and was not going to be fooled by me. To my surprise his voice came over the R/T telling me in a very forceful manner, 'Get back on to the runway and clear at the correct point,' which I did, with shame. I was on very good terms with this instructor, though, which I always appreciated as it was a great help, and he told me later on that he was actually very amused by the incident and had given me full marks for impudence!

Squadron Leader Dick Smerdon recalls of the Harvard:

This was my first introduction to brakes, a constant-speed propeller and an American radial engine. The usage of these items gave me a lasting preference for hydraulic brakes in contrast to the British pneumatics, and an admiration for the trouble-free radial engine – no overheating, even in the tropics. (The water-cooled engine of the Spitfire in desert training schools suffered from overheating). The Harvard had a lockable tailwheel, but if the wheel got to too great an angle, as in a tight turn, on the ground, or if the weight came off the tail, it could equally castor freely. This taught one to control the aircraft.

The Harvard behaved like many an operational fighter, and would flick off a turn if the control inputs were not sympathetic. While I was with No 11 Flying Instructors School at Shullafa in the Egyptian Canal Zone, we had No 351 (Yugoslav Partisan) Squadron Hurricane pilots sent to us, as they were losing aircraft on strafing attacks and rocket attacks. We took them up to no great altitude to show them how tightly a turn could be pulled and no tighter, and supervised their practices. This low level flying concentrated the mind wonderfully.

I did my B Advanced, A2 and A1 Instructor Recategorisation tests on the Harvard and spent quite a lot of time inverted during practise, which paid off when I was later required to patter an inverted spin recovery, albeit in the Magister. I thought the Harvard, although a stride from the Tiger, was only a little step forward on to the operational fighters, British or American.

Squadron Leader Don Brittain also had a fair amount of Harvard experience:

I enjoyed flying the Harvard. I don't remember many vices, except that if you relaxed after landing it would quickly ground-loop on you. Our aircraft had a Verey Pistol stowage and tube, but the pistol was never carried. We found a Coke bottle would fit in and, yes, silly and dangerous as it is now to me, we occasionally did drop the odd bottle. God, how stupid!

We flew in the front for normal training, and in the back for IF – genuinely under the hood, as a canvas pram-like hood stowed behind the seat came over and fastened to the coaming, enabling you to sit there and concentrate on the dials.

One of my pals got to the end of the runway for take off – was given control, then found there was no control column – how's that for awareness!

In Canada, because of the cold weather on the last trip of the day, you used the oil dilution switch – this put petrol in the oil to stop it freezing. I did this as a matter of course when I got back to the UK, to get the full wrath of the Flight Sergeant waiting to know which silly bugger had done it. I could never understand why they didn't wire the switch off if they didn't want it used!

One event which did scare me when it happened was the first time I went night flying in the UK. Canadian Harvards had a long exhaust pipe which they used to tap off heat for cockpit heating. The British ones had a short stubby exhaust. I didn't realise flames came out of the exhaust, as you couldn't see them during the day. Well you guessed it, when I went into a cloud at night, I thought the aircraft was on fire. I nearly shat bricks, and it took me some while to calm down.

I remember using the precautionary forced landing procedure to do a bit of illegal low-level flying – it's surprising how long it takes to find a suitable field!

While at Cottesmore, one of my mates on a solo cross-country at night, picked up his girl friend on the dark taxiway – flew the cross-country and then dropped her off after landing. I would never have the nerve to do that in a million years. I'd be too worried at getting found out or something going wrong. What if I was diverted to another airfield?

We used to do spinning on instruments, which is really quite simple – I carried this over on to piston-Provosts once I became an instructor. When you think about it, spinning is the worst that can happen to you, and it does give you confidence to know you can cope.

Frank Mares, DFM, a Czechoslovakian Spitfire Pilot in the Second World War was training on Harvards during May 1940 with other Czech pilots, while

North American Harvard IIB FT179 'C' of No 2 (Indian) Group Communications Flight at Yelahanka, near Bangalore in August 1946.

(Author)

attached to the French Air Force at Avord in south east France. Frank and three other pilots had taken off, and they were flying along in formation, thinking how grand life was. It was a very nice day; bits of cumulus about and very good visibility. Then Frank saw a twin-engined aircraft flying a few hundred feet below.

North American Harvard IIB FS753 'FBGG' of No 6 Flying Training School at Ternhill in formation during Operation Stardust in April 1950.

(Don March)

All four pilots, being made of the right stuff and wanting to be fighter pilots, made the obvious mutual decision – to dive down and beat the hell out of this French aircraft. At a great rate of knots, the four Harvards dived down (no guns or ammo, of course) and the range closed rapidly.

Frank and his fellows were in for the surprise of their lives when at close quarters, they espied great black crosses and swastikas all over this 'French' aircraft. What to do next? Almost instantaneously, great decision-making became superfluous – three parachutes blossomed from the Dornier, which was heading south west, in the vicinity of Avord. The German crew had baled out at the sight of these four fearsome 'fighters' diving down.

Frank reported this incident after landing, but due to language difficulty the French did not seem to comprehend the true nature of the episode. Their colleagues thought that Frank and his fellow pilots ought to have been credited with a quarter of a 'Jerry' each.

Squadron Leader Mike Sparrow trained on Harvards at 3FTS Feltwell:

I found it a lovely aircraft for training. RAF versions had the undercarriage horn disconnected, but a large red light

Above:
North American Harvard IIB FK977 'FBTA' of No 3 Flying Training School at Feltwell in formation during 1951.
(via Ray Hanna)

Below:
North American Harvard IIB KF292 'FBTK' of No 3 Flying Training School starting up in the snow at Feltwell in 1951.
(Ray Hanna)

would come on in the cockpit if the throttle were reduced below one-third open and the undercarriage was up. The exhaust flame always seemed to play onto the fuel filler cap and sometimes blinded one at night. I once landed one wheels-up at night flying a very skilful circuit in order to manipulate the throttle to keep that stupid red light out!

Cyril Smith was stationed at Thornhill in Southern Rhodesia, where Harvards were frequent visitors:

One night our flying programme was scrubbed due to thunderstorms and, with lightning flashes all over the place, something like 18 Harvards diverted in from Heany. Of course they all had to be hangared for the night, and after much pushing and pulling of both Ansons and Harvards in less than adequate space we managed to close all doors, then feeling very pleased with our efforts we retired to bed. Next day we received the biggest rocket ever, and suffered a humiliating lecture on the consequences of an undercarriage collapse causing untold damage in a hangar full of aircraft with wings and tails overlapping. Another lesson learnt – but no-one came forward with any constructive ideas on how to get x-number of aircraft safely tucked away in the circumstances. There was no second occasion – perhaps the Heany pilots felt that we had no respect for their charges and wouldn't take any further risks.

Eric Sharp was posted as an Engine Fitter to one of the Harvard flights at Cranwell in the early fifties:

Cranwell at that time, along with many other Flying Training stations, was a grass airfield. It had no runways, except for a vestige up at one end that was built for the Gloster-Whittle prototype jet. There were no taxiways, just a little strip road used to park the aircraft along and give access for the fuel bowser. Night flying was an experience of cold dark starry nights, navigation lights, whorling propeller discs, feeble marshalling wands and goose-neck flare taxiway and runway markers, pulling chock ropes and hauling trolley-accs.

I remember the Harvard with a certain affection. Ground running it had a bit of Biggles about it! It had a hand/electric inertia starter which wound up to a most satisfying scream, although I don't ever recall hand winding it. To get the engine started one set the throttle and pitch lever with the left hand, then manually pumped up five pounds pressure in the fuel line with a wobble pump on the left hand side of the cockpit, at the same time priming with the Ki-gass pump on the right-hand side with the right hand. The inertia start switch was in the centre of the dash behind the stick – down to wind, up to engage. So there you are, switch on the ignition. Wobble with left hand. Prime with right. Clutch stick back with thighs and nudge the inertia switch down with right foot. Wait for the starter to scream at the right pitch and nudge the switch up with the same foot The engine would rotate and fire, but often it would require continued effort from left and right hand to keep it going until sustained.

We had a lot of ignition problems caused by water in the front harness and plugs. I finally got round this by getting advice from my father, who worked at that time with the 2nd Royal Tank Regiment as a civilian Engine Representative. They filled the spark plug body with silicon grease to keep the water out. My Chiefy threw his hands up in horror at the idea, but we gave it a go and it worked!

Another ignition problem was radio interference. We spent ages on the wing root with heads in the engine cowling, engine running, and in contact with the bod in the cockpit by long lead and head set, shaking and poking to find the cause of crackle. The cause was finally found to be the magneto mounting; some sort of less than perfect earth contact between magneto and mount. This was cured by a Heath Robinson-type metal strip and bolt arrangement that squeezed the two together. Simple, but it took a long time to find.

Before stopping the engine on a Harvard, the propeller should be brought to coarse pitch, to protect the bracket prop ram which was exposed in the fine pitch, but this nicety was hardly ever observed. The mag contact breakers were dead easy to get at and set up, though quite prone to arcing and ozone corrosion. A good sniff round the mag if running rough was experienced, was a good pointer to the problem.

The riggers were pleased with a time delay valve in the hydraulic system. This was adjusted through a panel on the port side while the engine was running. I quite enjoyed it on cold days, sitting in the closed cockpit in the warm 'bending the throttle', while my pal was on the outside freezing in the slipstream making touchy adjustments.

One last thing comes to mind. At the onset of late autumn/early winter, oil dilution was carried out before the engines were shut down after the last sortie. This washed all the gum and sludge out of the oilways. The oil filter had also to be dropped and cleaned, which was an onerous task. We had lots of Harvards, and we had to do this to all of them before we could pack up and go to tea. (It was years before the last meal of the day for any airman was called anything but tea!) We hated the oil dilution system.

The Harvard continued in RAF service for some years after the war, being finally superseded by Vampire T.11s in 1954/55.

Percival Prentice

Specification

Power plant:	*One 251 hp de Havilland Gipsy Queen 32.*
Dimensions:	*Span 46 ft 0 in, length 31 ft 3 in, height 12 ft 10 in, wing area 305 sq ft.*
Weights:	*Empty 3,140 lb, loaded 4,100 lb.*
Performance:	*Maximum speed 150 mph at sea level, cruising speed 136 mph, initial climb 700 ft/min, range 466 miles, endurance 3.4 hrs, service ceiling 15,000 ft.*

Towards the end of 1943, Air Ministry Specification T.23/43 was issued for a new basic trainer to replace the Tiger Moth, which was by then becoming outdated, being a simple low-powered design, fitted with few instruments, and largely dependent on good weather. What was now required was an economical, all-weather monoplane, fully equipped with modern instruments and capable of providing the pupil with a much greater range of experience. Tenders were received from several firms including Miles, Percival, de Havilland and Heston. Percival and de Havilland were asked to construct five prototypes each of their respective designs, for testing purposes, but the de Havilland order was soon dropped leaving the field clear for Percival.

The first prototype machine, which adopted the name Prentice, flew on 31 March 1946, and was to provide the basic flying tuition for the early post-war influx of pilots. Its de Havilland Gipsy Queen engine delivered twice the power of the engine used in the Tiger Moth, and was fitted with a variable pitch airscrew. Its sturdy airframe was much larger than its predecessor and was of metal construction, except for the control surfaces, but retained the fixed undercarriage configuration. The forward fuselage was nearly rectangular in cross-section, and was of light-alloy sheeting covering a semi-braced structure. This blended into an after section of a tall elliptical shape of semi-monocoque construction with light-alloy frames and stringers.

The large, fully enclosed cabin incorporated VHF radio, electrical intercommunications and SBA blind-flying equipment with two-stage amber screens. It also had heating and ventilation. There was an excellent field of view from both front seats, and the standard of roominess and comfort was high, in stark contrast to its Tiger Moth predecessor. The intention of the third seat was to economise on instruction by having a second pupil seated behind the instructor and pupil in the front seats, looking over their shoulders, so as to gain some air experience and enable him to listen to the instructor's commentary on the electrical intercommunications system. In practise the idea proved unsatisfactory. The aircraft was underpowered for this purpose, and tended to waddle through the air, consequently it was largely used as a side-by-side two-seater.

Taxiing proved to be no problem, the all-round view combining with a well-sprung fixed undercarriage and pneumatic brakes which could be operated smoothly. The aircraft became airborne easily, and when in flight proved sufficiently sensitive on the controls. There was plenty of vibration warning of a stall, and recovery from a spin was not difficult. Both powered and glide landings could be made at about 75 mph, the steep angle of approach giving an excellent view of the landing path.

Above:
Percival Prentice VR218, a pre-production machine used by Blackburns prior to building these machines under sub-contract. Note the distinctive wingtips.
(Author's collection)

Below:
Percival Prentice VN691 '52', a pre-production machine later used by No 7 Reserve Flying School and seen here at Leicester East in June 1953.
(Author)

An early problem which came to light, however, was a tendency to flip over in a gentle turn, and this led to the wingtips being modified by being turned up at an angle of 30 degrees. There were also problems with spinning, but this fault was not so easily cured, only marginal improvement being brought about by fitting anti-spin strakes forward of the tailplane and increasing the rudder area. After only two or three turns the manoeuvre would develop into a flat spin from which recovery was difficult and took far too long, especially if the aircraft had insufficient height to start with. Various tail configurations were tried, including at one stage twin fins and rudders, but eventually the designers arrived at a compromise shape.

Deliveries commenced in 1947, and over 350 were produced for the RAF, 125 of these under sub-contract by Blackburn. Many more were exported to Argentina, Lebanon and India, and the type was also built under licence at Bangalore by Hindustan Aircraft for the Royal Indian Air Force. Despite their wartime design and manufacturing experience with the Proctor, however, problems were encountered by the makers, giving rise to criticism which later endangered their prospects for the next generation of trainers. However, the Prentice served for some years with the Central Flying School, the RAF College, Cranwell and several Flying Training Schools. It became one of the many trainers which over the years have become referred to as the 'clockwork mouse'. It was later used at Swanton Morley for training air signallers. The Prentice was withdrawn from pilot training in 1953, when it was superseded by the Provost, and large numbers were sold for civil use, though it was not the success in this role that had been envisaged, and many remained unconverted.

Squadron Leader Mike Sparrow flew the Prentice at 3 FTS Feltwell:

If held in a spin this aircraft became very stable, hence difficult to get out of the spin again. This led to several accidents – some were fatal, some people walked away. It was pleasant to fly straight and level, but a cow when doing aerobatics. A good slow roll seemed almost impossible, probably due to the stability imposed by the upturned wing tips.

Don March recalls of the Prentice:

As an *ab initio* pilot I looked at it, thought it looked a little antiquated, and had a slight twinge of sadness that I would not be flying the Tiger Moth. However, being so keen in those days, I dismissed that thought from my mind and was determined to like the aircraft, which I succeeded in doing very quickly.

The Prentice had a number of advantages over the Tiger. The instructor sat at your side, not behind, which was supposed to make for better instruction. The Tiger was more seat-of-pants type of flying, which was not a bad thing in itself, but it was also very necessary to become proficient on instruments, for which the Prentice was ideal, with its far

Percival Prentice T.1 VR267 'FDIO' of the Central Flying School at Little Rissington, seen at an air show in 1951.

(MAP photo)

superior instrumentation and well-designed instrument panel.

Open cockpit flying is very nice if the weather is fine, but the Prentice had the advantage of an enclosed cockpit, protected from all winds and weather. However, it had its disadvantages. It was underpowered, which was not very good for aerobatics, and gave it a slow rate of climb. It was very difficult, if not impossible, to do a decent half roll off the top of a loop.

The Prentice was designed for three pilots, the one in the rear seat being supposed to learn by observing, but this was not very successful. There was too much weight with a third pilot, and a consequent risk of getting into a flat spin from which one might not be able to recover. The three pilot concept was therefore abandoned.

Robin Brown was a pupil on Prentices at 22 FTS Syerston in May 1951:

I found the Prentice a pleasant aircraft to fly. It was a tiny machine. You sat side by side with your instructor, so he could watch you handling the controls. There was, as far as I recall, never a third person behind us. It always struck me as being a curious aircraft, first because of those turned-up wing tips, and then because of the platform just forward of the fin and rudder which had some effect on the spinning characteristics. I thought that any aircraft which needed comic little additions and attachments like that must have started life inherently unstable. Anyway, whatever vices it may have had to start with must have been eliminated, since it was a delight to fly.

By the time I moved on to Harvards I had done 60 hours in the Prentice, but it remains 'special' because I flew my first solo in it after 7 hours 50 minutes dual, about average on the course, and that great day always remains indelibly fixed in every pilot's mind. I did mine just down the Fosse Way on the grass airfield at RAF Newton, which is where first solos were always flown by Syerston pupils – probably because it was a quieter place with not so much going on in the circuit to distract the nervous. Your instructor simply unstrapped, got out, gave you a thumbs up and then went and hid behind the control tower, hardly daring to watch. You took off, did one circuit and one landing, taxied over and collected him and then flew back to base.

This was the time of the Korean war and there was a big RAF expansion programme. Lots of young men were being pushed through wings courses. I'm not so sure that the instruction was all that brilliant or as thorough as it might have been. In the early 1950s you were left to get on with it very much by yourself and it was assumed that you knew what to do and that you would do the sensible thing – of course in those days you could put an aircraft down almost anywhere and get away with it – but if you had never flown before you would not always know what the sensible thing was.

I remember having a final handling check with the Prentice Squadron Commander, Sqn Ldr Wilson, and we were somewhere near Grantham, when the squadron leader said, 'All right, set course for home. Show me your map and work out the course to get to Syerston'. Well, in fact you could almost see Syerston, and I knew the countryside like the back of my hand because I had lived there and had relations all round Lincolnshire and Nottinghamshire. It had never crossed my mind I needed a map! I said, 'Well I haven't gone one,' at which point Wilson nearly failed me. After that, of course, I never flew without a map, but it was so ridiculous that I could have reached the 60-hour stage without any instructor even bothering to tell me that vital fact.

One amusing thing that happened to me during my Basic

Training stage on Prentices was when I was flying with my instructor, Flt Lt Lines, a quiet capable man who I liked. We were in the Ossington Low Flying Area, north-west of Syerston, where we practised dead-stick landings and hedge-hopping. With piston-engined aircraft you always had to rev up during a practice forced-landing, about every hundred feet of descent, to be sure the engine would respond when you wanted to overshoot. We came quite low and Flt Lt Lines said 'I have control' at just about the last possible moment. As he opened up, of course, the inevitable happened, the engine didn't respond. We sank lower and lower into the standing corn when, at last, the engine came to life and staggered off into the air again. Nothing was said, he looked one way and I looked the other, both pretending nothing had occurred. It takes something like that to happen to your instructor to make you realise he is human after all and not infallible! We got back to Syerston and people walking this way and that in front of the line huts began to stop and stare at us. We got out of the aircraft and realised why – the undercarriage spats were festooned with sheaves of corn!

Another event that happened in the Ossington Low Flying Area concerned a pupil who actually did have engine failure. He coped very well and ended up just inside a very small field. They sent an instructor in another aircraft to pick him up, and when he arrived overhead he saw the stranded machine, and decided to land alongside, making the not unreasonable assumption that if a pupil pilot could land there, a trained instructor could. Instead, he shot through the fence on the far side of the field and ended up on his nose. When the pupil finally got back to base he was asked how he had managed to land in such a small space. 'Oh,' he said, 'I touched down two fields away – I bounced into that one!'

Nowadays either of those two incidents would mean a Board of Inquiry and a possible Court Martial, but in those days it was all part of the wonderful delight of flying, something to be laughed about in the bar that night, a lesson to be learned. Thus you were expected to get on with it and cope as best you could. It is sad that today's jet pilots probably know nothing about the sheer amusement and delight that has long since gone out of flying – dating from the time the new attitudes began to creep in during the late fifties and sixties, but there was an elan, a 'press on' spirit that was a requirement if you wanted to get your wings and reach a squadron.

One morning I was told to go and bring up an aircraft from the squadron hangar for the first trip of the day. This was a task that was sprung on you after you had done a few hours flying, and it involved starting a Prentice from 'cold'. Up until that day you had always done it with the help of your instructor – this time you were on your own; not only that but you had a crowd of airmen watching you. I suddenly thought, 'Oh, my God, do I really know how to start the damn thing'. One couldn't appeal for help from the groundcrew, that would be an admission of failure, you just had to get it right all by yourself! Also, like a car on a cold morning, you had to get the fuel mixture correct or you would flood the cylinders. Meanwhile, up on the flight line people would be waiting for you, anxious to start the day's flying! I think the desperation of that morning etched itself into my dreams for a long time afterwards.

In fact the Prentice was normally very easy to start. It was in the Harvard where you had to build up the pressure in the carburettor by pushing and pulling at a priming pump. Some later aircraft were started by a small cartridge, others

Percival Prentice T.1 VS270 'FAFJ' of the RAF College at Cranwell around 1949.

(MAP photo)

had to have the propeller swung, but most machines in those days needed a 'trolley-acc.' The trolley accumulator was a little trailer full of batteries on two solid metal wheels that was plugged in somewhere by a long umbilical cord and which gave you electrical power to start the aircraft without having to rely on the internal batteries. You could start on internals if you had landed away somewhere, but only in emergencies. As soon as the aircraft was running you waved away the trolley-acc. There were special rooms in the hangars where the trolley-accs were recharged, identifiable by a low humming noise that emanated from them.

One thing I disliked was having to fly the SBA (Standard Beam Approach) instrument let-down system. You had what were known as the 'two-stage amber' screens which, if you were down for an SBA sortie, you took along in the cockpit. When you were ready to start, you slotted these into the inside of the glass panels either side of the cockpit. The front windscreen remained clear, but to stop you peeping out you wore a special amber visor which, together with the side panels quite blacked out your view of the outside world. You let your seat down so you couldn't see over the coaming but only the instrument panel in front of you. It was just like flying at night.

The system was designed to make you concentrate entirely on your instruments. As far as I remember, you were set up in a downwind pattern and you had to make a procedural (Rate 1) turn to bring yourself round onto the outer marker beacon which was situated somewhere near Newton (I think you could only use SBA on one runway heading). In your earphones you started to pick up the signals, dots or dashes depending whether you were port or starboard of the required track, plus an occasional ident signal so you didn't home in on the wrong airfield. When you were bang on the centre line you got a steady note. Over the outer marker you started descending at a fixed rate and you should have been at, say, 500 feet over the inner marker. The object of the exercise was to bring you down to a certain height over the runway threshold – about 50 feet, from which point you could look up and make a normal visual landing. The SBA system was quite hard to fly, lots of perspiration and anguish, anyway for me.

Percival Prentice T.1 VR236 'FAEA' and other aircraft of the RAF College at Cranwell in 1951.

(Eric Sharp)

Percival Prentice T.1 VR230 'FBRE' of No 3 Flying Training School at Feltwell, seen at an air show in 1950. (MAP photo)

In those days (something of a cliche?) spinning was taught as quite a normal manoeuvre. I believe it is no longer taught unless you are a test pilot or something exalted, but in Prentices you were expected to be able to spin, and, naturally enough, recover. You went up to a generous height above ground level, about 10,000 feet, and you had to recover by about 5,000 feet, so you probably did four or five turns. There was no difficulty with the Prentice, what with all the gadgets stuck all over it. I felt sure, though, that whoever had tried to spin the Prentice in its prototype stage must have tent-pegged into the ground resulting in a concerted rush by the designers back to the drawing board! All through my flying career I tried to make a point of never flying an aircraft that had not been in RAF service for at least a while so as to ensure that most of the bugs had been ironed out of it!

Squadron Leader Stan Greenhow flew Prentices with 3 FTS at Feltwell:

I well remember the Sunday morning in August 1948 when the first aircraft of that name flew into Feltwell. I was the Station Duty Officer over that weekend, and it was my duty to meet all incoming aircraft as well as 'see-off' departing ones. When the Prentice taxied into the hardstanding, I was a bit appalled at its slab sides, enormous canopy, general lack of aerodynamic beauty and the feeling it gave of being very underpowered.

The CFI flew the aircraft that morning, and after he had landed I had a go, when all my suspicions were proved correct. On grass it was *very* underpowered, and I got the impression of a slow acceleration as we charged towards the far end of the take-off grass runway. It lumbered into the air, but was very stable and solid once airborne and doing circuits and landings, medium turns and stalls. Aerobatics were awful, however. Of course it looped OK, but for trainee pilots, slow and barrel rolls were only just possible and tended to be a bit disastrous. It flew like an airborne caravan, and landings were very positive with no tendency to bounce.

As a trainer it lacked 'feel' – unlike the other two trainer aircraft I was instructing on at that time, the Tiger Moth and Harvard. It was useful, though, in some flying exercises for night familiarisation, navigation exercises, and introduction to instrument flying and beam approach, because it had a third seat, and the 'non-piloting' student who occupied this seat could get useful experience in the exercises without actually flying the aircraft. The changeover of students

involved a bit of climbing about inside the canopy, but was quick and relatively easy. One had to match the students involved, otherwise inflated and deflated egoes could result if the 'piloting' student made a rubbish of an exercise virtually under the eyes of his partner – the 'observing' student in the third seat.

The extra seat was very useful when a staff pilot or other serviceman was being posted, and would easily accommodate luggage, fishing rods and guns, and even a small bicycle on occasion. I last flew the aircraft at Feltwell in January 1949, but flew it spasmodically over the next few months at CFS with trainee QFIs. The students were all mature pilots, and most of them thought the Prentice was some sort of bad joke.

A groundcrew viewpoint is provided by Eric Sharp, who worked on Prentices for a time with HQ flight at Cranwell in 1951:

The flight operated four Prentices, two Ansons and a Tiger Moth in the communications and general duties role for flying hour currency for some of the desk bound members of the staff.

The Prentice was a nice docile aeroplane which we used as a primary navigation trainer, the trainee sitting in the rear cockpit behind the dual side-by-side pilot seats. Between them was a whole host of radio and navigation equipment, consequently the plane was very underpowered with three up. The version of the Gipsy Queen fitted didn't seem to have half the poke of, say, that in the Devon. I remember cadging a lift with another lad to Manston one weekend, with a pilot who was going home for a couple of days – staff using the aircraft as personal transport was quite normal at weekends! We trundled off, the pilot being quite perplexed at needing the whole length of Cranwell South airfield to get in the air. What he didn't know was that as well as two passengers, the kit bag in the back had my motor bike engine in it!

Hunting Percival Provost

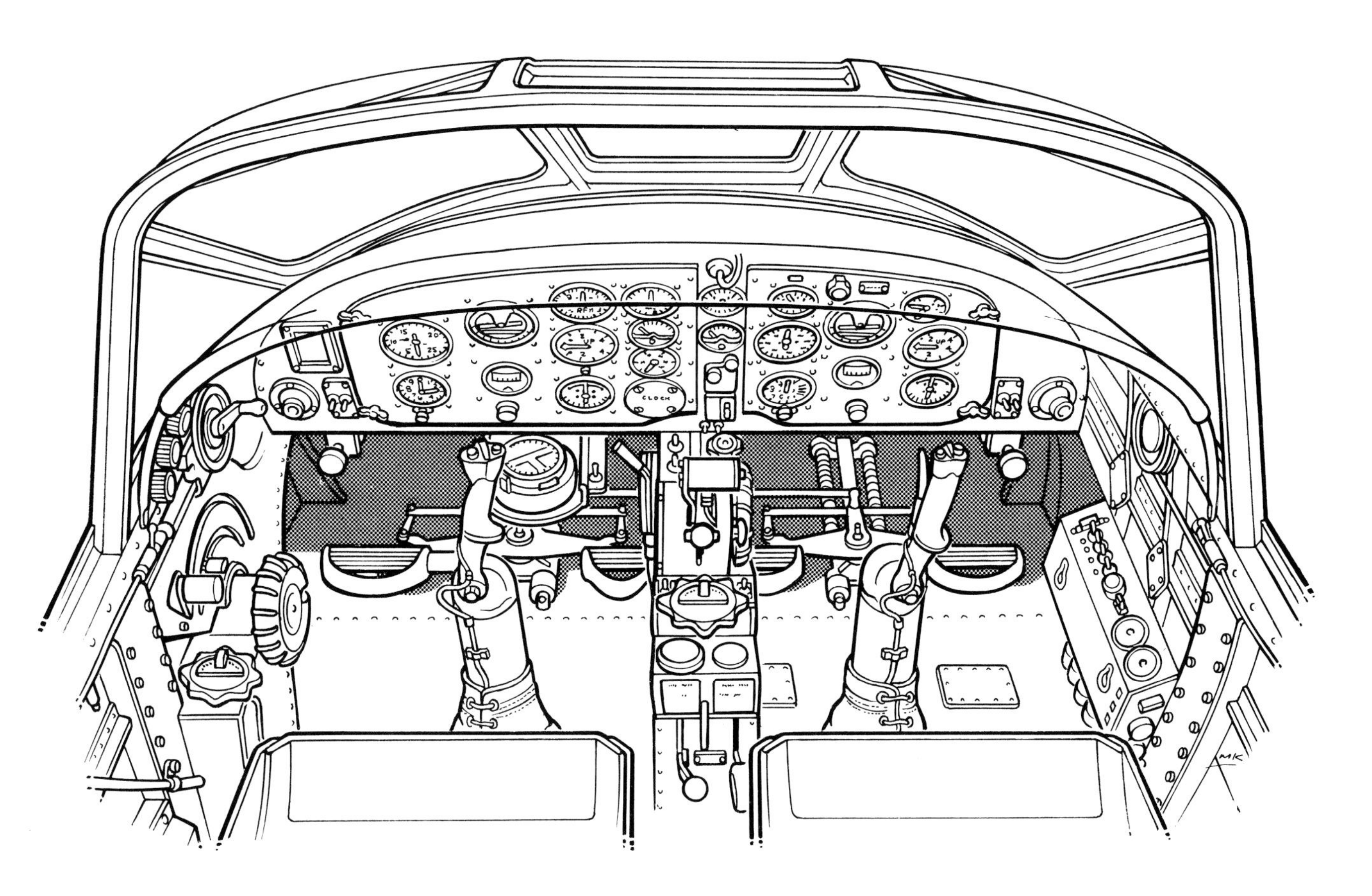

In July 1948 an Air Staff Operational Requirement (OR.257) was formulated for a new type of single-engined two-seater basic trainer with a fixed undercarriage and side-by-side seating in an enclosed cabin. It was initially intended for use worldwide, and therefore its construction would have to be sufficiently sturdy to be able to withstand long periods of exposure to all types of weather conditions.

Specification

Power plant:	*One 550 hp Alvis Leonides 126.*
Dimensions:	*Span 35 ft 2 in, length 28 ft 8 in, height 12 ft 2½ in, wing area 214 sq ft.*
Weights:	*Empty 3,350 lb, loaded 4,400 lb.*
Performance:	*Maximum speed 200 mph at sea level, cruising speed 162 mph, initial climb 2,200 ft/min, range 648 miles, endurance 4 hrs, service ceiling 25,000 ft.*

Speed was not seen as too important a factor, but it would have to be capable of maintaining a continuous cruising speed of not less than 110 knots. More crucial was its endurance, which was envisaged to be at least two hours, and somewhat more than this if it could be achieved without any detriment to performance.

The machine needed to be simple to fly. It would have to be highly manoeuvrable and fully aerobatic, yet at the same time free from vices or any peculiarities, the mastering of which might inculcate bad habits in the trainee pilots or call for special handling techniques. It was essential that adequate warning be given by the machine when it was approaching a stalled condition, either by elevator buffeting or judder. It would also be necessary for the design to allow a pupil to recover quickly and without much difficulty from any stage of a stall, spin or other unusual condition.

It was specified that the cockpit location and design had to provide the best possible all round view for instruction and pupil, both in the air and on the ground. The instrument layout was to be as simple as possible, with a standard blind flying panel located on the port side in front of the left-hand seat, which was to be used by the pupil. Immediately to the right of this panel were to be the engine instruments. The instructor, in the right-hand seat, was to be provided with an air speed indicator, an altimeter, and a turn and bank indicator.

The engine would have to be a tough design, if it was to survive the demanding conditions likely to be encountered in training in all kinds of climatics. Engine cooling arrangements would have to be such that it could run continuously at low altitudes and for lengthy periods of circuits and bumps without undue risk of suffering any damage. It must also be fully capable of coping with long periods of taxiing and waiting on the ground.

Of primary importance were ease of maintenance and servicing, with trouble-free operation. The design had to be simple in such respects, as it was highly likely in those early post-war days that a good proportion of the routine servicing would have to be carried out by semi-skilled personnel.

The requirement was developed and refined, eventually emerging in September 1948 as official specification T.16/48. Consideration was given to the firms likely to have the design capability for such a machine, and it was proposed at that stage that invitations to tender be sent out to Airspeed, Blackburn, Boulton Paul, General Aircraft, Percival, Scottish Aviation and Westland. De Havillands were also thought capable, but they were not included in this initial list as their design staff was considered to be already fully occupied with their DH.111 design, an intended three-engined tandem-wing development of the Vampire, though in the event this was later abandoned.

Meanwhile Percivals, one of those to whom invitations were to go, had anticipated events. Following their experience with the Prentice, they had

Percival Provost second prototype WE530, fitted with a Cheetah engine.

(Paddy Porter collection)

Percival Provost WG503, the Leonides-engined prototype, initially flown with the manufacturers marking G-23-1.

(Hunting photo)

seen the need for a more advanced design of *ab initio* trainer, and already embarked on a private venture design, designated the P.56. A mock-up had been constructed, and in fact on 20 October 1948 they had written to the Ministry of Supply proposing that one of their officials come to look at this, and also make a flight in their new Prince, which was then undergoing tests.

By the time invitations went out on 15 December, the list had been modified, and tenders were now sought from Boulton Paul, de Havilland, Handley Page (Reading), Percival and Westland. Handley Page (Reading) was a subsidiary of that firm, which had bought up the Miles company at Woodley. Probably more out of courtesy than real interest, copies of the specification were sent to a number of other firms, although even at that stage it was apparent that they were unlikely to receive much consideration. It was seen by the trade however, as a crucial contract, and tenders were received from no less than 15 firms, namely Air Service Training, Airtech, Auster, Blackburn and General, Boulton Paul, Chrislea, Elliots of Newbury, Fairey, Folland, Handley Page (Reading), Percival, Planet, Portsmouth Aviation, A.V. Roe and Westland. The Avro submission was of interest in that it would have saved design time by utilising Anson wings and an Athena tail.

An evaluation in April 1949 indicated that Percivals, thanks mainly to their private venture design work, were the only firm who could produce a prototype at a sufficiently early date for the project to be kept on schedule. Ideally, at least six months test flying was needed before placing a production order, if delivery of the first machine off the line was to meet the Air Staff requirement target date of mid-1952. It was possible that Handley Page (Reading) and Avros might also be able to meet that target, but this could only be achieved by placing a production order at the same time as that for the prototypes, a risk which was not easy to justify.

Despite the head start, some reservations were expressed about giving the contract to Percival. These centred round the difficulties they had previously encountered with the Prentice. They were considered to have been too weak aerodynamically, and also

The Handley-Page HPR-2, one of the main competitors for the Specification T.16/48 contract.

inexperienced on the design details that are necessary in order to make a sufficiently robust aircraft. Similar considerations virtually automatically ruled out most of the firms tendering to T.16/48.

Avro, not surprisingly in view of their history, were seen as being the best in experience, but their design team was already stretched with current work. Percivals, on the other hand, had the benefit of a private venture design which was well advanced, and had also taken to heart the lessons resulting from their earlier shortcomings, considerably strengthening their design staff. It was felt that the best course would be to take advantage of this and place an order with Percivals but, as a precaution, also order prototypes from one of the more experienced firms. Accordingly orders were placed on 21 July 1949 for three prototypes each from Percival and Handley Page.

The engine selected for the T.16/48 was the Armstrong-Siddeley Cheetah 17, in preference to the de Havilland Gipsy Queen 71 which had also been considered. The Air Staff remained adamant on this point, even though the new Alvis Leonides engine would also be available. They took the view that although the latter was a more modern design, the Cheetah had the advantage of reliability, it had a long life between overhauls, and spares for it were readily available.

At a progress meeting in July 1950, however, the Leonides option was again raised, and it was then decided that the second prototype of each design would now have this fitted. It was stressed at this meeting that the winner of the competition would have to be produced at the earliest possible date, the design being initially required at that time for replacement of ageing Tiger Moths with the RAF in Southern Rhodesia.

Meanwhile prototypes of both machines had flown, the P.56 in February 1950 and the HPR.2, as the other design had become, two months later. Tests of each had taken place at the Aeroplane and Armament Experimental Establishment, Boscombe Down, and the P.56 was markedly superior. Its handling trials were excellent, the design requirements were fully met, and no major critcisms had been made by the test pilots. The Handley Page design proved much less satisfactory, the trials revealing that it lacked the basic handling qualities essential in this class of training aircraft, and several months of redesign work would be necessary to make it acceptable. Nevertheless, one of each machine was sent to No. 3 Flying Training School at Feltwell for comparative trials.

Just before Christmas 1950, Percivals sought authority to fit a modified fin with dorsal and rudder mass balance, etc. The Handley Page design was by now in deep trouble, however, and the third machine had already been cancelled. The view from the rear quarter was poor. Care had to be taken to avoid the aircraft nosing over when the brakes were applied, particularly when solo. It had a marked tendency for self-stalling when the flaps were down and the power on, consequently requiring a good measure of speed when approaching to land. Even worse, deficiencies in the spinning characteristics were such that this manoeuvre was by then prohibited until further order. Fitting WE496, the first prototype, with a modified fin and rudder, which increased the rudder area, brought some improvement, but the results were still not acceptable.

Above:
Percival Provost T.1 XF685 '20' of the Empire Test Pilots School at Farnborough in 1957.
(RAF Museum Photo)

Below:
Percival Provost T.1 WV534 'MM' of No 22 Flying Training School at Syerston in July 1954.
(Author)

Time was by now pressing, and a final meeting at the end of January came to what by then was virtually a foregone conclusion. From an engineering viewpoint, the designs were considered to have equal merit. It was decided, however, that the P.56 had far superior flying qualities, irrespective of their respective spinning characteristics. The Handley Page design would, in any event, be more expensive to produce. The Ministry of Supply therefore recommended the Percival design to the Air Ministry, the name Provost being later adopted.

An initial order for 200 Leonides-engined machines was placed in May 1951, and WV418, the first machine off the line, was ready by 31 January 1953, only about six months behind the target date set by the Air Staff, though by then the RAF no longer needed any for use in Southern Rhodesia. The first few machines were reserved for trials purposes of various kinds, but on 28 May WV432 was delivered to the Central Flying School at Little Rissington, and the Provost thus became the last piston-engined basic training aircraft to enter unit service with the RAF.

Its introduction enabled the RAF to bring in a new Provost/Vampire training scheme to supersede the Prentice/Harvard system, which was no longer appropriate for pilots going to jet-equipped squadrons. As a consequence the schools were gradually regrouped, some being equipped entirely with Provosts and some with only Vampires.

As production continued, deliveries were made to No. 6 Flying Training School at Ternhill, commencing with WV426 on 1 July, being followed by 22 FTS at Syerston which received its first four machines, WV501-504, all on 19 November, building up within six months to a strength of 50. Subsequent deliveries were made from a second order for 55 aircraft, with 3 FTS at Feltwell getting its first aircraft on 23 September, followed by the RAF College at Cranwell on 19 October. Two final orders were placed, for 16 and 66 aircraft respectively, but the only other unit to receive the Provost in quantity was 2 FTS at Hullavington in May 1954, although a number were delivered in 1958 to both the Central Navigation and Control School at Shawbury and the RAF Flying College at Manby. Small numbers were flown by various other units, including several University Air Squadrons.

A number of Provosts went overseas. An unarmed version was designated the T.51, armed conversions of the T.1 were called T.52s, whilst new builds of armed aircraft were T.53s. Overseas orders went to Burma, Eire, Iraq, Malaya, Southern Rhodesia and Sudan.

In service, the Provost had the advantage over the Prentice of much higher performance. It was particularly fine in aerobatics, with excellent manoeuvrability and a rate of roll exceeding 90 degrees per second. Adjustable amber screens were fitted for simulating blind flying instruction.

Squadron Leader Don Brittain flew Provosts many times:

While in Malaya I was flying in a Provost with a big Indian Sikh who messed up a landing. He had partial power on, not enough to climb away but too much to stay down – he forgot all his English and wouldn't respond when I tried to take control. The control tower was getting close, and as he had frozen in the controls there was little I could do. So I hit him to make him let go, and I just cleared the tower. Had it not been side-by-side I would have been dead.!

I found the piston-Provost a very good trainer. On a trial I once flew one up to its absolute ceiling of 21,500 feet, fitted with oxygen of course, to see if it would be worthwhile fitting oxygen generally so as to get above the weather – it wasn't and none was fitted.

A colleague of mine, while doing circuits at Chetwynd Relief Landing Ground, had a *very* heavy landing – he took control and asked the student if there was any sign of damage. 'Wing's a bit wrinkled,' came the reply. After landing and shutdown, he walked around to have a look. The main spar had sheared – the wing had moved up about one inch and was only being held on by the skin!

Another time we learnt a student had got an engine failure and was about to force land. Naturally, being ghouls, we ran out just in time to see him apply 90 degrees of bank near the ground to change to another runway. The aircraft stalled, flicked and crashed wings level – the undercarriage broke off, as did the wings which went up and clapped over the cockpit. As they started to fall to earth the pilot was out and running. Afterwards he said he was worried about being burnt alive as he was trapped in the cockpit and couldn't get out. He wouldn't believe us that he was actually out and running before the wings had hit the ground!

Another instructor friend did a heavy landing at South Cerney, and as he overshot was surprised to see a tyre roll away from him – it was his own which had broken off. Yes, in case you are wondering – he did manage a successful one wheel landing.

I once had a student who on an IF [instrument] take-off, just after applying full power, applied full right rudder. I immediately took control, but not until I'd left the runway and gone around the control caravan – God knows what went through the controller's mind. On the next IF trip I was ready for him, and, yes, he started to do it again, but my size 9 boot prevented it. Why did he do it? He didn't know – perhaps a death wish.

When I was in the CFS course, I had finished the sorties but hadn't enough hours, so I was sent off with another trainee instructor to fly for 1½ hours to get a tick on the board. Where shall we go? I know, let's go down to Salisbury Plain to look at the badge carvings there – good idea. Off we went, lovely day, when suddenly flak-like smoke puffs appeared. What's that, I asked – don't know, came the answer – well never mind, nice sight seeing the badges. Let's go home – those funny smoke puffs again. It wasn't until

Facing page:
Percival Provost T.1 XF836 'JG' of the RAF College, Cranwell.

(MAP photo)

eleven years later, when instructing at Syerston, that I found out what the smoke puffs were – a warning that you were in a danger area – clear off sharp. Happy days!

Another pilot to train on Provosts was Chris Ashworth:

My first contact with the piston-engine Provost was at South Cerney in January 1955. I was at the RAF's Central Flying School (Basic) on the first stage of learning to become a flying instructor.

Percival Provost T.1 visiting a strangely deserted HMS Heron.

(Brian Lowe)

First impressions were of an aircraft of workmanlike appearance, neat and compact despite its side-by-side seating. Parked on the grass outside the flight hut it looked ready and eager, and so it proved for I had no reason to revise my initial reaction during the following weeks.

The Leonides engine started easily following the characteristic 'crack' of the cartridge starter, and the aircraft

handled well on the ground – always a good start. In the air the controls were well co-ordinated and crisp and there was plenty of power. The aircraft had good stalling characteristics, was stable enough for accurate instrument flying and yet capable of precise aerobatics and circuit flying – all 'plus' points in a basic trainer.

Of course the Provost did have faults. The position of the oil cooler shutter had to be watched carefully to maintain temperatures in limits, the spinning characteristics were rather erratic and, perhaps worst of all, fuel fumes in the cockpit were a problem during and after aerobatics, making many *ab initio* students feel very sick – with consequent loss of interest!

Overall, the Provost was a delight to fly, a first-class trainer in nearly all respects. It was difficult to believe that it was from the same stable as the Prentice!

Robin Brown flew Provosts on a CFS course late in his career:

I flew the Provost in August and September 1957, when I came back from RAF Germany. I was posted to the Central Flying School at Little Rissington, and flew something over 100 hours on Provosts. Once again these had side-by-side seating like the Prentice.

The only really frightening thing that happened to me during this time was when I was sent off solo one day to do spinning and aerobatics. I was upside down with negative-g when suddenly the parachute which was in the unoccupied right-hand (instructor's) seat floated up and started drifting around the cockpit. This was a very dicey situation because, first of all, you have to recover from the manoeuvre and, secondly, you have to grab the parachute and make sure it doesn't do something stupid like sailing out of the window, or worse, jam the controls (which was a very real possibility) and, thirdly, you have got to get it back into the bucket part of the seat whence it came. It was quite a dangerous few minutes, and I was very cross with myself for being so idle as not to have done my pre-flight checks properly.

When the aircraft was due to fly solo it was important to ensure that the harness in the unoccupied seat was connected and the straps pulled tight. If I had done this the lap straps would have prevented the parachute from going walkies by itself.

The Provost was a splendid little aircraft, with a nice wide undercarriage and the big radial engine that reminded me of the Fw 190. I liked it. My opinion of its potentialities went up when, after I had finished at CFS, I was posted to the Flying College at Manby and I saw in the hangar one day two Provosts being modified to go to a Middle Eastern country, having been transformed into very nice operational ground attack aircraft, by the addition of camouflage, machine guns in the wings, bomb racks, extra fuel and so on.

Robin goes on to give a fascinating insight in to his attitude to the CFS at that time:

There were two alternatives once you got your wings. You either went straight to the Central Flying School (even before doing jet conversion), in which case you were funnelled into the CFS empire and became branded as a QFI (Qualified Flying Instructor) for the rest of your life, or you went to a squadron, and became what I regarded as a normal pilot. Eventually, though, the CFS got you, but this might not be until you had done several tours on various types of aircraft, as in my case. I think it's correct to say that

Percival Provost T.1 XF541 'PG' of No 6 Flying Training School at Ternhill.

(MAP photo)

Cockpit of Percival Provost T.1 'PF' of the Central Flying School at Little Rissington in 1957.
(Robin Brown)

your career prospects were somewhat affected if you had never been to the CFS.

I was posted back to UK after having spent five or six very happy years in Germany boring holes in the sky, and I was sent to Little Rissington for the CFS instructor's course. However, I didn't get on with them very well. It was not what I wanted to do at all. I had always thought that QFI's were an odd lot, not quite as other folk, so to speak! Even if you managed to escape from the dreaded Flying Training Command and got back on a squadron you were always stuck with the QFI label and given the job of instrument flying rating – half your flying would be on two-seaters. I decided it wasn't for me.

As a trainee instructor one returned to basics. You went back into the classroom at CFS and relearned in far greater detail everything you had done on your 'wings' course. I imagine that CFS had the task of not only teaching you to teach, but also remedying the gaps in your knowledge that came from the rather elementary tuition at Flying Training Schools in the early fifties. This was caused by so many pilots being pushed through at the time of the Korean War. Although I'm glad I qualified that way – I don't think I would have been bright enough to succeed had I gone through Cranwell (I was/am hopeless at maths for a start).

So, when you went back to CFS you were really being put through the mill again, and being groomed for a far higher standard. It was like going back to school for the third time. It bored me to a certain extent, although I was fascinated by the lessons of flying instructional techniques.

Moreover I wasn't very impressed by the attitudes at CFS. I was sad that I failed the course, but glad in certain respects, even though it was the first time I had failed a flying course. The course was in two parts. First you had two months basic training flying piston Provosts, and then you were given instruction on various other types of aircraft. Finally you concentrated on the machine on which you would be instructing, either basic or advanced, whatever CFS thought you best fitted for.

After passing out at CFS, you would probably be sent to an FTS, and after a couple of tours you might manage to get back on a squadron. If you were a brilliant pupil you might end up instructing at CFS.

Here I think I ought to admit that my attitude to CFS is perhaps curious, but also natural. I admired a lot that went on at CFS, and I appreciated that the instructors were probably the best in the world, but, having failed the course, I tend to be critical and even laugh at CFS's attitudes. CFS had, and I suppose still has, tremendous kudos. It was obviously a show place, the station was immaculate. Students came from all over the world, particularly the 'emerging' nations who were building their brand new air forces from scratch. As well as being rather a bind it was, in a way, quite an honour to be chosen to go to CFS (not everyone even got that far).

The instructional blocks where, for instance, you learnt about aero engines, were splendid, big demonstration rooms where beautifully sectioned engines were on display. The instructors here were NCOs, and they, too, had been chosen for their knowledge and instructional skills. Lectures were always supported by films, colour slides, or whatever 'aid to instruction' was necessary.

It was a very efficiently run place, but for various reasons I didn't like it – it was not my cup of tea. It was something to do with the attitudes of the instructors, who seemed to think they were God's Gift to the Air Force. When you came back from an operational command like 2nd TAF where you didn't do things 'by the book', the niggling attention to detail was irritating. It was a standing joke in

Germany that the only take-off checks you needed were 'fuel and noise', you checked you had some fuel and if there was some noise from the engines you were all right! You went off and did hairy things in those days. On 79 Squadron you low-flew whenever you wanted, the lower the better. One did extraordinary scramble take-offs, or cobbled together huge 'Balbos' of aircraft, twenty or thirty from different squadrons and wings, to go and stir up the Americans for a fabulous dog fight! Things that would turn people's hair white these days, I fear. Then suddenly you went back to a very precise way of flying that was, unfortunately, the shape of things to come.

The chop rate in those days was still horrendous, five from 79 Squadron in the two and a half years I was on it. Admittedly it was something you had grown up with and took for granted in the rather blasé fashion of those days. When I was converting on to jets at Full Sutton I kept a page in my scrap book simply for newspaper cuttings reporting fatal crashes – in a very short time it was almost full. Many had been my friends. In the crewrooms in those days there were always course photographs stuck up so you knew who was who. It was customary, as someone killed himself, to draw a little halo over his head – grim humour! I once saw a 'bone dome' that belonged to a pilot on a Sabre squadron with 'Dig here for Charlie' written across the top.

Obviously it was slowly realised that this wastage of manpower had to be stopped, and this is where CFS came in. It was a return to reality after the post-war years, making people realise the limitations in themselves and their aircraft. People were brought to understand they had to fly in a more responsible and considered way. Nowadays, the chop rate is virtually nil, which proves the changes were right, but it has taken away much of the joy of flying. It was wonderful to be a pilot in the fifties – you were always doing things to prove you could do them, like flying under bridges or high tension wires. In one 2nd TAF exercise, for instance, word went round that if you flew down the autobahn you should keep to the right – so as to miss anyone coming the other way!

Kev Darling, now a Corporal A/T/A, first met the Provost at Halton:

When I first joined the RAF, the piston Provost was the main training aid at Halton. It was later replaced by the Hunter and the Jet Provost T.4, both of which are in turn being replaced by the Jaguar.

The sight of so many piston Provosts in various states of disassembly and reassembly was quite daunting, but as time wore on we became used to it. After our initial training, we moved to the airfield at Halton where we had to learn how to marshal a Provost. This particular beastie was driven by a pilot whose main aim seemed to be to induce in us trainees a respect for the turning propeller. He certainly succeeded; in fact, the result bordered on abject fear, as he appeared to us to ignore the marshallers' signals and chase the poor unfortunate across and around the airfield. It was not unknown for the airman to make a break for the hangar and go and hide there. He certainly kept us fit though!

My memory is that, like its jet-powered successor, the piston Provost's flying controls were operated by cables, control being entirely manually assisted by balance tabs on all five surfaces. Trimming assistance was provided by trim tabs at the ailerons and elevators, possibly the port aileron and starboard elevator as in their jet-powered cousins.

The hydraulic systems on the piston Provost were extremely simple, only being required for the brakes and the flaps. To ensure adequate reserved hydraulic pressure for engine-off brake and flap usage, accumulators were fitted in the hydraulic circuit. The accumulators were located in the rear cabin. Hydraulic power whilst flying was provided by an engine driven pump.

The aircraft electrical power supplies were 24-volt with external starting from trolley. Internal power was provided by a 24-volt generator, which also ran the hydraulic pump. Emergency power was available from 24-volt emergency batteries located in the port and starboard sides of the fuselage which were capable of being fully aerobatic with overflow drains fitted, as acid does nasty things to aluminium.

The fuel system comprised wing bags made of fuel resistant rubber compound, each fitted with a fuel contents sensor to provide both port and starboard totals plus an overall total. To ensure aerobatic capability, the fuel system would have incorporated a fuel booster pump, in addition to the normal item and a recuperator. A recuperator is a container with a rubber diaphragm fitted in the middle, on one side of which is a low pressure air supply of 5–6 psi, and on the other is maintained a small amount of fuel which is forced to the engine by the air pressure when the aircraft is inverted. Incidentally, the reason many aircraft have bag tanks is the habit that integral tanks (which are sealed portions of airframe) have of leaking – witness the Buccaneer and Lightning.

The Provost airframe was of standard all-metal stressed-skin construction, mainly single skin except for the wings which were of double skin construction to provide a smooth surface and also to increase structural integrity. Airframe systems consisted of windscreen de-icing, windscreen/canopy de-misting and a fairly crude (by today's standards) air conditioning system. Also fitted were windscreen wipers for use in inclement weather.

Overall, therefore, in comparison with the Jet Provost, the piston Provost was a much simpler aircraft to maintain, with those experienced on the latter able to transfer their skills to the former.

Boulton Paul Balliol

Around the end of the Second World War, Air Ministry Specification T.7/45 was issued for a three-seat advanced trainer to be powered by a turboprop engine. This attracted a number of entries, among them the Avro 701, Blackburn B.52, Boulton Paul P.108 and Miles M.70. The Avro and Boulton Paul entries were both accepted initially, and each firm was authorised to construct four prototypes, later cut back to three.

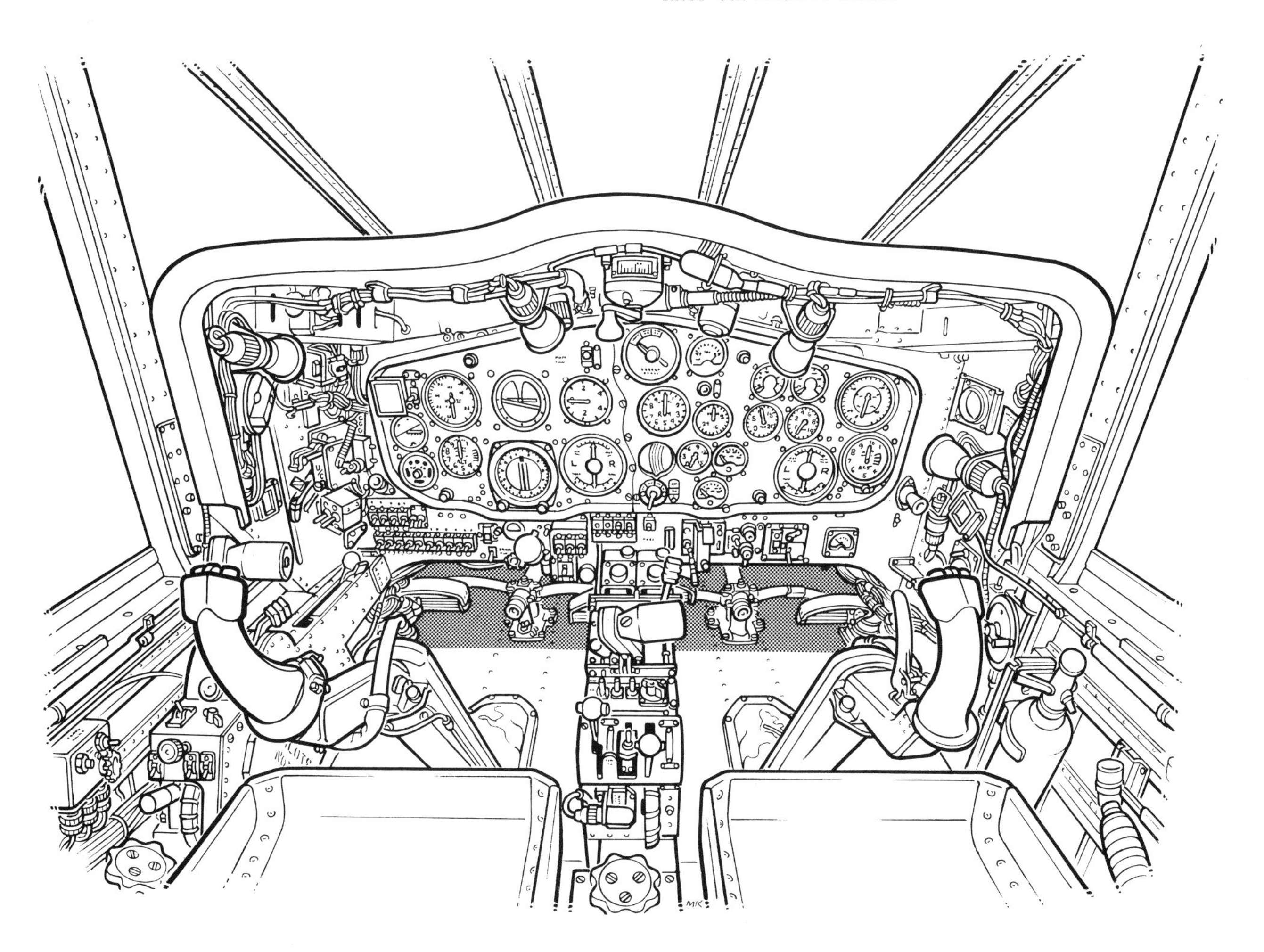

Specification (Balliol T.2)

Power plant:	*One 1,245 hp Rolls-Royce Merlin 35.*
Dimensions:	*Span 39 ft 4 in, length 35 ft 1½ in, height 12 ft 6 in, wing area 250 sq ft.*
Weights:	*Empty 6,730 lb, loaded 8,410 lb.*
Performance:	*Maximum speed 288 mph at 9,000 ft, cruising speed 220 mph, initial climb 1,790 ft/min, range 670 miles, endurance 3 hrs, service ceiling 32,500 ft.*

Such was the need seen for this new aircraft that in October 1946, before any of the prototypes could fly, the two firms were each asked to produce 20 pre-production aircraft under Specification 29/46P. Three months later this order was modified, and the Specification reissued in respect only of the Boulton Paul entry, now named the Balliol T.1. A new Specification, 47/46P, was issued to cover the Avro entry, which became the Athena T.1.

The original proposal had been for both types of aircraft to be fitted with the Rolls-Royce Dart, but at the end of 1946 it was decided to change this to the Armstrong-Siddeley Mamba. As this was not yet available in sufficient numbers, the first Balliol prototype flew in May 1947 with a conventional Bristol Mercury radial engine. On 24 March 1948, however, it became the first aircraft in the world to fly with a single turboprop engine, having in the meantime been refitted with a Mamba. Supplies of these had now become available, and the other two Balliol prototypes were similarly fitted. The Athena was longer in appearing, and the first prototype did not fly until June 1948, with a Mamba engine, but the next two prototypes reverted to the originally proposed Dart.

In the meantime, however, official interest in the turboprop concept had waned. Consequently a new Specification (T.14/47) had been issued in mid-1947 for modified versions of each design, to be conventional two-seat trainers fitted with Rolls-Royce Merlins, and the pre-production aircraft were to be completed to this formula, being redesignated Athena T.2 and Balliol T.2. In addition, four prototype T.2s were ordered from each firm, the first Boulton Paul machine flying in July 1948, and its Avro counterpart three weeks later.

By early 1950 the requirement was for a single-engined monoplane for advanced flying training leading up to operational training on both single-engined and multi-engined aircraft. It was to be of robust all-metal construction with modern handling characteristics, and was to be used either during the day or at night for dual flying instruction, including aerobatics. Advanced pilot training needs included long cross-country flights, dual front gun training and dual low-level, glide and dive bombing training.

Its construction was to be such that in the event of a wheels-up landing, the shock of impact would be taken by crushing the underpart of the body, which had to be capable of protecting the rest of the aircraft, so that the damaged parts could be easily repairable. The brakes had to be capable of standing up to repeated landings and long periods of taxiing.

Testing at Boscombe Down had led to a number of changes in the design of both machines, including an altered tailplane incidence in the Balliol and a new fin and rudder on the Athena. When competitively tested at the Central Flying School, the Balliol was considered crisper than the Athena, and allowed the student to exploit his ability better. It was considered that this machine would allow greater precision to be inculcated in the pilot. The Athena suffered from too high a weathercock stability, had less effective ailerons, and heavy foot loads were required which made aerobatics slovenly.

Boscombe Down agreed with these criticisms, and also made the point that in their view the longitudinal stability of the Athena was too great at high speeds, and out-of-trim stick forces were too high. Both machines met the night flying requirements, though the CFS preferred the Balliol. The spin on both types could be very unpleasant after the second turn, but here again the CFS preferred the Balliol – recovery was straightforward in both cases. From the engineering point of view there was little difference to choose between the two machines in normal servicing. The Athena, however, required one-third more man-hours than the Balliol. In addition, the Athena suffered greater tyre wear, and required more man-hours for each change. The overall conclusion was that the Athena was the better machine from the purely engineering point of view, but the Balliol had the advantage when it came to ease of servicing.

Boulton Paul Balliol P.109 prototype with Bristol Mercury engine at Radlett.

(Author's collection)

An engineering appraisal carried out at Boscombe Down on the second prototype Balliol T.2 (VW898) during July and August 1949 reported favourably on a number of features. Many of the components were interchangeable between port and starboard, there were built-in jacking and slinging points, and good defuelling arrangements. The undercarriage was designed to lower and lock by gravity, and there was a simple mechanical indicator to show that the wheels had locked down. Special attention had been given to the design of the undercarriage legs, so that strut bending would be minimal and tyre wear would not be a great problem. Whilst the undercarriage mechanism was satisfactory it would, however, require careful attention during servicing.

Above:
Avro Athena prototype VM125, unsuccessful contender for the advance trainer requirement.
(Author's collection)

Below:
The Balliol fitted, as originally specified, with the Armstrong Siddeley Mamba.

The machine was not entirely without criticism. In most areas there was ample access for inspection, but difficulties could be encountered in reaching the starter motor and various components behind the engine. During 100 hours of intensive flying, however, the only major defect encountered was a failure of the fuselage frame to take wheel loads, but this was not seen as a great problem, since it would be a relatively simple matter to modify the structure to overcome the weakness.

The general assessment of this machine was that it was pleasant to fly, but its pilot would be required to exercise a fair degree of skill, accuracy and concentration. It ought therefore to make a good training aircraft.

By the time a decision came to be made in February 1950, it was fairly obvious which way it would go. Despite the effort involved in winning the contract, however, the Balliol was destined not to fulfil its promise. An initial order for 500 machines had been envisaged under Specification T.14/47 Issue 2, but economy prevailed, and when the contract was placed it was actually for 100 Balliol T.2's under Specification T.14/47 Issue 3. Additional orders were placed in January 1951 for 138 machines to be built by the parent company, and a further 120 under sub-contract by Blackburns.

These had no sooner been placed, however, than there was a change in official thinking, it being decided that the piston-engine was outmoded for advance training, and would give way to the jet engine. The second Boulton Paul order was consequently cut back to only 40 machines, and the Blackburn order was reduced to 30. Five further replacement machines were later ordered, bringing total production up to 175 aircraft, but only one Flying Training School ever received them, this being 7 FTS at Cottesmore, though quite a number were used by other units, such as the RAF College at Cranwell and No 238 Operational Conversion Unit at Colerne. The Athenas saw little service, being mainly used by the RAF Flying College, before they were withdrawn.

The Royal Navy also had a requirement for a piston-engined trainer around this time, with deck-landing capabilities, and Specification N.102D was accordingly issued on 26 August 1950. Two pre-production Balliols were fitted with arrester hooks for trials in HMS *Illustrious,* a third such machine (VR599) being completed as the true prototype Sea Balliol T.21, having its maiden flight on 23 October 1952. This satisfied the requirement, and an order for 20 machines following, ten more being procured later. Balliols were largely withdrawn from service in 1956 and Sea Balliols in 1959.

In December 1949, Squadron Leader Stan Greenhow was one of several staff QFIs at CFS invited to fly both the Balliol and Athena, and to give their opinions as to which was the better of the two aircraft for subsequent use as a trainer to replace the ageing Harvard:

There was little to chose between them. They were solid, roomy and docile, and easy to fly. Moreover, the instructor sat beside the student and could observe checks and points of handling which were difficult to be aware of behind the student as in the Tiger Moth and Harvard. Lookout was good, climb, glide, circuits and landings, medium and steep turns were all good, and steep turn and aerobatics and spins were all that one could wish for from a trainer aircraft. The landings were particularly easy and very solid, with little tendency to bounce even on a tarmac, and my students appeared to like them both. Along with many of my fellow QFIs, I plumped for the Athena – of course it was the Balliol which eventually made its way into the flying training world, and the Athena disappeared into the mists.

Incidentally, I remember that both the Athena and Balliol suffered from the drawback of having a fairly flat windscreen which tended to mist over in fog and rain. I cannot remember if it iced over under freezing conditions.

It is now almost 40 years since I flew these types, and although clear recollection of handling characteristics is a bit difficult, I enjoy a contented feeling when I think of the Athena and Balliol, so they must have been all right.

Ray Hanna, a former Red Arrows leader, interviewed at Duxford, recalls of the type:

I wasn't instructed in the Balliol, but I remember it as being very noisy and a bit rattly. I had never flown in a Merlin-engined aeroplane before, and if I remember rightly the engine was derated, so one was immediately aware of lots of noise and rattles and bangs and pops and things, and as I recall worse than we have seen and heard here today with the Spitfire and the Mustang.

I only had two trips in it, but it was a very nice aeroplane. From what I have heard from students that flew in them, it was maybe a little bit over the top for some of them. Cranwell and Cottesmore had them for people who were going from Prentices to Balliols as opposed to Prentices to Harvards. They had air brakes fitted to teach people advanced flying before going on to aeroplanes such as Meteors and Hunters, and therefore accustom them to what was coming in the future. I think it was really a bit unnecessary. It had a relatively high wing loading.

From the instructor's point of view, I'm sure it was delightful, because it had a superb field of view. Sitting alongside the student, you could see exactly what was going on. I know they had one or two accidents, though, with students overshooting the runway because they had messed up the approach or whatever, giving it full power and going round the propeller and hitting the ground – the dreaded torque stall. I think the Balliol was perhaps a little bit overpowered for students at that stage in training. I've said for many years, though, that we would love to get our hands on one, to have here at Duxford, as it would be an ideal trainer for our sort of fun.

I do recall that around 1952 or 1953, when we were out in Germany on fighter reconnaissance in Meteors, three or four Balliols being sent out from one of the establishments for

ground attack trials. The Air Staff looked at it quite seriously, but obviously it didn't come off.

Commander Maurice Tibby had experience on both the Balliol and the Sea Balliol, the latter as CO of No 727 Squadron:

I first encountered the aircraft when I was a staff instructor at the Central Flying School, Little Rissington in the early months of 1950. That establishment was asked to carry out the comparative service trials between the Balliol and the Athena. I flew them both at the time, and seem to recall that they were extremely similar – rather like two peas in a pod. In fact the Athena seemed to be a more docile performer, and one can only presume that the Balliol got the vote for political or other reasons. At the time it was meant to herald a new era of side-by-side training to follow on from the piston Prentice, but it never seemed to catch on and only a few were ordered. Perhaps they were overtaken by the jet era.

When 727 Squadron recommissioned at Brawdy in January 1956, it was primarily tasked with providing air experience for Dartmouth Cadets which was a compulsory part of their training. We were equipped with Balliols for piston flying, Vampires for jet flying and Sea Princes for navigation, and therefore well placed to show a broad view of naval aviation.

The Balliol was a robust aeroplane and adequately powered by its Rolls-Royce Merlin. With its wide undercarriage it was not difficult to handle during take-off and landing, but was lively enough to ensure concentration during these key phases. In the air it was a versatile performer although somewhat unexciting; it was cleared for all aerobatic manoeuvres and spinning, and was flown both by day and by night. The cockpit was quite roomy with particularly good all-round visibility. We were not allowed to deck land them and the Balliols in 727 were not cleared for this; had they been so then this would not have presented any problems. In summary it was a strong, useful all-round trainer with no particular vices and much to commend it.

I suspect that at some time or other it was intended that the Balliol would be fitted with a gun and/or bomb sight for armament training – there was plenty of room for one – but the 727 aircraft were not so fitted. At the time (1958), the front-line squadrons used to carry out a concentrated period of training called a Front-Line Armament Practice School (FLAPS) when they concentrated entirely on various bombing/rocketing firing practices. During that year in 727 we had a three-week period without any Dartmouth Cadets, and I instituted our own Second-Line series of firing exercises (SLAPS). Without any gunsights we used a chinagraph pencil on the windscreen; the position had to be adjusted for each pilot, and with this basic device (+) we managed to achieve a similar standard to front-line squadrons.

It was also another way of demonstrating the capability of the Balliol since rocket firing and bombing gave us no serious logistic problems. I really cannot think of any other unusual attributes, it was a very versatile aeroplane and would undoubtedly have acquitted itself well if it had been more fully adopted.

Chris Ashworth recalls:

My acquaintance with the Balliol was comparatively short-lived and straightforward, for I neither trained nor instructed on this impressively bulky and powerful aircraft. The year was 1957 and the place White Waltham, the aircraft belonging to the Home Command Communications Squadron.

Perhaps it was the Balliol's angular wings, the way it sat on its wide track undercarriage, its four-bladed propeller, or more likely a combination of all three, that gave it the aggressive look which must have stretched the confidence of most pupils to the limit. In fact, despite tales of torque stalls and a vicious spin, it flew quite nicely if treated with respect.

The starting drill for the Merlin 35 was typical of the time and not unduly complicated. Once it was going, engine temperature control was normally automatic, which was a great boon though I was suspicious of it because the similar Griffon engine controls on Shackletons invariably leaked in 'Auto'. My concern was unfounded – they never gave any trouble on the Balliol.

The large nose completely obscured the view ahead whilst taxiing, so it was back to a Chipmunk-style 'weave', but the take-off was impressive, especially on White Waltham's uneven turf, a lot of rudder being needed to keep straight. The famous Waltham 'bump' threw the aircraft into the air in a most disconcerting fashion. This would not be a problem experienced by pupils at Cottesmore and Cranwell, but the incredible amount of trimming required once in the air undoubtedly was – the Balliol being the only aircraft I have come across on which aileron, elevator and rudder had to be retrimmed for every speed or power change. That must have been a nightmare for both pupil and instructor – though any of the former who mastered it would never be at a loss in any other aircraft.

Once airborne and trimmed, the Balliol was pleasant enough. Cross-country flying was great, economical cruise being about 180 knots which meant that at 2,000 feet or so the countryside really slipped past at a useful rate. Rudder and aileron controls were good, but I recall the aircraft as heavy on the elevators. I never pretended to be the world's ace at aerobatics but I could loop most aeroplanes pretty well. Not so the Balliol – and as for stall turns they were a disaster! At least the one I tried was, for instead of the aircraft gently rotating about its axis when vertical it refused to yaw, the propeller stopped turning and I 'hammer-headed' out of it. The ground began to look quite close as I pulled out of the ensuing dive and I only regained my composure when the engine spluttered into life again.

Circuits were great fun – the chance for frustrated would-be Spitfire pilots to try the famous curved approach. Once lined-up and in the 'round-out' the wide track undercarriage took charge and a gentle three-pointer was easy.

Flying the Balliol was an interesting experience, but I would not have liked to do my advanced training on it – thank the Lord for the good old Harvard!

Flight Lieutenant Peter Bouch, lately of the Battle of Britain Memorial Flight, also flew the Balliol:

I got about 50 hours in the Balliol and found it to be an

excellent advanced trainer, with a high-power Merlin 35 (the same engines now in use in the Hurricanes of the BBMF!), nicely balanced controls, a nice wide track undercarriage and a lockable tailwheel. These gave it predictable landing and ground handling characteristics, but it was demanding enough to be considered quite a handful. In fact there were several fatal accidents, most of which I seem to remember being put down to torque stalling on the approach or overshoot – torque stall basically meant the airframe revolving around the engine! This was one of the monthly practice requirements (at height I hasten to add!) and would occur if you got the speed low (approaching the stall), held the stick back and fully opened the throttle! It would not work if you eased the stick forward as the throttle was opened, so if it was the cause of the accidents then they were caused by either ignorance or poor instruction!

I liked the Balliol – there is something about having a Merlin in front of you – BBMF would jump at one for their trainer – but unfortunately there are none about.

Boulton Paul Balliol VW899, the third prototype T.2, tested at the Aeroplane and Armament Experimental Establishment, Boscombe Down.

(Author's collection)

Another Balliol trainee was Peter Raeburn:

I trained on the Balliol in 1955 at RAF Cranwell. Surprisingly it had only a limited span as an advanced trainer, replacing the long-lived American Harvard.

Initial training was on the Chipmunk, and the change to a more potent, heavier aircraft seemed most marked, especially as the Balliol was powered by the Merlin, albeit derated to a much reduced boost. Under normal circum-

Boulton Paul Balliol T.2 WG141 'N' of No 238 Operational Conversion Unit being serviced at North Luffenham around 1947.

(Eric Sharp)

Boulton Paul Balliol T.2 WN516 'CC' of the RAF College at Cranwell around 1955.
(Wing Cdr Robert Sage)

stances the aircraft was fun to fly, a really stable, manoeuvrable platform and an excellent introduction to advanced flying training. That being said, however, there are two particular points I will never forget. First, having come from the docile Chipmunk, which was virtually a powered glider, the Balliol's high rate of descent when gliding for practice forced landings etc, led to the usual description that 'it flies like a brick-built shithouse'!

A more alarming trait, with more disastrous potential and which was practiced at height to familiarise pilots with the problem, was the torque stall. When full power was abruptly applied from low revs at low speeds near a stalling configuration, the aircraft tried to revolve around the prop! So much power was applied, the prop could not absorb it fully. Consequently the excess torque started to affect the aircraft itself and it started to revolve. This was not dangerous at height, but when overshooting from a missed/bad approach to landing, ie close to the ground, in a near stalling configuration when full power application from near idling is paramount, problems could and in fact did occur. One student found himself cartwheeling down the runway wingtip first, luckily emerging unhurt from the wreckage.

Unfortunately for pilots destined for fighters, the Balliol was one's last acquaintance with piston engined aircraft, as on course completion and the award of wings, one was immediately posted to a jet conversion unit to update on to jet aircraft.

James McNamara worked on Balliols as an engine fitter during the summer of 1954, when he was one of several people 'volunteered' to supplement the ground crews for a University Air Squadron summer camp:

The Balliol itself was an aggressive sort of small aeroplane, often referred to as a sawn-off Spitfire. Those of us who had some experience of them quite liked them from the engineering point of view, as they were quite accessible. I myself was concerned with the engine, in this case the Merlin 35.

The airframe people either loved or hated it, depending on the particular tasks they had to perform. The pneumatics could be a bit strange. It had interchangeable control surfaces, so that you could exchange ailerons left to right, and it also had tailplane halves and elevators in common. It was quite a well thought out machine. One thing you had to be careful with, though, was the electrically-operated canopy, which was very heavy indeed, so you had to make sure you kept your fingers out of the way.

The installation of the Merlin was very, very straightforward, because it came built-up as a complete power unit. Using a crane and a big sling, you lowered the unit onto the front bulkhead of the machine, then lined up the top bearer attachment arms and looked through them to see if they were reasonably well aligned. There was a big temptation to poke one's finger in them, which of course was highly dangerous. I remember being told by my grizzled old Chiefy that it was a good way to stop anyone biting their nails! Once the top two attachments were in, the unit was lowered down a little more until the bottom ones were lined up. It was then simply a question of tying up all the wires, servicing the fuel system and so on, putting a propellor on the front, then checking it

Boulton Paul Sea Balliol T.21 on the deck of a carrier. (via Brian Lowe)

out. The propellor was a four-bladed de Havilland affair, a little over 11 feet in diameter. Installation was very, very straightforward. Just put it on, tighten it up and off you went. The installation of the Merlin was so neat and simple that it would only take us about three hours to have the thing in and running.

I remember on one occasion we had an example of what was known as the three-minute, or lightly-boiled, Merlin. We did all the usual checks on it for safety, but then decided to remove the engine just in case. We then put in a new one and I had an absolutely superb ride on the subsequent air test.

One thing common to all Merlins is that you have to make absolutely sure that the air intake for the radiator is clear of any foreign objects. It is very easy for it to get blocked up with things like bits of grass, straw and newspapers.

As regards ground running of the aeroplane, again one had to use one's loaf. One had to point the thing into wind and tie it all down and so on, because it was very tricky and one had to keep a very close eye on the coolant temperatures all the time.

I was very impressed with the Balliol, and thought it an exciting aeroplane. It was extremely noisy, though, and coming downhill it would dive very, very quickly. The ground really seemed to rush up at you, but it had powerful air brakes, and when they were deployed you were really grateful that you had a very good harness and a strong aeroplane around you.

It had its darker side. It had a fantastic stall which I'm afraid caused some quite horrendous accidents. I remember one day two young ashen faced chaps getting out of one and referring to the 'steaming little machine' as the Boulton Paul Bitch. Nevertheless, it was an aeroplane which was much liked by those who knew it well and could keep in control, but by the novice it was viewed with a certain amount of trepidation. It was an aeroplane that did require a great deal of respect – it wasn't a simple thing.

But what a superb noise it made, like any Merlin, of course, especially when landing. Over the fence, throttle back and then you heard this lovely, lovely popping sound as the power came off – it was quite something. I remember especially one lovely summer's day, with meadow larks singing and then the sound of a Merlin approaching. It was quite something and I don't think I'll ever quite forget that. I was privileged to have worked on one – I regard it as one of my better times.

Vickers Varsity prototype VX828 in September 1949.
(RAF Museum Photo No P100640)

Vickers Varsity T.1 WF331 'M' of No 5 Flying Training School at Oakington around 1971.
(Paddy Porter collection)

Hunting Percival Jet Provost prototype XD674 in August 1954. A comparison with the piston Provost, particularly of the rear fuselage and empennage, reveals notable similarities. *(RAF Museum Photo No P100113)*

Gloster Meteor T.7 taxying at Ta Kali, Malta in 1952. *(RAF Museum Photo No P100309)*

De Havilland Sea Vampire T.22 XA154 of the Flag Officer Flying Training at Yeovilton, visiting Culdrose around 1962. *(A.E. Hughes)*

BAC Jet Provost T.4 XP559 '73' of the RAF College at Cranwell around 1962. *(Author's collection)*

Hawker Hunter T.7 XL605 of No 92 Squadron at Leconfield, visiting RNAS Hal Far, Malta around 1962.
(A.E. Hughes)

Hawker Hunter T.7 XL565 '89' of No 4 Flying Training School at Valley around 1973. *(British Aerospace)*

Hawker Siddeley pre-production Gnat XM693, the first to be fitted with full dual control. (British Aerospace)

Hawker Siddeley Gnat T.1 XP541 '41' of No 4 Flying Training School at Valley. (British Aerospace)

RN Jetstream T.2 XX483 '562' of No 750 Squadron at Culdrose. *(RNAS Culdrose)*

RN Jetstream T.3 with manufacturer's marking G-31-659, first flown in May 1986 at Prestwick, and delivered a year later to No 750 Squadron at Culdrose as ZE440. Note the fuselage bulge housing the relocated Racal ASR 360 search radar. *(British Aerospace)*

British Aerospace Hawk T.1 XX304 and a T.1A fitted with Sidewinder missiles. *(British Aerospace)*

Army Gazelle AH.1 XX375.
(via Eric Myall)

RN Gazelle HT.2s of No 705 Squadron at Culdrose as mounts of the 'Sharks' display team.
(RNAS Culdrose)

Shorts Tucano prototype bearing manufacturer's mark-

de Havilland Chipmunk

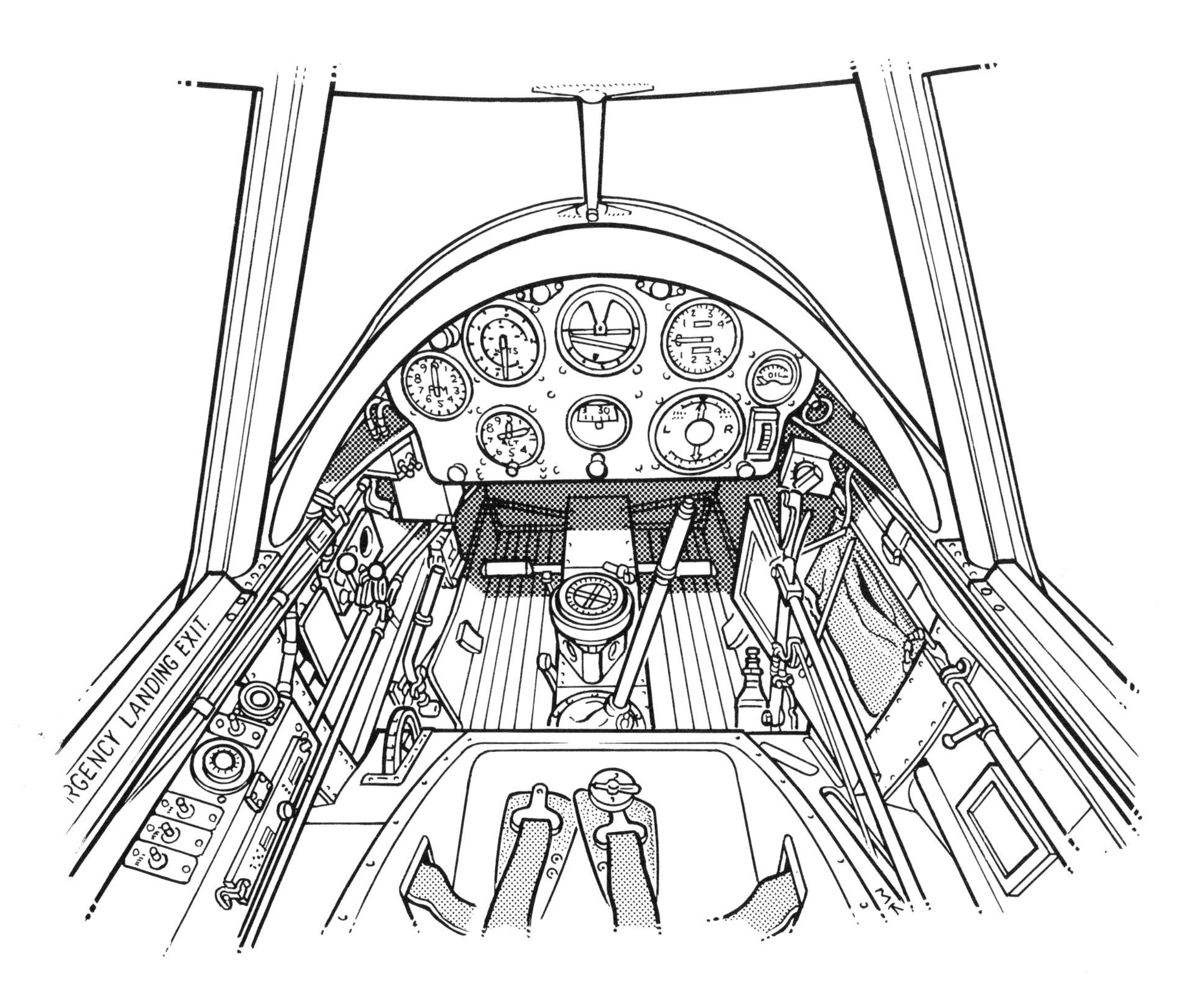

Specification

Power plant:	*One 145 hp de Havilland Gipsy Major 8.*
Dimensions:	*Span 34 ft 4 in, length 25 ft 5 in, height 7 ft 0 in, wing area 172.5 sq ft.*
Weights:	*Empty 1,417 lb, loaded 2,000 lb.*
Performance:	*Maximum speed 138 mph at sea level, cruising speed 119 mph, initial climb 800 ft/min, range 300 miles, endurance 2.3 hrs, service ceiling 16,000 ft.*

Shortly after the end of the Second World War, the RAF had a need to replace the ageing Tiger Moths initially issued to the numerous post-war Reserve Flying Schools and University Air Squadrons. Studies of the needs of these units led early in 1948 to the issue of Specification T.8/48 for a new elementary trainer of more advanced monoplane design, and two contenders emerged, the Fairey Primer and the de Havilland Chipmunk, both based on existing aircraft.

The Belgian-built Fairey Primer OO-POM, unsuccessful competitor to the Chipmunk for the T.8/48 specification. It was later given Class B registration G-6-1 before being dismantled at the Hayes factory for jigs to be made for intended UK production.

(RAF Museum)

The Fairey submission was a development of the Tipsy M, which had been built by their Belgian subsidiary company, Avions Fairey S.A. at Gosselies, to the design of E.O. Tips, who designed a series of Tipsy light aircraft both before and after the war. Hopeful of an order, Faireys brought over the first prototype OO-POM, which with manufacturers marking G-6-1 was flown briefly before being dismantled at the Hayes factory, where jigs were then made for its intended production.

The position at de Havillands was somewhat similar, their Canadian subsidiary having already built an elementary trainer as an intended replacement for the Tiger Moth in service with the Royal Canadian Air Force. By the time the Air Ministry Specification appeared, early examples of this machine were already in Britain.

The Ministry of Supply invited tenders on the basis of a minimum order for 100, with provision for further orders up to a possible ultimate 750. Both tenders were submitted in mid-May 1948, and Faireys offered to build 100 Primer airframes at £2070 each, this price reducing to £1405 each for the next 150, £1360 for a further 250 and £1320 for a final 250. The firm proposed delivery of the first batch within 13-14 months of a contract being signed.

De Havilland's first bid, submitted around the same time, was considerably more expensive. They could provide an initial 100 machines for £4400 each, deliveries commencing in April 1949 and ending in March 1950. If the order was increased to 250 machines, this could be completed within three years and the price for each machine would drop to £3135. An increase to 500 machines over four years would reduce the unit price to £2750, and an order for 750 over five years would bring a final reduction to £2620 each. The quotation in each case would include £100 per machine to help their Canadian subsidiary recover its design and development costs. These prices did not take into account fitments, such as engines, propellers, instruments, radios and harnesses, all of which would have to be provided by the Ministry.

Early in June, having learned that they were in danger of losing this contract, de Havillands had second thoughts. They wrote to the Ministry suggesting that they had not appreciated that their quotations were intended to be taken as a competitive tender, and said they were not yet in a position to put in a firm price.

They asked for an opportunity of reviewing their costs of manufacture to see if this could produce a lower production figure.

The outcome was a fresh letter to both companies in late July inviting formal tenders in competition. Before the tenders would be considered, however, an example of each machine, equipped to RAF standards, had to be provided for comprehensive evaluation and tests. De Havilland accordingly made available the tenth Canadian production machine G-AJVD. This was still to specification T.6/48, but it was decided to issue a fresh specification, T.17/48, for the Primer, the machine submitted being G-ALEW, which had the manufacturer's marking G-6-5, and was fitted with a 155-hp Blackburn Cirrus 3.

In the meantime both firms had taken a fresh look at costings, and Fairey had now increased theirs slightly, ranging from £2150 each for the first 100 down to £1380 each for the last 250. De Havillands, however, had evidently realised that their original pricing put them in danger of losing this prized contract, and were now quoting a much-reduced flat rate of £2100 each for 100 upwards, irrespective of the size of the order.

Both machines were delivered in November 1948 to the Aeroplane and Armament Experimental Establishment at Boscombe Down for an urgent test programme, and the evaluation reports were ready by mid-December. It emerged from this that the Chipmunk had a slight but definite superiority in both handling characteristics and ease of maintenance, though the Primer scored slightly in ease of repair. The only real criticism of the Chipmunk was that it would not spin very easily, but it was thought that this could be cured by a simple modification to the rudder.

De Havilland's costings still remained at £2100 per machine, but Faireys had in the meantime substantially revised their tender upwards, to give a new price, ranging from £2590 each for the first 100, dropping to £1750 for the last 250. Over a lengthy production run this would still work out less than the Chipmunk, but by now the initial need was seen as only 200 machines, at which number the Chipmunk came out substantially cheaper. Combined with the more favourable evaluation report this left no doubt as to which firm would win the contract, and on 25 February 1949 an order was placed for 200 Chipmunks T.10s.

The Chipmunk, which is still in service 40 years later, owed its origins to an idea by an exiled Polish designer, Wsiewolod J. Jakimiuk. He had been responsible before the war for a number of designs built by PZL, the Polish National Aviation Establishment, and had also worked on the de Havilland D.H.95 Flamingo. In June 1940 he was offered to the Canadian Government by the Polish Government-in-exile, and accordingly joined de Havilland Canada. By 1943 his desk carried a model of an idea for a low-wing monoplane trainer to replace the Tiger Moth.

With the end of the war in sight it was possible to devote design time to this concept. The first prototype Chipmunk, as it had become, flew at Downsview, Toronto on 22 May 1946 in the hands of Pat Fillingham, a test pilot sent from the parent Hatfield company. Registered CF-DIO-X, it was of all-metal stressed-skin construction, and had a typical de Havilland eliptical-shaped fin and rudder, similar to that of the Mosquito. The first flight was uneventful, and it looked from the start as if the firm had a potentially successful machine on their hands.

A few relatively minor problems were experienced. The metal fuselage was found to respond to the frequency of the engine, but the resulting vibration was cured by fitting firmer rubber engine mountings. A slight aileron over-balance was cured by a quarter-inch droop. The top was cut off the rudder at one stage to improve stability, but this idea was soon abandoned. After several attempts to improve stalling characteristics, stall bars were fitted immediately under the leading edge of the wings. After modification, the prototype was shipped to England, and on 15 January 1947 flew at Hatfield, being later re-registered G-AKEV.

Further modifications were incorporated in the British version. In place of the original D.H. Gipsy Major Ic engine, the RAF specified a 145 hp Gipsy Major 8 with a Coffman cartridge starter. Two 12 volt batteries were fitted in a special compartment aft of the luggage locker, and redesign of the panel and coaming was necessary to enable a standard RAF blind flying panel to be fitted. These alterations resulted in the Centre of Gravity moving forward, and there was now some tendency to ground-loop and stall recovery was inadequate. These problems were overcome, however, by raking the undercarriage forward three inches, increasing the rudder area, and fitting spinning strakes.

Initial deliveries to the RAF began in February 1950, but a second order had already been placed in May 1949 for a further 100 machines. The first units to receive them were the Oxford and Cambridge University Air Squadrons, quickly followed by No 22 Reserve Flying School at Cambridge, and by the end of 1951 most units of these two types had been re-equipped. Due to expansion of the RAF as a result of the Korean War, five Basic Flying Training Schools were set up in 1951 and 1952, and these too adopted the Chipmunk as standard equipment. Aircraft were also required for a rejuvenated Rhodesian Air Training Group, and further orders were consequently placed, eventually bringing total RAF production orders to 740 aircraft. The final order was placed in December 1951, though many became surplus when all the Reserve Flying Schools were closed during 1953 and 1954 for economy reasons. Four members of the Royal Family have so far flown solo on the Chipmunk – Princes

Above:
De Havilland Chipmunk prototype CF-DIO-X, which was later shipped to England to become G-AKEV.
(Author's collection)

Facing page, top:
De Havilland Chipmunk T.10 WB754 'H' of the Army Air Corps at Middle Wallop in 1958.
(School of Army Flying Museum)

Facing page, bottom:
De Havilland Chipmunk T.10 WP930 'J' of the Army Air Corps in formation with others near Middle Wallop in 1963.
(School of Army Flying Museum)

Philip, Charles, Andrew and Michael of Kent.

In addition to RAF service, small numbers have served with both the Army and the Navy. When the Army Air Corps was set up in September 1957, the Elementary Flight at Middle Wallop received 25 Chipmunks, and this unit still exists under the title Basic Fixed Wing Flight. The Fleet Air Arm did not get Chipmunks until 1966, however, when the Britannia Flight of the Britannia Royal Naval College at Dartmouth received 12 Chipmunks, these aircraft being still based at Roborough, Plymouth, giving air experience to naval officers.

From 1973 the Chipmunk was largely replaced in the RAF by the Bulldog, but numbers are still being flown by Air Experience Flights and the Flying Selection Squadron. The Chipmunk also fulfilled its original purpose as an RCAF trainer, and many went to other air forces, some of these also being still in service. The RAF plans to keep its surviving aircraft in service for another 20 years, a tribute to its original design.

Dick Smerdon recalls:

My logbook shows that I first met the Chipmunk in January 1953, and between that date and 1978 I put in quite a few hours on the aircraft. Three-pointing a Tiger Moth has prepared me for the landing problem, if any, and the Harvard tailwheel had taught me to be careful of castoring if there were a crosswind. I was used to the engine. Carburettor air on hot unless one broke the wire was a novelty. The method of setting the differential brake for taxiing was new to me, but I must admit that I never landed a Chipmunk with any brake set, in case I overdid the counting of clicks and because it was such an alien action in the pre-landing vital actions.

The cartridge starter was a godsend in single-crew operation without the benefit of groundcrew, when operating for Maintenance Command. Cartridge starting was also valued when visiting work services and ex-flying stations, when there was sufficient length of grass for safe landing and take-off.

The fact that I flew so many Air Training Corps and Cadet Force cadets, and that they were not to be subjected to negative g, resulted in my aerobatics becoming too smooth, with rolls being performed as 'chicken rolls'. That this kept the engine running was an added bonus.

I am not sure why eight turn spins had to be performed, but I recall that it took three more turns to recover – and quite a while for my eyeballs to return to normal.

Squadron Leader Don Brittain writes:

The Chipmunk was another aircraft which, like the Harvard, could ground-loop on you, but it did not have such a powerful engine. I remember checking out a 29 Squadron

3
3
ARMY
WB754

P
ARMY
D
ARMY
J
ARMY
WP930

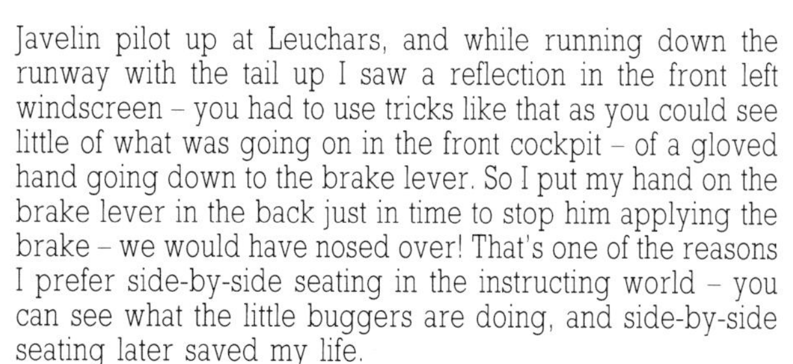

Javelin pilot up at Leuchars, and while running down the runway with the tail up I saw a reflection in the front left windscreen – you had to use tricks like that as you could see little of what was going on in the front cockpit – of a gloved hand going down to the brake lever. So I put my hand on the brake lever in the back just in time to stop him applying the brake – we would have nosed over! That's one of the reasons I prefer side-by-side seating in the instructing world – you can see what the little buggers are doing, and side-by-side seating later saved my life.

I remember doing a practice forced landing at Kirton-in-Lindsey. It was a nice summer's day, so I didn't bother clearing the engine – I thought this was only to keep the engine warm, but I soon learnt differently. When I did apply power, not a lot happened as the plugs had oiled up. It farted and coughed quite a bit, and I thought I was going to crash. The airfield boundary was pretty close, but the engine responded all of a sudden and once again my laundry bill went up a shade. This is one of several occasions when I can say I learnt about flying from that!

There is a fibre cog on the magneto which often sheds a few teeth which then buggers-up the timing. They always seem to go on take-off. I had one up at Leuchars, but the misfiring engine did get me round the circuit – just.

The Chippy used to have – I don't know if it does now – amber screens put in it for instrument flying with the pilot using blue goggles, and it is just like flying at night. The instructor of course can see nicely through the amber screens. If you look on the right-hand side of the Chippy in the front there is a hole which used to take a tube from your blue goggles to suck out any condensation and stop them misting up. Asking modern Chipmunk pilots what this tiny hole is can win you a pint.

I once changed a low-level aerobatic sequence without much thought. I put in an extra Porteous loop (roll of the top with flick – now forbidden), failing to take into account the extra height loss as the engine cuts out under negative-g. I quickly realised my error, though, when heading earthwards, as everything looked a bit close. Another thing I learnt . . .

Flight Lieutenant Peter Bouch flies the Chipmunk with the Flying Selection Squadron at Swinderby:

The squadron consists of 12 instructors and 10 aircraft tasked with giving elementary flying training to selected students – those without previous formal training, i.e, a Flying Scholarship or from a University Air Squadron. The course totals 63.15 hours – 44.15 dual and 19.00 solo. The syllabus comprises a full range of general handling, navigation, instrument flying and formation. When a student finishes our course he then undergoes a shortened course on the Jet Provost – thus saving a considerable amount of money!

The Chipmunk was chosen for the job, firstly because it was available and cheap, but much more important to the instructors was the fact that it was robust, simple to operate, yet because of its tailwheel configuration quite demanding in its handling – particularly on or near the ground. It is a very basic, simple little machine, with nicely balanced controls, fully automatic, spinnable (up to eight turns), and ideal for the full RAF primary flying syllabus. It is considered by most to be reasonably easy to fly safely but difficult to fly well. In fact I would rate it as the most demanding of all our training aircraft from the pure handling point of view – and I have flown them *all*, with the exception of the Tucano – and I don't think that would alter my opinion either!

On the plus side we have a simple, robust, light, cheap, reliable aircraft, easy to maintain, operating equally well from grass or concrete, and yet demanding of the student. Against, we have the fact that it is under-powered (slow to height and slow cruising speed), the engine will not run inverted (limiting the more advance aerobatics), and with a single radio fit is not allowed to penetrate more than 5/8 of cloud if the base is below the local safety height. Also the fact that it is light makes it vulnerable to strong winds and

De Havilland Chipmunk T.10 WB754 '21' of Hull University Air Squadron, seen at Leeming in June 1953. (Sqn Ldr D.W. Warne)

De Havilland Chipmunk T.10 WP967 'F' of the Glasgow and Strathclyde University Air Squadron at Perth in 1970.

(MAP Photo)

crosswinds, so we have to be fairly careful with it. Having said all that, it is still the best aircraft for the job! It is a much-loved old aeroplane – excellent for the task and likely to outlast many of its successors.

The school is the biggest Chipmunk user, all the Air Experience Flights use Chipmunks, and the Battle of Britain Memorial Flight, which I have recently left, has a Chipmunk which they use to train up their potential display pilots in the mysteries of tail wheel piston engine flying before they are allowed to get their hands on the priceless Hurricanes and Spitfires.

Squadron Leader Mike Sparrow flew the Chipmunk as a QFI with the University of Birmingham Air Squadron in 1965-68, and again with the Royal Navy Grading Squadron at Plymouth:

It is a superb and well-loved basic training aircraft. Well balanced, light on the controls and seemingly capable of absorbing for ever all the punishment student pilots can inflict upon it. The carburettor is prone to icing so most aircraft have carb heat control wired in the hot position. (The Navy Chipmunks at Plymouth are an exception as extra thrust is needed for take-off.)

On a UAS the squadron R/T call-sign was 'India', followed by a number – 01 to 10 for instructors, and 20 onwards for solo students. There came the inevitable day when a not-so-bright student found himself above cloud and, to put it kindly, 'uncertain of his position'. After much R/T chat he eventually got his compass and direction indicator synchronised and was given a heading to steer for base. At this stage the controller wanted to know whether the student was in cloud, so asked him, 'Lost student, are you on instruments?' After a long silence, he repeated the query. After yet, another lengthy silence, a puzzled voice, replied, 'No, I'm on a parachute'. The frustrated controller then snapped, 'Lost student, I mean are you IMC; that is India Mike Charlie?', to which he received the immediate, bright, sunny reply, 'No, I'm India 46!' The student landed safely.

Squadron Leader Michael Neill now flies Chipmunks with No 6 Air Experience Flight at Abingdon:

I started my flying training on Chipmunks in January 1952, and have had a soft spot for them ever since. After completing a tour in Germany I returned to the UK in 1956 and completed the CFS course, returning there in 1958 after a short tour instructing on the Piston Provost at the RAF College Cranwell. In 1959 I joined the Basic Examining Staff, and all the basic trainers were part of my responsibilities, and included examining instructors at flying clubs which were involved in the Flying Scholarship Scheme.

On one occasion I was tasked to examine the CFI at a flying club in the south of England. The test was conducted on a Tiger Moth and included a full general handling sortie. In the spinning exercise he told me 'to recover from the

spin: apply full opposite rudder, wait for the spin to stop, then move the control column forward to unstall the wings and recover from the dive'. It worked on the Tiger Moth, but it was not standard spin recovery and such action on the Chipmunk would be disastrous. I wrote the test report some time later, and stated that the spin recovery action was 'being incorrectly taught'. The CFI, on receiving the report, was extremely upset and insisted on a retest, on the grounds that should there be any sort of accident in the future my report could be used in evidence. My boss thought I had been harsh and he agreed to do the re-test himself, and wrote a suitable report afterwards.

I felt some concern that I could have been more diplomatic in my report, until one day I was examining a cadet pilot at a University Air Squadron, flying the Chipmunk. On this occasion, I asked the student to show me a prolonged spin and to call out the recovery action. After about six turns he said he was recovering and sang out, 'full opposite rudder, wait for the spin to stop . . .' Of course the spin did not stop and I had to take control. After landing I began my debriefing with three statements, all of which the student agreed with – I told him he had learnt to fly before joining the University Air Squadron; the name of his flying club; and the name of his instructor! After that I did not feel bad about the report I had written some months earlier. It also goes to show that first lessons learnt are hard to change.

Some years later I found myself as OC operations at RAF Gatow Berlin flying the Chipmunk once again. I was invited to give a low level aerobatic display at the American Base at Tempelhof during their 'Open House' celebrations. My wife was given a front seat and was escorted by an American officer's wife. During the display I got to a negative-g manoeuvre and, of course, the engine cut. The American wife, convinced disaster was about to ensue, dragged my wife from her seat saying that they must return immediately to the VIP lounge. My wife realised what was going on, and consoled the American by saying, 'Now don't you worry about a thing, it's a gravity feeds fuel system and the engine always stops under negative-g.' And sure enough, as they looked up at the Chipmunk again, it burst into life with its usual puff of black smoke. Both ladies sat down again with a big smile on their faces to enjoy the remainder of the display.

The Chipmunk is an attractive aircraft and super to fly, but not easy to fly well and always presents a bit of a challenge. Perhaps that's why even today all three services use it as a primary trainer, and it does sort out the men from the boys. Spinning has not been a problem in the Chipmunk, but if you fail to 'continue moving the control column forward until the spin stops' the recovery will not happen. The Chipmunk has the unofficial record of killing more senior officers than any other service aircraft, and it may be said that this stems from poor spin recovery technique.

'Over the years many have wanted to change the Chipmunk – put a new engine in or give it an inverted flight capability, but that original design, by W.J. Jakimiuk and his team, produced a machine which has stood the test of time, and those who know the aircraft well would not change it. On 22 May 1986, No 6 Air Experience Flight celebrated the 40th Anniversary of the first flight of the Chipmunk and Pat Fillingham, the original test pilot, attended the celebrations and flew again in the Chipmunk with OC the unit. Pat Fillingham had not flown the Chipmunk for 25 years – what was his comment? – 'it was like meeting an old girlfriend again'.

De Havilland Chipmunk T.10 fleet of No 6 Air Experience Flight lined up at Abingdon in 1986.
(RAF Abingdon)

The aircraft has proved easy to maintain, and John Norris, who was a rigger stationed for a time at Chivenor, recalls it with affection:

It was a simple little machine that could not hide its wheels. All the controls were manual except the brakes which were actuated by an enormous lever set to port of the cockpit. I was always tempted to shout 'Whoa' when hauling back on the brake lever, because it put me in mind of the wooden poles that stage coach drivers heave on in Western films. The Chipmunks I worked on were on loan from various UASs, and they were used to give air experience to ATC cadets. These used up a tremendous number of 'bags, sickness', but would often miss the bag and foul the cockpit, the canopy and even the driver up front. After such a mishap the aircraft would be returned to the line, the engine shut down, and the culprit ordered to clean up the mess with buckets of hot water and disinfectant. They seldom did it properly, though, and one of the ground crew would then be nominated – usually one of the riggers, of course. 'Get it clean', would be the command, and it really did have to be clean.

The pilots, who were often RAFVR types, would sometimes indicate to the waiting groundcrew to help the unfortunate occupant of the rear cockpit to dismount, which they were careful to do anyway because the cadet was quite likely to put a foot through the mainplane if there was no-one to steer him. When this happened there was much burning of midnight oil in the gloom of the hangar with two or three riggers frantically trying to repair the damage ready for the next day's flying. I particularly recall one dazed little chap who stepped out to starboard, and promptly dipped out of sight. The rigger tore around the tail to try to help him, only to find that he had put both feet through the wing, damaging his shins. The rigger felt sorry for him, but nearly as sorry for himself because he got a 'rollicking', and then had to effect the repair – he says his needlework was nearly up to GCE standard!

Apart from window cleaning there was little for a rigger

Facing page:
Pat Fillingham, the original British Chipmunk test pilot, with Sqn Ldr Mike Neill, cutting a cake on the 40th Anniversary of the type's first flight, during a visit to No 6 Air Experience Flight at Abingdon in 1986.
(RAF Abingdon)

A civil-registered De Havilland Chipmunk T.10 flown in the former marking of a Cambridge University Air Squadron aircraft WD379 'K', seen at Wroughton in 1986.

(Author)

to do on a Chipmunk. The brake reservoir was easily accessible and in any case rarely needed topping up. The occasional wheel or brake unit change was simple. To change a tailwheel, no jacks, trestles or assistance were needed; one simply applied the parking brake then, clutching a serviceable wheel, a 3/8 – 5/16 BSF spanner, a pair of pliers and a hank of locking wire, crawled under the tail, heaved upwards and got on with it.

Two men could easily move a Chipmunk to or from the line. It could be done by one man, but this was rather unwise. One windy day a man attempting it single-handed had it weathercock as he emerged from behind the hangers. It bowled him over and bobbed off at a canter down the road towards the MT section. By the time he was back on his feet it had a ten yard start on him and was gaining momentum, but fortunately it scraped a kerb and swung to a halt without damage. The only serious danger for groundcrew was the propeller, which was very easy to forget as it whirled away rapidly and invisibly.'

There is no inverted fuel system, so the engine always coughs and splutters during zero negative-g flight. It adds a bit of drama when one is doing a sequence of aerobatics at an air show! Although flick manoeuvres were and are prohibited the Porteous Loop was allowed between 1964 and 1968. This was a flick roll entered when inverted on top of a loop, called Avalanche in civilian flying circles. Most, if not all, Service aircraft are fitted with vertical acceleration recorders to give an accurate assessment of fatigue life.

Nevil Gardner also had some ground experience on Chipmunks:

Once, while preparing the aircraft for a repaint, I was relieved to discover that the paint stripper hadn't melted the spinner, when I realised that it was made of fibreglass, and not aluminium alloy as I had supposed.

At Duxford in the seventies there was no grass runway, and I once watched a Chipmunk taxi off the apron and take-off on the taxiway. The pilot had obviously considered it wasn't worth the long taxi to the runway!'

Kev Darling had the dubious distinction of nearly setting fire to a Chipmunk whilst under training at Halton.

I was detailed by a Chief Technician to remove the battery from a Chipmunk. Never having done so before, I asked how it was done. He explained in his forthright manner, and I then went off to do the job. Unfortunately for me, his explanation was incorrect. Having attached my ratchet handle and socket to the live terminal, I proceeded to short out the battery on the metal fuselage. This resulted in a bright blue flash, a bemused trainee mechanic (me!), an irate Chief, plus clouds of carbon dioxide, as someone had thought there was a fire and had set off a fire extinguisher! Thankfully, as I was a trainee, the matter died down rapidly.

Gloster Meteor Trainer

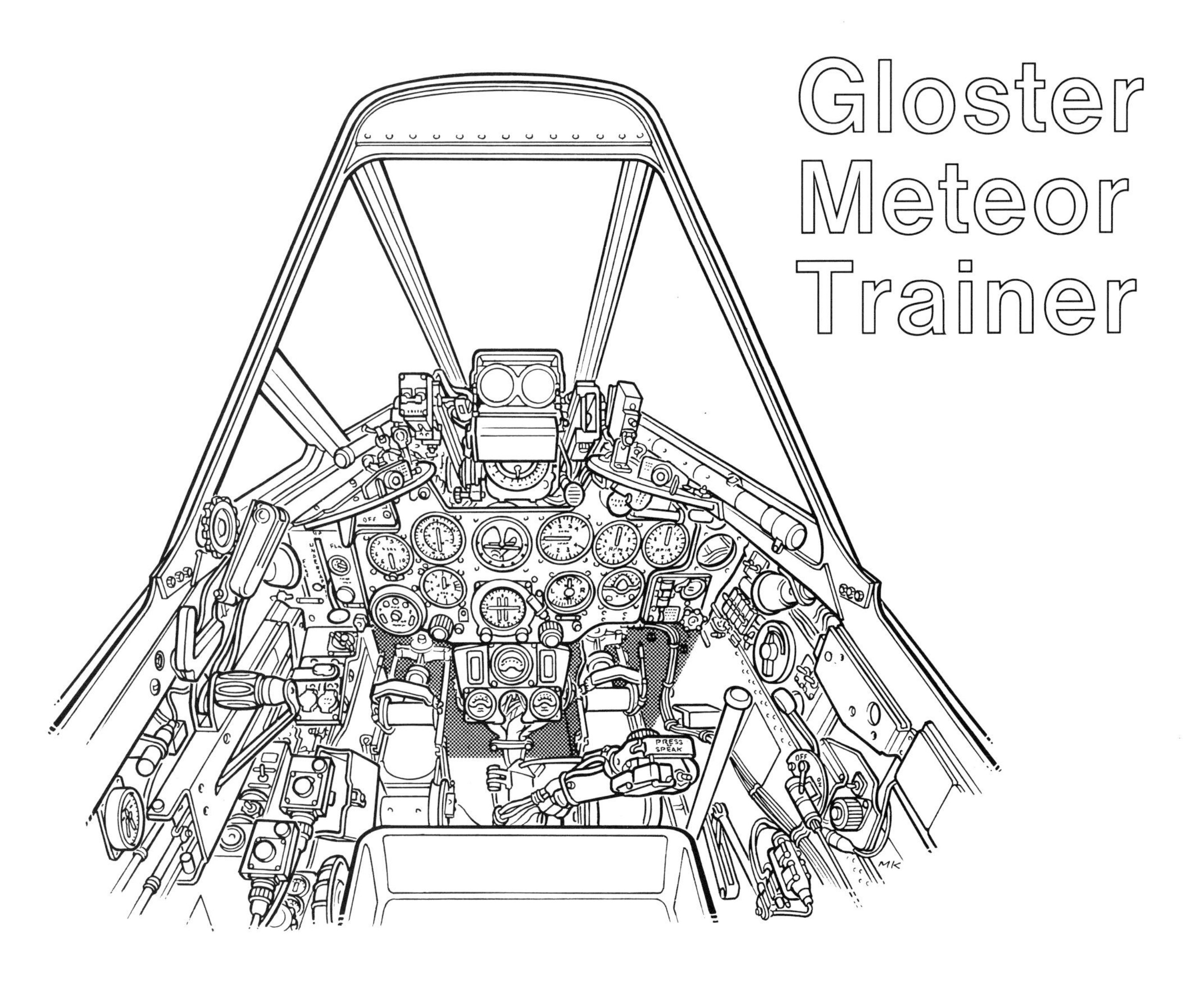

The Gloster Meteor Trainer first appeared as a private venture, demonstration aircraft G-AKPK making its first flight on 19 March 1948 from the manufacturer's aerodrome at Brockworth, and landing 26 minutes later at Moreton Valence. Painted in high-gloss red with yellow trimming, it took advantage of the wings, rear fuselage and tail of the Meteor F.4, and was similarly fitted with two Rolls-Royce Derwent 5 engines. Its length had been increased by 30 inches with the addition of a strong new two-seat cockpit, built to withstand speeds in excess of Mach 0.8, and containing complete dupli-

Specification

Power plant:	*Two 3,600 lb thrust Rolls-Royce Derwent 5 or 8.*
Dimensions:	*Span 37 ft 2 in, length 43 ft 6 in, height 13 ft 8 in, wing area 350 sq ft.*
Weights:	*Empty 10.540 lb, loaded 14,230 lb.*
Performance:	*Maximum speed 585 mph at sea level, cruising speed 535 mph, initial climb 7,600 ft/min, range 820 miles, endurance 1.5 hrs, service ceiling 35,000 ft.*

cation of the controls and flight instruments. It retained something of the clean lines of its predecessor, but was in reality a compromise so far as the visibility of pupil and instructor was concerned, though the view from the front seat was very similar to that of the Mark F.4, as it was ahead of the engine nacelles. Being lighter than its fighter counterpart, it had a better rate of climb, and three drop tanks gave it an excellent range.

It arrived on the scene at about the time Fighter Command had discarded the last of its piston-engined fighters, and in fact the Air Ministry had already decided to issue Specification T.1/47 for an RAF trainer version. A Meteor F.4 (EE530), which had previously been used by the record-breaking High Speed Flight, was converted for prototype trials. An order for 70 production aircraft had been placed in August 1947, the first of these (VW410) making its initial flight on 26 October 1948. Over 600 were eventually built.

Further trials to investigate spinning characteristics revealed additional cause for criticism. Positive action was required to initiate a spin, but once it had started there was immediate tail buffeting and violent aileron snatching. There was little problem over recovery in the first turn, though both hands would be needed on the control column. After the second turn, however, the rate of rotation increased, the controls became extremely heavy, and the control column snatched over to the side of the cockpit, in the direction of the spin. If left unchecked, the forces involved could become too great for the pilot's strength.

Despite the criticisms, there was nothing better available, and in any event production was already well under way. They came steadily off the line, for issue to the Central Flying School and numerous Advanced Flying Schools, being mainly used by the latter to convert pilots trained on piston-engined

Gloster Meteor Trainer private venture prototype G-AKPK.

(RAF Museum)

Handling trials at Boscombe Down with EE530 and VW411, the second machine off the line, showed the T.7 to have fairly similar characteristics to the F.4. This was not necessarily an advantage, except as an introduction for pilots progressing to that type in squadron service. It exhibited marginal longitudinal stability, and increased speed and thrust brought large changes of trim, serving to cast doubts on its suitability as a general high speed trainer. Several features of the cockpit layout came in for criticism, and there was concern at the ability of the crew to get out of the aircraft safely in the event of crash-landing or ditching. It was recommended that instructors on the type have some experience with flying it from the rear seat with the canopy removed.

Harvards or Balliols. When the Provost/Vampire sequence was introduced in 1954, many of the Meteor T.7s became surplus, but they continued in use for many years, giving refresher training at both RAF and RAuxAF units.

Don March was on one of the first courses to go directly from the Harvard to the Meteor:

It was thought by many of us that the direct step from Harvards to Meteors was a bit much, the old system being

preferred of going through Spitfires and then on to Oxfords for asymetric flying training. The results of this step showed in the fatality rate, in my opinion. If a pilot was killed, a red cross was put over him in his Course photograph, and when we first went to Driffield to start flying Meteors we saw that some of the previous Course photographs were almost completely obliterated by red crosses, which made us look at each other a bit.

I think it is true to say that the fatality rate was appreciable in the 1950s. My Harvard Instructor eventually became a Meteor Instructor, and it was his job to rewrite the Meteor training manual. He had the satisfaction, he told me years later, of seeing the fatality rate on Meteors fall by over 50 per cent – I wished he had rewritten the manual before I went on to them. In our end-of-course criticism, we said we thought we needed more training. Our target at Driffield was 30 hours, but I actually had only 27 hours which was an appreciable drop. One then went to Stradishall for OCU training for another 30 hours, then to a squadron. After my time these hours were increased to 50 at Driffield and 50 at Stradishall, which was a welcome increase; that is my own personal opinion, of course, but I heard it expressed by others. Looking back, I cannot understand how the RAF endured such a high rate of Meteor fatalities, which seemed a great waste of money. 200 previous flying hours were completely wasted every time a trainee pilot got the chop.

When the great day came to fly a Meteor for the first time with one's Instructor, the initial acceleration seemed terrific. We kept low at 290 knots, then pulled on the stick and went rocketing skywards – very impressive. On the initial circuit, to avoid shooting up through circuit height of 1,000 ft, it was absolutely necessary to wrench the power back about two-thirds, or one would inevitably shoot up past the desired height, doing a circuit at 1,500 or 2,000 ft.

Leaving the airbrakes out while turning finals was a killer. We used to join circuit after a sortie with a minimum of 80 gallons of fuel, which was only enough for an overshoot and one further circuit and landing, then you were out of fuel.

Undercarriage lights played up a lot, often giving two green lights instead of three. To try to ensure the undercarriage was locked down, we used to do a low flypass over the Tower, rocking the aircraft about. The chaps in the Tower would observe the undercarriage and inform you that it appeared to be down and locked. Fortunately that was always the case for me, but it was not really good practice.

Initially one had to determine one's own personal critical speed for keeping straight when an engine failed during the take off phase. If it were, say, 109 knots, you could fly on if you were above that speed, because you would have the necessary speed and rudder control. Below that figure it was impossible to keep straight as there was insufficient rudder control, so the drill was to throttle back on the good engine and belly land. Whilst determining this personal critical speed, however, one's leg would shake up and down uncontrollably, as it was exerting so much pressure to keep the Meteor straight on minimal speed with full power on one engine, but no power on the other, to simulate engine failure.

After a maximum rate descent from very cold temperatures to warmer moister air at low level, the whole cockpit would ice up or get wholly covered by condensation, and one could not see out at all. The drill was to career around at low level at high speed, and the heat would soon clear the ice or condensation, but meanwhile one was flying blind, which was rather undesirable.

In all other aircraft one had to learn to spin and recover, but for some reason we were not allowed to do this in the Meteor – a bad thing. Then I saw Zurakowski at Farnborough not only spin a Meteor from 7,000 ft, but prior to that perform his Zurabatic, personally invented by him. He did a vertical climb up to the stall, then full power on one engine only – the result, a cartwheel in the vertical plane.

Snake climbs were perfect in theory, but when one emerged at 30,000 ft expecting still to be in follow-my-leader style, one could usually not see another Meteor for miles.

Lastly, at Driffield, formation breaks used to be immediate, until the day one took place over the airfield, the formating pupil pulled too tight and hit the leader, and both then came down in no uncertain manner. From then on, three second breaks were introduced.

Robin Brown trained at 207 AFS, and he too had reservations:

The Meteor 'death dive' apparently didn't develop until quite late in the Meteor's life – around 1958-59. I don't know why it didn't manifest itself earlier, unless people started getting casual with an old and well-loved machine. My ex-CO on 112 Squadron, Sqn Ldr Hegarty, killed himself this way at Strubby.

It usually happened when the aircraft turned onto the downwind leg, at 1,000 feet above ground level. Suddenly, and without any warning, the aircraft would dive into the ground. From 1,000 feet there wasn't much you could do about it (not even eject; there weren't bang seats in the Mk7).

Because it all happened so quickly it took a little while for the Accident Investigation Branch to work out what was going wrong. It transpired that if you came into the circuit for an 'Operational' break (i.e. quite fast), turned downwind with air-brakes still out, and selected undercarriage down, there was complete loss of lift over the wing surfaces and you plummeted into the ground. The effect was worsened if the machine was allowed to yaw, but as this happened anyway as the undercarriage came down, it was difficult to avoid.

The solution was simply to do your downwind checks in the correct sequence: 1 – airbrakes 'in', 2 – undercarriage 'down'. It was only if you selected undercarriage down with airbrakes out that you were in trouble. I always made doubly sure by holding the airbrake lever forward as the undercarriage came down.

Squadron Leader Don Brittain also flew the Meteor T.7:

Flying at 33,000 feet unpressurised, the inside froze up and you had to scrape the ice off to see out. There were decompression sickness symptoms – the chokes, the creeps (formication), and others. Ignorance is bliss – nowadays we are more aware and limit cockpit altitudes to 25,000 feet. They believe we lost a few pilots because of this.

We did instrument flying in the 'Meatbox', sitting in the back seat with brasso on the sides and a weird coal scuttle contraption on your head to stop you looking out. I once did a sortie with a Pole, I think he was, and he flew the thing whilst I was supposed to be doing IF. He even had the cheek to criticise my IF when he was actually flying it.

Another reason for disliking the side-by-side cockpit: – you can't keep hold of the controls – it tends to put the student off. I did my dual on a T.7, and then solo in a Vampire FB.5. There was no resemblance at all in handling characteristics. They got three airmen to sit on the tail booms and said 'that's what it looks like on touchdown – off you go'. They forgot to say that the trim change in the Vampire was quite pronounced when you put down flaps – I had a hell of a job in my first solo getting it down safely.

A number of Meteors were used by naval training units, and Commander Peter Bagley has vivid recollections of these:

It was never a nice aircraft, having too many vices in my opinion. With a total of 400 gallons of fuel for its twin Derwent jet engines it burned 40 gallons at start-up and taxiing. Then another 40 gallons at take-off, whilst 60 gallons had to be conserved for use when joining the aircraft circuit as this was absolutely necessary for flying round again if a baulked landing or over-run occurred. Without this reserve it meant a possible forced landing and probable 'goodbye', so 140 gallons were spoken for out of 400 total. This gave just one hours flight time, so accurate navigation was imperative.

Let's assume the pilot had done his ground checks and all was well. He then climbed into the front of the large two-seater tandem cockpit, covered by an enormous perspex and metal-framed hood that weighed an absolute ton. The hood was hinged on its right side, held open by a hydraulic strut and closed by pulling it down from right to left.

Having strapped in (safety harness), connected oxygen bayonet fitting to aircraft supply, connected dinghy safety strap, the hood was closed by the pilot. Next, both he and the groundcrew checked the locks to ensure positive closure and locking, the pilot from inside, the groundcrew from outside. The twin Derwent jet engines were then started and left idling at around 7,500 revolutions per minute. Chocks were waved away after obtaining taxi clearance – usually done as the second engine fired up.

Most pilots did their take-off cockpit checks whilst taxiing out to the duty runway. The drill was to check fire warning lights, flaps up, air brakes in, all three undercarriage lights at green. Co-ordinate compass with direction indicator and uncage when lined up for take-off. Ensure correct radio channel selected. Set altimeter to airfield height so that it read zero height accurately. Ensure pitot head heater was on. Both low and high pressure cocks set on. Low pressure pumps set on. Then select one-third flap down, and ensure brake pressure is reading 450 psi. Recheck hood locks and request permission for take-off.

When lining the aircraft up with the centre of the runway, move sufficiently far enough forward to straighten the nose wheel. Apply full brake and open the twin throttles until 14,500 revolutions is shown on the rev counters. Then release brakes and keep straight by use of slight brake if required, and the aircraft would soon get to 80 knots at which point backward pressure on the control column raised the nose wheel to the nose-up attitude. At 125 knots the Meteor T.7 flew off, whereupon the pilot had to select

undercarriage up and remember to brake the wheels simultaneously. Holding the aircraft level until 165 knots, the flaps were then retracted. When 290 knots was reached, the climb could be started. Remember all of this procedure took 40 gallons of fuel.

When the required altitude was reached, the aircraft was allowed to gain air speed until a figure of 0.70 Mach was shown on the Mach meter. The ailerons tightened up considerably at such Mach, whilst at the same time there was a very defined nose-up tendency which, although the pilot could trim out to some extent, he nevertheless had to apply strong forward stick force to counteract fully.

The Meteor T.7 took about seven minutes to climb to 35,000 feet, and if flown to the maximum Mach of 0.70, the indicated air speed had fallen to 200 knots. If aerobatics were to be flown, an air speed of 300 knots was required for slow rolls, whilst a loop needed 380 knots entry air speed and bags of height to be flown round. Not a pleasant aircraft in any sense. Too heavy in handling. Too unstable in flight characteristics.

On rejoining the airfield circuit for landing some 180/200 knots was best for the downwind leg at 700 feet. Air speed was controlled by both use of the air brakes and the throttles. On the downwind leg the drill was to check brake pressure making sure of full at 450 psi, and at the crosswind leg, best flown as a descending curve, reduce speed to 160 knots and select one-third flaps down. Select undercarriage down and check for three green lights. Throttle back to 140 knots and as the final turn lined the aircraft up with the centre-line of the duty runway, ensure the throttles were giving engine revolutions of 7,500 minimum. This was to ensure rapid opening-up if either a baulked or badly judged landing run occurred and the engines were to get the aircraft airborne again. On crossing the runway threshold at 110 knots the aircraft had always to be landed on the two

Gloster Meteor T.7 WA634 fitted with non-standard tail unit, and used for Martin Baker ejector seat tests.
(British Aerospace)

main wheels and held in a nose-up attitude until speed dropped off and the nose wheel made contact at about 70 knots. During the landing approach and final touch-down the aircraft felt heavy and a 'bolter' (go-around) was never pleasant to do.

Perhaps my dislike of this aircraft was why one, VZ646, I was flying on 14 January 1952, decided to try to kill me! The weather was blowing a Force Nine gale at sea in the English Channel. I had been briefed to climb to 25,000 feet then carry out two radio-controlled descents, called QGH in those days. I did my take-off and climbed to 25,000 feet, then called for a controlled descent and got my first 'steer' and height and

Going up . . . *Gloster Meteor T.7 WL364 goes vertical.*
(British Aerospace)

Coming down . . . *Gloster Meteor T.7 aerobatic team of No 8 Flying Training School.*
(Author's collection)

speed from the ground controller. I had call sign *Culdrose Two Two Zero.* When the aircraft had descended to 18,000 feet I was ordered to start a left-hand descending turn at 220 knots. As I did so there was an almighty bang and the aircraft went wild throwing my hands off both stick and throttles and briefly winding me. The aircraft shot into a violent nose-up attitude and stalled as it also began to spin. In mini-seconds I realised the cockpit hood – that 2 cwt monster – had unlocked, somehow breaking the large hydraulic strut from its mounting point on the port side of the cockpit. Also the forward set of hinges was flailing around like a maddened helicopter blade.

I knew my end had come – but somehow The Almighty was with me on that terrible day. Realising the aircraft possibly was in an inverted spin, as I was thrown violently forward against my safety harness, I pulled the locking pin. Somehow I was thrown out, but having forgotten in the heat of the moment to undo both my oxygen tube and my radio plug, I nearly got hanged as my helmet tore off my head. It gave me a severe neck pain for two days.

When I suddenly realised I had baled-out safely without being hit by any part of the aircraft, especially the high tail, I lay on my back with my legs and arms spread-eagled, free-falling through very wet and cold cloud, calling the controller at Culdrose . . . *'Culdrose Two Two Zero,* give me a steer' . . . It then dawned on my befuddled mind that I had no helmet and was facing a most terrible death on hitting Earth or Sea, so my reflexes called on me to pull my parachute release handle. On first trying, it refused to budge, being badly misshapen, but survival strength is fantastic and I gave it a terrific heave and as it pulled out so my chute opened with another crack. I swung there full of joy and wonder, thanking The Almighty for deliverance – as I thought.

I must have been shot out of the aircraft at about 15,000 feet, whilst my chute opened at possibly 8-9,000 feet. Eventually I broke cloud at about 400 feet, sighting a raging sea below me: high waves and poor visibility. Somehow remembering what I had learned about parachute pull-off in earlier years on a training course I had attended, I turned to face into wind and at the same time hit the 'oggin'. I went under, and as I surfaced again saw that my still open parachute was going to take me a fast surfing ride. It did. I then tried to use the parachute harness quick release box, but it was bent and refused to budge. 'So not liking the look of the ocean, the waves were *far* from fiddling and small', to misquote an oldie record by Stanley Holloway, I tried to get one arm out of the shoulder strap. When after a furious struggle and having swallowed far too much salt water I succeeded, I was able to get my other arm out. With the chute only partially collapsed and my legs still in the harness I went for a rapid surf ride on my back. Somehow I got my legs out and then pulled my Mae West gas bottle cord. Nothing happened, so I tried my dinghy cord only to find it has been cut during the bail-out. What no dinghy?

Luckily I was a strong swimmer in those days, and I decided to tread water until I recovered some strength, but before I could do so I heard an engine thumping and at the same moment was hooked through my Mae West vest at the back by an enormous hook. This lifted me out of the water knocking me against a ship's wooden rail and deposited me straight into a fish cleaning tank. I threw up.

What had happened was that as I came out of the cloud, a Jersey Airways DH Rapide flying at 'nought feet' had sighted me and seeing a trawler making towards Newlyn Harbour had 'buzzed' her redirecting to my fast drowning body. I was grateful, but at that moment was being stripped naked and having Calvados forced down my throat. I vaguely remember some Flemish fisherman trying to take off my pilot's-type wrist watch and resisting that. I was dressed in very fishy blankets and eventually when the trawler got alongside in Newlyn Harbour had to climb up an iron-runged ladder to the waiting ambulance.

All rescuers and the parachute packer were rewarded and thanked, and within three days I got into another Meteor T.7 and flew it – but not with enthusiasm.

As I had to go out to Malta to command the Fleet Requirements Squadron which was equipped with a variety of aircraft types including the dreaded Mosquito TT.39, a long-nose type which could not maintain height on one engine, I had to smother my fears and feelings and get on by setting an example flying all types. In later years this affected my health and I began a terrible saga of nightmares so my doctors advised me to open up and tell the story sometimes. The first time I did so was to an old experienced Meteor T.7 OCU wing commander – who told me that no-one had ever survived a bail-out from this type! I did!

Dick Smerdon also has recollections of the Meteor:

My conversion to jets was not at an Operational Conversion Unit, with lectures on jet propulsion and lots of flying. Instead it was three hours on-the-Squadron training, and then away you go in a Meteor F.4. Because of my Instructor category, and the inception of the RAF Instrument Rating scheme in 1950, I was made an Instrument Rating Examiner, and spent many hours in the back of a Meteor T.7. At first I did Instrument Rating Tests, then some jet conversion for ex-University National Service officers, and later the conversion of a whole squadron from single-engined Vampires to twin-engined Meteors.

Although the Mk7 did not have a wing planform conducive to really high speed, fatigue failure was not a factor we had to reckon with; it was a robust aircraft. A Critical Mach Number of 0.86 was achieved at altitude in a shallow dive. At low level, however, the aircraft could be flown at full throttle. It was disappointing later when I flew the Javelin to find it placarded at 535 knots, although this was only at about half throttle. The method of demonstrating the Meteor T.7s rate of climb to my wartime piston-engined friends was a full throttle run at low level, then a pull up to level off at 10,000 feet.

Neither the pressurisation nor the heating in the Mk7 were very impressive. Consequently what flights to 35,000 feet did to us physically, I have no idea. It was certainly fatiguing, even for a younger man, but the question was postulated by a P2 Officer when I joined Fighter Command "Why do they send you old buggers to Fighter command" – I was 27!

The single-engined performance of the Meteor was so much better than any twin I had previously flown. I had short thick legs, and I could lock on full rudder against the live engine and carry out missed approaches above the committal speed and height. Then to save fuel, an engine

Above:
Gloster Meteor T.7 WH186 'MC' of No 215 Advanced Flying School at Finningley around 1953.
(MAP photo)

Below:
All-black Gloster Meteor T.7 WL353 '574/HF' of 728 Squadron at RN Air Station Hal Far, Malta around 1963–65.
(MAP photo)

used to be shut down and only restarted to taxi in – one usually managed to turn off the runway beforehand.

I note that I gave Norman Tebbitt an instrument rating test on 15 August 1954 . . .

A groundcrew point of view is given by John Norris, who helped service them as a rigger at Chivenor:

Working on the Meteor T.7 was a pleasure. There were very few components that could be even remotely regarded as inaccessible, other than some oxygen bottles. These were set to starboard and below the cockpit floor line, and to change them I had to tie on my spectacles and work hanging upside down. But then airframe tradesmen didn't meddle with oxygen systems before 1965, when the instrument trade relinquished their responsibility and oxygen systems became ours. The undercarriage, while having a rather novel shortening facility when retracting, was in all other respects a model of sturdy simplicity. Its levered or 'trailing arm' legs were capable of absorbing enormous thumping arrivals without damage. The wheels brakes were adequate but, being drum-type pneumatic units, rather prone to overheating if used too vigorously, even while taxiing, especially in hot weather. The advantage the occupants of a T.7 had during such weather was the ability to open the canopy whilst taxiing, so the crew could remain cool whilst the brakes got frazzled.

A hazard for the unwary ground crewman wandering about atop the inner mainplanes was that someone in the cockpit might select the airbrakes open. With no pressure remaining in the accumulators, the airbrakes would have to be pumped open using the handpump, which was located in the forward cockpit. Should there be pressure in the accumulators (or the port engine running), however, the airbrakes would slam open, which could launch anyone standing on them clear of the wing. A similar hazard existed beneath the wings, where the other set could dent an unwary head.

On the port side of the cockpit coaming, beside the front seat, was a little trigger at the end of a Bowden cable. Painted black and yellow in stripes, this was the undercarriage override which enabled the undercarriage to be retracted 'with weight on'. This would drop the aircraft on its belly and slow its progress in the event that the brakes should fail on the landing run. Unless this trigger had a 'tell tale' wire to indicate it had been operated, it could be operated and returned to the off position and no-one would be the wiser unless they inadvertently selected undercarriage up while the aircraft was on the ground. The mechanism could only be reset by going to the selector located in the fuselage behind the cockpit, and pulling back on the cable to engage a latch (ensuring that the trigger in the cockpit was set to the off/normal position). This little conundrum caught out at least one pilot at Chivenor, who dropped a Meteor on its nose while carrying out his cockpit checks after start up on the line. The main legs did not retract because the brakes were on, and the friction and weight on the wheels prevented it.

The worst task on the line for the rigger was to clean the windows, for the T.7 had lots of them, some being rather awkward to polish. There were twelve on the canopy, and a further four in the port sidelight.

Facing page:
Gloster Meteor T.7 aerobatic team from the College of Air Warfare at Manby in 1963, showing to good effect their 180 imp gal ventral drop tanks.
(via Ray Hanna)

Eric Sharp ended his career as a Flight Sergeant with the Battle of Britain Memorial Flight:

I was posted to Cranwell in 1951, after passing out at Halton, first employed on R & I (Repair and Inspection Flight), a name which gave way to ASF (Aircraft Servicing Flight) in the mid-fifties and is used to this day. There I was set to work with an 'aged' Corporal Fitter, who sported wartime medal ribbons, completing an engine change on a Prentice. I don't remember much about it, apart from being completely overawed at the world of real Airmen, Air Force and aeroplanes after the sheltered if rough life as an apprentice.

In the hangar was the station's one and only jet-engined aircraft, a Meteor T.7, WA619, which had been on an inspection for some time. Very few airmen at that time knew anything about the 'modern airplane' and I, full of bullshit and brimming with recently acquired knowledge (but no experience), was set to finish off the engine side of the inspection. I remember finding the fuel filter elements in the drip trays among the old lock wire cuttings and paraffin-soaked sawdust. After asking Chiefy to order replacements I explained the procedure I had been taught for replacing these items, and the technical workings of the half ball valves in the Lucas fuel pump governor to which the merest speck of dust or obstruction was death.

Of course the inspection came to an end and no replacement filters were in sight. Sticking to my guns, I refused to proceed any futher, treating the suggestion that I put back the old ones with scorn. To my horror, the Chief over-rode my juvenile and bum-fluff protests, retrieved the elements from where they still lay among the rubbish, gave them a quick rinse in a bucket of fuel, clapped them back into the bowls and bolted them on – where they flew perfectly, confounding my trained but immature technical soul!

It wasn't only the engine trade that lacked knowledge of the then high tech aeroplane, for on the post inspection test flight the pilot reported it flying a little one wing down. A most experienced Corporal Rigger, armed with a couple of spanners, went out on the line and gave it the aileron trim adjustment that years of working on Harvards and the like was judged about right. On take off the kite was noted to do a very swift and erratic circuit and landing and, after taxiing in, a very white-faced test pilot emerged, who when calmed down explained he had shot the circuit practically sitting sideways with one elbow braced on the cockpit wall in an effort to hold the stick central to stop a very high roll rate.

On reading the APs, the riggers found that Meteor aileron trim is adjusted with a jig incorporating a degree plate, and adjustments made only a fraction of a turn at a time. Anyway I found myself posted with the Meteor to HQ Flight, I suspect as much to get rid of me as the aeroplane.

Regarding servicing generally, odd things tend to stick in one's mind. For instance Meteor engine cowlings had

dozens of screws – I actually bought a Stanley Yankee Screwdriver to do the job, years before they were ever issued. Getting into the early small engine intakes was difficult, especially if wearing the awful kerosine suit, to check the gear box oil level during Before-flight Inspections. In those early days of jet aeroplanes, kerosine (later Avtur) was for some reason considered lethal, or likely to stunt your growth or something, and the answer was thought to be this one-piece rubber overall tightly fastened all round together with short rubber lace-up boots, for all who worked on or refuelled jet planes. They were dreadful things; the nearest I've had to endure since was the immersion suit, but for much better reasons.

James McNamara worked on Meteor T.7 engines:

On a Middle East Air Force squadron of which I was a member, we had three T.7s. These were coded V, W and X – known as the Venerable Virgin, Weary Willie and Xenon.

The T.7 was not the easiest of aircraft to work on, but very much the state of the Art in the fifties. Getting the two seats in or out was quite tricky, and smallish people (like myself) were 'volunteered' for this job. Loose-article checks were frequently carried out, and if someone announced they had lost a pencil, it was a major operation to find it. The owner was fined a nominal sum and the proceeds went to the Squadron Party Fund, the idea being that we tried to have no money in the kitty at the end of the year.

As the aircraft were used for communications and continuation training, we had many Senior Officers flying them, and it was quite something to present the Fine Book and Money Box to a Group Captain. I remember approaching one somewhat fearsome character with more than a little trepidation, and asked him for five bob. He considered this for a moment, then said "As a Scot, I'd like to point out that it wasn't a new pencil, so 4/6d should cover it"! Shared humour of this sort usually led to firm friendships, as was the case in this instance.

Much later, at an Open Day in the UK, I was looking after a T.7 and trying to answer the usual 'Joe Public' questions. How fast can it go? How much petrol can it carry? – and the really curly ones like, how many miles per gallon? The ones to be careful of were the ATC, who would want a quick answer to things like – 'What is the efficiency of the Derwent compressor over a range of RPM and altitude – density and so on? The standard answers to these questions was 'Sorry, that's classified'.

Anyway, towards the end of a tiring day, I was on a ramp-like stand, showing people the cockpit, when a commotion broke out. A small boy had decided to count the turbine blades in the starboard engine, and had managed to get himself impaled on the thermocouple probes. The ensuing noise was tremendous. However, I managed to get the very sooty and frightened blighter out of there. His parents immediately wanted to know who to sue, and what I would have done if I couldn't get him out. I resisted the urge to suggest I might have hit the starter! Anyway, we had him cleaned up and ice-creamed, and sat him up front for a few minutes.

For ages afterwards, I dreamed of being hung from the Air Ministry yard-arm – with full military honours. Even now, when I see a 'Meatbox', I always check the starboard tailpipe for wildly flailing grey-socked little legs!

Vickers Varsity

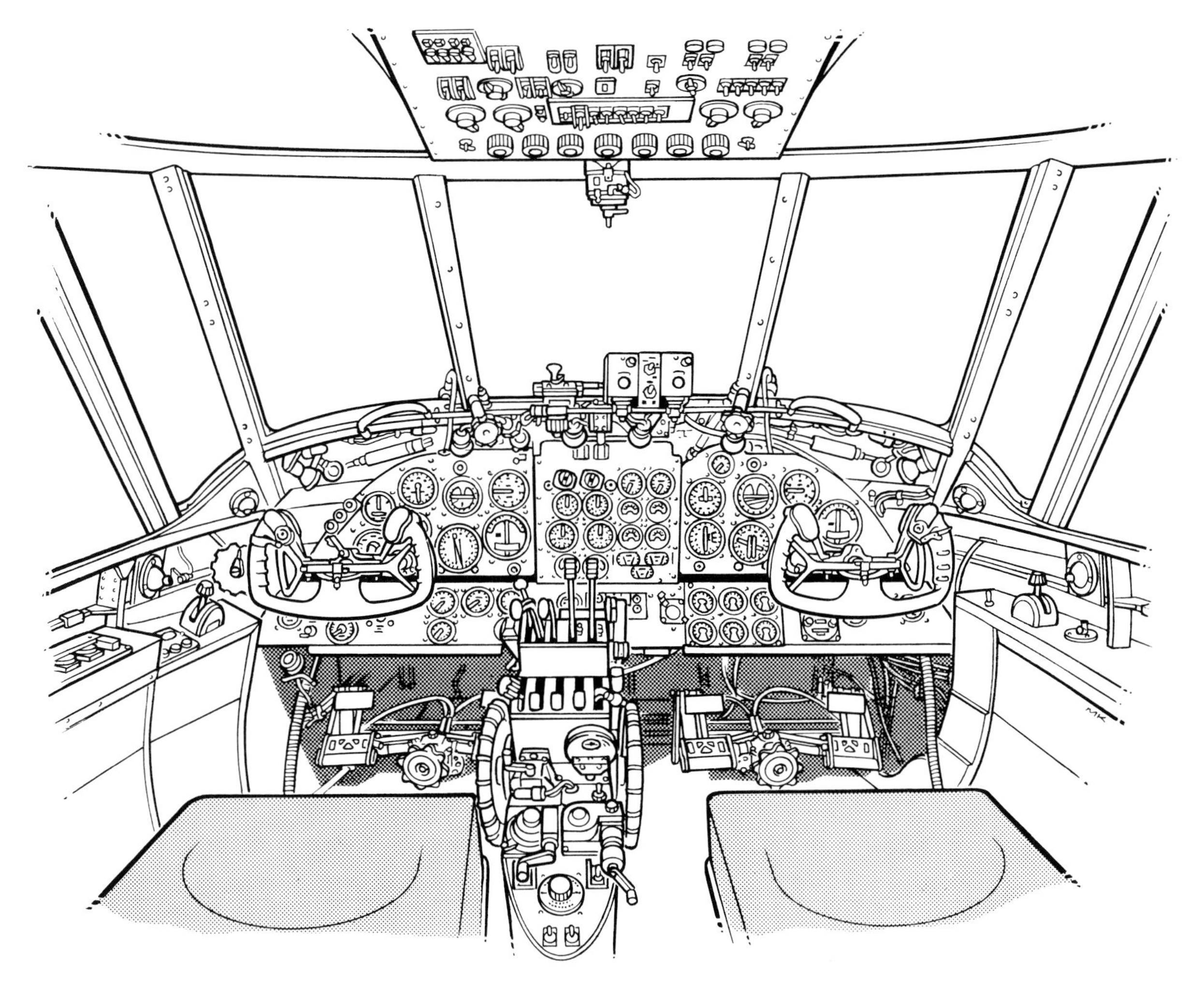

At the end of the Second World War, the RAF had a need for a medium-sized crew trainer, a role performed for much of the war by surplus Wellington bombers of various marks. From 1946, numbers of Wellington Xs were converted by Boulton Paul specifically as navigator trainers, the nose turrets being replaced by a streamlined fairing. In this guise they became the Wellington T.10, although the style Wellington T.19 was also considered for a time. They were a useful expedient but, not being

Specification

Power plant:	*Two 1,950 hp Bristol Hercules 264.*
Dimensions:	*Span 95 ft 7 in, length 67 ft 6 in, height 23 ft 11 in, wing area 974 sq ft.*
Weights:	*Empty 27,040 lb, loaded 37,500 lb.*
Performance:	*Maximum speed 288 mph at 10,000 ft, cruising speed 239 mph, initial climb 1,400 ft/min, range 2,648 miles.*

specifically designed for their task, they had many shortcomings, especially in the potential for an instructor to rescue a pupil from some of his worst mistakes.

These aircraft were only regarded as a stop-gap, and Operational Requirement number OR.249 was accordingly issued for a new post-war design. In the meantime the Vickers company had produced the Viking civil transport, and its military counterpart the Valetta, and therefore a logical next step was a derivative to meet the new requirement. Specification T.13/48 was issued on 20 September 1948, and Vickers were authorised to proceed with their Valetta classroom-type trainer, later to be named the Varsity, thus maintaining the tradition of academic names for RAF trainers.

The prototype (VX828) first flew on 17 July 1949, fitted with a tricycle undercarriage, which would be more appropriate for training pilots to take off and land post-war types of aircraft. Accommodating the steerable nosewheel entailed the addition of nearly five feet to the length, and the wingspan was also increased by six feet. A pannier, fitted under the centre fuselage section, incorporated a bomb-aiming position forward and stowage aft for twenty four 25-lb practise bombs in rows of six. A stowage rack had provision for remote equipment enabling the operation of Rebecca, radio compass, H2S, API, GPI and intercom.

The Varsity had a basic crew of three, comprising first pilot, second pilot/navigator and wireless operator, with six trainee stations. It could therefore train all crew members simultaneously. In the nose were the pilot-instructor and trainee separated by a pedestal, each having complete dual-flying controls, a big improvement over the Wellington T.10. Behind these were fitted side-by-side rearward facing seats for the wireless operators. Next came the bomb-aiming pannier, with provision for instructor and trainee, and having a mattress on which the pupil could lie prone. Aft of this came a station for an instructor and two navigator pupils. An astrodome in the roof was adjustable in height for use as a sighting platform.

Tests at Boscombe Down on the second prototype (VX835) included a trip to Khartoum, primarily to assess oil cooling and tropical suitability. The 60 hours flying involved in this exercise, including staging flights, also afforded an opportunity to obtain crew reports on the layout of the aircraft. There were a number of minor criticisms of detail, but in general the layout of equipment in both the cockpit and the cabin was well liked. Long cross-country flights were made by a single pilot, both by day and at night, and in a great variety of weather conditions, and none of these proved either difficult or tiring.

An initial order was placed for 60 machines, and RAF production eventually totalled 160. The first production machine (WF324) flew on 21 May 1951, and deliveries commenced on 1 October 1951 to No 201 Advanced Flying School at Swinderby, where by the following March it had completely replaced the Wellington T.10. At that time newly-winged trainee pilots came straight from single-engined Harvards or in some instances Balliols, to be taught the intricacies of flying twin-engined piston aircraft. They also learnt such skills as taxiing, asymmetric flight, single-engined overshoots and critical speeds and landings. The two 2,100 bhp Bristol Hercules engines gave ample power, and could easily cope with a single-engined baulked landing, even with a full load of trainees. Despite the big increase in aircraft size, it was found that it took only four hours to convert a pilot from dual to solo flying, though the ten-week course included a further nine hours of exercises.

The Varsity was gradually introduced into a number of units of Flying Training Command, giving advanced instruction to Pilots, Navigators and Bomb-Aimers, in addition to being used for signals training. Its range enabled it to undertake long-distance training flights, sometimes as far afield as North Africa. It also participated in annual air defence exercises, in which it took the part of an enemy bomber. Navigator training was given on Varsities at No 1 Air Navigation School at Topcliffe (later Stradishall) and 2 ANS at Thorney Island (later Hullavington then Gaydon), the task being taken over by 6 FTS at Finningley in 1960.

From August 1960, 4 FTS at Valley had a small number of Varsities for training Jet Provost-trained pilots destined for large propeller-driven aircraft, such as the Shackleton and Britannia. This function was transferred to 5 FTS at Oakington two years later. The Varsity was withdrawn from service in 1976.

Gordon Hodkinson had his first experience of the Varsity at the Bomber Command Bombing School at Lindholme in December 1953:

I was flying the Lincoln and converted locally to the Varsity, both aircraft being used for training bomb aimers. The Varsity was a tolerant aircraft, and ideal for pilot multi-engine conversion and navigation/bombing training. After the Lincoln, which was a bit difficult to enter (over the main spar or up a tall ladder), and which needed a fair amount of attention to produce a reasonable landing, the Varsity was a joy. A gentleman's aircraft, easy to enter, with a comfortable roomy cockpit, it was straightforward to handle in the air and, with the tricycle gear (my first), easy to land and taxi.

At Lindholme we flew student navigators who dropped 24 practise bombs per flight from a height of 4,000 to 8,000 feet. The aircraft was very manoeuvrable when required, and a good bombing platform when straight and level. Up at 20,000 feet for high-level bombing, on oxygen and with the engines in 'S' gear, performance was still good but not so comfortable, being unpressurised and decidedly cold in winter. I seem to remember 'changing gear' in the climb – at about 12,000 feet the boost started to drop so we levelled off, throttled back to zero boost, selected 'S' gear, opened the throttles and continued the climb.

The bomb-aimer's position provided a marvellous view, but was not supposed to be occupied during landing, being about 18 inches above the runway. People would try it, of course, and get quite a shock the first time.

Vickers Varsity T.1 WJ939 'Q' of No 201 Advanced Flying School based at Swinderby in 1953.
(Author)

The single-engine performance was good provided the speed was 115 knots or above. It was a knee-trembling exercise keeping straight with rudder against full power on one engine, and trying to hold climbing speed of 115 knots. Things became a little easier at circuit speed.

A memorable demonstration of controllability was the glide landing from 1,000 feet. One turned finals level at 1,000 feet, waited until the runway disappeared under the nose, then throttled back to idle, selected Full Flap and pushed the nose down to about 30 degrees (it seemed vertical) to hold 130 knots. It worked a treat providing one rounded out in time! Most people tended to round out early and had to ease on a bit of power.

The short take-off was impressive. Select full flap, throttles to full power on the brakes. brake off, lift off at 80 knots after a very short run, then fly level above the runway, accelerating to 115 knots, then climb.

The Hercules engines were powerful and dependable. They certainly took quite a lot of 'hammer' without complaining, in the pilot conversion role. They never sounded happy when idling on the ground though, clanking like an old steam engine – something to do with the sleeve valve, perhaps. I only remember one case of engine failure (loss of oil pressure) during my time. One design fault was putting both Idle Cut-off switches side by side on a panel above the pilot. Incidents occurred in training when the wrong ICO was switched off and caused a flurry of hands in the cockpit to sort things out. A guard was later fitted between the switches to reduce the possibility of error.

The anti-icing system worked well to keep the wings clear, but the engine intake guards used gradually to ice up until completely covered. Then a flap automatically opened to allow hot air to be drawn from behind the engine. This hot air could also be selected if required, but this resulted in a loss of power, so engine speed had to be increased to maintain height and speed. This happened to me once in the Berlin Corridor at a medium level, but fortunately we were able to maintain our level and the engines accepted the increased fuel consumption. Generally though, icing never seemed a great problem.

The aircraft was roomy, and would carry a fair load, but care was needed to balance the load to prevent the tail sitting on the ground! A metal rod was supplied to be hung under the rear fuselage whilst loading, to prevent such a thing happening, and it was needed once when picking up a Sea King engine from St Athan. There was no problem loading this item, but it was heavy and aft of the main spar, putting the rod under compression. We moved all the parachutes and everything loose forward of the spar, and two of us sat in the front whilst the third crew member removed the rod (now free) and came up front with us. The balance must have been right because she flew well!

Squadron Leader Dick Smerdon recalls:

When I took command of the Home Ferry Squadron in 1956, my taxis were three Ansons and two Varsities. I spent most of my time ferrying aircraft ranging from Oxfords to Spitfires, and from Hunters to Javelins, leaving the taxiwork to those qualified to do so. However, I had a few dual sorties in the Varsities. I liked the tricycle undercarriage, and the power-weight ratio seemed such that the performance was impressive. I recall viewing through the bomb-aimer's window the nosewheel during the exit from the landing runway on to the taxiway, and being surprised to see how much the nosewheel hub and axle could move from the position of the centre of the tyre in contact with the ground.

Warrant Officer Paddy Porter worked on Varsities for a period of over six years early in his career, both

M E
WJ908

H
ROYAL AIR FORCE SIGNALS
WJ945

V
V

Vickers Varsity T.1 WJ608 'ME' of the Central Flying School at Little Rissington in 1960.

(MAP photo)

at first-line servicing on the squadron and second-line servicing in Aircraft Servicing Flight (ASF). After completing 18 months' boy entrant training as an Air Wireless Mechanic, but still being five months too young for Man's Service, his first posting in March 1956 was to No 2 ANS at Thorney Island:

On arrival at Thorney I was posted to the Radio Servicing Flight (RSF), but was quickly moved into the ASF to help out. I was so keen that I hadn't even changed a pair of my studded boots for shoes (ex-Boy Entrants were not issued with shoes until they arrived at their first unit). I soon latched on to a National Service mechanic who was carrying out an inspection on a Varsity, but as I was under age I couldn't sign for any work that I completed. I spent the first couple of weeks fetching, carrying and generally learning the ropes. On my first day in ASF I was helping this lad to do his inspection, and he sent me to get a tool, but in the meantime someone had moved the access ladder to the entry door, so when I returned I couldn't get back in. While I had been

Vickers Varsity T.1 WJ945 'H' of No 115 Squadron, RAF Signals Command, based at Tangmere in 1961.

(MAP photo)

away the Varsity had been jacked up as part of the inspection routine. I eventually climbed up a set of step ladders near a wing tip and walked right along the wing, over the engine to the fuselage, studded boots and all. None of the emergency windows were out, but the astrodome blister on top of the fuselage had been removed. Yes, I clambered up the side of the fuselage and in through the astro hatch. The sound of my boots was heard throughout the interior of the aircraft, and that afternoon I got my first pair of RAF shoes – after a short lesson in the English language from the Hangar Flight Sergeant!

From the groundcrew point of view the Varsity was a good aircraft to work in. There was plenty of room, with easy access for most jobs, even to the Hercules engines, whose cowlings unfolded and hinged backwards. Entry to the aircraft was through a door just aft of the trailing edge on the port side of the fuselage. A metal ladder, which could be folded in half for stowage, was carried in the rear of the aircraft when flying.

Originally the RAF training Varsities carried yellow bands around the rear fuselage and on both wings, but this was changed when 'dayglo' was introduced. I think it was around 1959–60 that the first 2 ANS Varsity appeared in the

Vickers Varsity T.1 WL638 'V' of the Bomber Command Bombing School at Lindholme in 1963.

(MAP photo)

new colour scheme. Silver overall with 'dayglo' nose, fin and wing tips.

As a navigation trainer, the Varsity was fairly well equipped, being fitted with the following items: two 10-channel VHF transmitter/receivers, TR.1985 and 1987, operated by the pilots via independent control units, fitted in the centre of the cockpit, above the instrument panel; one High Frequency/Medium Frequency (HF/MF) transmitter and receiver Type Tx1154 Rx1155, with its associated power units, Pu 33B/Pu 35A, this was operated by the Air Signaller, for voice or morse communication; two intercom systems, one for crew and one for students each having its own A1134 amplifier, Pu 173 vibrator pack and 2 volt accumulator; One radio compass installation with a remote control unit at the navigator's position. One Gee II navigation radar, one Rebecca MkIV radar (Eureka homing, BABS approach), and a Sperry G4B gyro compass were also fitted at the navigator's position.

A remote radio compass bearing indicator and G4B indicator were fitted into the pilot's instrument panel. One astro compass which, when needed by the navigators, could be removed from its storage bracket and fitted into the perspex astrodome. One type P12 compass fitted in the roof of the cockpit above the pilots. One drift sight was fitted on a special mounting, on the port side of the fuselage between the main entrance door and navigator's position. One Aldis signalling lamp with clear, red and green glasses was stowed at the signaller's position, and when required a Mark IX bubble sextant was carried by the navigators. Some years later the Varsities were completely updated with modern wireless and radar equipment.

The Varsity carried a selection of different types of radio aerials, each being coupled to a specific equipment. The VHF, radio compass sense and Gee II aerials were solid whip types, similar to those used on cars. The Rebecca IV had blade aerials fitted each side of the nose, just below the cockpit and on both outer wing tips. The radio compass rotating-loop aerial was mounted in a loop housing on the top centre-line of the fuselage aft of the astrodome. There were two HF/MF stainless steel wire aerials, one being fixed like a clothes line from the top of a mast, which was mounted on the fuselage above the signaller's position, to a tensioned insulator at the top of the fin. The other was a trailing aerial which comprised a reel of wire terminated at the free end with a string of lead ball weights. The reel was fitted onto a ratchet assembly at the side of the signaller's position, and when required he would reel it out through a fixed tube which protruded below the lower fuselage on the starboard side of the aircraft. It was not uncommon for a trailing aerial to be lost during flight or for it to part company with the aircraft on landing if the signaller had forgotten to reel it in. It was a wireless man's job in ASF to make up trailing aerials and one's fingers could become quite sore splicing the steel wire. To ensure the correct length you had wire stretched right down the hangar, one hell of a job because it if kinked you had to start again.

I think it was about 1957–58 that the new type blue cloth flying helmet entered service as a replacemernt for the WWII leather type. A bone dome fitted over the top for protection. This new helmet also introduced a smaller mic/tel plug and socket, plus the mic/tel lead which plugged into the aircraft was quite short, being tailor-made for ejector seats. To overcome this problem in the Varsity and Valetta, I was one of a two-man team tasked with fitting the first trial installation of long extension leads. These mated with the new helmets, to every intercom position throughout the aircraft, and could be stowed away when not in use. Eventually pigtail adaptors were introduced as part of the aircrew's flying kit.

One other trial modification I did while in ASF was to fit a second radio compass control unit into the cockpit roof between the two pilots. This enabled the pilots to tune into homing beacons instead of having to rely on the navigators. Several trial flights were carried out, but for some reason this modification was never accepted, and I had to remove all the extra kit. I never did find out why.

In those days, when an aircraft had been through an inspection in ASF, it was an unwritten rule that members of the servicing team would fly on the Air Test, and I have 27 Varsity flights recorded in my log book. A flight test crew would consist of a pilot and co-pilot, the remainder of the crew being made up of several mechanics and fitters, usually of corporal rank and below, from the various trades which had equipment to check or set up during the flight. The co-pilot, if not another pilot, would usually be an Air Signaller, and I seem to remember that the majority of Air Signallers at Thorney were trained to take off and land, and many flew regularly as co-pilots.

The first thing you did when you knew you were going on an air test was to visit the safety equipment section and book out a parachute, harness and Mae West. A flight test normally lasted about 50 minutes, and during this time lots of individual checks were carried out. I used to test the T.1154 R.1155, but I never did risk letting the training aerial out. Then I would move down the back to the navigator's position, next to the radar man who would be running both radars, and test the radio compass. The electrician would check and monitor various voltages with an avometer and adjust regulators etc. When the pilot was satisfied that all was well, both up front and in the back, he would order everyone to strap in, in preparation for clean and dirty stalls.

For this, the pilot would throttle back the engines until the aircraft buffeted and began to drop its nose in a stall; he would then catch it just in time with the throttles and all would be normal again. A clean stall is one with wheels and flaps up, and a dirty stall is one with them down. On one particular flight, I was sitting next to the radar mechanic. The pilot had just called over the intercom 'I am throttling back for a dirty stall'. I think everyone was a little tense on these occasions, even if you had done many such trips before. Just as the Varsity was about to drop its nose, it suddenly flipped over, almost on its back. I remember seeing the radar mechanics' watch, which he had on the desk to time something, plus several parachutes, floating in the air. How

Vickers Varsity T.1 WJ945 of No 5 Flying Training School at Oakington.

(Paddy Porter collection)

Vickers Varsity T.1 WF371 'S' of No 5 Flying Training School at Oakington in 1973.

(Map photo)

the pilot pulled us out and regained control I shall never know, but he did. I think we were at about 6–8,000 feet at the time. The problem was caused by a flap either jamming or having been set incorrectly, which caused it to act like an aileron, i.e one flap was fully down and the other jammed up or only partially down. As I was quite young at the time it was just a bit of excitement, but if it happened to me now, I'm sure I would have to change my underpants!

The rear crew seats, comprising two signallers, one screen navigator, two student navigators and any spare seats that were fitted down the back, all faced rearwards. Consequently, there was a tendency to leave your seat and go and stand behind the pilots to see out front. In this position, however, you were standing on the escape hatch. In an emergency the front crew could lift open this hatch and vacate the aircraft. I believe it folded in half, hinged along the middle, and, when activated, a door on the outer skin would swing inwards making a kind of slide. I remember on one test flight we had a navigator on board and he told me always to be careful when standing behind the pilots, because he had seen the emergency hatch open by itself a couple of times. Unfortunately, this same navigator died in a Varsity crash a few weeks later. I was a trumpeter in the Thorney Island band at the time, and I played the Last Post and Reveille at his funeral. The Varsity was on a navex, and crashed somewhere in the north of England killing all the crew.

Work on the squadron flight line consisted mainly of carrying out routine servicings, such as before flight, after flight and turn round inspections; plus the rectification of any faults that occurred. Until about 1960, a pre-flight inspection for a wireless man included a functional check of all VHF channels except the two tuned to the distress frequency. Every radio man had his own call sign, and nine channels on each set were checked against a standby radio rig which was installed in the RSF. If you were the only wireless man on early shift, and ten plus aircraft had to be prepared for flight, you really had your work cut out trying to get them ready.

You were supposed to have a 24 volt trolley accumulator plugged into the aircraft before you switched on any radio equipment, but there were never enough trolley-accs to go round. In these circumstances you were expected to push trolley-accs between aircraft as they were needed. This didn't work very well because the various trades, especially if faults cropped up, required power for different lengths of time. One short cut was to switch the aircraft ground-flight switch to the flight position and then carry out your checks quickly using the aircraft's batteries. If the electricians caught you, though, it normally meant an ear-bending.

A before and after flight inspection also included a physical check of all the aerials. The whip aerials were fixed rigidly to mounting plates in the roof of the aircraft and they were poked out through rubber grommets. When a pilot reported one of the VHF sets unserviceable with no transmit or receive, especially in very cold weather, investigation would often find an aerial missing. Vibration during flight could cause hairline cracks at the base of the aerial rods, moisture would then seep in and freeze, causing the aerial to break off. Quite often the aerial would just be lying on top of the fuselage still attached to the rubber grommet.

The HF/MF mast and loop aerial were also affected by water, and in extremely wet weather, especially when aircraft were parked in the open for any length of time, water would seep into both. As the aircraft climbed or dived the mast aerial had a nasty habit of drenching the signaller. Water in the loop aerial would often drip through the drive tube into the base of the loop drive unit, just above the navigators. It was quite common to look through the small window at the desyn indicator, to check a reading, and see it immersed in water.

One of the main problems with the intercom system in the early days (I believe it was modified with two A1961 amplifiers with their own internal motor generators around 1959–1960) was a loud whistle, which normally happened at start of flying in the morning, shortly after a crew had climbed on board and plugged themselves in. The heaters for the valves in the A.1134 intercom amplifier worked off 2 volt accumulators, and when these ran down, low voltage caused the system to go ape. The intercom system was greatly improved after the 1961 Amps were fitted.

When an aircraft landed, especially at night after a navigation exercise, there was a distinctive smell inside – a mixture of stale oxygen, chewing gum, hydraulic oil, rubber and warm radio equipment. We usually waited for all the crew to depart before we climbed on board to commence our checks, unless it was pouring with rain. Then we would get inside and stand at the back out of the way. As soon as the crew had left, we would rummage through the discarded flying ration boxes, hoping to find the odd Mars bar or packet of chewing gum. The student navigators were favourite, because they had to work hard during the flight and didn't get much time to eat their rations.

I sometimes had a funny feeling when I climbed into a Varsity or Valetta at night by myself, especially if it was shortly after the aircraft had landed. The creaking and spluttering from the engines as they cooled down always seemed that much louder. If I was clearing a radio fault, I would soon be in a world of my own, headset on and voices or music in the earphones. About 1957 we had a newly promoted Wireless Corporal posted in. I can't remember his name, but I did work with him for quite a spell before he was discharged. He came to us from the Far East, I believe, and was recovering from a nervous breakdown. His brother had been an air signaller and had been killed in a Valetta crash somewhere in Malaya. This lad was servicing radio sets in his section one day, when he suddenly thought he heard his brother's voice screaming at him. Evidently he went berserk and smashed the place up, including the radios. He told me about it several times when we were working together, and as I was quite young at the time I suppose it had an effect on me for a while.

Towards the end of their course, student Navigators would be let loose on an overseas navigation exercise, usually to Gibraltar. Normally four to six aircraft would make the trip, leaving on a Thursday or Friday and returning on the following Monday. Ground crew would be selected from volunteers, and a senior non-commissioned officer (SNCO) with authority to oversign all trades would be in charge. The rest of the team would be made up of corporals and below. Everybody, air and ground crew, would attend the flight briefings so we all knew what was going on. Two or three of us would fly as supernumary crew in each aircraft and distribute rations and coffee during flight.

On one of these trips, in WL683 'Q', we headed into bad weather over the Bay of Biscay, so the other mechanic and I went down to the back of the aircraft. Using our parachutes as pillows, we stretched out on the floor between the extra seats and aircraft spares, then both fell into an unintended deep sleep. Some time later the crew decided they would like some coffee so the pilot called over the intercom, 'Coffee lads' – no response – 'How about some coffee' – still no response. The Varsity was not pressurised, so if it went above 10,000 feet the crew plugged into oxygen. Unknown to us, the pilot had climbed way above this to get out of the bad weather, but no one had thought to tell us to put oxygen masks on. By now the pilot had descended to the normal operating altitude, and he was puzzled when neither of us answered him over the intercom. A dig in the ribs and a whiff of oxygen soon brought us round, however, then after a bit of leg pulling from the crew we dished out the coffee.

This was quite an eventful trip, because as we approached Gibraltar all the wireless equipment started packing up, even the intercom. When the crew realised I was a wireless man they gave me a free hand to try to get something working. The trouble was, the screen navigator on this trip was the Wing Commander in charge of navigator training, and he became rather interested in what I was doing, watching closely every move I made. All the major items of wireless and radar gear were easily accessible, the VHF sets were mounted in trays in a crate between the main spar and the signaller's position on the starboard side. Access to the bomb aimer's position was via two doors positioned in the centre of the floor, in line with the radio crate. The Varsity floor was soon like a radio workshop, I had covers off the sets swapping valves and crystals, tweeking variable resistors etc, but all in vain. I even had a go at fixing the Tx1154 and Rx1155, but that would not work either.

Eventually I got all the kit back together, and asked the pilot to try to contact Gibraltar. No joy at all, we couldn't even contact the other aircraft in front and behind us. At this point we were getting dangerously close to Gibraltar, and especially Spain. The Wing Commander, realising I wasn't getting anywhere, decided to leave me and go up front to consult with the pilot. I think they had decided to fly overhead and waggle the wings, which was the usual 'NO RADIO' ident. By this time I had used up all my special vocabulary, and as no one was watching, I decided to vent my frustration by giving the radio crate the boot treatment – whereupon both VHF sets started working, I couldn't believe it, and the crew thought I was ace!

At Thorney, 24 volt trolley-accs were normally used to provide power to the aircraft for ground servicing purposes, but overseas it was more common to use petrol electric sets, whose power leads terminated in a standard NATO plug. This meant we had to use a special adaptor which was plugged into the Varsity socket, located on the starboard side of the nose under a small hinged flap, to enable us to get a 24 volt supply. Everything went fine on engine start, until the pilot signalled – remove external power. If you were not extremely careful, the power lead would pull out of the adaptor and leave it plugged into the 24 volt socket. This happened to us as we were preparing to leave Gibraltar. As the lead pulled away, the flap sprang down and shorted out on the large brass pins that were left protruding from the rubber adaptor. The length of fine rod down the centre of the hinge glowed, sparkled and then melted, allowing the small flap to fall on the deck. Luckily no serious damage was done, and it didn't delay us from leaving Gibraltar.

On the way back to the UK, I spent the first part of the flight down in the bomb aimer's position, then when it became too dark to see anything I decided to return to my seat. I had just got back into the main cabin and was closing the bomb aimer's entrance doors when the co-pilot tapped me on the shoulder. He asked me if I would sit in his seat and act as co-pilot for a couple of hours. I think he had had a good time in Gibraltar. The pilot briefed me on the main instruments and controls, but as the aircraft was being flown on George (automatic pilot) I didn't have much to do really. I remember seeing the Channel Islands in the moonlight, 10,000 feet or so below us, and the shimmer on the sea and the beams from a lighthouse – a truly beautiful sight.

de Havilland Vampire Trainer

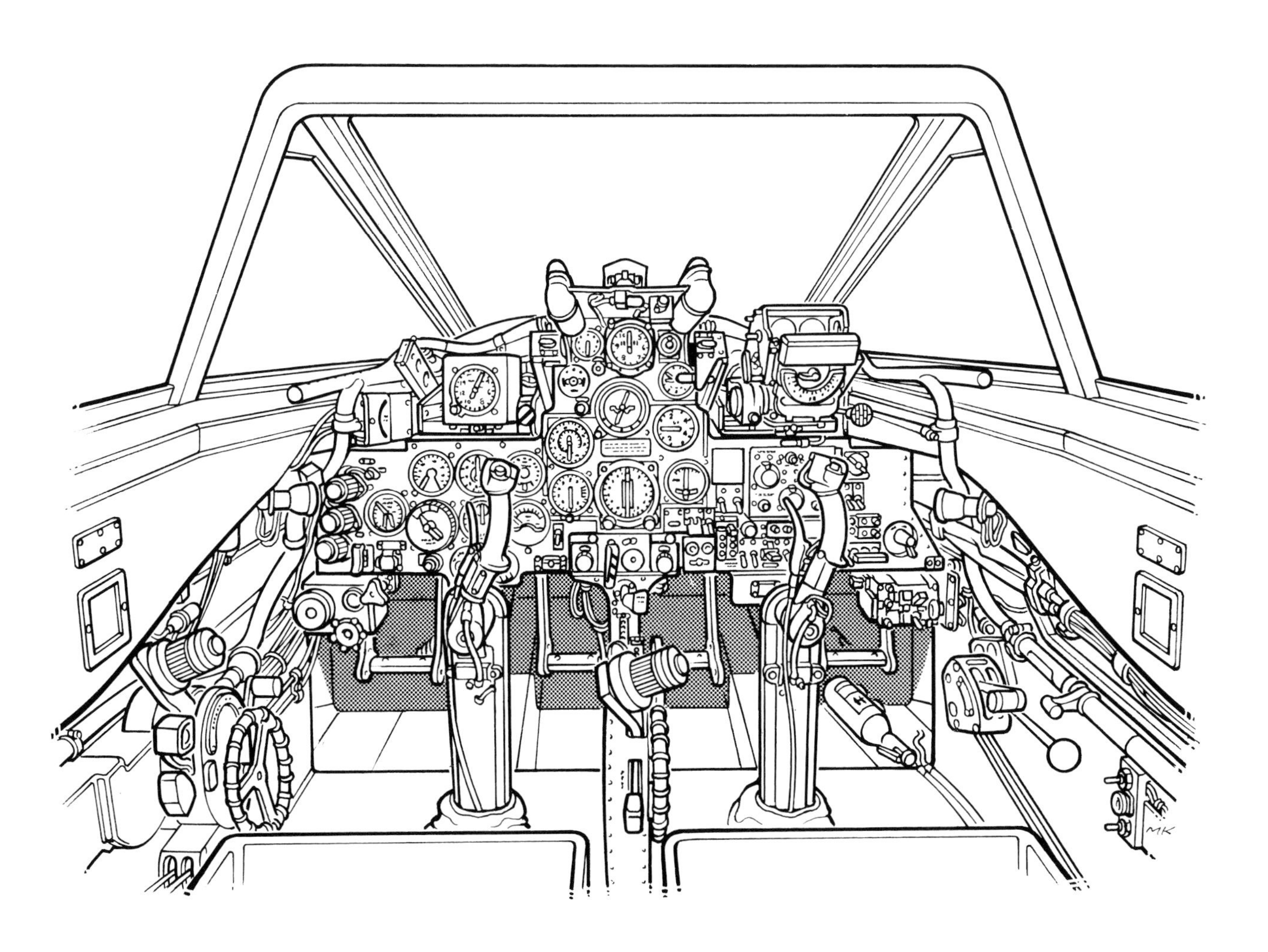

Specification

Power plant:	*One 3,500 lb de Havilland Goblin 35.*
Dimenisons:	*Span 38 ft 0 in, length 34 ft 6½ in, height 6 ft 2 in, wing area 261 sq ft.*
Weights:	*Empty 7,380 lb, loaded 12,920 lb.*
Performance:	*Maximum speed 549 mph at 20,000 ft, cruising speed 403 mph, initial climb 4,500 ft/min, range 850 miles, endurance 2.3 hrs, service ceiling 40,000 ft.*

The introduction into service of the de Havilland Vampire T.11 brought about a revolution in RAF flying training. For the first time pilots were able to qualify on a jet aircraft.

The prototype Vampire Trainer was a private venture aircraft built by the Airspeed Division of de Havillands, who undertook the design and tooling at Christchurch. It was exhibited in the static park at the 1950 Farnborough Show with the manufacturers' marking G-5-7, and made its maiden flight on 15 November 1950. De Havillands had already sold many Vampire fighters to overseas air forces, and saw a market for a two-seater trainer version. The new conversion was based on the Vampire FB.5 fighter-bomber, but took advantage of the experience gained in designing the Vampire NF.10 night fighter. The wings and tail booms of the Trainer were identical with those of the FB.5 but it was fitted with a wide cockpit, which was straightforward and uncluttered, with side-by-side seating, dual controls and dual instrumentation. The cockpit canopy had a welded tube framework, with a large single-piece optically correct front screen flanked by two direct-vision panels.

Alterations were made to the tail surfaces to compensate for the effects of the extended nose. The de Havilland Goblin engine differed from that used in the FB.5 only in having cabin pressure tapped from an engine compressor instead of needing a separate cabin supercharger. Designed as an all-purpose trainer, the machine had the four 20 mm Hispano cannon of the FB.5, which enabled it to be used for gunnery instruction at both high speed and high altitudes. In addition there was provision for two 1,000 lb bombs or eight rockets.

The Ministry of Supply, then responsible for aircraft production, took an interest and Specification T.111 was issued, an order being placed on 5 July 1951 for two pre-production machines, to be designated the Vampire T.11. The first of these (WW458) flew on 1 December 1951, but in the meantime there was sufficient confidence in the concept for two full production orders totalling 147 aircraft to be placed on 3 October 1951, the first (WZ414) being delivered in February 1952. Further production was authorised under Specification T.111P on 17 April 1952, over 500 being ultimately produced for the RAF. The Royal Navy also took an interest, drawing up naval requirement NR/A36, leading to the Sea Vampire T.22 variant, of which 72 were delivered under Specification T.111P2, issued on 28 May 1952.

Tests were carried out between February and April 1952 on WW458, to establish its general suitability as a trainer, and to see if there was any notable difference in its handling characteristics compared with the private venture prototype. It was found to have very similar performance capabilities to those of contemporary jet fighters and was pleasant to handle, making it eminently suitable for both advanced and operational training, and likely to inspire confidence in the pupil.

Spinning was rather unpleasant, but for an intermediate trainer this was not necessarily a

Top:
An early production de Havilland Vampire T.11 WZ421 of the Armament Practice Camp at Acklington in July 1953.
(Sqn Ldr D.W. Warne)

Bottom:
De Havilland Vampire T.11 XD426 just off the production line in December 1953. This is a late version showing to good effect the dorsal anti-spin extension to the fins, and the one-piece canopy.
(Ministry of Supply)

drawback, as pupils would gain an early introduction to circumstances similar to those they were soon to encounter in current fighters. There was now a sharp wing drop at the stall, however, which, if uncured, would rule out its use in that role, as trainee pilots would have insufficient experience at that stage to cope safely. Further tests however, on the second production machine (WZ415), showed that the problem had already been overcome by the manufacturers.

The T.11 was very suitable for armament training, its side-by-side seating being especially welcome as the instructor and pupil had similar sighting systems, which would be of considerable help in gun-firing, rocketry and bombing. Absence of ejector seats was a major disadvantage, however, as was non-duplication of the undercarriage lever, which could prove embarrassing on occasion. A minor fault was optical distortion by the curved roof panels, which could lead to difficulties in the closing-in stages of formation flying.

The arrival of the Vampire T.11 in Flying Training Command enabled the sequence of pilot training to be radically improved. Hitherto pilots had received *ab initio* training on Provosts at a Flying Training School, then progressed to an Advanced Flying School for jet training on Meteor T.7s before going on to Operational Conversion Units. With the arrival in 1953 of this new machine at the FTSs, it became possible to complete the early stages of their training at the one unit. However, the change from the Prentice/Harvard/Meteor sequence to the new Provost/Vampire sequence added £10,000 to the cost of training a pilot.

Initial deliveries of the Vampire T.11 were mainly to AFSs, but these were gradually closed down and their function taken over by the FTSs, the first to do this being 5 FTS at Oakington, whose first all-through course commenced in May 1954. The syllabus for the Vampire T.11 comprised 110 hours of training, which included dual flying instruction, instrument flying, aerobatics, navigation exercises, formation drill and night flying.

Later production batches of Vampire T.11s incorporated a number of improvements recommended after evaluation at Boscombe Down. The earlier machines had some tendency towards rudder overbalance, which was cured by limiting rudder travel, but this in turn tended to impede recovery from a spin. To overcome this, the fin surfaces were increased by fitting dorsal fairings extending forward along the tail booms. Visibility from the cockpit was also a problem, and interim modifications to the framed canopy were later superseded by fitting a new moulded single-piece canopy. The safety aspects were considerably enhanced by the fitting of Martin-Baker fully automatic ejector seats.

The aircraft was eventually phased out with the arrival on the scene of the Gnat, but by then more than 3,000 pilots had taken their wings on it, the last unit to use it for all-through training being 3 FTS at Leeming.

Squadron Leader Dick Smerdon was one of many pilots to fly both the fighter and trainer versions of the Vampire:

I first flew the Vampire 5 at the Day Fighter Leaders School. By that time I had flown about 65 hours in the Meteor. The most noticeable difference in performance was in acceleration, to the Vampire's detriment. We used the Vampire for Air-to-Ground firing, and for low level and dive bombing. It was a handy and responsive aircraft.

Two years later, I joined a Squadron still equipped with Vampire F.3s. I well remember the poor acceleration and slow rate of climb as we took off for Malta with drop tanks fitted. In aerobatics however, the Vampire was delightful to fly. In March 1956, I did a little training in the Vampire T.11. The side-by-side seating was novel for a single-engined trainer, but looking back there was a bonus over the Meteor of an ejection seat. I am not sure that I worried about that at the time. Being a bulky chap, I found the cockpit a rather tight fit.

De Havilland Vampire T.11s of No 5 Flying Training School at Oakington around 1954.
(Author's collection)

I never liked IRTs (Instrument Rating Tests) much, but this was probably because I never liked being supervised. I suppose I was perhaps slightly under-confident when being tested – not that I ever failed my test so far as I can remember. Moreover, I preferred being tested on the Meteor since I was more at home in it than the Vampire, which I had not flown very much. Sometimes you didn't have the choice, one or other of the machines in the IR Flight being unserviceable.

It was a very cramped machine to fly in – two blokes side-by-side in a cockpit that had originally been designed for one. Admittedly it had been widened considerably, but it was still rather a squeeze.

Previously I had been Personal Assistant (PA) to Air Vice-Marshal 'Zulu' Morris, who was SASO (Senior Air Staff Officer) at 2nd TAF under Harry Broadhurst. He announced one day that he intended to fly up to Ahlhorn in a Vampire 5, so I asked if I could go too, never having flown a Vampire in my life. I had to dash off down to Wildenrath and get checked out. In those days all you had to do was sit and digest Pilot's Notes, be shown round the aircraft by someone who told you how it started, what speed it stalled at and various other simple pieces of information. You clambered in and off you went! It was all very relaxed. As far as I can recall the only warning they gave me was to be careful on finals. As the speed dropped off you had progressively to push the control column further and further forward until it almost touched the instrument panel, otherwise you would stall it. The nose up change of trim must have been quite severe. I did four trips as No 2 to 'Zulu' Morris (ex-Battle of Britain pilot! I felt very proud), to Ahlhorn and back to Laarbruch and back.

When you took off and landed you rattled down the

Robin Brown also flew both versions:

I first flew the Vampire T.11 in 1955 when flying Sabres with 234 Squadron at Geilenkirchen in Germany. There was no two-seat Sabre, so we had our periodic instrument rating checks either on Meteor T.7s or one of the two T.11s of the Instrument Rating Flight attached to Flying Wing Headquarters.

When your rating was due, once a year, you had to be checked out on a series of exercises (one of which was instrument take-off) so as to retain your instrument rating (either 'White', 'Green' or 'Master Green'). On every squadron there was an IRE (Instrument Rating Examiner) who had done the CFS course and who had probably been an instructor at some stage. They were quite fair and gave you a thorough check, but if you weren't up to standard you had to keep going back until they were satisfied.

De Havilland Vampire T.11 WZ610 of No 45 Squadron at Butterworth, Malay in 1955.
(Eric Sharp)

runway on those tiny little wheels in a tiny little machine that was a sort of pram with wings. It was really comic.

Squadron Leader Don Brittain flew Vampires with 4 FTS:

The first T.11s that came into service at Valley had no ejector seats, had a small lid on top to get in and out, and did not have the extra finning. They were very stable in a spin, and prone to enter one from aerobatics. One crew on my course went into a spin deliberately at 22,000 feet (it was normally 20,000 feet), and the aircraft wouldn't come out. They tried to jettison the canopy, but couldn't get the restraining strap off – it was on the floor and had been constantly trodden on – so they sat there with full anti-spin control on waiting for the end – it came out at 2,000 feet and they overstressed it recovering. The student quit and the instructor was given some leave!

Because of the spinning, I never did a roll-off-the-top solo until I had been on a squadron some considerable time. Another of my friends got into a spin and couldn't get out. He jettisoned the canopy, undid his straps and went out like a cork out of a bottle – he was in an inverted spin and out he shot!'

Squadron Leader Mike Sparrow also flew the Vampire T.11 at FTS Valley:

These aircraft had just arrived at Valley. They had a very solid canopy with several bars across the top of one's head. These first machines had no ejector seat, but later ones did.

At Valley I received my first met lectures on high altitude conditions. I was told of a student who got airborne from Valley on a normal training high-level exercise. He climbed through the usual cloud and carried out his briefed manoeuvres which included high speed runs, aerobatics, etc. On descending through cloud he could not get Valley on the R/T but came out over a sea which he assumed was the Irish Sea. He turned onto 090 degrees, crossed an unfamiliar coast and, with tanks almost dry, landed at the first airfield he came to – in Belgium! He had, of course, hit a jet-stream.

Chris Ashworth recalls:

The Vampire was the first aeroplane I flew which was truly three-dimensional in that it had a decent service ceiling. It took a fair time to get up to 40,000 feet, mind you, but it could be done and in reasonable comfort, unlike the roughly contemporary Meteor T.7 in which it was difficult to even talk to the pupil at altitude because the cockpit was not pressurized. It was also an advantage to be able to see what he was doing – or about to do – a facility which did help prevent such mistakes as using the undercarriage instead of the airbrakes to recover from a 'high speed' run.

The aircraft was easy to start, taxi, take-off and land. The view from the cockpit was very good and the controls well co-ordinated. The Vampire was an excellent instrument flying trainer because it needed a light touch to be flown accurately, a useful cross-country machine because it was

De Havilland Vampire T.11 aerobatic team of No 4 Flying Training School at Middleton St George in 1955. (Author's collection)

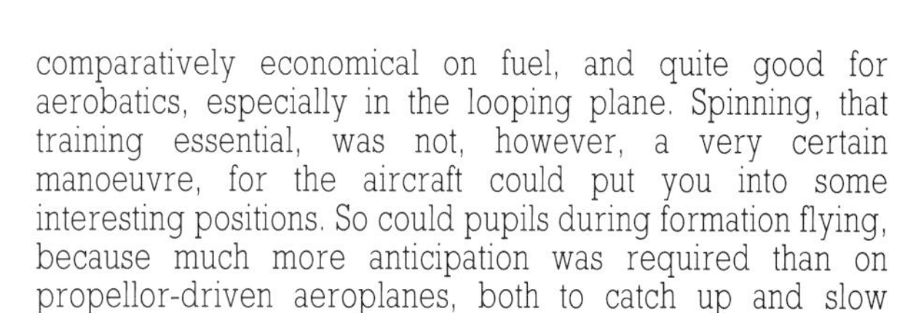

comparatively economical on fuel, and quite good for aerobatics, especially in the looping plane. Spinning, that training essential, was not, however, a very certain manoeuvre, for the aircraft could put you into some interesting positions. So could pupils during formation flying, because much more anticipation was required than on propellor-driven aeroplanes, both to catch up and slow down.

Circuit flying was straightforward unless it was raining. Then it could be difficult to see forward through the flat windscreen, especially at night. The undercarriage gave a hard ride on the ground, and, unless the landing was a 'greaser' (now discouraged but then thought desirable), on touchdown as well. Perhaps one of the most off-putting features was the strange noise sometimes produced by the Goblin engine.

The T.11s which I flew whilst instructing did not have ejector seats and we all risked incipient back trouble climbing in and out with parachutes strapped to us. Later I

Facing page, top:
De Havilland Sea Vampire T.22 XA107 '681' of Station Flight Lossiemouth around 1966 seen here fitted with long range tanks.

(MAP photo)

Facing page, bottom:
De Havilland Sea Vampire T.22 XG743 '798/BY' of Station Flight Brawdy around 1970.

(MAP photo)

Below:
De Havilland Vampire T.11 'N' of No 238 Operational Conversion Unit being serviced in the Aircraft Servicing Flight hangar at North Luffenham around 1957.

(Eric Sharp)

flew Vampires with 'bang seats', but wasn't very impressed because space was so tight that the seat back leant forward making it very uncomfortable.

Altogether I thought the Vampire an excellent trainer, if a little on the flimsy side – certainly the condescending name of 'kiddy-cars' much favoured by Meteor 'drivers' had some justification, for their aircraft had a Rolls-Royce feel about it which was not only due to the make of engine.

John Norris, who experienced the Vampire T.11 as a rigger at 233 OCU Pembrey in 1957 recalls:

I was first involved with one on a ground run after an engine change. After preliminaries – intake guards fitted, trolley-accumulator connected, etc. – an engine corporal made to light up and begin the run. The electric starter wound up the Goblin engine nicely, but as the starter revolutions peaked, fuel surged out of the jetpipe, forming a large puddle between the tail booms. Grey fuel mist also emerged briefly, then there was a flash as the igniters woke from their slumber, and the whole issue burst into flames. The occupant of the cockpit became rather agitated and indicated to myself and others present that he would rather like us to push the aircraft forwards, away from the burning fuel. With a roaring inferno enveloping the tail booms and tailplane, I had no desire to go behind the aircraft. Those with me indicated how the push should be applied – at the wingtips. But first the chocks had to be removed. Braver souls than I did this, then we pushed and rolled the aircraft clear of the fire, which burned itself out quite quickly. A second start was then tried with the same result and the same rolling forward. A tow back to the hangar, and a new set of igniters effected a fix, and some time later a successful restart raised the whistling wail of an angry Goblin.

In time, wet starts became routine to me, and I affected a casual nonchalance about them, staring about with a bored expression. Inevitably I ended up with Wadpol and rags cleaning the soot off the singed rear ends because such chores fell to the sprog. Even raised on jacks the Vampire hardly towered above you. They were quite simple airframes and while some things, like the engine, uncowled, were easily accessible, others were most definitely not. For example, the elevator and rudder cables inside the tailbooms called for a blind dexterity when they needed attention. One could either peer through the access panels at them or thrust one's hands inside and fiddle away at the guides.

The undercarriage and its retraction system was sturdy, neat and simple, rarely giving trouble and relatively easy to service. Component changes were straightforward, as was the 'setting up' and adjustment afterwards. The cockpit pressurisation system was simple and rather crude by comparison with systems I had to cope with in later years. The ejector seats in the T.11's crowded cockpit always gave me pause for thought, and no-one could have been more cautious than I about checking the safety pin positions before entering. Sprog as I was, my work was always carefully monitored and generally the more menial tasks fell to me, except for one brief period of acclaim when I made up and spliced two steel cables for the undercarriage mechanism of one particular aircraft. Fresh from training as I was, I did the job in a day. Feeling rather pleased with myself after words of praise from Chiefy, my balloon was pricked when one of the 'old sweats' told me 'Sergeant Smith usually does them. He can make up a pair in an hour'. He could, too, as I saw for myself later on.

Something extraordinary happened one day at Pembrey during an 'air firing phase'. It was a fine day with clear skies and the flight line was very busy, the Armourers especially so, arming up and galloping about with truckloads of live rounds all belted up. I had been assigned to assist with 'straps in', 'seeing off' and 'turn rounds'. A Vampire was returning from the range after a 'stoppage', its guns having jammed during firing, when eight or ten rounds suddenly loosed off inland in the general direction of Carway and Trimsaran. Everyone on the line heard it and, as one man, we took refuge, myself grovelling under a fuel bowser along with its civilian driver. At the end of its landing run the offending Vampire braked to a halt and sat there with engine running, while a gaggle of rather pale-faced armourers set off for it in a Land-Rover at a rate of knots to make it safe. Those stray rounds passed unnoticed by the local community, and by God's good grace presumably did no damage wherever they landed.

Geoff Cruickshank was a rigger with 5 FTS in the mid-fifties:

The Vampire was quite an easy aircraft to service, certainly from a rigger's point of view. Almost everything was at eye level – hydraulics and pneumatics were grouped together in the gun bay.

The bane of a rigger's life was the oil and water trap situated in the gun bay. This had to be cleared twice a day, which meant unscrewing gun doors on non-modified single-seaters. These had very long screw threads quite easy to undo, but line-up afterwards was always a chore. Luckily most aircraft were later modified with three clips, and were very easy to clip up.

Wheel changes were a doddle, the main wheels having just a single large nut and split pin. I remember one sunny day in 1956 at Oakington, a student pilot landed his Vampire with brakes on and both main tyres burst on touchdown. He slewed the aircraft across the main runway and cut his engine. There were about twenty other aircraft in the circuit. The duty corporal and I loaded two spare wheels and a jack into the squadron Land-Rover, and took off across the grass. We jacked up one side, changed wheels, then the other side, hooked up the towing arm and drove off to the first exit – total time five or six minutes!

Hunting Jet Provost

Specification (Jet Provost T.4)

Power plant: *One 2,500 lb Armstrong Siddeley Viper 202.*

Dimensions: *Span 36 ft 11 in, length 32 ft 5 in, height 10 ft 2 in, wing area 213.7 sq ft.*

Weights: *Empty 4,650 lb, loaded 7,400 lb.*

Performance: *Maximum speed 410 mph at 20,000 ft, initial climb 3,400 ft/min, range 700 miles, endurance 2.5 hrs, service ceiling 30,000 ft.*

The Jet Provost entered service with the RAF in 1955, to become the first basic jet trainer to operate with any of the world's air forces. It says much for its design that over 30 years later it is still in service, though likely to be replaced before long.

It was in March 1952 that the idea was first mooted of fitting a jet engine to the Percival Provost. Jet-powered aircraft were then rapidly becoming standard, and some means was being sought of speedily introducing jet engines into the initial stages of flying training.

The first reaction to the proposal was that a strightforward conversion would be unlikely to prove practicable. The change in engine weight would have a considerable effect on the balance of the aircraft, and in turn this would almost certainly have a serious effect on the aerodynamic characteristics.

Nevertheless, interest was maintained, and in December 1952 the Directorate of Research decided the idea should be pursued as it offered the possibility of making a practical trial at a comparatively low cost, as compared with a completely new design. There was the added advantage that if the experiment proved a success, it would be possible to convert existing follow-up orders for piston-engined Provosts into Jet Provosts. A basic jet trainer would consequently be in service considerably earlier than would otherwise have been the case.

It was agreed that on this basis an order for ten Jet Provosts for trials be placed, under Specification T.16/48 Issue 4, this being an extension of the Provost specification to meet Operational Requirement OR.321. Some expense was inevitable, however. The fixed undercarriage of the Provost would have to go, and fitting a retractable undercarriage would be much more expensive. The new Viper engine which was to be fitted would also be expensive, as the Jet Provost would have to bear the high cost of the early engines, as opposed to sharing the cost with other Viper-engined designs which would probably have been possible later. Accordingly an order was placed for ten machines, and the first of these, XD674, flew at Luton on 26 June 1954 with a 1640 lb static thrust Armstrong Siddeley Viper 101.

This emerged as a side-by-side machine with unswept low aspect ratio wings, manual controls and hydraulically-assisted services. As had been anticipated, it proved necessary to compensate for the weight of the engine, which was now behind the crew. The cockpit had therefore been moved forward and the fuselage lengthened. To compensate for this, the side area of the tail had been increased and additions were later made to the fin surfaces. D-shaped air intakes had been fitted each side of the fuselage immediately ahead of the wings, and it had also been necessary to adapt the wing structure to incorporate a retractable undercarriage and additional fuel capacity, with provision for wing-tip tanks. Spoiler/air brakes were fitted both above and below the wings, whose profile had to be redesigned near the roots as the absence of slipsteam from an airscrew affected the low-speed handling characteristics.

The first Jet Provost T.1s to enter service went initially in August 1955 to the Central Flying School (Basic) at South Cerney, then soon afterwards to 2 FTS at Hullavington for service trials. Eighteen pupils were arbitrarily chosen for the first jet trainer course, going on afterwards to complete their training on Vampire T.11s, thus becoming the first RAF pilots to have done so without ever having flown a piston-engined aircraft. The Jet Provosts on which they had flown were later transferred back to the Central Flying School to continue this experiment at its main airfield at Little Rissington, when 2 FTS moved to Syerston in November 1957.

Since then, the Jet Provost has been periodically upgraded. The first change was the fitting of a 1750 lb thrust Viper 102 (ASV.8) in the T.2 version, which first flew on 1 September 1955 and had other modifications. Its undercarriage, flaps, air brakes and wheel brakes were now controlled by a hydraulic system, the undercarriage was about 3 feet shorter, and the rear fuselage had been redesigned to allow for a larger tailpipe and to improve airflow.

The T.2 was only built in small numbers, however, and the first version to be used by the RAF in quantity was the T.3, which had its maiden flight on 22 June 1958, production eventually totalling 199 aircraft. In addition to the engine change, this incorporated a number of improvements from the T.1, including the shorter undercarriage, Martin-Baker Mk4 ejection seats, clear-vision cockpit canopy and wing-tip tanks, UHF radio and Rebecca Mk8. It first equipped 2 FTS at Syerston in September 1959, followed later by the other similar schools.

This was followed by the T.4, first flown on 15 July 1960 and featuring the 2500 lb thrust Viper 200. To enable the RAF to evaluate the machine with this increased power, two early machines in the second batch of T.3s were completed with Viper 200s for trials. It was found that the extra power made the aircraft more versatile and, far from offsetting its capabilities as a basic trainer, actually enabled pupils to attain a higher standard of flying. Orders were placed for an eventual total of 187 of this variant.

Finally came the T.5, first flown on 28 February 1967 as a private venture, prototype XS230 being a conversion from a T.4. Initially designated the BAC.145, this version had an extended nose, a rather bulbous single piece canopy, a larger jet pipe, additional integral wing fuel storage and an extra radio. It also featured a pressurised cabin for high altitude training, the system being controlled automatically and coming

into operation when the aircraft had climbed to 8,000 feet. Ancillary equipment included a hood seal, a new altimeter and a cabin-pressure warning light. In addition there were various export versions produced under the name Strikemaster. 110 T.5s were built.

Many T.3s and T.5s have been brought up to T.3A and T.5A standard respectively, these incorporating newer avionics such as ILS, VOR and DME. In the meantime the makers have undergone a series of name-changes, first to Hunting Percival in 1954, then plain Hunting in 1957, next British Aircraft Corporation in 1960 and finally British Aerospace in 1977.

Squadron Leader Allan Corkett was involved in the introduction into service of the Jet Provost:

The world's first *ab initio* jet training experiment was carried out at 2 FTS, RAF Hullavington, Wiltshire, which became the only Flying Training School to operate both the Piston and Jet Provost at the same time.

The first course of pupil-pilots to fly the Jet Provost commenced their training in September 1955, and there were to be a further two courses completed before the end of the flying training experiment in November 1957. This unique trial, to evaluate the concept of pupil-pilots' flying training being carried out only on jet aircraft, was carried out by eight flying instructors and eight aircraft. I was fortunate to be instructing on the aircraft throughout the two years.

The Jet Provost was a most pleasant aircraft to fly, with no handling problems. Its very small Armstrong Siddeley Viper engine was first rate, with a very unusual characteristic for a jet engine of that time, in that (if need be) the throttle could be operated – in like manner to a piston engine throttle – without the slightest tendency to 'flame-out'.

Early in 1955 two Jet Provosts had been used at the Central Flying School during the preparation of a provisional basic syllabus. However, the fact that the training of the first course of pupil-pilots commenced as soon as the flying instructors familiarisation trips had been completed, meant that service trials of the aircraft were being undertaken at the same time. It would, therefore, have been quite remarkable if 'teething troubles' had been absent during the most intensive flying, often undertaken (as usual during flying training) by very inexperienced and quite often ham-fisted pilots.

Nevertheless, I recall that although there were the usual minor problems, which were soon dealt with, three even more serious snags (which were design problems) resulted in only minor damage to particular aircraft, and were sorted out without any serious disruption to the flying programme.

In a lighter vein, I remember that one of the more serious problems came to light at our relief landing ground. I had positioned my aircraft on the grass alongside the runway prior to demonstrating to my pupil a short take-off, and we were waiting for another Jet Provost to land. It touched down, and as it passed my aircraft its port undercarriage collapsed. The aeroplane gyrated behind us on one wing-tip, almost completing the circle and finishing with its wing tip just behind mine. Having noted from the aircraft's letter who was the instructor, I called over the R/T, '*Good* afternoon, Douggie'. I heard his reply '—, and a good afternoon to you Allan', just as I switched my engine off and went to his assistance. The leg pivot was later redesigned and fitted to all aircraft without further problems.

The training experiment was to prove a complete success, and the production mark Jet Provost, with its ejector seats and refinements which emanated from these trials, has together with later marks been the basic jet trainer in the Royal Air Force for over thirty years. Also, it should be remembered that this aircraft has been used for military purposes by several countries over the years, especially in a ground-attack role. Its robust construction has enabled it to carry the weaponry, and the dash and superb manoeuvrability must have made it quite a useful striker.

Peter Middlebrook was a pupil with 2 FTS at Syerston from June 1961:

The course proper started with ground school, and drills done on a static rig, which consisted of a Jet Provost fuselage with switches and toggles on it, and fuses which could be pulled to simulate various failures. We went through all the usual things – theory of flight, engines, instruments, etc. – and in a surprisingly short period of time we found ourselves sitting next to our instructors in the cockpit of a Jet Provost T.3, quite a new aircraft at the time.

Throughout my time at Syerston, I don't think I ever had any problem flying the Jet Provost. What I did have a problem with was getting it back on the ground. It was an extremely light aircraft with a great desire to fly.

The first exercises we did consisted of gently taxiing the aircraft out, turning left, turning right, watching the instruments move, doing the checks, rumbling round the peritrack to the marshalling point. Lessons seemed to be based on imparting skills, imparting technical knowledge and combining these with basic airmanship. We always, as far as I remember, flew with full internal tanks and full tip tanks. Once at the marshalling point one carried out one's pre-take-off checks and checked the approach to see if any aircraft were close to the airfield. If the approach was clear, one called for line-up and take-off. It was a very easy aircraft to taxi. Once lined up, one hit the brakes, opened the throttle, checked engines, pressures, temperatures, JPTs etc, and if all was well, off you went.

It was a very easy aircraft to keep directionally straight on the ground, and at the appropriate speed, one applied gentle back pressure and it took off quite easily. I remember it as a straightforward aircraft to handle with no vices that I encountered, and early exercises consisted of steep turns, 30 degree banked turns and then on to more advanced exercises such as spinning and a little bit of cross-country navigation.

Once back in the circuit, one turned downwind and did the downwind checks. I think I can even remember these still. A – airbrakes in; U – undercarriage down, three greens; F – flap take-off, the fuel 400 lb at least; H – harness tight and locked; B – brakes 'on', 'off' exhausting. My problem started once I turned finals. I think what I had basic trouble with was the notion that if you were going to undershoot, this was corrected by opening the throttle, whereas if the speed were too high, this was adjusted using the stick. This is, of course, a very simple and sound principle in retrospect, but as a young lad in my teens, flying a jet aircraft for the first time, I

XD676
XD677

XD693

Hunting Percival Jet Provost T.1s of No 2 Flying Training School at Hullavington banking over cliffs in 1955.

(Author's collection)

found it very difficult to put into practice. I also found that once I had placed it firmly on the ground, it didn't necessarily stay there, and I think on my second solo trip on the aircraft I bounced all the way down the Syerston runway from one end to the other in what I now know to be a pilot-induced oscillation, whereby I was out of phase with what the aircraft was doing, worsening the problem. I survived that particular near-accident.

I was not the only pupil with problems. On my second familiarisation, I was taxiing round the southern peritrack, when I suddenly became aware that my instructor was extremely agitated. He kept shouting things like 'put the nose down'. As we hadn't left the ground yet, this clearly didn't relate to my activities, so I looked where his eyes were pointing and I saw a Jet Provost at about 1,000 feet over the end of the runway in what looked like a semi-stalled condition. It did at that moment stall, and fell all those thousand feet back on the end of the runway with a great BANG. It didn't catch fire. The next thing I noticed was the student jumping out of the aircraft and running across at full speed back to the Crew Room, passing on the way the fire crew who were intent on dowsing any flames that did appear.

I had been taxiing the aircraft all this time, and it was a miracle that I was still on the peritrack. We went round to the marshalling point, but it was quite clear the airfield was going to be closed for some time, so we taxied back down the main runway, past the heap of wreckage which had moments earlier been a Jet Provost. We turned into dispersal, closed down, went into the Crew Room, and found that the student involved had been taking off on a solo cross-country with a full fuel load. It had been a hot day, and he had tried an extremely steep climb and just stalled the aircraft in. Apart from a scratch to the side of the head he was completely unhurt. The Jet Provost, however, I don't think survived.

I also remember another incident when a friend of mine was taking off solo in the Jet Provost on the short runway at Syerston. This started by the main Newark road and ran off the far end into the Trent. As we passed the aircraft on the peritrack, I noticed that he had left his airbrakes out. We immediately radioed him, and he closed them, shot off down the runway and took off successfully. I've often wondered exactly what would have happened if he had left his airbrakes out while he tried to take off on a short runway with full fuel load. Almost certainly he would have ended up in the river.

Hunting Percival Jet Provost T.1 XD693 'QZ' of No 2 Flying Training School being refuelled at Hullavington around 1955–57. Note the very long undercarriage legs; a hangover from having to keep the prop tips clear of the ground.

(Sqn Ldr A.H. Corkett)

It gradually became apparent that the course was moving into two distinct groups. There were those that had progressed quickly into solo, and were moving on with few problems. There was a second group, of which I was a member, who were having problems. I remember it took an inordinate length of time for me to go solo, and this was only achieved by changing instructor to a very nice chap called Flight Lieutenant Sweet. As I was having trouble going solo, he took me over, and we set off in a Jet Provost together to Wymeswold, which was one of Syerston's Relief Landing Grounds. We spent about 35 minutes in the circuit. He then asked me to land the aircraft and stop it at the end of the runway as he was too frightened to carry on, and I had better get on with it myself. The moment for the first solo had arrived. I remember he got out of the aircraft, he made up the seat so that it could be flown with only one pilot, and I set off gingerly round the peritrack. I stopped, did all the checks at the marshalling point, parked on the runway and realised that this was it. I opened throttles, let the brakes go and off we went.

I can remember to this day the surprise I felt when the speed built up much faster than normal. Before I knew where I was, I was at rotate, I pulled back on the stick and the aircraft went up like a rocket, about 400 yards earlier than I had been used to. It was only half way round the downwind leg that I suddenly realised that minus one pilot, the little Jet Provost flew even more readily than with two pilots. It certainly was a major surprise, and I don't remember being warned about it. Anyway, I flew a creditable circuit, and put the aircraft down for my first solo. The instructor then got back into the aircraft, and we flew back to Syerston. He seemed well pleased. I certainly was.

Once having gone solo, however, progress still seemed to be slow. A disaster occurred to me when Flt Lt Sweet was posted after a few sorties. I then had another instructor, whom I loathed. According to him, the centre line of the runway ran all the way round the world, and met at both ends of the runway, and if he said I should be on the centre line, I should be on the centre line, wherever I was in regard to the airfield. It was apparent from the start that he and I were never going to make it together. As an instructor he had more chance of staying than I did.

About this time I noticed members of the slower part of the course starting to disappear. They were what is known as 'suspended' from the course, and made their way back to Hornchurch. It became apparent that I was heading down the same road when I came up for 'review'. This involved a check ride with the Wing Commander. He had obviously been badly burned in an aircraft accident at one time because he was heavily scarred, and I remember when flying with him that he was meticulous in making certain that not one extra inch of skin was exposed to any potential fire-risk.

I have to say that my 'chop' ride was actually inspirational. We set off in the aircraft, climbed above a cloud and he put the aircraft into some unusual attitudes, which I promptly recovered from. We then motored on for a while doing nothing in particular, and he suddenly handed over to me and said, 'Right, find your way back to the airfield'. I have to confess I hadn't the slightest idea where we were. But I do remember taking the situation well in hand, and I flew the aeroplane on a particular heading for a particular period of time, and then at the end of what I

Hunting Jet Provost T.3 XM384 '26' of No 2 Flying Training School at Syerston around 1960. Improvements over the T.1 and T.2 include an uprated engine, clear-vision canopy, ejector seat and tip tanks. (Hunting photo)

thought was the right amount of time pointed down through the clouds and said, 'The airfield, I think, is down there'. He said, 'OK, let's have a look'. We descended through the cloud smartly, and sure enough there was the airfield directly underneath us. I don't know what his feelings were about the whole thing, but I was absolutely amazed.

We then joined the circuit, and I did some creditable circuits and landings. Eventually I turned off the runway, taxied the aircraft back to the pan, closed down and scuttled off to make a coffee for the Wing Commander. What I found encouraging was that he was debriefing me all the time, and we actually had a very thorough debrief during the next hour and a half. This was widely interpreted as a good sign. The efficient flying training system would not waste time on people who were about to be chopped. My future hung in the balance for about two days, and then I remember being smartly suspended. I was not told this by the Wing Commander, in fact I never saw him again. If I remember rightly, I was one of about five people chopped during that week. We all found our way back to Hornchurch for reselection, and three months later I started navigation training.

BAC Jet Provost T.4 XR697 '33' of No 3 Flying Training School at Leeming, during Wright Jubilee Trophy competition at Little Rissington in May 1966. (Dave Watkins)

Squadron Leader Don Brittain, an instructor who has flown nearly 5,000 hours on the Jet Provost, recalls:

I first flew JPs in 1961 at Cranwell, and have been flying them almost continuously since except for two years on piston Provosts in Malaya and two years on Buccaneers.

On a final navigation test a student told me we were overhead Diss (we were at 25,000 feet or so at the time). 'How do you know?' I asked. He whipped on 90 degrees of bank and pulled to the stall, in a series of semi-controlled stalls we sank, earthwards and he said, 'Cos I went to school in Diss and that's it down there'.

Once, I was leading two students in Vic formation and as was the norm I told them to ease out for a breather. When I told them to rejoin into close, they both slapped on too much bank, and came in like bats out of hell. Doing my chameleon act, trying to look at both of them at once, I saw them both reverse bank to stop coming in. Seeing two aircraft belly up coming my way, I decided it wasn't a safe place to be, so I

BAC Jet Provost T.4 XP571 of the Red Pelicans aerobatic team from the Central Flying School around 1963–64. (Dave Watkins)

pulled back smartly on the control column, and the two students just missed each other where I should have been.

At Cranwell, the Station Commander, who only had one good eye, used to like formation. We calculated that if we only put him into Number 3 position (echelon port) it would keep him out of mischief and make use of his one good eye. It wasn't until just before he was posted that he commented, 'Do you know, it's a funny coincidence that I always seem to get echelon port in formation, and it's bloody awkward as my good eye is on the left!' We never did let on to him though!

When a course graduated we used to do a flypast forming the course number, eg '96' would be flown – the number actually being flown in reverse to appear correct as viewed from the ground. On one I was in, I was on the inside of the number, looking right of course to formate, when in my peripheral vision a tip tank appeared from the left. The two leaders had got too close and the two numerals had intermeshed. My opposite number was looking the other way as well. I had someone with me at the time, but he never said a word.

Another student who had been doing very well caught me on the hop as he had lulled me into a false sense of security – motto 'never relax!' Whilst doing a normal powered approach, instead of rounding out as normal he suddenly jerked the control column hard back. Adrenalin flowed remarkably quickly and I moved like greased lightning onto the controls, but too late. Luckily the aircraft stalled wings level instead of flicking, and a heavy landing on all three wheels ensued. As with other students, he couldn't explain why he did it.

Another of my students (who is now a Squadron Leader) checked three greens on the aircraft on finals, when in fact he hadn't got any lights at all. Why? Who knows? That's why I think there will always be accidents, all humans make mistakes. I know this is a fact – I remember making one in 1951!'

Ground crew also had their problems. Nevil Gardner recalls:

During Apprentice training at Halton on the airfield, an instructor, who had been given dispensation to taxi in order to provide an element of realism, bogged down his Jet Provost on the far side of the airfield. Needless to say, it was some time before he reappeared on foot. Neither the digging out team nor his flight commander were impressed!

Another Instructor demonstrated a dry start in the 'old workshops'. The noise in the confined space was very impressive. So much so, the Flight Sergeant made one of his rare appearances in the bay, to say a few pithy words!

David Watkins serviced Jet Provosts at the Central Flying School at Little Rissington during 1966-68:

I arrived at the CFS in the spring of 1966 from a tour with Javelins (ugh!!) of 228 OCU, Leuchars. The unit comprised No 1 Handling Party with Jet Provost T.3s and T.4s, and No 2 and 3 Handling Parties with respectively Varsities and Chipmunks, plus a detached Flight at Fairford (later Kemble) that flew the dreadful Gnat. The Engineering Wing also operated a Scheduled Servicing Squadron and Rectification Squadron.

To my horror I was detailed for No 1 HP – the sight of three, sometimes four, lines of Jet Provosts (normally 10 aircraft to a line) was awe-inspiring! The CFS operated a Composite Trained system, which meant that we had to be conversant with not only our own trade (I was an Airframe Fitter), but also Engines, Electrics and Instruments.

The CFS, of course, trained seasoned pilots to become QFIs, and their course was quite intensive, often flying 10-15 aircraft per 'wave' per day, so the Jet Provost proved a rugged and forgiving aircraft. We often flew with an Instructor if a spare seat was available. I found the cockpit quite roomy and well laid out, and the view from it was excellent. The aircraft seemed easy to fly provided the nose was kept well up.

The JP was a basic aircraft, and looked rather toy-like, but it was easy to work on for servicing and rectification, having plenty of access panels. The engine was equally easy to work on, having two large hinged panels on top of the fuselage. The nose cone was also hinged to facilitate access to the radio equipment and to replenish the oxygen system. Tyres were frequently changed (especially at the beginning of a course), and the engine would occasionally suffer a 'wet start' due to heavy-handed pilots. This was easily remedied by removing the two drain plugs on the underside, although this invariably meant a soaked sleeve if you were slow removing the drain plug. Refuelling between sorties was

BAC Jet Provost T.5 XW296 '57' and others of No 1 Flying Training School at Linton-on-Ouse banking in formation near Fylingdales early warning radar station around 1970–73.

(British Aerospace)

simply achieved by two filler caps in the wings (one each side) and the tip tanks.

Little Rissington was sited on what must have been one of the highest spots in the Cotswolds – in summer you roasted and in winter you froze. I recall one airman who was detailed to act as starting crew to the 'weather kite' on an early January morning. Plugging in the trolley-acc, he clambered upon the wing to jump in the cockpit, but slipped on the ice and fell. Scrambling for a handhold, his hands literally stuck to the metal on the wing due to the sub-zero temperatures. A medic had to be called to release him to prevent the skin tearing from his hands. Two weeks later, still suffering from minor frostbite, he was posted to the Middle East!'

Kev Darling is a Corporal A/T/A at Cranwell, with four years experience of working on Jet Provost T.5As:

At Cranwell I first spent one year in an airframe component servicing bay, then the last three years as Junior NCO in

charge of Primary, Primary Star and Equalised Servicing (Nos 1-4). The T.5 is the version with tip tanks, no nose strakes and higher tyre pressures, and the T.5A is the reverse.

The Jet Provost on first sight is definitely a compact little beast, sometimes known as the 'Dinky Toy', part of 'Teeny Weeny Airways'. First impressions should of course always be treated as such, as the Jet Provost is definitely designed for those of short stature and slightly deformed shape. Being 6 ft 2 in and fairly normal, the JP came as rather a shock, especially for one used to the room available in the Vulcan, Victor and even the Buccaneer.

Even fully raised on jacks, the JP isn't very high off the ground, as many people can testify, with cut heads and lumps missing out of their backs. The most common complaint from this aircraft is the infamous 'JP knee', an affliction that eventually hits everybody in the Airframe Trade. Though a very simple aircraft, most points of access are located underneath.

Fitted with a cable operated undercarriage, a carry-over from earlier JP marks, the JP5 would have benefited if the cable, jack and mechanical locking presently fitted had been replaced by the installation of a totally hydraulic system. This would have simplified the servicing of this awkward system.

Other hydraulic systems fitted include the airbrakes/lift spoilers, each side having an individual jack. The flaps are also hydraulically operated, having one jack connected to the starboard operating lever and connecting to the port lever by cables, the original rods having been removed by modification action. Flap operation is by hydraulics with Teleflex follow up, and indication is provided by desyn transmitter.

Flying controls are manual and cable operated, except

in the case of the rudder and elevator, for which rods are employed in the area of the jet pipe. All flying controls have balance tabs, with the starboard tab on the elevators and the port tab on the ailerons acting as balance tabs, their operating wheels being located in the cockpit. Part of our servicing includes climbing up the jet pipe area to inspect the control rods and the forward fin mounting. Apart from becoming very dirty, the whole area can give you a cramped feeling and it is always a relief to reach the outside again.

Flight Sergeant Sam Mullen had Jet Provost experience with 2 FTS at Syerston:

I joined the Air Force in March 1960 and trained as an Airframe Mechanic. In December 1962 I was posted to Syerston, and there worked on Jet Provosts as a junior technician. There were about 50 JPs on the station, mostly Mark 3s, and the flying was on a centralised system from a single flight line. I spent most of my time working on the rectification team in the hangar, where we carried out major, minor and primary servicings etc, and also rectification of any faults which were beyond the capability of flight line crew. The JP was a smashing aircraft to work on. Most of the problems were fairly easily dealt with, and there weren't too many difficult jobs.

One of the more awkward and complicated ones was wire locking of the undercarriage jack. The JP being close to the ground, one had to lie on one's back working upwards through a small panel, and when adjustments were required on the eye end, it meant breaking the wire-locking and then relocking it, which was quite an involved job. The diagrams in the AP showed a view looking down on it, whereas of course when you were actually wire-locking it you had to look upwards, which added to the problems. The first time I did this particular job, my NCO ripped it apart and made me do it again!

All flying controls on the Jet Provost were operated by cables except for the undercarriage, which had one hydraulically operated jack, which in turn operated cable and pulleys to raise and lower the tricycle undercarriage. During my time working on the Jet Provost, they had a problem with the undercarriage cycling. A pilot coming in to land would lower his undercarriage, it would go down, show three greens on the instrument panel – then retract of its own accord. On occasion this would happen just as the pilot was about to touch down. Several incidents occurred from this malfunction, on one occasion when an aircraft was coming in to land at our satellite station at Wymeswold, and of course the pilot touched down on the underside of the aircraft. I was part of a team tasked to go Wymeswold, dismantle the aircraft and load it on a Queen Mary trailer to bring it back to Syerston for repair. This was another new experience for me, to go to another station, which was virtually just a runway, and recover an aircraft. Dismantling the JP was no problem, nor was loading it once we got the crane into position, but following the Queen Mary back along the A46 to Syerston doing about 50 mph with a police escort in front and behind was certainly novel! This undercarriage problem was eventually resolved.

Another problem we had with the JPs on the flight line was when refuelling through an open-line bowser. The hoses and nozzles on these were similar to those on standard garage pumps, hand-held nozzles being controlled by the operator. After a spate of aircraft fuel leaks, an investigation was carried out and the problem was traced to the nozzles being too long. If the nozzle was pushed in too far, it nipped the flexible bag type fuel tanks that were fitted in the wings. To remedy this, all the bowsers on the station had their nozzles shortened. We operated for quite a time without further problems, then suddenly the fuel leaks started again. It transpired that a new bowser had been delivered to the station, and nobody had realised that it had not been modified. This oversight resulted in further tank changes.

While I was at Syerston they had a Mark 2 JP, which gave a double bang in a certain attitude of flight, and Hunting representatives were called in to try to find out the reason. The aircraft was given several test flights, and each pilot reported the same double bang in the same attitude of flight, and at first it was thought these were coming from the undercarriage area. Eventually, after a series of checks by the representatives, the aircraft was grounded. After some months investigating the problem, Huntings came back with the answer that the skin just forward of the intake was panting at particular attitudes of flight. I was then given the task of stiffening the skin by riveting a stringer to the skin on the inside. Once this had been done on one side it was decided to give the aircraft an air test, and as I had done the work I was given the option of flying on the test flight, which was quite a novelty for me.

British Aerospace Jet Provost T.3A of the Central Flying School coming in downwind to land at Scampton in October 1984.

(John Lewis)

British Aerospace Jet Provost XW299 T.5A '60' of No 1 Flying Training School at Shawbury. This type represents the ultimate development of the Jet Provost in training guise having, amongst other improvements, a pressurised cockpit.

(Richard Keefe)

We got airborne, and it took some time for me to settle down to flying as it was my first flight, but eventually I was able to pick up this bang. There was no doubt that this was the solution, as at this stage we had only re-stiffened one of the panels and there was now only one bang. After landing, I was just taking off my flying suit when it was decided that another aircraft was going up on air test, and I was given the option of flying again on this one, to see if it made a bang in the same attitude of flight. It didn't of course, but I got my first two flights in the same afternoon, and I enjoyed them thoroughly. The second one in particular because it was going up primarily on stall checks, and it was quite an experience for me to see the wings start to vibrate as the Jet Provost reached the stall speed. Unfortunately I didn't get the opportunity to fly in the Mark 2 after the second panel was stiffened, but there was no doubt that the problem was solved.

All through my time at Syerston, working on the rectification section, I thoroughly enjoyed working on the aeroplane, and thoroughly enjoyed the station. At that time we were working the longest hours in Flying Training Command and it wasn't until right at the end of my 2 years 11 months stay at Syerston that they eventually cut the hours to 8 o'clock in the morning to 5 at night. Prior to that we had been working a full five day week from 7.45 am to 5.30 pm.

Being Flying Training Command, everything was done very meticulously. The JPs were stored overnight in a hangar, and towed out by the line team each morning for flying. Land-Rovers were used for towing, it being a light aircraft, but for the final manoeuvring, especially in confined spaces, such as when parking in the hangar at cease flying, it was good old manpower push and shove. We had one incident where a lad lost a button off his blue service dress jacket while towing the aircraft out in the morning. This necessitated a loose article check of every JP on the flightline, which obviously took some time, and delayed flying by about three hours. We checked every aircraft, every cockpit, but couldn't find the button. Then we started to search the areas over which the aircraft had moved that morning. The button was eventually found on the hangar floor from which we had removed the JPs!

Hawker Hunter T.7

The first production Hunter F.1 made its maiden flight on 16 May 1953, and in that same year the Hawker design team began work as a private venture on a dual control trainer version. By that stage orders had been placed for around 500 Hunter fighters, to be built both by the parent company and by Armstrong Whitworth at Coventry, and a potential market could be seen for an instructional version.

The idea of a two-seater version had been mooted from the early days of the Hunter design, and these thoughts now formed the basis of the Type P.1101. Initially a modified variant of the F.6 was considered, but production of this was some way off, and therefore the F.4 airframe was selected as a basis for the prototype machine.

Specification

Power plant:	*One 7,700 lb Rolls-Royce Avon 122.*
Dimensions:	*Span 33 ft 8 in, length 48 ft 10½ in, height 13 ft 2 in, wing area 349 sq ft.*
Weights:	*Empty 12,950 lb, loaded 17,200 lb.*
Performance:	*Maximum speed 610 mph at 36,000 ft, climb 12½ min to 45,000 ft, range 1100 nautical miles, service ceiling 50,000 ft.*

Hawker P.1101 prototype XJ615, during trials in 1956. (British Aerospace)

Contemporary service thinking was that side-by-side seating was best for tuition, necessitating a new nose and cockpit assembly. This was to be attached to a transport joint bulkhead immediately forward of the wing-root air intakes, and its overall width would be dictated by that of the two Martin-Baker lightweight ejection seats which were to be fitted. The soundness of the basic design led to all this being accomplished without detriment to the handling and stability characteristics, nor to the original clean looking design.

There were some fears that the broader front fuselage might lead to adverse effects on the engine performance, especially the possibility of flame-out under some circumstances, though this later proved not to be the case. The sliding canopy of the fighter variants had to give way to a new two-piece hinged Perspex canopy, with a hood-jettison system connected to the seat-ejection mechanism.

Meanwhile, official thinking had caught up with Hawker's concept, Specification T.157D being issued in January 1955, and when the Avon-powered prototype machine first flew on 8 July 1955 it had the service number XJ615. During trials its handling characteristics were found to be generally similar to that of the fighter, but at high subsonic speeds it suffered from airflow stability problems. The pilot would hear a noise like an express train in a tunnel, and see hazy blue shock waves forming outside, gradually moving towards the tail as the speed increased. Various hoods were tried, but the problem was eventually cured by modifying the shape of the cockpit canopy rear decking. The machine then became even quieter than the fighter version, itself considered very quiet.

A second prototype (XJ627) flew in November 1956 with a more powerful Avon engine and twin Aden guns in the nose, but when production orders were placed the lower powered Avon 122 was specified, and only a single Aden gun fitted on the starboard side of the nose. The type went into service as the T.7 and a batch of 55 was laid down based on the F.6 fuselage, but ten of these were completed for naval use, as the T.8. In addition, 31 F.4s with low airframe hours were converted to T.8 standard.

The T.7 entered service with No 229 Operational Conversion Unit at Chivenor, near Barnstaple in August 1958, being later used by a number of RAF units for instrument flying training, weapons training and other purposes. In 1967 it was issued to 4 FTS at Valley, to give advanced pilot tuition alongside the Gnat trainer, and was later used by No 1 and 2 Tactical Weapons Units at Brawdy and Lossiemouth (later Chivenor) respectively.

The naval T.8 variant stemmed from the Fleet Air Arm's need for a suitable trainer for its second generation of jets. It was fitted with an arrester hook, though only stressed for airfield emergency use and not for carrier landings. The aircraft were used for weapons delivery training, some being later fitted with TACAN equipment, and were designated either T.8Bs or T.8Cs, depending on whether they had the full or partial equipment. Assorted Hunters, including trainers, are still in service with the civilian-operated FRADU at RNAS Yeovilton.

Lieutenant Commander Don Pugh, later to become CO of 759 Squadron, had his first encounter with the Hunter T.7 at RNAS Lossiemouth, where he familiarised in October 1958:

I found it very exciting, supersonic downhill and generally a big step in performance from the Sea Vampire T.22 and Meteor. Returning to my base at RNAS Yeovilton I was able to start the ball rolling with a Hunter capability there.

At that time the main use of the Hunter Trainer was to back-up the new Buccaneer and Sea Vixen squadrons with instrument flying and testing facilities. The Sea Vixen Intensive Flying Trials Unit (700Y Flight) had just formed under the command of Cdr Malcolm Petrie, and the Hunter was ideal in providing general flying practice with the doubtful serviceability of the squadron aircraft in those early days. By then we were flying the naval T.8 version – arrester hook, brake chute and Avon 122 giving 7,575 lb static thrust.

In 1961 a trainer was fitted with OR946 instrumentation and based at RNAS Lossiemouth. This was the Buccaneer type MRG (Master Reference Gyro) system, consisting, as I remember, of a central, large and accurate gyro stabilised platform from which was electronically fed information on attitude, heading and yaw rates. This meant that instead of instruments having their own little gyros, they could be servoed electrically from the common source. In addition, an Air Data Unit provided performance data for the new type of strip displays. This aircraft afforded a very necessary training facility for safe familiarisation and instrument flying practice on the new style panel and for training in the weapon delivery manoeuvres appropriate to the Buccaneer in those days.

Hunter Trainers were usually held in the Station Flights and available to squadron pilots as the training needs and general flying practise requirements arose.

In February 1963, HMS *Ark Royal* got a little perturbed with a T.8 making determined attempts at the deck, though not hook down and always managing a late overshoot. I had taken Hawker's Hugh Merryweather out for a preliminary look at deck approach problems before the P.1127 was landed on for trials!

1 August 1963 was significant in the Hunter T.8 story. 759 Squadron was commissioned at RNAS Brawdy and given the task of slotting into the training pipeline to give advanced pilot training between the Jet Provost and the Hunter GA.11

Hawker P.1101 prototype XJ615 showing broadened front fuselage.

(British Aerospace)

and the Vixen, Buccaneer and Gannet OCU. No great experience of flying training existed on the type. The RAF used it for weapon training and first-line, of course, but no one had taught people how to fly with a Hunter syllabus. Now we had to write the book, the instructor's manual. Many hours were spent flying the lessons, finding the clearest, most economical way to put the message over. Drop tanks gave us a 50 minute sortie with sufficient reserve and a 60 sortie syllabus was designed.

The instructional staff arrived, the biggest gathering of naval QFIs ever. They mostly needed conversion to type, then standardisation and categorisation. Then the great moment, the first students arrived – and didn't they do well. What a marvellous aircraft, so sweet to fly, with safe reliable systems. Training proceeded with little modification to syllabus and none of the incidents that would excite the reader – just hard training, thoroughly enjoyed by all. The availability of the hook which on an over-run could engage the arrester wires at the far end at up to 75 knots, saved many an incident where the student had come in hot and high. The barrier which the RAF would use to stop a T.7 could write-off the aircraft.

Hawker Aircraft spent a lot of time and money making a spinning case for the trainer; you could sell an all-spinning advanced trainer around the world. At first it was out because a badly handled entry could go inverted, and I remember recovery required stick forward as in the erect spin. An average-size pilot could not have reached to full control when out on the end of his straps. We got the negative-g restraint, but still could not find time or forceful reason to spin the students.

I never flew the Gnat, but I know that whilst the RN was having great success with the Hunter at Brawdy, the RAF at Valley could not get useful serviceability from the Gnat to do the same job, and eventually they formed a Hunter T.7 squadron to back up the Gnat.

Above:
Hawker Hunter T.7s of No. 229 Operational Conversion Unit at Chivenor around 1959.

(George Ruby)

Hawker Hunter T.8c WT702 '874/VL' of the Fleet Requirement and Air Direction Unit at Yeovilton in August 1980. This example is unusual in having a nose-mounted Harley light, fitted to aid visual acquisition during gun crew training.

(Author)

Lt. Louis Beardsworth, RN has flown Hunter T.8s more recently with FRADU, the Fleet Requirement and Air Direction Unit operated at Yeovilton by Flight Refuelling Ltd:

FRADU is responsible for Fleet tasks, providing aircraft for the Fighter Controllers School and also for giving air experience flights for pupils on the Junior Officers Air Course. All its Hunters are maintained by civilian staff.

Naval fixed-wing standards flights are now co-located with FRADU and use the Hunters held by them. Fixed wing standards, apart from testing and examining ('trapping') all fixed wing squadrons, use the Hunter for the SMAC309 Sea Harrier assessment course, continuation flying for RNR aircrew and training tasks of fighter evasion against Yeovilton-based helicopter squadrons.

The SMAC309 course is aimed at assessing the suitability of current rotary wing pilots for retraining to fly the Sea Harrier. It comprises 15 hours assessed flying, during which the pupil should achieve solo standard, and then continues on to cover low and high level navigation instrument flying and close formation.

Hunters are also used at Yeovilton by the Sea Harrier training squadron. 899 Squadron hold two T.8Ms fitted with the Blue Fox radar from the Sea Harrier. These are used for a small number of the radar training trips and occasionally for dissimilar air combat training.

Below:
Hawker Hunter T.7 of No 12 Squadron at Lossiemouth around 1984.
(Paddy Porter collection)

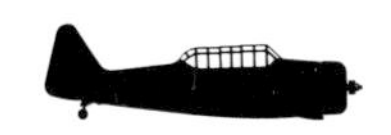

Mark Hanna flew the Hunter T.7 with 2 TWU at Lossiemouth:

I was on one of the last Hunter courses, having already flown the Hawk at Valley. I remember how surprised we were that initially we had just a two-day ground school and that was it, whereas at Valley on the Hawk it would have meant one or two month's work. Most of all, however, we were surprised in the two-seater Hunter at the shambles of instruments after the Hawk. Coming from the Hawk, which was a nice modern aeroplane with fancy layout, and bits and pieces, and all the right avionics and so on, the Hunter really was quite confusing and, compared with the single-seater, all the instruments were in different places.

I don't know how the design logic as a trainer went, but everything was different to the fighter. The starting system was different and it was cartridge as opposed to Avpin. The basic T-layout of the instruments was exactly the same, but all the engine speeds were different because it was a different sized engine – 7,500 pounds thrust instead of 10,000 in the single-seater, so threshold speeds and all that sort of thing were different. All you can say is the actual basic handling was similar, though obviously there was less thrust.

We never flew them as single-seat, though I believe they did at Valley. Primarily we flew them for initial weapons training, just to make sure you were getting the angle of dive right for dive bombing or for rocketing. Then you would be cleared solo, and safe to go in a single-seater. I always felt that it wasn't really an instructional aeroplane by the time I was flying them at the TWU, being by then more a safety check aeroplane. For example, we did one or maybe two dual rides before we went solo on the single-seater. It was basically just to make sure you had some idea, and weren't likely to spear in on the single-seater, when you would be going on to rocket attacks, for instance. You would have an instructor with you, who would check you dual, making sure you were getting in the angles correct, and that you weren't exceeding the minimum ranges or anything. Then, pow, up you would go in the single-seater.

We didn't deliberately practise formation flying in them, or anything like that, because we were already competent to do formation in single-seaters. As students, none of us liked flying in the two-seater. The view out was awful, with the strutwork, and of course looking out to the right across the instructor was never very nice, with someone sitting next to you monitoring what you were doing.

David Watkins serviced Hunter T.7s with 229 OCU at Chivenor in 1969-70:

The Hunter was a beautiful aircraft, and technically something of a challenge to work on. The pilots loved it, because of its dog-fighting qualities and the fact that it was an excellent weapons platform. It was sleek, powerful and, before they started adding little bits on it, a joy to work on.

The OCU operated two servicing squadrons on a pooled basis, and the three Reserve squadrons (Nos 63, 79 and 234) were divided up between them. In practice, the Hunter fighters of 63 (part) and 234 Squadrons were operated by No 1 Servicing Squadron, whilst 63 (part) , 79 and Towed Target Flight were the responsibility of No 2 Squadron. The T 7s were also under the aegis of No 2 Squadron.

I was detailed to one of four teams in the Scheduled Servicing Flight of No 1 Squadron, and carried out Primary, Primary Star, Minor and Minor Star servicing. Anything more than this was given to the resident 71 MU or Hawker working parties.

The cockpit of the T.7 was fairly well laid out and, once seated, I felt as if I was in a powerful sports car. I flew in one on several occasions, and at first I was terrified at the power of the aircraft and sensitivity of the controls. Eventually, the exhilaration of flying in a T.7 at 20,000 feet over the Bristol Channel became a greatly anticipated event during my time at Chivenor.

To work on, especially in the undercarriage wells when changing filters (I seem to recall we changed a lot of filters), one required 12-inch fingers and the ability to be double-jointed! The rear fuselage was removed with monotonous regularity, to enable the engine fitters to work on the Avon engines.

In 1969 the OCU replaced the West Raynham Hunter commitment of 'guarding the Rock' at Gilbraltar. Most days a Spanish Air Force Heinkel flew a 'Milk Run' sortie up the border of Spain and Gibraltar, and we scrambled a Hunter to escort it. I still laugh as I remember the sight of a Heinkel flat out and a Hunter almost at stalling speed flying alongside it!

David also tells a rather sad story about a troublesome Hunter:

We had two resident 'Hangar Queens', an F.6 and a T.7. The T.7 was probably a rogue aircraft with hydraulic problems, which affected its brakes, and I think we eventually changed everything vaguely connected with the hydraulics. After being air tested, a student was detailed to take it up for the next exercise. Returning 45 minutes later, he landed normally, but the brakes failed and he overshot the runway, entered the barrier and went into the safety area. I was on Duty Crew at the time and we raced to the scene of the accident, only to find the cockpit unoccupied. After a short search we found the pilot, who had dashed off to the bushes for a rather urgent call of nature. As the intrepid aviator stumbled past us, he was heard to mumble, 'I didn't want to be a pilot, my mother wanted me to be a pilot – I wanted to be an estate agent'.

Hawker Siddeley Gnat

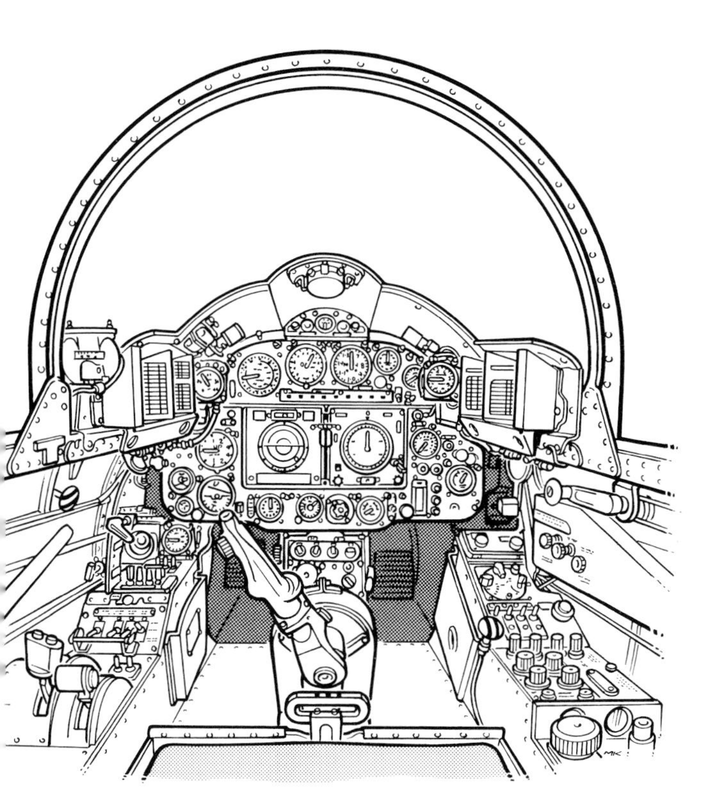

The Gnat started life as the Folland Fo.140 design for a lightweight fighter, which was preceded by the Fo.139 Midge aerodynamic test aircraft. Both were private ventures by this Hamble-based company, which had only limited experience of aircraft building, but foresaw a market for such a concept.

Folland's chief designer was W.E.W. Petter, who had previously worked for Westlands and later English Electric. With the latter company he had been responsible for the design of both the Canberra and the prototype Lightning. He had misgivings about the trend towards ever more technically complex and therefore costly interceptor fighters, and saw in the new small turbojets being developed an opportunity to reverse this.

The Midge prototype G-39-1 appeared on 11 August 1954, powered by a 1640 lb thrust Armstrong Siddeley Viper 101. This was followed by G-39-2, the prototype Gnat, which had its maiden flight on 18 July 1955 at Boscombe Down, powered by a 3,285 lb thrust Bristol Orpheus B.Or.1 engine. The test reports led to an order for six development machines with Orpheus B.Or.2 engines giving 4,520 lb thrust, the first of these (XK724) having its first flight at Chilbolton 26 May 1956. They weighed less than half the Hunter, for a little over half the cost, but arrived on the scene too late, production of the Hunter being by then in full swing. The Gnat was considered in the ground attack role as a Middle East replacement for the de Havilland Venom, but the Hunter was selected because of its range and its ability to carry heavier warloads. The fighter version of the Gnat was, however, sold to both Finland and India, and the latter country built over 200 under licence as well as a development named Ajeet (Invincible).

Despite the setback of not being selected by the RAF in the fighter role, the aircraft offered potential as a two-seat advanced trainer with supersonic capability, and design work had in the meantime been undertaken on this.

The proposal met with official approval, and specification T.185D was issued in January 1958, leading to a production order for 14 pre-production machines. The prototype Gnat T.1 (XM691) first flew at

Specification

Power plant:	*One 4,230 lb Bristol Siddeley Orpheus.*
Dimensions:	*Span 24 ft 0 in, length 31 ft 9 in, height 10 ft 6 in, wing area 175 sq ft.*
Weights:	*Empty 5,900 lb, loaded 8,400 lb (with full external tanks).*
Performance:	*Maximum speed 640 mph at 36,000 ft, initial climb 8,044 ft/min, range 1,180 miles, endurance (with drop tanks) 2 hr 20 min, service ceiling 48,000 ft.*

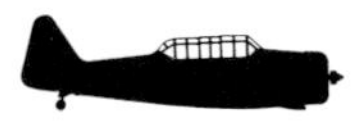

Chilbolton on 31 August 1959, powered by a 4,230 lb thrust Orpheus 100, this having been derated slightly to give longer periods between overhauls and improved fuel consumption figures. To meet specification requirements, the airframe was strengthened to reach a stipulated fatigue limit of 5,000 hours flying over ten years. In theory it had a simplified structure, designed so that comparatively major components could be replaced economically during this period – but in practise, RAF ground crews took a rather different view.

The lengthened fuselage accommodated an additional seat in tandem, the RAF having by now dropped its previous stipulation that advance training should be side-by-side. This had the advantage of giving the pupil pilot in the front seat a view more approaching that to which he would have to become accustomed in squadron service, and was especially necessary for formation flying.

The wings were of greater area than the fighter version, and therefore reduced the landing speed, but to maintain high speed performance their thickness/chord ratio was reduced from 8 per cent to 7 per cent. They incorporated additional fuel storage in the leading edges, outboard ailerons and conventional inboard flaps, which provided sufficient drag for a comfortably slow approach, especially when using ILS, yet the machine could reach supersonic speeds in a dive. It had larger upright tail surfaces, and redesigned intakes. The engine provided enough power for it to reach 40,000 ft in only seven minutes.

Shortly after the first flight, the parent company became absorbed into the Hawker Siddeley Group, and consequently the aircraft became the Hawker Siddeley Gnat, production being later transferred to Dunsfold.

The first eight pre-production machines were earmarked for evaluation at Boscombe Down and Farnborough, the remaining six being delivered to the Central Flying School at Little Rissington in early 1962 for service trials. Specification T.185P had meanwhile been issued in February 1959 for a production version, resulting in an order for 30 machines, followed by further orders for 20 and 41 respectively. Although the Gnat was a small machine, the contract required it to have much of the equipment which would be fitted in operational types then under development. This included new flight and navigational instrument presentation, engine anti-icing, liquid oxygen and many other items including a centralised failure warning system. Two of Folland's own 4GT lightweight seats were used in the new ejection escape system,

Folland Gnat T.1 XM691, the first pre-production aircraft, powered by a 4,230 lb thrust Bristol Siddeley Orpheus 100.

(RAF Museum)

these being capable of operating at runway level if necessary, and at any speed from 90 knots upwards. OR.946 flight instrumentation was fitted, similar to that used in Lightnings and other operational types of fighter, and this made it necessary for the cockpit to be redesigned, including a new windscreen omitting the gunsight and bullet-proof frame.

The Gnat was fully aerobatic with drop tanks in place, and a variety of underwing stores could be carried. Possible armament loads included two 500 lb bombs, two rocket pods, two Sidewinder or Bullpup missiles and two Aden gun pods. Alternatively, reconnaissance camera pods could be fitted. Its flying slab elevators had emergency follow-up elevators, and it was fitted with anti-skid brakes, drag parachute and eleven fuel tanks.

Further Gnats were supplied to the CFS, but the majority went to equip 4 FTS at Valley, and from November 1962 the Vampire T.11 began to be superseded as the standard advanced pilot trainer in the RAF. One big factor in the selection of the Gnat was its comparatively low price, which offered the prospect of reducing the steadily increasing cost of training a pilot. The Provost/Vampire sequence, for instance, had raised this bill by around £10,000 compared with the previous Prentice/Harvard/Meteor sequence. Pupils now completed 160 hours flying on Jet Provosts, then went to Valley for 70 hours on Gnats before proceeding to an Operational Conversion Unit. These times were later varied, and by 1973 direct entry students were undertaking 100 hours on Jet Provost T.3s, followed by 45 hours on T.5s, then 85 hours on Gnats.

In service, the Gnat was found to have its faults. It was not particularly stable, but had sensitive controls which made it very manoeuvrable, and challenging to fly. It was a great success with the Red Arrows aerobatic team, which formed in 1965, but for normal training its economy in operating costs was offset by a number of severe drawbacks. Its design was complex, despite the original concept, and caused engineering problems, particularly in respect of the systems and longitudinal control. The small cockpit gave the instructor in the rear seat an extremely limited forward view. It was of little practical use for weapons instruction, and pitch control difficulties were never satisfactorily overcome. It was eventually withdrawn in 1978 in favour of the Hawk.

Flight Lieutenant Rod King was a Gnat student at 4 FTS Valley in 1965, and an instructor there in 1972:

4 FTS in both 1965 and 1972 was based in a combined Station Headquarters and ground school, occupying a large number of wooden huts located at the back of the old control tower. The Station Commander's office overlooked the taxiway, and therefore there was some incentive to control one's taxiing speed as one went past the window. If one didn't, questions would be asked.

There were two Gnat squadrons at Valley, each with two flights. Each squadron was commanded by a Squadron Leader, and each flight by Flight Lieutenants, there being four or five instructors in each flight. There was also a Standards Squadron, responsible for the quality control of standards of instruction and seeing that people were teaching the right things. There was a further squadron, operating Hunters, and this was for foreign and Commonwealth training, because many nations, particularly Gulf States, operated this aircraft until the late seventies.

In 1965, students came from the Jet Provost with some 160 hours on type at the end of their year on basic flying training. The first three weeks were spent purely in Ground School at Valley, learning the complexities of the Gnat. In

Hawker Siddeley Gnat T.1 XM708 of the Central Flying School at Little Rissington in 1962.
(British Aerospace)

particular the electrical system, the hydraulic system and the longitudinal control system, of which the last two systems dominated the life of every student and instructor who ever encountered the Gnat. Allied to these systems were two emergency drills, STUPRE and CUBSTUN, burned vividly into everyone's memory.

In the next 16 weeks, students flew a total of some 76 hours, of which some 21 hours 10 minutes were solo and 48 hours 20 minutes were dual by day, and some 3 hours were solo and 4 hours were dual by night. The official syllabus length was some 70 hours, but there is always Incidental Allowance (IA) in such syllabuses to cater for aircraft that go unserviceable, bad weather or even 'failed' sorties.

There were also some 13 hours in the Gnat simulator. This was built in vans which were fully mobile, the intention being that one could redeploy the simulator at short notice. There were some problems, however, when it was first installed, as the lorries were found to be too wide for the Menai Bridge. They were therefore driven to Liverpool, then put on a ferry for Ireland, from where they were re-shipped to Holyhead. Having got these expensive vans to Valley, they were put on a concrete plinth, but it was quickly discovered that Force 8 gales and rain gave problems, and therefore wouldn't it be a good idea if a roof was put over these vans? After a little while, someone said – if we've got a concrete base and a roof, why don't we put walls around them – and we ended up with these expensive vehicles totally enclosed. This proved to be no problem until about 1977, when the Gnat was phased out and we tried to get the vans out to install the Hawk simulator and associated equipment. We found the only way was to deflate the tyres, and they would then just get out under the door lintel!

My next encounter with the Gnat was in 1972, when I became an instructor at Valley, having done the Gnat refresher course. I had done this because I had been a Jet Provost instructor, and it was easier to make me a Gnat instructor than to hew someone out from square one. The CFS refresher course on the Gnat was about three months long, and was really geared to instructors who had previously flown the Gnat some time in the past. It was some 50 hours long, of which 9 hours or so were solo by day, 35 hours dual by day, with 1 hour 40 minutes night solo and 3 hours 30 minutes night dual. At the end of this course, which was carried out at Kemble, one went to Valley, which was the only FTS then using the Gnat, and in the next two years I flew some 700 hours on the Gnat.

It was a complex aircraft, which students found difficult, and instructors equally so. As some seven years previously, life was dominated by STUPRE, which had now become STUPRECC. This is the drill for going manual from hydraulically-operated controls, whereby you get the aircraft **S**peed below 400 knots (or .85 Mach); you **T**rim the feel trim to the ideal sector set, which puts the stick into the middle of the cockpit. You **U**nlock the elevators, using an umbrella-shaped handle on the left hand side of the cockpit; **P** is for power to put the cock off to make sure that if the hydraulic pump subsequently recovers, you don't get a pulse of hydraulic fluid or pressure through the system. You **R**aise the guard of the standby trim so that you can motor the tail electrically, which provides your main source of controlling pitch, your fine control then being provided by the very small elevators. So it is a reverse of the normal way of controlling an aircraft.

One also then had to **E**xhaust the accumulators, which were built into the hydraulic system and enabled you, if the pump failed, to recover the aircraft to straight and level flight before you went through the full drill for putting in to manual. With the accumulators exhausted, the control surfaces then froze in the right positions. Finally, one then had to **C**heck that one had **C**ontrol in pitch and roll. This was a consequence of some embarrassing examples of people rolling or completing a landing and take-off with the tailplane absolutely frozen. There were various other incidents with the longitudinal control system which were required to be brought into this check. We also had a changeover system whereby we could move the standby trims from operating on the console to the normal feel trim switch on the stick.

The CUBSTUN drill was to cater for failure of an alternator, which meant that you lost all electrical power. You were then running the aircraft, which was essentially an electrical aircraft, on battery power alone, and the main batteries would only last you 20 minutes. So you now had a drill called CUBSTUN, which was **C**abin altimeter to static, **U**HF to standby, **B**ooster pump off, **S**peed, **T**rim and **UN**lock,

Facing page, top:
Hawker Siddeley Gnat T.1 flight line of the Central Flying School at Little Rissington around 1962–63.
(British Aerospace)

Facing page, bottom:
Hawker Siddeley Gnat T.1 formation of No 4 Flying Training School at Valley in 1964.
(British Aerospace)

Below:
Two Hawker Siddeley Gnat T.1s of the Central Flying School at Little Rissington in 1962.
(British Aerospace)

96
95
XM709
92
XM706

in the same way as you did with the STUPRECC drill. This put you into a condition called UNLOCK, whereby the hydraulic system was still working, but by unlocking ended up with extremely light control loads and no necessity to trim. As you had no need to use the electrical trim, you didn't drain the battery. A lot of time was spent in the early stages of the course, teaching these two drills to the students.

My own view was that if you could get a student through the first fortnight, which was essentially first solo on type, then he really had got the course cracked. Much of the 70 hours of the course was spent on learning to fly the Gnat, to handle its peculiarities and to cope with the emergencies that could arise from either failure of the hydraulic system, or the engine flaming out. This was necessary because if the engine flamed you lost both the hydraulics and the electrics. So you were going to go through both those drills again of STUPRECC and CUBSTUN.

The pace of work for the student on the first part of the course was very high. There was a phase briefing nearly every night, this being a mass brief on an aspect of operating the aircraft. In the case of 'manual', you had not only a mass brief, but also a hangar demonstration in which the aircraft was jacked up in the hangar with a hydraulic rig on it so that you could demonstrate what happened at various stages of failure or various conditions of flight. This took some 30 minutes, followed by a phase brief of some 40 minutes. In addition to this, with regard to manual, the student must also have done a certain number of exercises in the simulator. There were therefore a number of critical points that had to be fulfilled before a student could be sent solo. It was not unknown in fact for students never to go solo on the Gnat, as they didn't reach the required standard, and in practise solo proved to be the big weeding out point.

Half way through the course, as indeed we have now on the Hawk, we had an Instrument Rating Test, to test the ability of the student to fly the aircraft on instruments. There was also a progress check to evaluate a student's ability to fly the aircraft doing general handling – stalling, spinning, aerobatics, forced landings and circuits. The second half of the course, which was about the last 30 hours, covered high- and low-level navigation and formation and some 7 hours of night flying.

A major problem of instructing on the Gnat was the view from the back seat, particularly with the aircraft in manual, as this required a flapless approach to the airfield with a high nose attitude, resulting in a restricted view from the back cockpit, especially in conditions of no crosswind. Because the Gnat is a swept wing aircraft, it generates large amounts of drag at low speed and this is particularly important on the approach. The aircraft must not be flown too slowly, and the approach path should not become too steep. Either of these conditions could lead to a heavy landing, a bounce and perhaps a pilot-induced oscillation. The only corrective action for this was to hold the stick in the middle, keeping the wings level, apply full power and blast the aircraft away from the runway before getting into too much harm. If one persisted with a PIO, and didn't take the right corrective action, one could end up with quite severe damage to the aircraft. Perhaps, also, a situation whereby one tried to eject, but the aircraft had been damaged, and ejection seat performance degraded such that one might not survive, because it was only a 90 knot seat straight and level.

The view on the approach from the back seat was exacerbated at night by large areas of double reflections in the large bubble canopy. There were similar reflections from the blast screen which separated part of the rear cockpit from the front cockpit, and was intended as a measure of protection for the instructor in the back seat if the main canopy shattered for any reason such as a bird strike. At night, therefore, in manual or on a flapless approach, if the student started to get high, one lost complete sight of the runway. The only remedy was to tell the student to overshoot and go round again for another approach, because you couldn't be sure exactly where the aircraft was in relation to the runway.

The swept wing characteristics of the Gnat also showed up in buffet handling, which was nice and smoothly graduated from light to very heavy buffet. Like all true swept wing aircraft in heavy buffet, the aircraft would pitch very, very well, but it would lose performance very rapidly. This was shown in two demonstrations that we used to fly, of a loop starting from the same speed of 350 knots and using full power. In a loop on a light buffet the diameter of the loop would be some 6,000 feet, but in heavy buffet with wing rock the diameter of the loop could be reduced to some 4,500 feet. The only difference was that on the loop with the light buffet, the speed of exit from the loop was the same as when one went in, but after the loop in heavy buffet one came out some 100 knots slower. So one had reduced the diameter of the loop by some 1,500 feet, but had lost 100 knots of overall performance.

Another demonstration that had to be flown was to reinforce the problems of getting slow on the final approach. We decelerated the aircraft with undercarriage and flap down, towards the stall, with the engine at idle. Then, some 7 knots before the stall, slammed the throttle open, and it took the engine take some seven seconds to wind up. In that time, the aircraft decelerated to 115 knots, one had the maximum angle of tail applied, some 15 degrees, with the stick on the back stops, and one had full power applied and one was at 115 knots. You were unable, therefore, to accelerate the aircraft, you were unable to stop it going down, and you were effectively in a jam – you were stuck. This was a very convincing demonstration, but it took a lot of flying and one concentrated perhaps too much in the rear cockpit on the vertical speed indicator, sometimes called the RCDI (Rate of Climb and Descent Indicator), to make sure that you were flying this demonstration exactly level, because unless you did that the demonstration did not achieve its full impact.

Another interesting aspect was that from 1965 to 1972 we had lost a number of aircraft in accidents of various sorts, usually related to the longitudinal control system. Consequently there were a number of areas which one was allowed to practise as a student in 1965, but which by 1972 had become the sole prerogative of 'A' category instructors, the most notable being forced landing in manual. Normally, if the engine flamed out, one would be able to glide the aircraft back to an airfield and carry out a forced landing. Provided the engine remained windmilling at about 10 or 15 per cent rpm, this was sufficient to keep the hydraulic pump on line, and therefore the flying controls in power. This meant that one had a reasonable degree of control over the aircraft, and provided one didn't thrash the stick around and therefore make excessive demands on the hydraulic system, enough control would be available to land the aircraft without problem. One or two incidents occurred, however,

whereby the judgement required proved too much for the student and a heavy landing ensued. Thus, by 1972, this was one of the exercises which was restricted to instructors only.

Another problem with operating the Gnat as a teaching instrument, was its endurance. Although it carried some 3,000 lb of fuel, the Orpheus was a very thirsty engine. In conditions of bad weather where one might have, say, a 200 ft cloud base at Valley and a visibility of approximately half a mile, one could require fuel to go to a diversion airfield, perhaps some 200 miles away, a good example being Leuchars. Under these circumstances, the maximum length of sortie one would do with a Gnat was a climb to 20,000 feet, and an instrument recovery straight away, a total sortie length of some 20 – 25 minutes. Therefore the diversion airfield that the Gnat was almost totally orientated toward was Shawbury, some 70 miles away just over the border in England, and consequently our activities were closely interrelated with that airfield. It was therefore necessary to show the student a practise diversion to Shawbury in the early stages before he went solo, and also for him to do a night sortie where, again, one did a practise diversion to Shawbury.

The other problem with the Gnat was that with its swept wing, and narrow track undercarriage, it was very susceptible to crosswinds, and therefore the maximum crosswind component that could be accepted in normal operations on a dry runway was some 20 knots. If the runway were wet, this dropped to 10 knots, although if the runway had a friction surface it could be increased to 15 knots. For a student, however, the maximum crosswind limit was 15 knots dry, and some 10 knots wet. In a strong crosswind the Gnat proved something of a handful. It wanted to lean out of wind, it wanted to drift sideways on the runway and, because of the peculiarity of its braking system, it was very easy for the pilot to get his feet out of synchronisation with the braking required. This was due to a component of the system called response valves which delayed the application of brake pressure when one planted one's foot on the brake pedal, but also kept the braking pressure applied after lifting one's foot off the brake pedal. If one got out of synchronisation, the aircraft went down the runway rocking and rolling as well as drifting sideways in the crosswind.

There could also be problems with the Maxeret anti-skid system components which were prone to fail, leading to a complete loss of brake pressure on one side. As the Gnat was steered on the runway or the taxiway by differential braking, this meant that you were unable to turn one way or the other. The Gnat was also fitted with a brake parachute. This was really a training aid because the Gnat had originally been intended as a stepping stone from the basic trainer to the Lightning. The brake parachute was not terribly reliable, although it was quite helpful as a training aid, but it only knocked some 600 feet off the normal ground roll, which is a comparatively small amount in relation to a ground roll of some 4,800 feet!

Ray Hanna, former leader of the Red Arrows recalls:

I was posted to the CFS and the Red Arrows from instructing on Meteor T.7s and F.8s at the College of Air Warfare, having flown Meteors previously on squadrons, and suppose I had about 1,000 hours instructing on the T.7. Transitioning from the Meteor, which really was a first generation jet, to something like the Gnat which was second, maybe third generation, with powered flying controls, swept wing, etc., and with all sorts of modern avionics very similar to the Lightning, my first impressions of the Gnat were just that it was totally delightful, and very, very sensitive after the Meteor.

In a sense it was much nicer to fly than, say, the Hunter, and of course the two aircraft were always being directly compared. The Hunter was bigger and more substantial, had more power, and at height had a better power-weight ratio. The Gnat's altitude performance was disappointing from the excess thrust point of view. The Orpheus had about five and half thousand pounds of thrust at sea level, and at anything over 25,000 feet it seemed to me the aeroplane suffered a lack of thrust. But low down it had all that was necessary.

It had the same sort of low-level performance as the Hunter or the Swift, and was much nicer to fly, more sensitive, but being so light (seven and a half thousand pounds), it had a very, very low wing loading for a swept wing aeroplane. Somewhere around 40 pounds as opposed to 50 or 60 on the Hunter, and even more on the Swift, so the wing loading was down about the same as the Meteor. This made it a very manoeuvrable aeroplane, particularly at low altitude, but it did bump around in turbulence.

From another handling point of view, of course it wasn't supersonic straight and level, and had to be dived to achieve speeds over Mach 1, but in not quite such a determined dive as the Hunter or the Swift. If one rolled over, and literally pulled through vertically, the aircraft could achieve almost 1.2 Mach, something more than either the Hunter or the Swift.

I never instructed on the Gnat, but flew in the back seat from time to time checking other people on the aerobatic team. Of course the back cockpit was fully equipped and was fully dual. We were so confident in our days on the Arrows. I think things have changed a little bit since then; things seemed to be more relaxed and more free and easy in the Air Force in those days, and for example we frequently flew photographers in the front seat. They were obviously given a very close briefing on the undercarriage and various bits and pieces generally, in a sense it was very similar to taking a student on his first trip. My memory of the back seat was that it was quite difficult to get into, it was a very confined space, but once you were in it was very comfortable.

The Folland seat was exceptionally comfortable. The back seat had a visor arrangement around it in case you lost the canopy, so that the instructor had this fixed perspex visor in front of him basically to stop wind blast, and you could see through that very clearly. You could see left and right of the student's position. The only problem was that you were sitting with the coaming more or less level with the shoulders, such that the view downwards and forwards tended to be restricted. Looking aft, the top surface of the wing again obscured vision.

One could override anything. The aeroplane was fully dual, though you couldn't see what the other chap was doing in the front.

The Gnat did have a rather complicated flying control system. It was fine when it was in the normal hydraulic mode, with the aeroplane flying as it was designed to do, that is with the tailplane in the slab mode, powered. Other modes were: powered 'follow up', elevators disconnected from the

Yellowjacks aerobatic team of No 4 Flying Training School at Valley inverted over Holyhead in 1964. The display team, led by Fl Lt Lee Jones, was formed to display the RAF's new trainer.

(British Aerospace)

tailplane – very sensitive; and 'manual', electrical operation of tailplane and elevators via stick. Therefore instructing in this aeroplane could have its moments. There were occasions at Valley, particularly when emergency procedures were being taught. Problems arose, not because of any failure in the hydraulics, but because the teachers were instructing for the day when there was a failure. One of the problems with the tailplane was that it was very light and sensitive. It was possible on take-off or landing, if one wasn't careful, to porpoise quite severely.

In summary, it was a totally delightful aeroplane, and during the five years I was with the Red Arrows team we never suffered any major failure, any major accident. We had one hydraulic failure in the five years, and I recall one aircraft which had a persistent niggling brake problem, but on second thoughts it may have been the pilot – a heavy footed fellow – nice chap in those days! Of course, we had superb maintenance. Whilst I was with the team we never had anyone jump out, and we had complete confidence in the Folland seat. Later, two or three people ejected, and they never had the slightest problem, everything worked as advertised. Similarly, Valley had several ejections for whatever reason during flying training, and some very, very low level ejections, but I don't think there was ever one fatality ejecting from the Gnat. The seat was much maligned initially by industry and some people in the service, but in my opinion there has never been a better one!

Hawker Siddeley Gnat T.1 XP537 '100' of the Central Flying School at Little Rissington together with a de Havilland Vampire T.11 of the same unit around 1964–65. The problematical narrow undercarriage track can be seen clearly here.

(British Aerospace)

Squadron Leader Mike Sparrow also flew the Gnat, both as CO on No 2 Squadron at Valley and later as CO of No 4 Squadron of the Central Flying School at Kemble. His assessment is:

It was a good high speed advanced flying training aircraft, with complicated electronics and flying control systems. The roll rate was exceptional, being 210 degrees per second

with 16 degrees aileron movement. This 16 degrees was increased to 28 degrees at speed below 150 knots by electrical withdrawal of aileron pins so, by taking out a certain fuse, the rate of roll *could* be increased dramatically.

The aircraft was designed as a single-seater. When two seats were put in, the Centre of Gravity altered dramatically with the undercarriage lowered, so that an automatic datum shift had to be included in the lowering sequence, giving an automatic minus 3½ degrees on the tailplane (all-flying). If the powered flying controls failed, a manual back-up system was available. This was very complicated and several fatalities were caused by incorrect use of this system. Once the systems were mastered, however, this aircraft was loved by its pilots. Ejector seats were of Folland design and very different from Martin-Baker types.

The engine was very reliable – I never knew one to fail in 4½ years of flying the aircraft. I did have a potential engine failure once when I took a Gnat up for an air test. At 30,000 feet the engine failed to meet the time limit for a slam open from idle check. I returned to base where the flight line engineer fiddled with a screw and asked me to re-test the aircraft. I did so and had the same result. The aircraft was wheeled away to the hangar for a complete check, where it was found that two of the seven stages of the compressor had disintegrated completely and a further two were so badly damaged as to be of little use. A loose bolt had caused the damage.

The narrow track undercarriage took a bit of getting used to, particularly in crosswind conditions. Whilst at CFS, I was training a pilot to Gnat instructor standard on crosswind landing techniques. The wind was just within limits and the student instructor (SI) was having a bit of a problem. After several not-so-good attempts, the fuel state dictated a full stop landing. I told the SI that he was to land and that if he got into difficulties I would take over and complete the landing. All went well until just after touch down when the SI seemed unable to control the aircraft as it headed for the side of the runway, I took over control – and found there was no control. The aircraft charged through the runway lights, onto the grass, then back onto the runway, eventually coming to a halt well into the country on the other side of the runway. I leapt out of the aircraft (where a white faced SI was muttering something about brandy and three-wheeled jet skateboards that didn't) and found that our Gnat had only two. One main wheel had apparently dropped off on the final touch down, taking the brakes with it, hence the lack of control. The SI eventually passed the course and became an above average instructor.

The Gnat's serviceability rate was poor. We used to start with 30+ aircraft at first launch, but were invariably reduced to 20 or less by lunchtime.

Ground handling could have its problems. John Norris had a rather nerve-shaking experience at Chivenor, when a visiting aircraft dropped in from 4 FTS at Valley:

The Gnat's Orpheus engine had a compressed air starter which required copious quantities of air at about 50–60lbs psi. We lacked the proper air trolley at Chivenor, and instead had to use a cobbled-up affair of the type so common on every RAF flight line. It consisted of four large bottles at 3,000 lb psi, which in this case were all coupled to a large 'chamber'. This was welded up from steel plates and was nothing more than a crude box with a pressure gauge set on top of it. To this chamber was also connected a pukka air starter hose with 'connector, aircraft' at its other end. A desperate affair, but we didn't want the place cluttered up with dead Gnats. They had to be got rid of, legally. I was delegated to the start-up team and given a briefing. 'When the jock is strapped in and happy, watch for his thumbs up signal and reciprocate by giving him the 'clear to start engine' signal [raise the right arm, first finger extended and rotate it]. Then whop all four bottles open with the four keys provided and await results.'

At the appointed time the aviators arrived suitably clad, mounted up and gave the signal. I responded with 'clear to start engine', and my man B hastily slammed open all four air valves on our starter. There followed a sound of rushing air, the hose twitched and went taut then began to quiver. The air gauge registered 20 – 40 – 60 psi in a rapid ascent of pressure, then there was a loud report, the roar of escaping air and the fleeting impression of flying fragments. Man B and I dived to the ground just as the large hose reared up and flew over the Gnat and settled across its wings and fuselage like some monstrous expiring snake.

When events had stabilised a little, man B and I arose and turned off the air bottles to silence the roar of escaping air which was persisting, and took stock of the situation. First we helped the two visibly shaken pilots from their cockpits, then all four of us carefully examined our starter and their aircraft for damage. The Gnat was unscathed, no damage whatsoever, but our welded box/air chamber had disintegrated, blown to bits before our very eyes, and no sign of the fragments. Some parts of it had probably landed in Cornwall, the remainder in Somerset. The air gauge, which presumably went straight up, was found some days later, many hundred of yards away from its point of departure. The two pilots wandered off shakily in the direction of the Officer's Mess, muttering something about needing a pint. Man B and I set about explaining to Chiefy, who had by now come across from his office to investigate the loud and unfamiliar noises. Very red and cross he was, too, arriving in the van of the rest of the line personnel – who all seemed to find the situation hilarious. After tearing us off a strip he directed man B and me to go and have a cuppa and bit of rest for five minutes – no more!

The sequel to all this was that an air starter trolley was brought by road from Valley the next day. Speedily put to use it sent the Gnat on its way. We didn't have many visits from the same quarter again, nor did we ever receive a 'trolley, aircraft, starter, for the use of'. The 'Red Sparrers' always brought their own ground crews and ground equipment when they came to perform on Open Days. Our 'starter trolley' was demodified and reverted to its proper role and anonymity on the flight line. It was a miracle none of the four of us was killed or maimed in the debacle.

Nevil Gardner also has recollections of the Gnat, while Apprentice training at Halton:

I enjoyed my training on these, they could be a little fiddly, but were quite interesting. Some of the 'quick release fasteners' should really have just been called fasteners, or

Hawker Siddeley Gnat T.1 XP504 '04' of No 4 Flying Training School at Valley with airman wearing protective gear whilst recharging the liquid oxygen system.

(via Dave Watkins)

perhaps thay had seen better days. The cockpit was very hard to squeeze into unless you were a midget, so goodness knows how the aircrew coped. Once you had got comfy there was the Ejection Seat safety handle poking between your shoulder blades to remind you the seat was safe. Although a discomfort on the ground it seemed an improvement over all those seat pins in other aircraft, but I have only seen this arrangement on the Gnat.

Despite being so low slung and looking so compact, the Gnat appeared a bit stranded when jacked and trestled for an engine change. The rear fuselage split at the main engine bearer mounts, quite a common design feature of the time. The flying controls and the brake chute operating cable were disconnected, and this invariably left the brake chute streamed on the hangar floor in a bundle. With the rear fuselage wheeled away on a trestle complete with fin and tailplane, the engine became exposed. There were two main bearers, that looked like small conrod caps; interestingly they were made, I think, of carbon-fibre and not steel as I would have expected. A previous entry had actually managed to break one of these, and a rather overbearing instructor laboured on this point so much we felt rather insulted. As this wasn't the first time, we planned our revenge. Pocketing the original broken bearer, my team of four 'confessed' to breaking another as we pulled out our engine just before tea break. Gloating, our instructor scurried off to tell his mates what clowns we were. When we 'unconfessed' after tea, his fellow instructors ribbed him so much that he became half decent towards us.

Once we had to change both aileron PFCUs [Powered Flying Control Units], and after some time the instructor came to see what was taking us so long. He noticed that the last team had put the left and right PFCUs in the opposite wings. They went in really easily by comparison with removal!

At one stage we did some fault finding. This was well planned, with linkages or valves disconnected so that we could reproduce faults. Then we could take the symptoms to the manuals and correct them first time. This turned out to be quite a bit different to some of the snags I came across later, which were either intermittent or couldn't be reproduced, but nevertheless it was valuable experience.

David Watkins refers to the aircraft as the 'dreadful Gnat', and explains:

I spent a short time with the CFS detachment in early 1966. Most people liked the Gnat; fast, agile and easy to maintain. I personally disliked them because every evening I returned from work stained with dye (mainly red and blue) *à la* Red Arrow. I also treated the LOX replenishing system with the greatest of respect, as I had heard stories that it could be dangerous if mistreated. During recharging, the airmen were supposed to wear protective gear, but in practise, or during a heavy AF/BF or Turnround commitment, one sometimes 'forgot' to put it on.

Cutting corners could lead to dangerous situations. During the summer of 1967 we were given a particularly heavy flying task with about 60+ serials to fly that day. We went into work early to 'Before Flight' all the aircraft. One particular airman was foolishly preparing three aircraft at the same time, and left the tyre pressure gauge in the cockpit. When the pilot took off and went into loop as part of his detailed aerobatic exercise, the tyre gauge hit the pilot on the eyebrow and temporarily knocked him out. He needed seven stitches, and the airman disappeared off the unit. Whose fault was it really – the airman's – or the system's?

British Aerospace Hawk

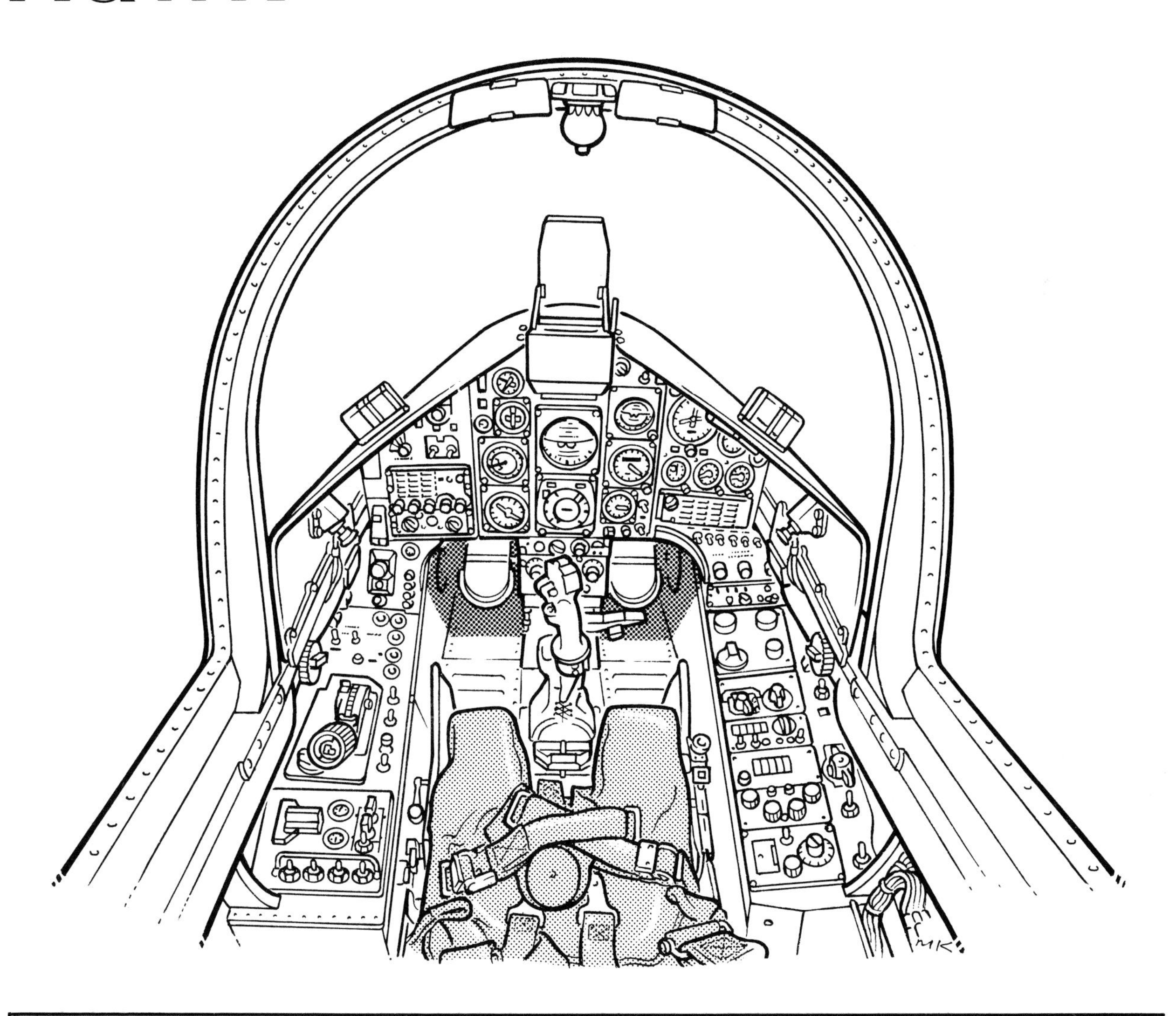

Specification

Power plant:	*One 5,340 lb Rolls-Royce/Turbomeca Adour Mk151.*
Dimensions:	*Span 30 ft 9¾ in, length 36 ft 7¾ in, height 13 ft 5 in, wing area 180 sq ft.*
Weights:	*Empty 7,450 lb, loaded 16,260 lb.*
Performance:	*Maximum speed 647 mph, initial climb 6 min 20 sec to 30,000 ft, range 1,500 miles, endurance 3 hrs, service ceiling 50,000 ft.*

The Hawk started life as another of the many private venture concepts from the Kingston stables. By 1968, Hawker-Siddeley saw a market for a cheap tandem-seat basic trainer, to replace such types as the Vampire, Jet Provost, MB.326 and T-33. The type designation HS.1182 was allotted, and a number of designs were considered. Meanwhile the Central Flying School had been having similar thoughts, and had put forward proposals for a Jet Provost replacement, around which Air Staff Target AST.397 had been formulated.

This Target adopted new terminology for RAF training aircraft, the terms primary and basic being superseded by basic and advanced respectively. The design was to be for an advanced day and night trainer, suitable for instruction in formation flying, high- and low-level navigational exercises, and weapon training. Several options were built into the Target. Flying controls could be either powered or manual, the wings might be either straight or slightly swept, and there could be either one or two turbojets or turbofans. Seating could be either tandem or side-by-side, but for the former the forward view from the pupil's seat had to be 15 degrees below datum, whilst that from the rear seat had to be 5 degrees. Zero-zero ejection seats and an airstream director detector (ADD) were specified, but there was no specific armament provision. It would also be the first British fixed-wing aircraft to adopt the metric (ISO) measurement system.

The Target in the meantime became Air Staff Requirement ASR.397, and the EEC team at Warton submitted their P.59 design. In addition there was Australian interest from the Commonwealth Aircraft Corporation, but in October 1971 the HS.1182 design was awarded the contract. The variant selected for development was known as the HS.1182AJ, the 'A' indicating an Adour engine, and the 'J' that it was submitted in July (1971).

Orders were placed for one prototype and 175 production machines, the first five of the latter being earmarked for initial use as development machines before being refurbished for RAF service. The prototype XX154 made its maiden flight on 21 August 1974, powered by a 5,350 lb thrust Rolls-Royce/ Turbomeca Adour Mk 151, just in time for it to appear at that year's Farnborough Show. By that time it had been named the Hawk T.1, thus abandoning the long tradition of scholastic names for RAF trainers. The flight was premature, in that full instrumentation was not fitted, but this would have delayed its appearance until after the show, leaving this field clear for the French-German Alpha Jet.

It demonstrated an excellent rate of climb, good manoevrability and an outstanding endurance for its class. It was capable of exceeding Mach 1.0 in a dive and, after some modification, developed superb spin characteristics. There were, however, a number of

British Aerospace Hawk T.1 XX280 of the Tactical Weapons Unit, at Yeovilton in July 1982, fitted with the centreline 30 mm Aden Cannon and a Matra 155 rocket pod on the starboard wing.

(Author)

shortcomings in its handling characteristics, including slow aileron and flap operation. To overcome the difficulties, a number of modifications were made to the wing, after trying various alternatives. To give a good natural stall warning, two breaker strips were fitted to the leading edges of each wing, other additions being an outboard fence and a series of vortex generators.

By the end of its flight trials the British Aerospace Hawk, as it became in April 1977 with the merger of its parent company, easily met the requirements of ASR.397. Due to the effects in 1974 on British industry of a 'three-day week' imposed during a fuel crisis, production began about six months later than scheduled, but thereafter proceeded at a steady pace, the first machine (XX156) making its maiden flight on 22 April 1975. Initial deliveries of 25 machines to 4 FTS at Valley began in November 1976, though it was not until two years later that the last of their Gnats departed, except for those flown by the Red Arrows, which were not replaced by Hawks until 1980. Next to receive the type was the Tactical Weapons Unit at Brawdy from January 1978. Poor weather conditions in South Wales soon led to this unit being divided, the Hunter element being detached on 31 August 1978 to Lossiemouth on the Moray Firth as 2 TWU, the parent unit then becoming 1 TWU. Deliveries of Hawks to Chivenor

British Aerospace Hawk T.1 XX168 of No 4 Flying Training School from Valley at Yeovilton in August 1985. The wing fence, which is very evident in this shot, was fitted to production Hawks to reduce wing drop rate at the stall.

(Author)

commenced on 1 August 1980, this being by then the new home of 2 TWU. Losses were few, but no replacement orders have been placed, despite post-Falklands optimism that this might be the case.

Painted in the new red and white (or 'raspberry ripple') colour scheme, the Hawk made an immediate favourable impression. It had an impressive rate of acceleration on take-off, and an excellent turn rate, particularly in low-level flight. The engine was so economical that pupils tended to overlook their fuel gauges, but bad weather became much less of a problem as most UK stations could be reached in the event of a sudden worsening. Servicing was much simpler, and accessibility considerably improved, compared with the Hunter and the Gnat.

The contract for the first 175 machines was a fixed price one, and a number of items of equipment were omitted to keep the cost down. There were, for

British Aerospace Hawk T.1 XX345 'Y' of No 2 Tactical Weapons Unit at Chivenor in July 1986.
(MAP photo)

instance, no stop watches, no directional gyro in the rear cockpit, no standby UHF radio and no standby compass. The compass system, although suitable for low performance aircraft, was inadequate for high performance aircraft using large angles of bank. The brakes had originally only two plates, though these have since been replaced by three plate brakes offering a higher performance. Although there have been various modifications to minor parts of the system, the aircraft have remained basically unchanged since they were first delivered. A number of machines have, however, been fitted with Sidewinder air-to-air missiles for second line UK defence, and in this form it is redesignated the Hawk T.1A.

The aircraft has attracted a number of export orders, being fitted out to whatever standard the customer requires. These are considerably more expensive, though, than those of the original RAF fixed-price contract, and an aircraft incorporating all the latest modifications could possibly cost in the region of £3,000,000.

Flight Lieutenant Rod King has had considerable experience as a Hawk instructor:

I began instructing on the Hawk in August 1979, having previously been a Gnat and a Jet Provost instructor. Since that time I have flown some 2,500 hours on the aircraft in tne advanced flying training role. At present I am Flight Commander on Standards Squadron, 4 FTS, which is still at Valley. Thus I am still flying and instructing on the Hawk.

My first impressions of the aircraft were that the systems were very simple, and therefore this led to uncomplicated emergency procedures – somewhat in contrast to the Gnat. The aircraft has a lively response, and requires sensitive handling. The wing of the Hawk is very cleverly designed and able to produce a lot of lift at a relatively low speed, and this contributes greatly to the aircraft's manoeuvrability. This wing also has straight-wing behaviour at the stall and at low speed, and this enables one to fly the aircraft relatively easily in the circuit.

From the QFIs point of view, the outlook from the back seat is exceptional; indeed, it is almost possible to forget that there is a student in the front seat. This applies whether in the circuit, at low level, or during tail chases. The cockpits are virtually identical with respect to the main controls, and thus there are no problems in monitoring students' checks or changing from one cockpit to another between sorties.

The aircraft has impressive fuel economy. It is possible to fly a whole hour's sortie and still have diversion fuel for an airfield some 200 miles away – typically Leuchars, up in Scotland, is used as a weather diversion from Valley.

The other advantage after the Gnat is the high crosswind limit, and when one considers that the average wind speed on Anglesey is some 15 knots throughout the year, and that 'Gale Force 8 in the Irish Sea' means Valley, this is a significant contribution to the ability to operate the aircraft.

From the point of view of the student and the syllabus, the simple systems and straightforward handling permit the student to go solo two sorties earlier than he did in the Gnat, and there is less emphasis on aspects of pure Hawk flying. This enables the instructor to graduate and control the pressure on students, rather than the aircraft itself generating an unbalanced amount of pressure early on in the course. This control of the pressure enables the development of airmanship and operating a fast jet to be effectively controlled by the instructor, never overloading the student, but always keeping him at full stretch throughout the course.

The syllabus is now only 76 hours, which compares very favourably with the Gnat, and yet it is now possible to include tactical, formation and more navigation sorties which range much further, and thus Hawks operating from Valley can be seen in Scotland, East Anglia or the South West of England.'

Mark Hanna gives a pupil's viewpoint of the Valley course:

When the Hawk first came in, about a year before I went through flying training, a lot of people said it's not like a Gnat, it's like a Jet Provost 'Mk 6'. Personally, when I flew it, I could not believe the performance improvement over a Jet Provost, and I thought, God, there's no way I'm going to be able to handle this. On my first trip, which was just a familiarisation ride sitting in the back seat, I distinctly remember seeing the rate of climb indicator go beyond the top stop, so I guess it was going up at about 6,000 feet per minute. This was certainly not very much compared to Phantoms and other operational aircraft, but at the time it was dramatic. The aeroplane climbs like a lift, in that the attitude appears quite flat, the nose isn't up in the heavens, but the ground is just falling away from you.

As a student, not having flown Gnats, I found the controls terribly sensitive and light, though maybe Gnat people would say the Gnat is lighter. It is a very lovely handling aeroplane, and as far as I can remember completely viceless, which is probably why people refer to it as a Jet Provost 'Mk6'. It's not like a Gnat – if you make a screw-up round a finals turn in a Gnat, you will, perhaps, kill yourself; the Hawk has basically a straight wing, which is much safer.

British Aerospace Hawk T.1 XX235 of No 4 Flying Training School at Valley.

(British Aerospace)

The difficulty with the Valley course, which is the advance flying training course, is not that the aeroplane is difficult to fly, but rather that the work load you are under is extremely high. For the first time you are flying an aeroplane at operational type speeds, in low-level navexes, transiting at 420 knots, which is 7 miles a minute, and having to worry about attacking targets on time. Also, it is not just low level, it is high level into low level, back into high level, and all the timings are critical. All along the routes the instructors are throwing wobblies, like, 'Break right, there's a bandit coming at . . .' Of course there isn't, but you have to go for it and pretend to defeat this imaginary bandit. By which time you are a minute or two behind track, so you then have to do a mental calculation and stick the speed up to 460 knots or so in order to make the time on target. I remember the workload being phenomenally high – I know other people did better than I did, but I found it a really high workload, and compared to Jet Provosts a real advance.

Having said that, when I got on to the single-seater Hunter, it was a quantum jump ahead of the Hawk, in that it was the first time you were flying a real warplane, with four 30-mm cannon and green-grey camouflage, and it really does go like hell compared with the Hawk. One thing about the Hawk, having flown it more recently, out of training, its air speed is limited. Whereas in a Hunter you could do 600 knots, for example, at low level, the Hawk is all getting pretty bumpy, and it's generally not a nice flying aeroplane at very high speeds (I think 550 knots); it bounces around a lot. We didn't make a habit of flying at that sort of speed, the fastest we would fly being generally about 500 knots. To somebody who had just done 150 hours on Jet Provosts, however, the Hawk is a fantastic aeroplane.

I think they have lowered the g-limits now, but the Hawk was the first aeroplane I had ever flown where, at the time, you were allowed to pull either 7½ or 8 g, and that was considered OK. You returned from aerobatic sorties with all the blood vessels in your arms and legs broken, rather like a prickly heat rash. Lots of people get it – you get it in F-15s and F-16s and other high performance aircraft, but there aren't many RAF aeroplanes that you can do it in; just the Hawk really. You would go off and do what we call sustained max-rate turns. At low level in a Hawk you could easily sustain 6 or 7 g, and you came back completely exhausted. Then about an hour later you would see this rash on the insides of your arms. I remember that fairly distinctly because I had never seen it before. It always amused me because the doctor would say it was all right and didn't do you any harm, but I often wondered.

The other thing I particularly remember about flying the Hawk at Valley was being totally tired, because you would fly maybe two trips a day – a very high mental workload, also physical with all this g, and I felt completely creased the whole time. I also remember feeling that I was nearly failing the course at each of the successive hurdles, but overcoming them each time by just a hairsbreadth and carrying on.

I had a lot of confidence in the aeroplane, I didn't ever think the engine was going to pack up or anything like that. We didn't like the windscreen, though, because it was not the armoured type, and therefore very susceptible to bird strikes. It's the only RAF aeroplane I've ever flown with my visor down the whole time, which is the recommended technique for all RAF flying, but in aircraft such as Phantoms and Hunter with an armoured windscreen, there's no way a bird is going to come through. I feel that even wearing clear visors cuts down vision, but in a Hawk, even solo where there was no instructor watching, I would have the visor down because there have been several incidents where birds have hit Hawk windscreens and gone straight through. I always felt that was a bit of a weak point on the Hawk and maybe they should have stuck an armoured windscreen on it, and accepted the fact that you would have a couple of extra struts.

One thing I distinctly remember about the Hawk was its appalling compass system. If you used more than about 30 or 40 degrees of bank doing low levels, and went over a ridge and overbanked to keep the altitude, the compass would totally desynchronise. This was terrible, because at a turning point you obviously need to use 45 to 60 degrees bank to get the turn coming round fairly swiftly in a fighter, but then it would desynch, with the result that you would roll out not really sure what heading you were on. So you then had to go through the performance of resynching it, which isn't generally difficult, just flick a little switch, but sometimes it

wouldn't resynch straight away, so there you would go firing off 10, 20, maybe 30 degrees of error, shall we say. It increased the workload dramatically. They do have a better compass system in it now, but this was in the late seventies.'

John Norris had experience as a rigger on the Hawk with 2 TWU at Brawdy:

The Hawk began to arrive at Brawdy in 1978. The initial deliveries had gone to 4 FTS at Valley. In preparation for their arrival, a few people of various aircraft trades had undergone the manufacturer's course at Kingston. They were drawn from the strength of Station Maintenance Flight and were Hunter experienced. As Hawk numbers increased, the few people trained on type were augmented as others came from the Kingston course, a few at a time. Evidently the output of Hawks was greater than anticipated, as they kept arriving regularly, exceeding the turnover of Hawk-trained personnel. Our fleet of Hunters remained at its original number, flying about the same hours, and requiring the same scheduled servicing and occasional rectification of snags, so the butter of manpower was thinly spread. Some compromises had to be made, which is how I came to gain my working experience on the Hawk.

There was no possibility of me having the manufacturer's course, being in my last year of service. My small minor (and minor star) team had just turned out a Hunter 6A well within the allotted time, and for our efforts we were allotted a 'Hawk acceptance check'. One Hawk-trained rigger was loaned to us for advice and assistance, but unfortunately his help was worth no more than the garbled advice we got from him. Using the Volume One and other APs, the acceptance check took longer than normal. A short while later however, yet another acceptance check fell to us and this was completed in an acceptable time. Other tasks concerning the Hawk fell to me, as more arrived, such as the embodiment of modifications like the fitting of fixed/foldaway stopwatches to the cockpit port side coamings, and modifications to the toe brake pedals.

I found the Hawk to be well designed for servicing, with easy access to most components. The cabin pressurisation and conditioning system was built into the upper fuselage and easily removable as a 'palletised' pack. Wonderful! The components of the flying control system were accessible and relatively easy to set up. The undercarriage appeared sturdy with levered (trailing link) legs like the Meteor, making for good 'arrival' absorption. Everything was so clean and new, delving within dark holes did not result in one getting covered with grease and grime. And yet I had misgivings. What I was looking at did not appear nearly as tough as the Hunter. I had, and still have, doubts that the Hawk will survive twenty-five years of the sort of use the Hunter had to contend with.

The worst enemies of the access panels are the line armourers. They remove them then toss them over their shoulders. They then stand on them, push heavy trollies over them and finally pound them back into place using brute force and obscenely large screwdrivers (which also serve as hammers, levers, throwing knives, drain clearers and as spoons to stir tea). Naturally these mutilated panels will not fit back into place due to their dog-eared and crumpled shape and mangled fasteners. Whereupon a rigger is summoned to effect a secure panel fit. There never being any spares available at such times, much galloping to and from workbench stores and the line office to sign up is the rigger's lot. The sortie gets delayed, tempers flare, and guess who gets the blame . . .?

The Hawk's designers must have known a thing or two about armourers, because they banished the Aden gun from within the airframe and hung it beneath the fuselage a few inches above the ground. I envisaged a new breed of dwarf armourers beating the bejasus out of this appendage, using a new and shortened version of their ubiquitous screwdriver, and was only fearful that they might set about the undercarriage on their way in.

'Another Hawk oddity was its metrication. New tool kits had to be made up. Gone were BSF, UNF and Rolls-Royce's own! Spanners, sockets *et al* bore the inscription MM. Very odd! But the engine had parts with A/F threads for variety.

Along with the Hawk came a new multi-purpose servicing trolley. One powerplant provided AC and DC electrics of varying potential: hydraulic power at 3,000 psi and compressed air at any poundage one required. This wondrous device replaced the PE (petrol/electric generating) set, the hydraulic rig (a cranky and noisy brute) and the compressor Type 'L'. Marvellous – except it didn't bloody work! After a few minutes of admittedly quiet working, the volts would fade, or an ominous pool of DM15 (hydraulic oil) would spread from beneath it. Even the Hawker-trained experts couldn't get one to run successfully for more than a few minutes. Ground equipment specialists spent many hours tinkering and probing without success. A man from the makers was sent in to spend a few unhappy days poring over the reluctant beast, before slinking away totally demoralised, ostensibly to summon up reinforcements. When I left Brawdy some months later, these new and shiny 'wonder machines' were still parked, idle and useless in the corner of a hangar.

It came as something of a surprise that the Hawk had a gaseous oxygen system, when I would have expected a LOX pack, which would have been lighter. It would also have been more compact and given better endurance. Maybe there remained a stockpile of new and unused oxygen bottles and trolleys at some MU which had to be used up. Our old line equipment was decidedly workworn and weary, having endured years of adverse weather and hard use at Chivenor before being carted to Brawdy, yet nothing new appeared on the line when the Hawks arrived, except for the large 'portable rostrums' which were the Hawk's cockpit access steps.

Nevil Gardner tells of one rather hairy incident:

The MDC (Miniature Detonating Cord) of one Hawk had been stuck to the canopy with what may not have been the right type of glue. Whilst flying in a sunny climate, the cord came adrift and draped itself around the pilot's shoulders. Considering its normal purpose, which was to blow off the canopy in an emergency, this must have given him much food for thought on the way home!

Aerospatiale /Westland Gazelle

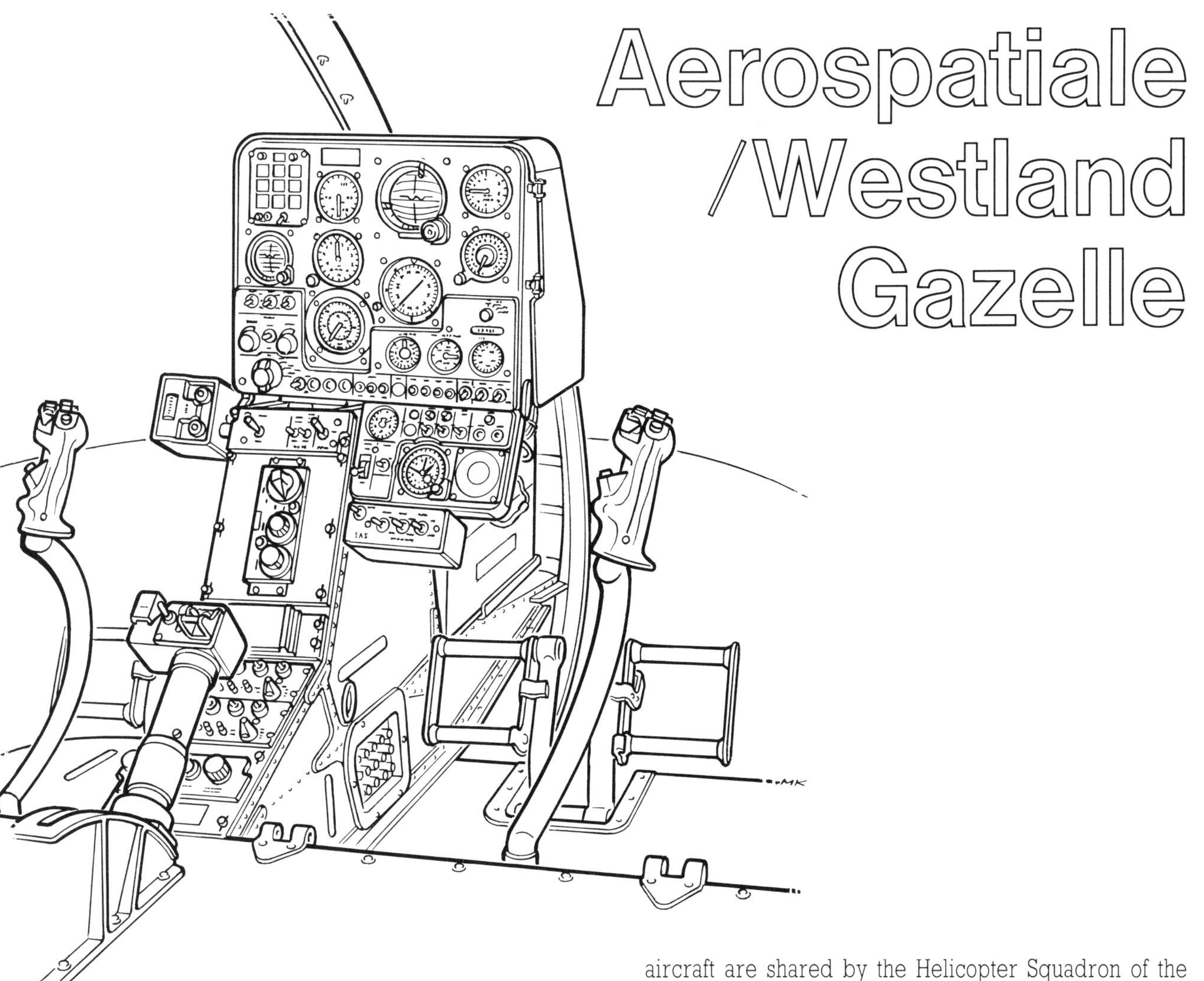

The Gazelle is currently the standard training helicopter for all three of the main armed services. It is operated at RAF Shawbury by No 1 Squadron of No 2 Flying Training School, whose aircraft are shared by the Helicopter Squadron of the Central Flying School. The Fleet Air Arm's No 705 Squadron, otherwise known as the Helicopter Training Squadron, flies the type at RN Air Station Culdrose, as does the Advanced Rotary-Wing Squadron of the Army Air Corps Centre at Middle Wallop.

Before looking more closely at the Gazelle, it is

Specification (HT.3)

Power plant: *One 590 shp Turbomeca Astazou IIIA.*

Dimensions: *Rotor diameter 34 ft 5½ in, fuselage length 31 ft 3 in, height 10 ft 2½ in.*

Weights: *Empty 2,022 lb, loaded 3,970 lb.*

Performance: *Never exceed speed 192.5 mph, maximum cruising speed 164 mph at sea level, economical cruising speed 144 mph at sea level, maximum rate of climb at sea level 1770 ft/min, range 416 miles, service ceiling 16,400 ft.*

useful to look at the background to British military helicopter training. Unlike the Fleet Air Arm, which formed the first all-helicopter squadron in this country, specifically for training purposes, as far back as 1947, the RAF was comparatively slow to adopt its own training programme for helicopters. In the late 1940s and early 1950s RAF pilots were trained either in a civilian flying school by Air Service Training, or by the helicopter manufacturers, then Bristols and Westlands. Some were also trained by the Fleet Air Arm.

It was not until 1954 that the Central Flying School at Little Rissington began to receive helicopters, these being Westland Dragonfly HC.4s, the first modern British-built helicopter to have served operationally with the Royal Air Force, in Malaya from 1950 onwards. They were followed into service in the training role by examples of the Bristol Sycamore, Westland Whirlwind and, briefly, the Saro Skeeter. None of these types was a 'dedicated' training helicopter, being merely adaptations of operational machines.

It was not until the mid-1960s that a special mark of helicopter was built for the CFS, by then based at Ternhill. This was the Westland Sioux T.2, and an order was placed for 15 of these machines. Prior to this the CFS had employed a small number of borrowed Army Air Corps Sioux AH.1s for training purposes. The Sioux, basically the Bell Model 47G built under licence by Westlands (and by Agusta), was used primarily by the Army Air Corps for air observation post duties. The type was also suitable for training, however, although the basic training of Army pilots at this stage was done by a special version of the Sioux (also built by Westlands), bearing civilian registrations and operated for the Corps by Bristow Helicopters Ltd under contract.

For a number of years, the training of RAF helicopter pilots was carried out on the Sioux HT.2 in tandem with the turbine-engined version of the Westland Whirlwind, the HAR.10. By the late 1960s, however, plans were under way to replace the Sioux in general Army service, and eventually to replace it in the RAF training programme, together with the Whirlwind. Similarly the Fleet Air Arm was looking to replace its own obsolescent training helicopters, by then the American Hiller HT.2 and Whirlwind HAS.7, and gradually all these factors became intertwined.

The Army Air Corps wished to replace its Sioux from 1969 onwards, and its thinking was much influenced by the contemporary American 'LOH' programme. This Light Observation Helicopter contest had involved three designs, the Bell Jet Ranger, the Hiller FH100 and the Hughes 500, the contract being won by the latter. Based on the LOH concept, an operational requirement (OR.3336) for a Sioux replacement was drafted by the Land/Air Warfare Directorate.

Sud Aviation was very interested in further UK sales, and accordingly designed a helicopter (the X-300, later the SA 340) for this requirement, even

Facing page, top:
RH Gazelle HT.2 XW861 '563/CU' of No 705 Squadron at Culdrose showing the fenestron tail.
(RNAS Culdrose)

Facing page, bottom:
RN Gazelle HT.2 XW886 '548/CW' of No 705 Squadron at Culdrose flying over Goonhilly Down.
(RNAS Culdrose)

Below:
An Army Gazelle AH.1 visiting RAF Wyton around 1982.
(Paddy Porter collection)

though at that time there was no similar proposal for a light helicopter for the French services. Although the OR was specifically for an Army training helicopter, there was from the outset an interest in a variant of the SA 340 for use as a trainer by the Fleet Air Arm and Royal Air Force. It was by no means a foregone conclusion at this stage that Sud Aviation would get the order, as Hughes were also taking a keen interest with a view to promoting their UH-6/Model 500 in Europe, and for some time competed for this order, with Westlands evaluating the type for possible UK production.

Political considerations had now begun to enter the scene, however. Proposals for various joint aviation projects between Britain and France, of which the Concorde was another, led to the respective governments signing a memorandum of understanding on 22 February 1967. This covered the joint development of three helicopters, the Sud Aviation SA 330 Puma, the SA 340 Gazelle and the Westland WG.13 Lynx. From that time onwards the Gazelle was the undisputed choice, both as an Army observation/liaison helicopter and, equally importantly, as a basic training helicopter for all the three major British services, as well as for the Royal Marines.

This is not to say that there were not many problems, both political and technical, while development commenced and the two manufacturers concerned began to implement the joint programmes. At the outset, the potential purchases for Britain and

France were in the ratio of 600 to 100, and there was strong opposition from Britain to both a French airframe and engine – in this case the Turbomeca Astazou IIN, later IIIA. The British would have preferred the Bristol-Siddeley BS360 (later Rolls-Royce Gem) in derated form.

Perennial arguments also surfaced over size/ weight and, of course, costs. The latter were estimated to have increased from £40,000 per unit to £90,000 per unit by 1969. The dimensions and weights were very soon much greater than those originally envisaged, and certainly in excess of the LOH concept which had generated the project.

Economic problems generally also caused misgivings, and by 1969 the Army Air Corps order was scaled down from 600 to 300. Even so, financial considerations continued to create tension between the two governments, and a revised cost-sharing agreement was reached in May 1970. From that time onwards, the programme moved forward without too many problems, either technical or political.

The prototype Gazelle first flew at Marignane on 7 April 1967, with the civil registration F-WOFH. When the second prototype, F-ZWRA, flew in May 1968 it incorporated the distinctive 'fenestron', which was to become the Gazelle's main recognition feature. Given the name because of its window-like appearance, this inset tail rotor installation was designed so as to achieve a smooth airflow, and as a protection for the relatively vulnerable conventional blades. Other recognition features on the Gazelle are its extensively glazed cockpit and a fixed skid undercarriage.

The prototypes were followed by four pre-production models (F-ZWRH/L/I/K), and the third of these was allocated to Westlands for UK development work, the serial XW276 being applied following delivery to Yeovil on 6 August 1969. After modification and fitting out to British Army standards it flew again on 28 April 1970, and was utilised for manufacturers' development trials at Yeovil and at the Aircraft and Armament Experimental Establishment at Boscombe Down. Although the main development work was, naturally, carried out in France, with feedback to this country, XW276 played a valuable part in eliminating the usual teething problems.

The relative size of the British and French orders for the Gazelle, by now designated the SA 341 – 300 against 100 around this time – meant that the major share of production came to Westlands and amounted initially to 65 per cent of the airframe. Production was begun at their main works at Yeovil, but switched in 1977 to their factory at Old Mixon, Weston-super-Mare, so as to leave Yeovil clear for Lynx production. The British components for the first production Gazelle (F-WIEP c/n 1001) were delivered to France in late 1971, and it made its first flight early the following year.

By this time the first British machine (XW842 c/n 1002) had arrived in France. Initial engine runs brought to light serious vibration/ground resonance problems, and these were traced to the larger cabin doors fitted on production aircraft. Shipped to Marignane in December 1971, XW842 was flown for the first time on 28 January 1972, being then retained in France for further tests and development work.

These trials continued with subsequent aircraft (XW843/4/5/6/8). The Army's Gazelles were designated AH.1, the Royal Navy designation was HT.2 and the RAF had HT.3 machines. XW847 was the first Army aircraft to be delivered to an Intensive Flying Trials Unit at Middle Wallop, arriving at the end of April 1973. It was joined there by XW849, XW850 and XW851. XW845 had been the first HT.2 for the Navy, and XW852 was the first RAF HT.3, being delivered to the Central Flying School at Ternhill on 16 July 1973. Uniquely, there were no separate serial batches for the individual service machines, all three versions being intermixed on the production line. This was, and remains, an exceptional feature, and serves to emphasise the very small technical differences between the respective marks.

When the Gazelle was introduced at CFS in 1973, trainees would complete 145 hours fixed wing flying on Jet Provosts before going on to Gazelles for 90 hours helicopter training.

By the time Westlands ceased production in February 1984, they had produced 294 machines, of which 282 were delivered to the various British services. However, production of major Gazelle components continued at Westlands for some time for continuing Aerospatiale deliveries.

Squadron Leader Barrie Simmonds, now commanding a Wessex squadron in Hong Kong, recalls:

I was a staff instructor with the Central Flying School (Helicopters), where I taught new instructors their skills. Latterly in my time in UK I was the Deputy Chief Flying Instructor (DCFI) when my job also encompassed *ab initio* training. Perhaps, however, my most significant memories of the Gazelle's handling came from my two seasons as the RAF's Gazelle display pilot!

The Gazelle was a delightful aircraft to fly: light and responsive with well-harmonized controls. Indeed, this could be a problem for advanced training, as an able student could not be excessively 'loaded' because of the Gazelle's simple systems and precise handling – hence the need for the Wessex! From the instructor's point of view, the Gazelle was very pleasant to fly and precise to handle; engine-off landings (with practise!) were simple and bestowed considerable confidence on a student when he was shown them. Experienced rotary pilots initially found the hover a little tricky because the Gazelle used to 'sit on its ground cushion' rather delicately, and a 5 ft hover, which intensified the effect, was quite wobbly until one got used to it. To ameleriorate this problem, the RAF introduced the Stability Augmentation System (SAS) – a limited authority autopilot in

Top:
RAF Gazelle HT.2 XZ933 'T' of No 2 Flying Training School at Shawbury practising a confined-space landing.
(I.L. Forshaw)

Centre:
RAF Gazelle HT.3 XW858 of the Central Flying School at Shawbury.
(Author's collection)

Bottom
RAF Gazelle HT.3s of No 2 Flying Training School at Shawbury around 1984.
(Paddy Porter collection)

pitch, roll and, below 48 knots, yaw. A very characteristic effect on RAF Gazelles was the distinct kick as one passed 48 knots increasing and the yaw channel of the SAS disengaged.

All, however, was not totally benign in terms of handling (is it ever with any aircraft?). Display flying soon approached the limits of the flight envelope and two aspects stand out in my memory. The first was jack stall as it was known; if the aircraft load on the blades exceeded the hydraulic power then the controls locked! The aircraft pitched up and rolled right uncontrollably until blade pitch angle was reduced. An interesting way to start a display pull-up if a little too spirited! The second, a rather complex aerodynamic phenomenon, was known as Vortex Ring (or stall) of the Fenestron (tail rotor). This, by conservation of angular motion, led to a further increase in yaw rate. This divergent situation could obviously lead to disaster and prevention was very much in order rather than cure!

Nevertheless, with proper handling and observance of the rules, the Gazelle is a very safe aeroplane, as its record shows.

A groundcrew viewpoint is given by Sergeant Mick Fowen, who joined the RAF in September 1967 as an A/Tech/P (Aircraft Technician Propulsion), and worked on Gazelles at Shawbury from March 1981 to December 1983.

It was a smashing aircraft from my point of view as an engine fitter, working in the Base Engineering Flight which was very similar to an Aircraft Servicing Flight. In the engine bay we did services up to and including majors on both the Gazelle and Wessex helicopters. We had four Gazelles in at any one time, taking up half of the hangar, with normally a Sergeant Rigger in charge of each aircraft and a Chief Tech. Rigger in charge of the whole servicing. I was then a corporal, and I used to enjoy working on the Gazelles far more than the Wessexes because to me they were a lot easier to work on. The Astazou engine was perfectly positioned for me, being at just the right height for me to be able to stand there, take the covers off and there it was right in front of my face.

Regarding routine work, we used to do primary star servicings and upwards. For an engine fitter on the Gazelles this would involve a few minor tasks, such as oil filter

changes and checking the throttle conduits. Also LP (Low Pressure) filter replacement, which was perhaps the one job which everyone used to hate, as you inevitably got an armpit full of Avtur. The LP fuel filter was situated in the tail section of the aircraft, reached through a little gauze manhole cover underneath. It would have been all right to work on if one were about three foot tall and very thin, but for me it was a case of getting down on bended knees, twisting up through the hole, and trying to get two hands in, one with the torch, and one to do the filter itself. One little ruse that we used to try was to put a big polythene bag over the whole lot, undo the clip and the clamp, and then let it drain out – but it never worked! That was the one awkward job we had on the Gazelle.

I suppose the most time-consuming job engine-wise could be setting up the throttle. This was a teleflex control which went from the centre of the cockpit above the pilot's head, through the teleflex control system, then wriggled its way alongside the engine. Quite often the teleflex ends would wear, so we would have to replace the whole lot. It was then a case of getting the old one out, measuring it alongside the new one, cutting the new one off, trimming it down, then trying to set it up again. Whereas you could do a major servicing in about four hours, a throttle would sometimes take a day to a day and a half just to get it inch perfect. The tolerances were fairly critical. You had to have the right bounce at either end, and the right bounce to me wouldn't be right for somebody else. It was a time-consuming job, but when it went together first time it was a bonus.

The aircraft themselves and the engines in particular were very reliable, and gave us very little trouble. We used to give them regular compressor washes, for which we had a little rig. We would soak the water mix, strap the seam round the engine intakes, start up the rig, flick a little lever over and then about a pint and a half of this soapy mixture would go down and blow bubbles all over the pan.

The Astazou was a particularly noisy engine, so there was a hearing conservation programme for people working amongst them. We were only allowed about ten minutes in any one hour inside the circle, which is basically the diameter of the blades plus a little bit more. We were only allowed so many ten minute sessions in one day, and so many hours per week total. We always wore the double ear protection, both the internal and the outer, and we had to sign a book for however long we were inside the circle with the engines running. The Astazou was a really high revving engine; it idled at 24,450 rpm, and I think maximum rpm was 43,000. This was tremendous when you had worked on piston engines doing 2,750 rpm, like the Griffon engines in the Shackleton.

Power supply was a 24-volt battery at the front, rather similar to a car battery. There was one little Dzus panel at the front, a couple of connections, then out would come the battery. During servicing, when the batteries were taken out for charging up, we used to replace them with a big lead weight, otherwise the Gazelle could drop on its tail.

Fuel on the Gazelles was the normal Avtur, the filler cap being on the right-hand side, just behind the cockpit and the cabin. The open line method of refuelling was used, and I think it took about 370 gallons.

The colour scheme was white and training dayglo red, which suited the Gazelle very well. I remember the aircrew saying one day when they flew both the Wessex and the Gazelle, the old Wessex was like a taxi cab and the Gazelle was like a sports car. They used to love flying them.

Once, during an exercise, we had to disperse from one side of the airfield to the other. We had taken off and were hovering about 10–15 feet above the deck, the pilot radioed Air Traffic Control and they gave permission to go low and fast across the airfield. He did, too – stick forward and away we went at about 80 knots, ten feet off the deck. The pilot loved it, and so did I!

We used to have a couple of guys who were passed out as flight test observers. They would go up with the unit test pilots after the major servicings, and take notes. They got flying pay for that, but it was limited to only about three on the camp, and unfortunately I couldn't get in on it.

When we used to operate out of Germany, we took our own kit with us. This included a set of ground-handling wheels to fit to the back of the skids on the Gazelles. We had to fit these wheels into some holes located there, and they worked on a sort of cantilever effect. You would stick them in, pull a jacking handle backwards and that raised the skids about three inches off the deck. At cease flying, we parked the Gazelles in a variety of locations, including aircraft hardened shelters (HASs), MT yards or wherever dictated by the local controller.

One of the other things we used to have out there was like a big fur coat. During the winter, when it was very cold and there were frost problems, we fitted this gigantic zip-up fur coat to the Gazelles, covering the whole front of the aircraft and up round by the blades. These covers apparently cost thousands of pounds, but they were really well made – the sort of thing you would like a coat made out of!

We had some good flights over there. At the end of the detachment they would sometimes give us a few flights. I managed to get on one flight myself. The pilot went up to about 1,000 feet, then said "OK there's your direction, there's your height, have a flight round", and I flew it for about a quarter of an hour. It was really great fun, as it was the first time I had actually flown a helicopter myself. I didn't make a bad job of it, and I'd love to do some more.

There wasn't any special ground equipment, apart from the compressor spray rings. The wheels we used to take with us, covers and locks, they were all basically standard stuff. We used a trolley-acc for starting, or you could use the internal battery if you didn't have one available. There were no special tools that I can remember, mostly standard metric stuff. We were all composite trained, so when we went on detachment we used to cover the airframes, electrics and, of course, the engines. We used to go abroad with a Sergeant and a couple of blokes, which would suffice to see us through, because the Gazelles were so reliable it was hardly worth taking anybody, but we were always glad to go.

British Aerospace Jetstream

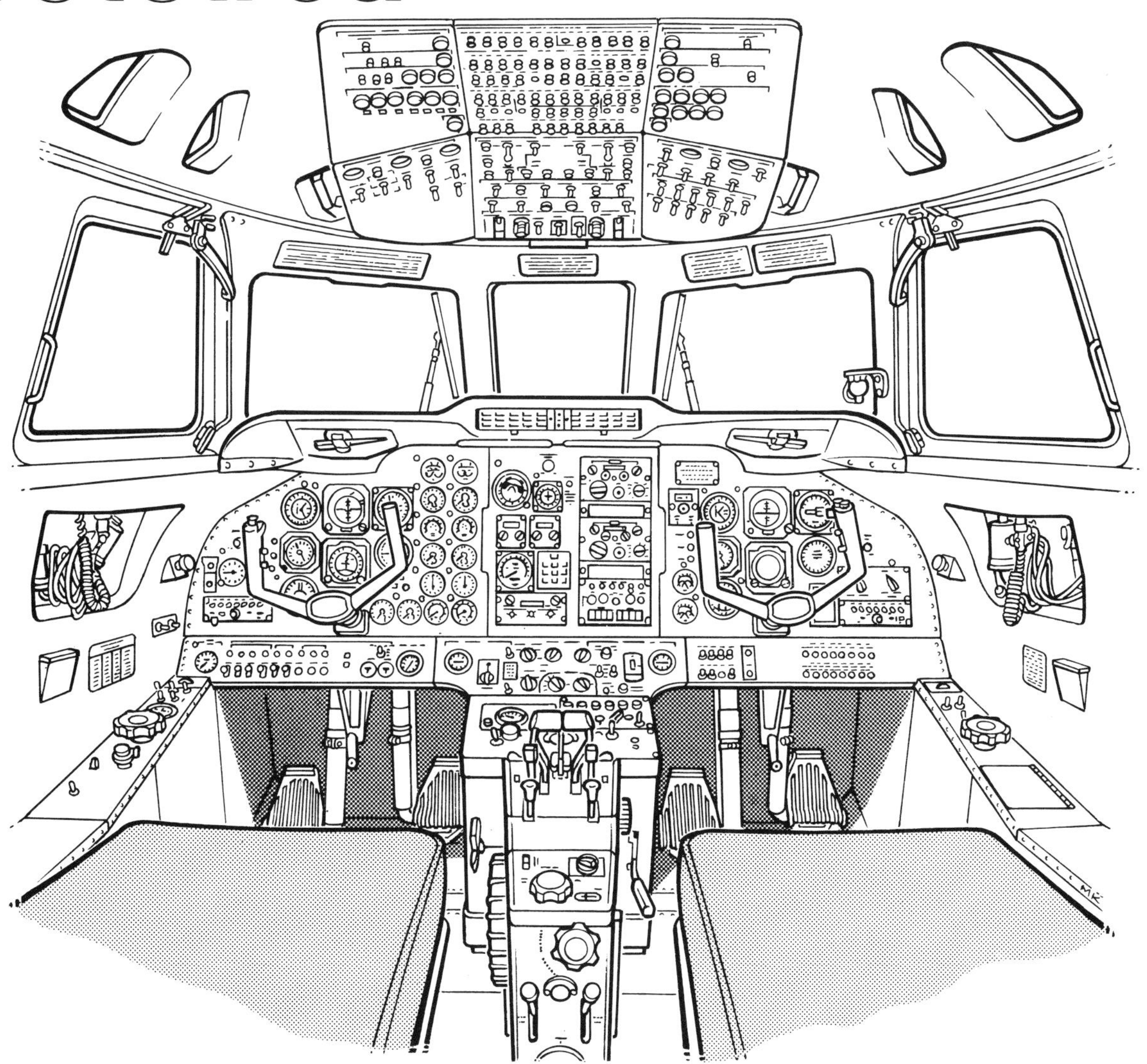

Specification (T. Mark 1)

Power plant:	*Two 940 shp Turbomeca Astazou MkXVI.*
Dimensions:	*Span 52 ft 0 in, length 47 ft 1½ in, height 17 ft 5½ in, wing area 270 sq ft.*
Weights:	*Empty 8,741 lb, loaded 12,550 lb.*
Performance:	*Maximum speed 285 mph at 12,000 ft, cruising speed 278 mph, initial climb 2,500 ft/min, range 1,382 miles, service ceiling 26,000 ft.*

The Jetstream was originally designed by Handley Page, as a means of staying in business after the Government of the day withdrew its support because they had refused to join either of the enforced consortiums which eventually combined to form British Aerospace. The firm had been largely dependent on military orders, culminating in the Victor bomber, and they found themselves in great difficulties filling the gap. They attempted to keep afloat by undertaking civil aircraft work, and some non-aviation engineering, but eventually failed and went into receivership.

The Jetstream was the final hope for their survival as aircraft manufacturers. Its origin can be traced back to an American-inspired proposal to modernise the de Havilland Dove by replacing its Gipsy Queen engines with two small turboprops. It soon became apparent that a major redesign would be required to make it into a high speed jet-engined executive aircraft. Initial studies by Handley Page led to the conclusion that the difficulties in achieving the requirements, including pressurisation, were such that it would be preferable to undertake a totally new design.

Given the company designation HP.137, development costs were estimated to be of the order of three million pounds, of which the Ministry provided half, on the agreement that this would eventually have to be refunded from sales profits. The first of four prototypes (G-ATXH) made its first flight at Radlett on 18 August 1967 powered by two Turbomeca Astazou XIV engines. The fifth machine (G-AWBR) flew on 21 November 1968 with Garrett TPE331 engines.

The concept was not altogether unsuccessful, and production was under way even before the first machine had flown. A number of orders were received, including eleven Garratt-engined machines for the United States Air Force, but things were not going too well. The firm had little experience of building small aircraft, and was learning lessons in this field the hard way. As a consequence the Jetstream not only slipped behind schedule, but was becoming overweight. Added to which its appearance coincided with an unexpected international fuel crisis, which completely upset the economics of operating such an aircraft, causing potential customers to postpone orders. This in turn sapped the confidence of the money markets and, despite having a potential winner on their hands, Handley Page went into liquidation.

RAF Jetstream T.1 XX498 'F' of No 6 Flying Training School at Finningley around 1984.
(Paddy Porter collection)

By this stage, 38 machines had been delivered, and

Above:
RAF Jetstream T.1 XX495 'C' of No 6 Flying Training School at Finningley around 1984 showing well the characteristically neat cowling of the Astazou XVI engine.

(Paddy Porter collection)

Below:
RN Jetstream T.2 ZE111 '574/CU', a late delivery machine for No 750 Squadron at Culdrose fitted with nose-mounted radar.

(RNAS Culdrose)

RAF Jetstream T.2 XX500 'H' of No 6 Flying Training School at Finningley around 1984.

(Marion Hamilton)

components were available for a further ten. These were taken over by a firm known as Jetstream Ltd, which in turn was bought in 1972 by Scottish Aviation Ltd on the understanding that an RAF order would be forthcoming. Despite the fact that the latter firm, like Handley Page, were outside the two consortia, they were allowed by the Government to undertake military work, and orders were placed for the Jetstream, and the Bulldog primary trainer which they had taken over from the liquidated Beagle company. No doubt the fact that it was a Scottish-based company was a factor in this decision.

The Procurement Executive of the Ministry of Defence had in fact been seeking a replacement for the now elderly Varsity, and they wasted no time in taking advantage of this new situation. On 27 June 1972, Specification number 283 D&P was issued for the development and production of the Series 200 variant of the Jetstream to meet Air Staff Requirement number ASR.398 for a badly-needed twin-engined crew trainer. An order was placed for 26 aircraft, the first being XX475, a conversion of AWVJ, built as a civil machine, as were several early machines in the order. This service version, the Jetstream Series 201, was designated the Jetstream T.1, and XX475 first flew as such at Prestwick on 13 April 1973.

The military version was fitted with the more powerful Astazou XVI engines, which improved performance, and met the RAF's needs for higher operating weights. XX475 was flown to the Central Flying School on 26 July 1973, to be followed by several others of its type. Then on 12 December 1973 XX479 was delivered to No 5 Flying Training School at Oakington as the first Varsity-replacement.

The intention was that pilots, after completing 145 hours training on Jet Provosts, would undertake an 80-hour multi-engine course on the Jetstream. Once again, however, politics entered the picture. A Defence Review resulted in a considerable reduction in RAF pilot requirements for multi-engine turboprop aircraft. 5 FTS disbanded on the last day of 1974, and its

Jetstreams went into storage at St Athan, as did those of the CFS towards the end of the following year. In January 1976, however, XX496 was sent to 750 Squadron, the Fleet Air Arm's Observer Training Squadron at Culdrose, for evaluation as a possible replacement for the Sea Prince, which they had by then been flying for 23 years.

The RAF were also still interested in the type, however, and on 25 November 1976, XX497 went to Leeming as the first of eight (later 11) T.1s for the Multi-Engine Training Squadron (METS) attached to 3 FTS, until being transferred in 1979 to Finningley where its allegiance was changed to 6 FTS. The Navy, in the meantime, had decided on the Jetstream for Culdrose, subject to certain modifications, and 14 aircraft were given a special refit to bring them up to T.2 standard, the first being delivered to 750 Squadron in October 1978. Two more T.2s were later delivered, then in 1986 the squadron received four new T.3s, these having their radar in a bulge under the centre section instead of in the nose.

At Finningley, although technically part of 6 FTS, METS largely operates quite separately from the parent unit. After having completed a basic training course on Jet Provosts, pupils undertake the 20-week Advanced Training course, which includes 45 hours simulated flying on the ground, and 47 hours practical flying in the Jetstream, including four night sorties. Training flights are made to such places as Cranwell, Waddington and Topcliffe. Re-training courses are also given to pilots withdrawn from helicopter or jet fighter training, whether for medical or unsuitability reasons, these being known as MEXO (Multi Engine Cross-Over).

Commander Neville Featherstone was heavily involved with the introduction of the Jetstream into naval service in replacement for the Sea Prince:

I was CO of 750 Squadron from 26 October 1976 to 13 July 1979, rather longer than is usual, so that I could see the Jetstream into service.

I was frankly appalled by the Sea Prince when I took over – and continued to be so. It was a harsh contrast to my previous job of flying the VIP HS 125's at Northolt. But in any case by the mid-seventies, or even the mid-sixties, the Sea Prince had become an aeronautical anachronism.

It was therefore a great pleasure and challenge to take on the task of introducing the Jetstream into naval service. Unlike the major operational aircraft types, we did not indulge in the luxury of an IFTU (Intensive Flying Trials Unit), of which I had had previous experience with the Phantom. The transition was very much an in-house process between the Squadron and the Observer School at Culdrose, DNAW in London and Scottish Aviation (later to become part of British Aerospace) at Prestwick.

I cannot remember the exact date on which the RN acquired the Jetstream from the RAF, but I think that financially it was a satisfactory arrangement for which DNAW, in particular the Project Officer Lt Cdr Ian Neale and his boss Cdr Dusty Miller, deserve credit. The aircraft has proved, I think, to be a satisfactory flying classroom. There will always be arguments about whether helicopter observers should train in a fixed-wing aircraft which can operate up to 25,000 feet and at more than double helicopter speeds. The principal argument in favour of fixed wing aircraft is their comparatively low operating costs. From the pilot's point of view, the Jetstream was a great step forward in terms of performance and modern equipment, including a complete airways-type avionics fit.

Reverting to personal reminiscences, I see from my log book that I spent October 1977 at RAF Leeming converting onto the RAFs Jetstream T.Mk1 with the METS (Multi-engine Training Squadron). This armed me with the necessary knowledge and experience of the aircraft to get things going.

The ten or so ex-RAF aircraft were taken out of storage and returned to Prestwick for refurbishing and modification to the Observer training role. Our major task was the design and installation of a Radar/Navigation console, two of which would fit comfortably in the spacious cabin. Lt Cdr Mike Boumphrey, the Chief Instructor at the Observer School, and I, spent considerable time on this design and in specifying the instruments and navaids with which it should be fitted. TANS was one of the better navaids that we stipulated, especially as it is fitted in the Lynx and ASW Sea King helicopters. The radar, however, was less of a success since it did not really equate to the Sea King's radar either in display or performance. Outwardly the bulbous radome was an aesthetic disaster which quite spoiled the lines of an attractive aircraft!

A year after my Leeming conversion I spent a few days at Prestwick flying the T.Mk2, the naval version, under the supervision of Captain Houston, Chief Test Pilot (I suspect the only TP) for Scottish Aviation.

26 October 1978 was the big day when the first aircraft was handed over to the Navy. There was an impressive unveiling ceremony in the hangar at Prestwick, Vice Admiral Sir Desmond Cassidi, the then Flag Officer Naval Air Command, being principal guest. After the ceremony I then flew XX481 down to Culdrose with the Admiral on the jump seat. Mike Boumphrey demonstrated all the goodies in the back to other VIPs, and Lt Cdr Ned Stone was co-pilot. Although it was early evening when we arrived, we did a couple of passes across the airfield to show off the shiny new toy. Unfortunately my landing was less than perfect and I uttered a considerable expletive; the Admiral remained poker-faced.

Meanwhile pilot and staff observer training was already well under way. We set ourselves the task of keeping the student pipeline churning through at maximum capability on the Sea Prince, although many aircrew were undergoing Jetstream conversion at Leeming. The maintainers, too, in the shape of Airwork Ltd and Chief Engineer David Rollo, took it all in their stride. With the exception of one small reduction in one student course, we fully met the task.

My logbook tells me that the last student training sortie in the Sea Prince was on 1 May 1979, but before that the students had already started on the Jetstream. Not surprisingly, they found the new aircraft a quantum jump in all directions, and the navigation equipment was clearly overwhelming. Indeed some navaids were not made available to them until the final stages of their course. The

RN Jetstream T.3 ZE438 '576', fitted with 940 shp Garrett TPE 331-10UF engines, soon after delivery to No 750 Squadron at Culdrose in May 1986.

(RNAS Culdrose)

aircraft was infinitely more comfortable than the whale-like interior of the Sea Prince. Goon suits, bonedomes and parachutes had given way to shirtsleeves, lightweight headsets and coffee at one's elbow.

Later in May 1979 we took six Jetstreams down to Gibraltar via Porto, returning via Hyères. The following month we proved the route to Berlin for a long weekend. The morale of the students perked up noticeably with these foreign jollies, even if they had little clue on the intricacies of airways flying. These and similar trips are now well-established features of the Basic Observer Course.

Finally the aircraft itself: probably the most significant thing the pilot had to get used to was the Astazou XVI turbo-prop engine driving a fairly large reverse-prop. The engine was basically that which powers the Gazelle helicopter, but the Jetstream version is encumbered with all sorts of electrically operated safeguards, microswitches, interlocks etc. The result was a complex engine to handle; when it went, it went very well indeed, like the proverbial sewing machine, but speeded up to something like 55,000 RPM. If it malfunctioned it could prove difficult to troubleshoot! In testing the various safety devices on the ground, prior to take-off, it was embarrassingly easy to shut an engine down by mistake!

On landing, too, the throttles had to be closed with a fine sense of timing – too early and the blades went to flight fine pitch, the aircraft ceased moving forward and moved abruptly downwards onto the tarmac. But once on the runway, selection of reverse pitch was always a good pilot-pleaser as the aircraft juddered to a halt in an incredibly short distance.

Finally it is worth mentioning that, apart from a cadre of experienced fixed-wing pilots, the bulk of the squadron pilots came straight from helicopters (via a short Sea Devon course) to the Jetstream. They coped admirably and it was always a pleasure when the best amongst them used this back-door entrance to the fixed wing world in order to graduate to the Sea Harrier.

Shorts Tucano

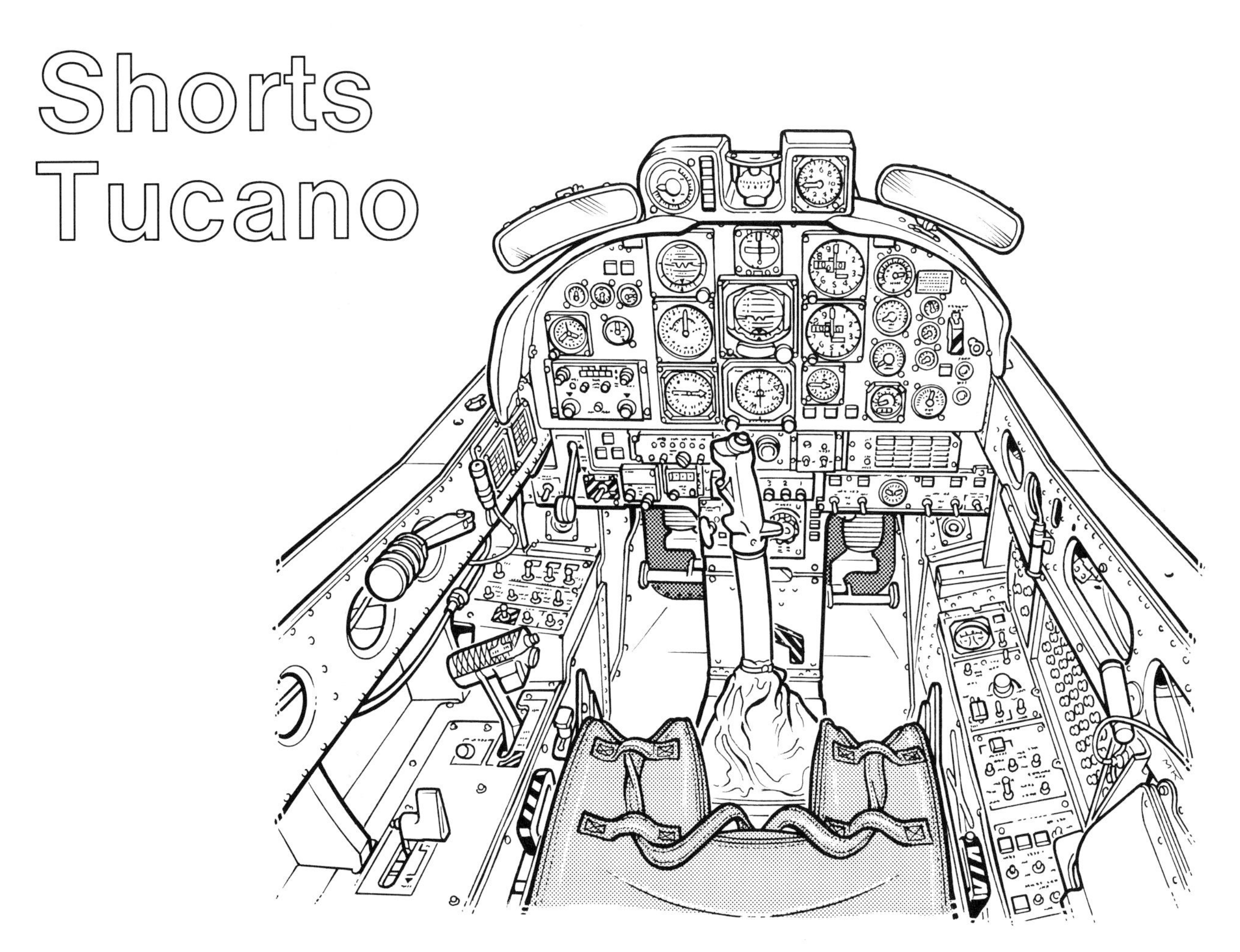

In March 1985, after much political dispute and lobbying, the British Government placed an order for an anglicised version of the Brazilian Embraer EMB-312 Tucano, as a replacement for the now ageing Jet Provost. The British version, of which 130 are being built, is fitted with an American 1,100 shp Garrett TPE331-12B turboprop, built under licence by Rolls-Royce.

The official requirement, Air Staff Target number AST.412, had been for an inexpensive high-performance turbo-prop trainer. Changing from pure jets to turbo-props was seen as the best means of reducing the rapidly escalating cost of turning a recruit into an operational pilot, already around £2.5m. It was also decided to revert from the long fashionable side-by-side seating to tandem seating, the view being taken that a student would more quickly develop the necessary skills and attitudes required for fast operational aircraft – and his instructor would find out sooner whether he was unlikely to do so.

Specification

Power plant:	*One 1.100-shp Garrett TPE331-12B.*
Dimensions:	*Span 37 ft 0 in, length 32 ft 4 in, height 11 ft 2 in, wing area 208 sq ft.*
Weights:	*Empty 4,447 lb, fully loaded 5,842 lb.*
Performance:	*Maximum speed 280 TAS at 15,000 ft, cruising speed 252 mph, initial climb 5,100 ft/min, range 1,200 miles, endurance 3.5 hrs, service ceiling 35,000 ft.*

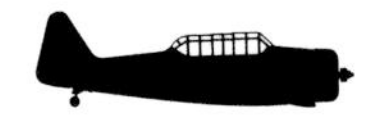

By October 1984 four main contenders had been short-listed. The Ministry of Defence fairly quickly narrowed the options down to two, eliminating the Hunting Turbo Firecracker and the Australian Aircraft Consortium/Westland A.20 Wamira designs. It then called for best-and-final tenders from the remaining two firms, British Aerospace and Shorts, both of whose designs centred round existing foreign-built trainers, the former being based on the Swiss Pilatus PC-9, and the latter on the Tucano.

Shorts claimed that the Tucano would be the most economical of the two in operation, especially if judged over the whole life-cycle, and their final offer had the attraction of a total overall saving of £60 million over the initial fiscal allocation for this requirement. This cost-effectiveness was undoubtedly an important aspect of winning the order, an announcement being made by the then Defence Minister, Michael Heseltine, that Shorts had been awarded the contract. The outcome also had the added benefit of creating jobs in a province with unemployment running at around 20 per cent.

Production was to be at Shorts Light Aircraft Company subsidiary, Shorlac, and would benefit from an agreement with the trade unions which would help overcome possible demarcation difficulties. This was seen as vital, if delays in working on such a small aircraft with only very few access points were to be minimised. The basic airframe would be entirely built in Belfast, and as many components as possible would be of British manufacture. Garretts had similarly agreed to the engines having a significant British content.

The original Tucano was designed from inception around a turboprop powerplant, being fitted with a 750 shp Pratt and Whitney PT-6A-27 engine. It made its first flight in 1980, and in this form production was well in excess of 200 at the time of writing, a further 80 being sold to Egypt in kit form to be assembled for the Egyptian Air Force. The first production Tucanos entered service in 1983, and these soon gained a reputation for reliability and suitability for their training role, as well as proving economic in operation.

Once the outcome of the British requirement had been decided, work commenced in Brazil on a Garrett-engined Tucano, and this made its official maiden flight there on 14 February 1986. It was piloted by Shorts' Chief Test Pilot, Allan Deacon, who was accompanied by Embraer's Gilberto Schittini, a graduate from the Empire Test Pilots School at Boscombe Down. Initial reaction was that the aircraft had felt right, and the engine ran perfectly during the test. None of the good flying characteristics of the basic machine appeared to have been lost, and some had actually been enhanced. It was found to be extremely easy to fly in all flight conditions, with no apparent vices, and by 21 February six hours testing had been completed.

Due to adverse weather conditions, the aircraft was subsequently airfreighted back to Belfast on 29 March, and within ten days had been reassembled by Shorlac at Sydenham, where the order for 130 production machines would be completed, powered by the TPE331-12B. Deacon tested it there on 11 April, and during a flight lasting an hour was able to fly the prototype to its maximum speed of 268 knots ISA at sea level, as required by the specification. The machine was origjnally registered PP-ZTC but now carried the Class B registration G-14-007, based on the Brazilian constructor's number 312007, the Tucano being Embraer Type 312.

To enable production to get under way fairly rapidly, the Embraer parent factory was responsible for component manufacture of the first ten machines, subsequent manufacture being shifted progressively to Belfast. A peak production rate was envisaged of four or five machines per month by the end of the decade, of which about half would be delivered to the RAF, the remainder being intended to meet hoped-for export orders.

It had not originally been intended to fly the prototype at Belfast with a prototype TPE331 engine, but plans were changed. Fitting a production engine enabled the manufacturer's flight testing programme to be accelerated, and by August 1986 this was more than one third complete. It was reported to be crisp in its responses, had a very good aerobatic capability and was easy to fly throughout the flight envelope. It was well suited for ILS approach training, and had excellent spinning characteristics. It was stressed for regular operation up to +6g and −3g.

The excellent handling characteristics of the aircraft were ably demonstrated on the evening of 26 August. Now registered G-BUTC, Deacon took the aircraft up from Sydenham for a test flight, but had to shut down the engine due to a rising oil temperature. With no airfield in the immediate vicinity he glided the aircraft until he was over Mullaghmore airfield, Co. Londonderry, then made a successful dead-stick landing on a strip only 400 yards long. On subsequent inspection, there was found to be no actual damage to the airframe, only some blistering of the paint where the overheated oil had vented. The problem was subsequently pinpointed to the failure of an engine scavenge pump following a period of inverted flying. This was then modified by Garretts, and no further trouble was experienced.

Following an engine change, G-BTUC was flown back to Sydenham on 29 August. It had been hoped that it might make an appearance at the 1986 Farnborough Show, but in the event it was being worked on at that particular time, and could not be spared without consequent delay to the programme.

The first of the initial batch of 11 Shorts-built

Pilatus PC-9, the unsuccessful short-listed contender for the AST.412 requirement.
(British Aerospace)

aircraft, serialled ZF135, made its first flight on 30 December 1986, and no problems were experienced during the 45 minute flight. To meet RAF requirements, the leading edges of the wings and empennages on production machines are strengthened to afford some protection against the inevitable bird strikes. The consequent redesign of the wings, especially the ribs, resulted in there being not a single item in common with the Brazilian machine, despite the general outline being unchanged. The basic structure is of twin spar design, with integral fuel tanks. The wings are joined together, and bolted to the fuselage immediately underneath the cockpit. The cockpit, which is fitted with a new reinforced canopy, has been completely redesigned to be similar to that of the Hawk, to assist transition, having the now-common stepped tandem seating arangement, and being fitted with new instrumentation and a revised avionics suite which includes VHF, UHF and TACAN. It also has Martin-Baker Mk8 LC ejection seats. Both fuselage and empennage have been designed to meet increased stiffness criteria, and the machine is intended to endure 12,000 hours of arduous RAF training.

Low-level speed is substantially below that of the Jet Provost, but the Tucano is more versatile, and in general performance it reaches well into the Hawk/advanced trainer performance envelope. If necessary it can climb rapidly into training airspace above the weather, and the fitting of dive brakes enables it to descend rapidly. Its internal fuel capacity and low fuel consumption enables it to complete two full training sorties, with a diversion allowance of 120 nautical miles and 10 per cent fuel reserve.

One modification introduced by Shorts was to the shape of the wing tips, necessary to meet an RAF requirement that the Tucano be capable of maintaining a 2g turn at 20,000 feet in level flight. Changes were also made to the leading edges of the mainplanes, as in their original form it was found that when landing the pilot experienced no buffet to warn him when he was near the stall. This later modification increased the stalling speed, however, so instead, artificial forms of warning were fitted, the main one being a stick shaker for the flaps/undercarriage down situation.

The basic Embraer design of the Tucano was found by Shorts to be extremely efficient aerodynamically, but the original Pratt and Whitney engine fitted lacked sufficient power to meet the RAF's speed requirements in level flight. 007 was therefore flown back to Brazil by Embraer, via the Azores, in the autumn of 1985, to be fitted with a Garrett TPE331-10 development engine. After only six hours of test flying in Brazil, however, it was decided to return 007 to Belfast, because the high

Shorts Tucano prototype.
(Shorts)

Shorts Tucano T.1 ZF135, the first production machine. (Shorts)

temperatures in Brazil were preventing the engine from delivering full power. The aircraft was therefore dismantled, crated and airlifted back to Belfast by a Heavylift CL-44 on 29 March 1986. It was reassembled in ten days at the Shorlac facility, and test flown on 11 April. Eventually the TPE331-10 engine was replaced by the standard TPE331-12B which has a number of refinements, including an electronic engine control unit. The new engine resulted in additional torque, but this was only significant if a 30 knot crosswind from the right happened to be experienced during full-power run up against the brakes when, initially, there was some tendency for the starboard wing to lift. Providing the propellor with a negative torque system facilitated feathering in the event of an engine failure.

Fitting the Garrett engine produced different spinning characteristics from the original Pratt and Whitney-engined version. Left-handed spins were near to the classic mode, a turn of about 3-4 seconds duration resulting in a loss of around 500 feet in altitude. A spin in the opposite direction was rather more nose down, and therefore slightly quicker. Recoveries were no problem, full opposite rudder being applied and the control stick eased gently off the stop. Inverted spin capabilities were also good.

After completing its manufacturer's trials, ZF135 was flown to Boscombe Down for service assessment and final clearance. The second Short-built machine, ZF136, made its first flight without incident on 10 March 1987, and by the following month the first three production aircraft were all at Boscombe Down. One of these is being flown by a Tucano Course Design Team to devise a new basic syllabus for the type. Further production is initially planned at the rate of 30 completed machines per year, but there is potential to double this if export sales are forthcoming. In addition to the firm RAF order for 130 machines, there is an option for 15 more.

Boscombe Down trials were due to end by mid-September, and Shorts are optimistic that, after all the work they have put into redesigning the aircraft to meet the stiff RAF requirements, no further drastic changes will be necessary. The first service aircraft ought therefore to be delivered shortly afterwards to the Central Flying School at Scampton, where RAF instructors will start to gain experience on the new type. By the summer of 1988 at least 30 production machines should have been delivered, and within five years the Jet Provost will then have been gradually replaced at CFS, 7 FTS Church Fenton, 1 FTS Linton-on-Ouse and the RAF College at Cranwell. All of these stations gained their first real sight of their new mount in mid-July 1987, when '007' spent several days visiting each of them, as well as calling at RAF Wyton for the benefit of nearby Support Command Headquarters as Brampton.

The Shorts' sales organisation is now very busy seeking possible overseas orders, though inevitably this takes time. Interest has been expressed, for instance, by the RNZAF, which needs to replace its Strikemasters by about 1989. Due to the drastic redesigning to meet stiff RAF requirements, Shorts' version of the Tucano is very different from its Embraer parent, and is therefore seen as likely to interest a different class of customer.

Allan Deacon says:

The effect of installing the Garrett engine has proved wholly beneficial. In the words of an experienced RAF instructor "This aircraft is going to put the fun back into training". The torque effect has increased, but directional stability is so good that a slam acceleration can be made at threshold speed on 'Go round' with the feet off the rudders, and only a small amount of aileron is required to keep the wings level in the ensuing side-slip. Power response is linear and the whole unit is exceptionally smooth. It is only during large power increases at speeds below 150 knots that the pilot is conscious of the propellor and torque effects. The stalling characteristics have been described by a CAA test pilot as impeccable.

Unlike many previous RAF trainers, the ailerons remain effective in the conventional sense, with inner wing fully stalled, and even if the stick is held fully back the nose will eventually drop. The spinning characteristics both erect and inverted, are slightly different from the Embraer 312, due possibly to the fixed shaft turbine and four-bladed propellor in the place of the free turbine and three blades, but recovery remains just as immaculate.

One of the virtues of the aircraft apparently is that whilst it is extremely lively with very rapid response to control inputs, it has a very pleasant instrument flying platform. A draft Operating Data Manual has already been submitted to the customer and bettering specification performance requirements are expected.

Appendix 1 Trainer Contract Specifications

Number	Designs
A.2(d)	BAT Baboon
5/24	Float seaplane (not issued)
5A/24	Float seaplane – Blackburn Sprat, Parnall Perch, Bickers Vendace
32/24	Avro 504N
5/25	Avro 504N with Gnome
30/26	Bristol F.2b (dual control)
3/27	Avro 504N update
12/28	Armstrong Whitworth Atlas (dual control)
4/29	De Havilland Gipsy Moth
5/29	Hawker Tomtit
3/30	Avro 621 Tutor
6/30	Avro 504N production
8/31	Armstrong Whitworth Atlas (dual control)
15/31	De Havilland Moth II (not issued, replaced by 23/31)
17/31	Westland Wapiti VI
18/31	Avro Tutor (succeeded by 25/32)
21/31	Fairey IIIF Mk.IIIB(DC)
23/31	De Havilland Tiger Moth I
8/32	Hawker Hart Trainer
12/32	Bristol Bulldog (T)
24/32	Fairey Seal (T)
25/32	Avro 621B Tutor (full production)
26/32	Avro 646 Seatutor
6/33	De Havilland Tiger Moth float seaplane
7/33	Westland Wallace (T)
26/33	De Havilland Tiger Moth II production
13/34	Bristol Bulldog (T)
24/34	Avro 621B Tutor production (Lynx IV)
26/34	Avro 646 Seatutor
32/34	Avro 626 Prefect
7/35	De Havilland Tiger Moth II production
8/35	Hawker Hart (T) production
3/36	Avro Anson (T) (not proceeded with)
6/36	Single seat trainer – DH Don, Miles Kestrel (Private venture). [Other designs – Avro 676, 677]
23/36	Airspeed Oxford
24/36	Miles Mentor
40/36	Miles Magister
T.1/37	*Ab initio* trainer – Heston JA.3, Heston JA.6, Parnell 382. Designs not built – Airspeed AS.36, Fairey, General Aircraft GAL.32, Miles M.15, Percival P.20 (specification not proceeded with)
27/37	Hawker Hind (T)
28/37	De Havilland DH.86B for E&WS
37/37	Miles Magister I production
T.39/37	Airspeed Oxford I production for New Zealand
40/37	Airspeed Oxford I production for RAF
T.4/38	Twin-engined trainer (not proceeded with)
16/38	Miles Master I
29/38	De Havilland DH.89A Dominie I wireless trainer
T.3/39	Twin-engined trainer and communications (not proceeded with)
T.4/39	Airspeed Super Courier
2/40	De Havilland DH.98 Mosquito trainer (not proceeded with)
T.24/40	Airspeed AS.49 fighter trainer (cancelled)
T.9/41	Percival Proctor (improved) (not proceeded with)
13/43BR	Bristol Buckmaster
T.21/43	Fairey Spearfish dual control trainer (cancelled)
T.23/43	Elementary trainer – Percival Prentice. Designs not built – DH.105, Heston JC.1, Miles M.53
T.7/45	Advanced trainer – Avro Athena, Boulton Paul Balliol. Designs not built – Blackburn B.52, Miles M.70
20/46P	Percival Prentice T.1 (Percival production)
21/46P	Percival Prentice T.1 (Blackburn production)
T.24/46	Avro Anson T.XX (overseas navigational trainer)
T.25/46	Avro Anson T.21 (home navigational trainer)
T.26/46	Avro Anson T.22 (radio trainer)
47/46P	Avro Athena T.2 production
T.1/47	Gloster Meteor T.7
T.1/47/2	Gloster Meteor T.8
T.11/47	B.3/45 trainer (replaced by T.2/49)
T.14/47	Avro Athena T.2, Boulton Paul Balliol T.2
T.14/47/3	Boulton Paul Balliol T.2 production
T.8/48	DHC.1 Chipmunk T.10
T.12/48	Westland Wyvern T.3
T.13/48	Vickers Varsity T.1
T.16/48	Single-engined basic trainer – HPR.2, Percival Provost. Designs not built – Air Service Training, Airtech, Auster A.9, Avro, Blackburn & General B.80, Boulton Paul, Chrislea, de Havilland, EEC, Elliotts, Fairey, Folland, General Aircraft, Heston, Miles, Planet, Portsmouth Aviation, Scottish Aviation, Slingsby, Westland
T.17/48	Fairey Primer
T.1/49	Vickers Valetta T.3
T.1/49/2	Vickers Valetta T.4
T.2/49	EEC Canberra T.4
T.3/49	Avro Anson flying classroom (cancelled)
T.17/49	Percival Sea Prince T.1
T.111P	De Havilland Vampire T.11
T.111P2	De Havilland Sea Vampire T.22
T.118P	F.4/48 trainer (cancelled)
T.117D&P	Fairey Gannet T.2
T.121D&P	Percival Pembroke C.1 navigational trainer (not proceeded with)
T.130D&P	Handley Page (Reading) Marathon T.11
T.147T	Advanced jet trainer (not proceeded with)

T.157D&P Hawker Hunter T.7
T.178D&P EEC Lightning T.4
T.185D&P Folland Gnat T.1
T.205D&P EEC Lightning T.5
T.220 Reservation only
T.233D&P HSA Dominie T.1
T.259D&P HSA Harrier T.
265D&P BAC Jet Provost T.5
277D Westland WG.13
281D HSA HS.1182
282D&P SAL Bulldog T.1
283D&P SAL Jetstream T.1
284D&P BAC Jet Provost T.3A
285D&P BAC Jet Provost T.5A
291D&P SAL Jetstream T.2

Appendix 2 Trainer Production since 1919

The following list gives all production batches of British service trainers ordered since the end of the First World War, and the training units with which each type of aircraft served as all or part of its main equipment. The list does not include prototypes or the many conversions, nor does it include overseas production.

Airspeed Oxford
Serials:
L4534 – 4669 (136 a/c); L9635 – 9660, 9680 – 9703 (50 a/c); N1190 – 1194 (5 a/c); N4560 – 4609, 4630 – 4659, 4681 – 4700, 4720 – 4739, 4754 – 4803, 4824 – 4853 (200 a/c); N6250 – 6299, 6320 – 6349, 6365 – 6384, 6400 – 6439 (140 a/c); P1070 – 1094 (25 a/c); P1800 – 1849, 1860 – 1899, 1920 – 1969, 1980 – 2009, 2030 – 2059 (200 a/c); P6795 – 6819, 6831 – 6880 (75 a/c); P8822 – 8868, 8891 – 8931, 8964 – 8998, 9020 – 9046 (150 a/c); R4062 – 4067 (6 a/c); R5938 – 5979, 5991 – 6038, 6050 – 6059, 6070 – 6114, 6129 – 6163, 6177 – 6196 (200 a/c); R6211 – 6248, 6263 – 6299, 6317 – 6458, 6371 – 6403 (150 a/c); R9974 – 9988, T1001 – 1028, 1041 – 1082, 1097 – 1141, 1167 – 1215, 1243 – 1288, 1308 – 1348, 1371 – 1404 (300 a/c); V3145 – 3194, 3208 – 3247, 3267 – 3296, 3310 – 3359, 3375 – 3404, 3418 – 3442, 3456 – 3480, 3501 – 3540, 3555 – 3604, 3623 – 3647, 3665 – 3694, 3719 – 3748, 3768 – 3792, 3813 – 3862 (500 a/c); V3865 –3914, 3933 – 3957, 3972 – 3996, 4016 – 4065, 4079 – 4103, 4124 – 4173, 4192 – 4241, 4259 – 4283 (300 a/c); W6546 – 6995, 6608 – 6657 (100 a/c); X1038 – 1040 (3 a/c); X6520 – 6564, 6589 – 6623, 6643 – 6692, 6726 – 6750, 6764 – 6813, 6835 – 6884, 6932 – 6981, 7031 – 7075, 7107 – 7156, 7176 – 7200, 7231 – 7265, 7278 – 7317 (500 a/c); AB639 – 668, 685 – 729, 749 – 773 (100 a/c); AP387 – 436, 451 – 500 (100 a/c); AP654 – 657 (4 a/c); AR756 – 790, 804 – 853, 870 – 889, 909 – 953, 968 – 982, AS144 – 188, 201 – 230, 254 – 278, 297 – 331, 347 – 396 (350 a/c); AS474 – 523, 537 – 571, 591 – 640, 665 – 709, 726 – 745, 764 – 813, 828 – 877, 893 – 942 (350 a/c); AT439 – 488, 502 – 536, 576 – 625, 641– 685, 723 – 742, 760 – 799 (240 a/c); BF782 – 831, 845 – 889, 904 – 953, 967 – 999, BG100 – 101, 113 – 132, 149 – 183, 196 – 245, 260 – 304, 318 – 337, 349 – 398, 415 – 459, 473 – 522, 541 – 575, 588 – 637, 649 – 668 (600 a/c); BM671 – 720, 737 – 785, 801 – 844, 871 – 877 (150 a/c); DF220 – 264, 276 – 314, 327 – 367, 390 – 433, 445 – 489, 501 – 536 (250 a/c); EB414 – 461, 483 – 518, 535 – 584, 599 – 640, 654 – 677, 689 – 703, 717 – 761, 777 – 826, 838 – 870, 884 – 930, 946 – 975 (420 a/c); EB978 – 999, ED108 – 157, 169 – 204, 215 – 236, 251 – 300 (180 a/c); HM603 – 650, 666 – 700, 721 – 767, 783 – 813, 827 – 875, 889 – 918, 945 – 990, HN111 – 149, 163 – 212 (375 a/c); HN217 – 239, 254 284, 298 – 346, 363 – 386, 405 – 441, 467 – 495, 513 – 554, 576 – 614, 631 – 671, 689 – 738, 754 – 790, 808 – 855 (450 a/c); LB401 – 429, 442 – 462 (50 a/c); LB469 – 492, 513 – 538 (50 a/c); LW727 – 759, 772 – 799, 813 – 835, 848 – 879, 891 – 930, 945 – 973, 985 – 999, LX113 – 152 (240 a/c); LX156 – 199, 213 – 245, 258 – 289, 301 – 333, 347 – 369, 382 – 401, 415 – 448, 462 – 489, 502 – 541, 555 – 582, 595 – 617, 629 – 648, 661 – 699, 713 – 746, 759 – 777 (450 a/c); MP275 – 314, 338 – 376, 391 – 430, 444 – 474 (150 a/c); NJ280 – 322, 345 – 382, 397 – 400 (85 a/c); NM217 – 254, 270 – 314, 329 – 370, 385 – 429, 444 – 488, 509 – 550, 571 – 615, 629 – 676, 681 – 720, 736 – 760, 776 – 810 (450 a/c); PG925 – 956, 968 – 999, PH112 – 157, 169 – 215, 227 – 268, 281 – 327, 339 – 379, 391 – 425, 447 – 489, 502 – 527 (391 a/c); PK248 – 269, 282 – 309 (50 a/c); RR321 – 367, 380 – 382 (50 a/c); VB861 – 869 (9 a/c). Total 8584 a/c.
Main units:
RAF: 2, 3, 6, 11, 12, 14, 15, 18 – 21 (P)AFU. 2, 3, 8, 11, 13, 14, 15, 16, 17
FTS. 2, 3, 4, 5, 6, 7, 8, 12, 14, 15, 16, 17 SFTS.
Central Flying School.
RAF College. 1, 2, 3, 7, 11 FIS.
FAA: 758 Squadron.

Armstrong Whitworth Siskin III(DC)
Serials:
J7549 – 7554 (6 a/c); J9190 – 9236 (47 a/c). Total 53 a/c.
Main units:
3, 5 FTS. RAF College.

Armstrong Whitworth Atlas DC and TM
Serials:
J9435 – 9477 (43 a/c); K1172 – 1197 (26 a/c); K1454 – 1506 (53 a/c); K2514 – 2566 (53 a/c). Total 175 a/c.
Main units:
1, 2, 3, 4, 5 FTS. RAF College.

Auster T.7
Serials:
VX926 – 929, 934 – 936 (7 a/c); WE534 – 572, 587 – 616 (69 a/c). Total 76 a/c.
Main units:
227 OCU. Central Flying School. Light Aircraft School.

Avro 504K
Serials:
J8331 – 8380 (50 a/c).
Main units:
1, 2, 4, 5, 6 FTS. Central Flying School.

Avro 504N
Serials:
J8496 – 8595 (100 a/c); J8676 – 8775 (100 a/c); J8975 – 9024 (50 a/c); J9253 – 9292 (40 a/c); J9415 – 9434 (20 a/c); J9683 – 9707 (25 a/c); K1038 – 1062 (25 a/c); K1242 – 1253

(12 a/c); K1798 - 1823 (26 a/c); K1956 - 1990 (35 a/c); K2346 -- 2423 (78 a/c). Total 511 a/c, excluding conversions from 504K.
Main units:
1, 2, 3, 4, 5 FTS. Central Flying School. RAF College.

Avro 621 Trainer
Serials:
K1230 - 1240 (11 a/c); K1787 - 1796 (10 a/c). Total 21 a/c.
Main units:
3 FTS. Air Pilotage School.

Avro Tutor
Serials:
K2496 - 2513 (18 a/c); K1389 - 3371 (183 a/c); K3380 - 3474 (95 a/c); K4798 - 4837 (40 a/c); K6087 - 6126 (50 a/c); K8168 - 8172 (5 a/c). Total 391 a/c.
Main units:
1, 2, 3, 5, 6 FTS. RAF College. Central Flying School. 2 CFS. 1, 2 FIS.

Avro Anson 1
Serials: (includes some early aircraft not built as trainers)
K6152 - 6325 (174 a/c); K8703 - 8847 (145 a/c); L7046 - 7073 (28 a/c); L7903 - 7932, 7945 - 7977, 7991 - 7994 (67 a/c); L9145 - 9165 (21 a/c); N1330 - 1339 (10 a/c); N4856 - 4899, 4901 - 4948, 4953 - 4989, 4995 - 5044, 5047 - 5094, 5096 - 5125, 5130 - 5178, 5182 - 5220, 5225 - 5274, 5279 - 5318, 5320 - 5359, 5361 - 5385 (500 a/c); N9526 - 9575, 9587 - 9621, 9640 - 9689, 9713 - 9752, 9765 - 9790, 9815 - 9858, 9870 - 9919, 9930 - 9956, 9972 - 9999 (350 a/c); R3303 - 3351, 3368 - 3413, 3429 - 3476, 3512 - 3561, 3581 - 3587 (200 a/c); W1505 - 1524, 1529 - 1540, 1544 - 1570, 1576 - 1618, 1627 - 1676, 1690 - 1736, 1751 - 1800, 1814 - 1863, 1875 - 1924, 1932 - 1971. 1986 - 2025, 2031 - 2072, 2078 - 2099, 2109 - 2158, 2163 - 2212, 2216 - 2245, 2252 - 2291, 2298 - 2347, 2355 - 2398, 2403 - 2452, 2457 - 2496, 2499 - 2548, 2554 - 2592, 2598 - 2646, 2651 - 2665 (1000 a/c); AW443 - 492, 506 - 540, 586 - 635, 653 - 697, 739 - 758, 778 - 812, 833 - 882, 897 - 941, 963 - 982, AX100 - 149, 163 - 187, 218 - 267, 280 - 324, 343 - 372, 396 - 445, 466 - 515, 535 - 584, 607 - 656 (750 a/c); AX748 - 752 (5 a/c); DG689 - 737, 750 - 787, 799 - 844, 857 - 880, 893 - 942, 956 - 987, DJ103 - 149, 162 - 190, 205 - 248, 263 - 298, 314 - 361, 375 - 417, 430 - 478, 492 - 529, 545 - 589, 603 - 639, 656 - 700 (700 a/c); EF805 - 839, 858 - 890, 903 - 941, 952 - 993, EG104 - 148, 165 - 195, 208 - 246, 251 - 280, 293 - 335, 350 - 396, 412 - 447, 460 - 507, 524 - 561, 583 - 616, 629 - 655, 672 - 704 (600 a/c); LS978 - 999, LT112 - 160, 175 - 210, 231 - 258, 271 - 307, 334 - 378, 410 - 459, 472 - 503, 521 - 549, 575 - 610, 641 - 682, 701 - 745, 764 - 797, 823 - 849, 872 - 899, 921 - 961, 978 - 999, LV122 - 167, 199 - 230, 252 - 300, 313 - 332 (750 a/c); MG102 - 147, 160 - 199, 214 - 256, 270 - 314, 327 - 368, 381 - 423, 436 - 478, 490 - 536, 549 - 596, 613 - 656, 669 - 701, 714 - 757, 770 - 813, 826 - 874, 888 - 928, 962 - 999, MH103 - 135, 149 - 196, 210 - 237 (799 a/c); NK139 - 149, 152 - 187, 199 - 244, 260 - 303, 315 - 351, 355, 370 - 406, 419 - 425, 429 - 431, 434 - 437, 440 - 442, 444 - 445, 450 - 462, 475 - 486, 494 - 516, 535 - 568, 581 - 623, 636 - 656, 662 - 663, 669 - 679, 692 - 694, 697 - 698, 701 - 702, 704, 707 - 721, 723 - 724, 726 - 727, 729 - 730, 732 - 733, 735 - 736, 738, 750, 752 - 765, 773 - 774, 776 - 777, 779 - 780, 782 - 783, 785, 788, 792, 806 - 818, 821 - 822, 825 - 826, 829 - 830, 833 - 834, 836 - 837, 839 - 840, 842 - 843, 845 - 846, 848, 861, 863 - 864, 866 - 869, 876 - 906, 910, 922 - 923, 926 - 929, 936 - 939, 941 - 958, 970 - 985, NL117 - 124, 126 - 127, 130 - 131, 134 - 135, 138 - 139, 142 - 143, 146 - 147, 150 - 151, 155, 169, 173 - 174, 177 - 178 (592 a/c). Total 6991 a/c.
Main units:
1, 2, 3, 4, 6, 7, 8, 9, 10 (O)AFU. 1, 2, 3, 4, 7, 8, 9, 10, 11, 12, 13 AGS. 1, 2, 3, 5, 7, 10 ANS. Air Navigation & Bombing School. 1, 2, 3, 4, 5, 6, 8, 9, 10, 11 AONS. 1, 2, 3, 4, 5, 6, 7, 9, 10 AOS. 6, 12 SFTS. 3, 10, 11, 12, 14 RS.

Avro Anson T.20
Serials:
VM410 - 418 (9 a/c); VS491 - 534, 558 - 561 (48 a/c). VS866 - 867 (2 a/c).
Total 59 a/c.
Main units:
3 ANS. 5 FTS.

Avro Anson T.21
Serials:
VS562 - 591 (30 a/c); VV239 - 264, 293 - 333 (67 a/c); VV880 - 919, 950 - 999 (90 a/c); WB446 - 465 (20 a/c); WD402 - 418 (17 a/c); WJ509 - 519, 545 - 561 (28 a/c). Total 252 a/c.
Main units:
1, 2, 3, 5, 6 ANS. 1, 2 BANS. Central Navigation School. Central Navigation and Control School.

Avro Anson T.22
Serials:
VS592 - 603 (12 a/c); VV358 - 370 (13 a/c); WD419 - 422, 433 - 436 (8 a/c).
Total 33 a/c.
Main units:
1 AES. 1, 2 ASS. 4 RS. Empire Radio School. RAF Technical College.

BAC Jet Provost
Serials:
T.3. XM346 - 387, 401 - 428, 451 - 480 (100 a/c); XN137 (1 a/c); XN458 - 466, 469 - 473, 492 - 512, 547 - 559, 573 - 607, 629 - 643 (98 a/c). Total 199 a/c.
T.4. XN467 - 468 (2 a/c); XP547 - 589, 614 - 642, 661 - 688 (100 a/c); XR643 - 681, 697 - 707 (50 a/c); XS175 - 186, 209 - 231 (35 a/c). Total 187 a/c.
T.5. XW287 - 336, 351 - 375, 404 - 438 (110 a/c)
Main units:
1, 2, 3, 6, 7 FTS. Central Flying School. RAF College. College of Air Warfare.

Blackburn Botha I
Serials:
L6104 - 6345 (242 a/c); L6347 - 6546 (200 a/c); W5017 - 5056, 5065 - 5114, 5118 - 5157, 5162 - 5169 (138 a/c). Total 580 a/c.
Main units:
3, 4, 8 AGS. 3 AONS. 2, 4, 10 AOS. 2, 4, 8 B&GS. 3 SGR. 1 (0) AFU. 3, 11 RS.

Boulton Paul Balliol T.2
Serials:
VR590 - 606 (17 a/c); WF989 - 998, WG110 - 159, 173 - 187, 206 - 230 (100 a/c); WN132 - 171 (40 a/c); WN506 - 535 (30 a/c); XF672 - 673 (2 a/c); XF929 - 931 (3 a/c). Total 192 a/c.
Main units:
7 FTS.RAF College. 238 OCU.

Boulton Paul Sea Balliol T.21
Serials:
WL715 - 734 (20 a/c); WP324 - 333 (10 a/c). Total 30 a/c.
Main units:
FAA: 702, 727, 765, 796 Squadrons.

Bristol Bulldog TM
Serials:
K3170 - 3186 (17 a/c); K3923 - 3953 (31 a/c); K4566 - 4576 (11 a/c). Total 59 a/c.
Main units:
3, 5 FTS. Central Flying School. RAF College.

Bristol Beaufort II(T)
Serials:
LS130 - 149 (20 a/c); ML430 - 476, 489 - 524, 540 - 586, 599 - 635, 649 - 692, 705 - 722 (229 a/c). Total 249 a/c.
Main units:
17 SFTS. 132 OTU.

Bristol Brigand T.4
Serials:
WA561 - 569 (9 a/c).
Main units:
228, 238 OCU. A.I. School.

Bristol Buckmaster T.1
Serials:
RP122 – 156, 170 – 215, 228 – 246 (100 a/c); VA359 – 368 (10 a/c). Total 110 a/c.
Main units:
228 OCU. Empire Central Flying School.

De Havilland Moth
Serials:
J8030 – 8032 (3 a/c); J8816 – 8821 (6 a/c); J9103 – 9121 (19 a/c); J9922 – 9932 (11 a/c); K1103 – 1112 (10 a/c); K1198 – 1227 (30 a/c); K1825 – 1907 (83 a/c). Total 162 a/c.
Main units:
5FTS. Central Flying School.

De Havilland Tiger Moth
Serials:
K2567 – 2601 (35 a/c); K4242 – 4291 (50 a/c); L6920 – 6949 (30 a/c); N5444 – 5493 (50 a/c); N6443 – 6490, 6519 – 6556, 6576 – 6625, 6630 – 6674, 6706 – 6755, 6770 – 6812, 6834 – 6882, 6900 – 6949, 6962 – 6988 (400 a/c); N9114 – 9162, 9172 – 9215, 9238 – 9279, 9300 – 9349, 9367 – 9410, 9427 – 9464, 9492 – 9523 (300 a/c); R4748 – 4797, 4810 – 4859, 4875 – 4924, 4940 – 4989, 5005 – 5044, 5057 – 5086, 5100 – 5149, 5170 – 5219, 5236 – 5265 (400 a/c); T5360 – 5384, 5409 – 5433, 5454 – 5503, 5520 – 5564, 5595 – 5639, 5669 – 5718, 5749 – 5788, 5807 – 5856, 5877 – 5921, 5952 – 5986, 6020 – 6049, 6094 – 6138, 6158 – 6202, 6225 – 6274, 6286 – 6320, 6362 – 6406, 6427 – 6471, 6485 – 6534, 6547 – 6596, 6612 – 6656, 6671 – 6720, 6734 – 6778, 6797 – 6831, 6854 – 6878, 6897 – 6921, 6942 – 6991, 7011 – 7055, 7085 – 7129, 7142 – 7191, 7208 – 7247, 7259 – 7308, 7325 – 7369, 7384 – 7418, 7436 – 7485, 7509 – 7553, 7583 – 7627, 7651 – 7700, 7723 – 7757, 7777 – 7821, 7840 – 7884, 7899 – 7948, 7960 – 8009, 8022 – 8066, 8096 – 8145, 8166 – 8210, 8230 – 8264 (2000 a/c); DE131 – 198, 192 – 224, 236 – 284, 297 – 323, 336 – 379, 394 – 432, 445 – 490, 507 – 535, 549 – 589, 603 – 640, 654 – 697, 709 – 747, 764 – 791, 808 – 856, 870 – 904, 919 – 957, 969 – 999, DF111 – 159, 173 – 214 (750 a/c); EM720 – 756, 771 – 819, 835 – 884, 893 – 931, 943 – 989 (222 a/c); NL690 – 735, 748 – 789, 802 – 847, 859 – 898, 903 – 948, 960 – 999, NM112 – 158, 171 – 214 (351 a/c); PG614 – 658, 671 – 716, 728 – 746 (110 a/c). Total 4698 a/c.
Main units:
RAF: 1, 2, 3, 4, 6, 7, 8, 9, 10, 11, 12, 13, 14, 16, 17, 18, 19, 20, 21, 22, 24, 25, 26, 28, 29 EFTS; 1, 2, 3, 6, 7, 10, 11, 12, 13, 14, 16, 17, 18, 19, 20, 21, 22, 24, 31, 32, 33, 34, 35, 38, 42, 43, 46, 47, 48, 50, 56 E & RFTS. 4, 5, 6, 10 FIS. 4 FTS. Central Flying School. RAF College. 1, 2, 3, 4, 5, 6, 7, 8, 9, 10, 11, 12, 13, 14, 15, 16, 17, 18, 19, 22, 23, 24, 25 RFS.
FAA: 727 Squadron.

De Havilland Dominie I
Serials:
R5921 – 5934 (14 a/c); R9545 – 9564 (20 a/c); X7320 – 7354, 7368 – 7417, 7437 – 7456, 7482 – 7525 (149 a/c); HG644 – 674, 689 – 732 (75 a/c); NF847 – 896 (50 a/c); NR669 – 701, 713 – 756, 769 – 815, 828 – 853 (150 a/c); RL936 – 946 (11 a/c). Total 469 a/c.
Main units:
2 E & WS. 2, 4 RS. 1, 2 SS.

De Havilland Don
Serials:
L2387 – 2436 (50 a/c). None used as trainers.

De Havilland Mosquito T.3
Serials:
HJ851 – 899 (49 a/c); HJ958 – 999 (42 a/c); LR516 – 541, 553 – 585 (59 a/c); RR270 – 319 (50 a/c); TV954 – 984; TW101 – 119 (50 a/c); VA871 – 894, 923 – 928 (30 a/c); VP342 – 355 (14 a/c); VR330 – 349 (20 a/c); VT581 – 596, 604 – 631 (44 a/c). Total 358 a/c.
Main units:
RAF: 8, 13, 16, 51, 54, 60, 132 OTU. 1655 Mosquito Training Unit. 204 AFS. 226, 228, 231, 237 OCU. Central Flying School.
FAA: 762, 790 Squadrons.

De Havilland Vampire T.11
Serials:
WZ414 – 430, 446 – 478, 493 – 521, 544 – 593, 607 – 674 (147 a/c); XD375 – 405, 424 – 463, 506 – 554, 588 – 627 (160 a/c); XE816 – 823, 848 – 897, 919 – 961, 975 – 998 (135 a/c); XH264 – 278, 292 – 330, 357 – 368 (66 a/c); XJ771 – 776 (6 a/c); XK582 – 590, 623 – 637 (24 a/c). Total 538 a/c.
Main units:
1, 3, 4, 7, 8, 10 FTS. RAF College. 226, 229, 233 OCU. 202, 206, 208 AFS. Central Air Traffic Control School. Central Flying School. Central Navigation and Control School.

De Havilland Sea Vampire T.22
Serials:
XA100 – 131, 152 – 172 (52 a/c); XG742 – 748, 765 – 777 (20 a/c). Total 72 a/c.
Main units:
FAA: 702, 718, 727, 736, 759 Squadrons.

De Havilland Chipmunk T.10
Serials:
WB549 – 588, 600 – 635, 638 – 662, 665 – 706, 709 – 739, 743 – 768 (200 a/c); WD282 – 310, 318 – 338, 344 – 365, 370 – 397 (100 a/c); WG271 – 289, 299 – 336, 348 – 364, 392 – 432, 457 – 491 (150 a/c); WK506 – 523, 547 – 591, 607 – 643 (100 a/c); WP772 – 811, 828 – 872, 893 – 930, 962 – 988 (150 a/c); WZ845 – 884 (40 a/c). Total 740 a/c.
Main units:
RAF: 1, 2, 3, 4, 5 BFTS. 5 FTS. 1, 2, 3, 5, 6, 8, 9, 10, 11, 12, 14, 15, 17, 18, 19, 22, 23, 24 RFS. RAF College. Central Flying School. University Air Squadrons. Air Experience Flights. Flying Selection Squadron.
FAA: Britannia Flight.

De Havilland Dominie T.1
Serials:
XS709 – 714, 726 – 739 (20 a/c).
Main units:
1 ANS. 6 FTS.

EEC Canberra T.4
Serials:
WE188 – 195 (8 a/c); WH839 – 850 (12 a/c); WJ857 – 881 (25 a/c); WT475 – 492 (18 a/c); XH583 – 584 (2 a/c); XK647, 650 (2 a/c). Total 67 a/c.
Main unit:
231, 232 OCU.

EEC Lightning T.4/T.5
Serials:
T.4. XM966 – 974, 987 – 997 (20 a/c).
T.5. XS416 – 423, 449 – 460 (20 a/c); XV328 – 329 (2 a/c). Total 22 a/c.
Main units:
Lightning Conversion Unit. Lightning Training Flight. 226 OCU.

Fairey IIIF MkIIIM (DC)
Serials:
S1454 – 1463 (10 a/c).
Main unit:
Seaplane Training Flight.

Fairey IIIF MkIIIB (DC)
Serials:
S1845 – 1851 (7 a/c).
Main units:
RAF Base Leuchars. 1 FTS.

Fairey Battle (T)
Serials:
P6616 – 6645, 6663 – 6692, 6718 – 6737, 6750 – 6769 (100 a/c); R7356 – 7385, 7399 – 7448, 7461 – 7480 (100 a/c); V1201 – 1250, 1265 – 1280 (66 a/c). Total 266 a/c.
Main units: 1, 7, 11, 12, 16 FTS. 4, 7, 8, 10 B&GS. 4, 5, 10 AOS. 3 AGS.

Fairey Firefly T.7
Serials:

WJ154 – 174, 187 – 209 (44 a/c); WK348 – 373 (26 a/c); WM761 – 779, 796 – 809, 811 – 822, 824 – 832, 855, 864 – 879 (71 a/c). Total 141 a/c.
Main units:
FAA: 719, 750, 765, 796 Squadrons.

Fairey Gannet T.2
Serials:
XA508 – 530 (23 a/c); XG869 – 881 (13 a/c).
Main units:
FAA: 719, 737 Squadrons.

Fairey Gannet T.5
Serials:
XG882 – 890 (9 a/c).
Main unit:
FAA: 849 Squadron.

Gloster Grebe (DC)
Serials:
J7519 – 7538 (20 a/c).
Main unit:
Central Flying School.

Gloster Meteor T.7
Serials:
VW410 – 459, 470 – 489 (70 a/c); VZ629 – 649 (21 a/c); WA590 – 639, 649 – 698, 707 – 743 (137 a/c); WF766 – 795, 813 – 862, 875 – 883 (89 a/c); WG935 – 950, 961 – 999, WH112 – 136, 164 – 209, 215 – 248 (160 a/c); WL332 – 381, 397 – 436, 453 – 488 (126 a/c); WN309 – 321 (13 a/c); WS103 – 117, 140 – 141 (17 a/c); XF273 – 279 (7 a/c). Total 640 a/c.
Main units:
RAF: 202, 203, 205 – 211, 215 AFS. 226, 229 OCU. 4, 12, 211 FTS. Central Flying School. Fighter Command Instrument Training School.
FAA: 728, 759 Squadrons.

Gloster Javelin T.3
Serials:
XH390 – 397, 432 – 447 (24 a/c); XK577 (1 a/c); XM336 (1 a/c). Total 26 a/c.
Main units:
228 OCU. Fighter Command Instrument Rating School.

Handley Page Marathon
Serials:
XA249 – 278 (30 a/c).
Main units:
1, 2 ANS.

Hawker Tomtit
Serials:
J9772 – 9782 (11 a/c); K1448 – 1452 (6 a/c); K1779 – 1786 (8 a/c). Total 25 a/c.
Main units:
3 FTS. Central Flying School.

Hawker Hart Trainer
Serials:
K2474 – 2475 (2 a/c); K3146 – 3158 (13 a/c); K3743 – 3763 (21 a/c); K4751 – 4770 (20 a/c); K4886 – 5052 (167 a/c); K5784 – 5897 (114 a/c); K6415 – 6550 (136 a/c). Total 473 a/c.
Main units:
1, 2, 3, 4, 5, 6, 7, 8, 9, 10, 11, 12, 13, 14, 15 FTS. Central Flying School. RAF College.

Hawker Hind Trainer
Serials:
L7224 – 7243 (20 a/c). Plus conversions.
Main units:
1, 5, 6, 10, 11, 12, 14 FTS.

Hawker Sea Fury T.20
Serials:
VX280 – 292, 297 – 310 (27 a/c); VZ345 – 355, 363 – 372 (21 a/c); WE820 – 826 (7 a/c); WG652 – 656 (5 a/c). Total 60 a/c.
Main units:
FAA: 736, 738, 759 Squadrons.

Hawker Hunter T.7
Serials:
XL563 – 579, 583, 586, 587, 591 – 597, 600, 601, 605, 609 – 623 (45 a/c).
Main units:
229 OCU. 1, 1 TWU.

Hawker Hunter T.8
Serials:
XL580 – 582, 584, 585, 598, 599, 602 – 604 (10 a/c).
Main units:
FAA: 738, 759, 764 Squadrons.

Hawker Siddeley Gnat T.1
Serials:
XM691 – 698, 704 – 709 (14 a/c); XP500 – 516, 530 – 542 (30 a/c); XR534 – 545, 567 – 574 (20 a/c); XR948 – 955, 976 – 987, 991 – 999, XS100 – 111 (41 a/c).
Total 105 a/c.
Main units:
4 FTS. Central Flying School.

Hawker Siddeley Harrier T.2/T.4
Serials:
T.2. XW264 – 272 (9 a/c); XW925 – 927 (3 a/c). Total 12 a/c.
T.4. XW933 – 934 (2 a.c); XZ145 – 147 (3 a/c); ZB600 – 606 (7 a/c). Total 12 a/c.
Main unit:
233 OCU.

Hawker Siddeley Hawk T.1
Serials:
XX156 – 205, 217 – 266, 278 – 327, 339 – 363 (175 a/c).
Main units:
4 FTS. 1 TWU.

Hiller HT.1
Serials:
XB474 – 481, 513 – 524 (20 a/c).
Main unit:
FAA: 705 Squadron.

Hiller HT.2
Serials:
XS159 – 172 (14 a/c); XS700 – 706 (7 a/c).
Main unit:
FAA: 705 Squadron.

Hunting Percival Provost
Serials:
WV418 – 448, 470 – 514, 532 – 580, 601 – 648, 660 – 686 (200 a/c); WW381 – 398, 417 – 453 (55 a/c); XE506 (1 a/c); XF540 – 565, 591 – 614 (50 a/c); XF678 – 693 (16 a/c); XF836 – 854, 868 – 914 (66 a/c). Total 388 a/c.
Main units:
1, 2, 3, 6 FTS. Central Flying School. Central Navigation and Control School. RAF College.

Miles Magister I
Serials:
L5912 – 6001 (90 a/c); L6894 – 6913, 6915 – 6916, 6918 – 6919 (24 a/c); L8051 – 8095, 8127 – 8176, 8200 – 8237, 8249 – 8295, 8326 – 8359 (214 a/c); N2259 (1 a/c); N3773 – 3817, 3820 – 3869, 3875 – 3914, 3918 – 3945, 3951 – 3991 (204 a/c); N4557 (1 a/c); N5289 – 5438 (50 a/c); P2150 (1 a/c); P2374 – 2400, 2426 – 2470, 2493 – 2510 (100 a/c); P6343 – 6382, 6396 – 6424, 6436 – 6466 (100 a/c); R1810 – 1859, 1875 – 1924, 1940 – 1984 (145 a/c); T9669 – 9708, 9729 – 9768, 9799 – 9848, 9869 – 9918, 9943 – 9982; V1003 – 1042, 1063 – 1102 (300 a/c). Total 1230 a/c.
Main units:
3, 4, 8, 14, 15, 19, 23, 25, 26, 27, 28, 29, 30, 39, 40, 43, 44, 45 E&RFTS. 5, 8, 15, 16, 21, 24, 29, 30 EFTS. 2, 4, 5, 6, 7, 10 FIS. 16 (P) SFTS. Central Flying School. Empire Central Flying School.

Miles Master
Serials:
Mk.I. N7408 – 7457, 7470 – 7515, 7534 – 7582, 7597 – 7641, 7672 – 7721, 7748 – 7782, 7801 – 7846, 7867 – 7902,

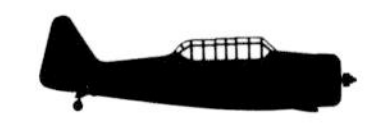

7921 – 7969, 7985 – 8022, 8041 – 8081, 9003 – 9017 (500 a/c), T8268 – 8292, 8317 – 8351, 8364 – 8412, 8429 – 8469, 8482 – 8507, 8538 – 8581, 8600 – 8640, 8656 – 8694, 8736 – 8784, 8815 – 8555, 8876 – 8885 (400 a/c). Total 900 a/c.
Mk.II. T8887 – 8923, 8948 – 8967, 8996 – 9037 (99 a/c); W9004 – 9039, 9050 – 9099 (86 a/c); AZ104 – 143, 156 – 185, 202 – 226, 245 – 289, 306 – 340, 359 – 383, 408 – 457, 470 – 504, 519 – 563, 582 – 621, 638 – 672, 693 – 742, 773 – 817, 832 – 856 (525 a/c); DK798 – 843, 857 – 894, 909 – 957, 963 – 994, DL111 – 155, 169 – 204, 216 – 256, 271 – 309, 324 – 373, 395 – 435, 448 – 493, 510 – 546 (500 a/c); DL794 – 803, 821 – 866, 878 – 909, 935 – 983, DM108 – 140, 155 – 196 (212 a/c); DM200 – 245, 258 – 295, 312 – 361, 374 – 407, 423 – 454 (200 a/c); EM258 – 304, 317 – 355, 371 – 409 (125 a/c). Total 1747 a/c.
MK.III. W8437 – 8486, 8500 – 8539, 8560 – 8599, 8620 – 8669, 8690 – 8739, 8760 – 8799, 8815 – 8864, 8880 – 8909, 8925 – 8974, 8990 – 9003 (414 a/c); DL552 – 585, 599 – 648, 666 – 713, 725 – 753, 767 – 793 (188 a/c). Total 602 a/c.
Main units:
RAF: 5, 7, 9, 17 (P)AFU. 5 FTS. 1, 5, 8, 9, 16 SFTS. 1 – 5 GTS. Central Flying School. 2, 3, 7, 10 FIS.
FAA: 736, 759, 760, 761, 762, 794 Squadrons.

North American Harvard
Serials:
Mk.I. N7000 – 7199 (200 a/c); P5783 – 5982 (200 a/c). Total 400 a/c.
Mk.II. AH185 – 204 (20 a/c); AJ538 – 987 (450 a/c); BD130 – 137 (8 a/c); BJ410, 412 – 415 (5 a/c); BS808 (1 a/c); BW184 – 207 (24 a/c); DG430 – 439, 442 – 444 (13 a/c). Total 521 a/c.
Mk.IIA. EX100 – 846 (747 a/c).
Mk.IIB. FE267 – 999, FH100 – 166 (800 a/c); FS661 – 999, FT100 – 460 (700 a/c); FX198 – 497 (300 a/c); KF100 – 999 (900 a/c). Total 2700 a/c.
Mk.III. EX847 – 999, EZ100 – 258 (312 a/c); EZ259 – 458 (200 a/c); FT955 – 974 (20 a/c); KE305 – 309 (5 a/c). Total 537 a/c.
Main units:
RAF: 1, 2, 3, 4, 5, 6, 7, 9, 10, 12, 14, 15, 16, 17, 19, 20, 21, 22 FTS. 2, 3, 6, 11 FIS. 1, 2, 3, 6, 7, 10, 15, 16, 17, 22 SFTS. 5, 9, 21 (P)AFU. 71, 73 OTU. Central Flying School. RAF College.
FAA: 758, 759, 766, 767, 798, 799 Squadrons.

Percival Proctor (RN)
Serials:
Mk.IA. P5999 – 6037, 6050 – 6079, 6101 – 6113, 6131 – 6145, 6166 – 6167 (99 a/c).
Mk.IIA. X8825 – 8859, 8898 – 8912 (50 a/c); BV535 – 573, 586 – 612, 625 – 658 (100 a/c). Total 100 a/c.
Main units:
FAA: 752, 754, 755, 756, 758 Squadrons.

Percival Proctor (RAF)
Serials:
Mk.II. Z7193 – 7222, 7237 – 7252 (46 a/c); BT278 – 281 (4 a/c). Total 50 a/c.
Mk.III. R7530 – 7539, 7559 – 7573 (25 a/c); DX181 – 201, 215 – 243 (50 a/c); HM279 – 324, 337 – 373, 390 – 433, 451 – 485 (162 a/c); LZ556 – 603, 621 – 663, 672 – 717, 730 – 771, 784 – 804 (200 a/c). Total 437 a/c.
MK.IV. MX450 – 455 (6 a/c); NP156 – 198, 210 – 254, 267 – 309, 323 – 369, 382 – 403 (200 a/c); RM160 – 197, 219 – 230 (50 a/c). Total 256 a/c.
Main units:
1, 2, 4 RS. 1, 2, 4 SS.

Percival Prentice T.1
Serials:
VR189 – 212 (24 a/c); VR218 – 253, 257 – 296, 301 – 324 (100 a/c); VS241 – 290, 316 – 338, 352 – 397, 409 – 414 (125 a/c); VS609 – 654, 681 – 698, 723 – 758 (100 a/c).
Total 349 a/c.
Main units:
1 ASS. 1, 2, 3, 6, 7, 22 FTS. 5, 6, 7, 9, 11, 16, 22, 23, 25 RFS. Central Flying School. RAF College.

Percival Sea Prince T.1
Serials:
WF118 – 134 (17 a/c); WF934, 949 (2 a/c); WM735 – 742 (8 a/c); WP307 – 320 (14 a/c). Total 41 a/c.
Main units:
FAA: 727, 750 Squadrons.

Scottish Aviation/British Aerospace Jetstream
Serials:
XX475 – 500 (26 T.1, of which XX475, 476, 478 – 481, 483 – 490 modified to T.2); ZA110 – 111 (2 T.2); ZE438 – 441 (4 T.3). Total 32 a/c.
Main units:
RAF: 3, 6 FTS.
FAA: 750 Squadron.

Scottish Aviation Bulldog T.1
Serials:
XX513 – 562, 611 – 640, 653 – 672, 685 – 714 (130 a/c).
Main units:
2 FTS. University Air Squadrons. Central Flying School. RN. EFTS.

Shorts Tucano
Serials:
ZF135 – 145 *et seq.* Total 130 a/c.
Main units:
7 FTS first.

Vickers Valetta T.3
Serials:
WG256 – 267 (12 a/c); WJ461 – 487 (27 a/c). Total 39 a/c.
Main units:
1, 2, 6 ANS. 228 OCU. RAF College.

Vickers Varsity T.1
Serials:
WF324 – 335, 369 – 394, 408 – 429 (60 a/c); WJ886 – 921, 937 – 950 (50 a/c); WL621 – 642, 665 – 692 (50 a/c); XD366 (1 a/c). Total 161 a/c.
Main units:
1 AES. 1, 2 ANS. 5, 6, 11 FTS. 201 AFS. Central Flying School. Central Navigation and Control School. RAF College.

Westland Wapiti
Serials:
K2236 – 2247 (12 a/c).
Main units:
501, 502, 503, 504, 601, 602, 605, 607, 608 Squadrons.

Westland-Bell Sioux HT.2
Serials:
XV310 – 324 (15 a/c)
Main units:
RAF: Central Flying School.
AAC: Advanced Rotary Wing Flight.

Westland/Aerospatiale Gazelle HT.2/HT.3
Serials:
XW845, 852 – 864, 866 – 868, 870 – 871, 884, 886 – 887, 890 – 891, 894 – 895, 898, 902, 906 – 907, 910 (21 HT.2, 10 HT.3); XX373, 382, 391, 396 – 397, 406, 410, 415, 431, 436, 441, 446, 451 (9 HT.4, 4 HT.3); XZ930 – 942 (2 HT.2, 11 HT.3); ZA801 – 804 (4 H.T.3). Total 61 a/c.
Main units:
RAF: Central Flying School.
AAC: Advanced Rotary Wing Flight.
FAA: 705 Squadron.

Glossary

AAC	Army Air Corps
AAS	Air Armament School
Ab initio	From the beginning
ADC	Aircraft Disposal Company
ADD	Airstream Direction Detector
AES	Air Electronics School
A/F	After flight servicing (when aircraft not to fly again for a period)
AFS	Advanced Flying School
AGS	Air Gunnery School
AI	Air Interception (airborne radar)
ANS	Air Navigation School
AONS	Air Observer and Navigator School
AOP	Air Observation Post
AOS	Air Observers School
AP	Air Publication
API	Attitude Position Indicator
ASF	Aircraft Servicing Flight
ASP	Aircraft Servicing Pan
ASR	Air Staff Requirement
ASS	Air Signallers School
AST	Air Staff Target
A/T/A	Aircraft Technician Airframe
ATC	Air Training Corps
A/T/P	Aircraft Technician Propulsion
ATS	Armament Training School
BABS	Blind Approach Beacon System
BANS	Basic Air Navigation School
BBMF	Battle of Britain Memorial Flight
BCATP	British Commonwealth Air Training Plan
BE	Bleriot Experimental
B/F	Before flight servicing (carried out on aircraft due to fly)
BFTS	Basic Flying Training School
B&GS	Bombing and Gunnery School
bhp	Brake horse power
BSF	British Standard Fine (screw thread type)
CANS	Civil Air Navigation School
CDT	Coast Defence Training
CFI	Chief Flying Instructor
CFS	Central Flying School
Clutch	Group of RAF stations
CO	Commanding Officer
CU	Conversion Unit
DCFI	Deputy Chief Flying Instructor
Desyn Indicator	Remote indicator driven electrically from master transmitter
DME	Distance Measuring Equipment
DNAW	Directorate of Naval Air Warfare
D&P	Development and Production
EFTS	Elementary Flying Training School
E&RFTS	Elementary and Reserve Flying Training School
Eureka	Ground transmitter used in conjunction with Rebecca for guiding aircraft to target
E&WS	Electrical and Wireless School
FAA	Fleet Air Arm
FIS	Flying Instructors School
FLAPS	Front-line Armament Practice School
FRS	Flying Refresher School
FTS	Flying Training School
GCA	Ground Controlled Approach
Gee	Navigation and target identification radar
George	Automatic pilot
GPI	Ground Position Indicator
GTS	Glider Training School
HF	High Frequency
HMS	His/Her Majesty's Ship
HP	Handling Party
hp	Horse power
HQ	Headquarters
H2S	Target finding radar
IA	Incidental Allowance
i/c	In charge
ICO	Idle cut-off switch
IF	Instrument Flying
IFTU	Intensive Flying Trials Unit
ILS	Instrument Landing System
Intercom	Intercommunications
IRE	Instrument Rating Examiner
IRT	Instrument Rating Test
ISA	International Standard Atmosphere
ISO	International Standards Organisation

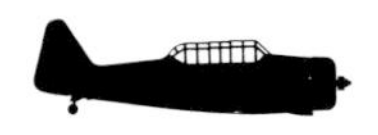

JP	Jet Provost
JPT	Jet Pipe Temperature
Kite	Aircraft
LOH	Light Observation Helicopter
LOX	Liquid Oxygen
LP	Low Pressure
MDAP	Mutual Defence Assistance Programme
MDC	Miniature Detonating Cord
Met	Meteorology
METS	Multi-engine Training Squadron
MEXO	Multi-engine Cross-over
MF	Medium Frequency
mic/tel	Microphone/telephone
MRS	Marine Reconnaissance School
MT	Motor Transport
MU	Maintenance Unit
Navex	Navigation exercise
NCO	Non-commissioned Officer
NM	Nautical Mile
(O) AFU	(Observer) Advanced Flying Unit
OC	Officer Commanding
OCU	Operational Conversion Unit
OR	Operational Requirement
ORP	Operational Readiness Pan
OTU	Operational Training Unit
PA	Personal Assistant
(P) AFU	(Pilot) Advanced Flying Unit
P/E	Petrol electric
PFCU	Powered Flying Control Unit
PIO	Pilot Induced Oscillation
psi	Per square inch (pounds pressure)
PSP	Perforated Steel Plate
QFI	Qualified Flying Instructor
QGH	Radar-controlled descent
RAeC	Royal Aero Club
RAF	Royal Air Force/Royal Aircraft Factory
RAS	Reserve Aeroplane Squadron
RCAF	Royal Canadian Air Force
RCDI	Rate of Climb and Descent Indicator
Rebecca	Aircraft navigation device used in conjunction with Eureka
RFC	Royal Flying Corps
R&I	Repair and Inspection
RN	Royal Navy
RNAS	Royal Naval Air Service
RNR	Royal Naval Reserve
RPM	Revolutions per minute
RS	Reserve Squadron/Radio School
RSF	Radio Servicing Flight
R/T	Radio Telephony
Rx	Receiver
SAN	School of Air Navigation
SAS	Stability Augmentation System
SASO	Senior Air Staff Officer
SBA	Standard Beam Approach
SFTS	Service Flying Training School
SGR	School of General Reconnaissance
shp	Shaft Horse Power
SI	Student Instructor
SLAPS	Second-line Armament Practice School
SMAC	Short Maintenance Air Course
SMF	Station Maintenance Flight
SNCO	Senior Non-commissioned Officer
SS	Signals School
S of TT	School of Technical Training
TACAN	Tactical Aircraft Navigation system
TANS	Tactical Air Navigation System
TAS	True Air Speed
TDS	Training Depot Station
TP	Test Pilot
Trolley-acc	Trolley-accumulator
TWU	Tactical Weapons Unit
Tx	Transmitter
UAS	University Air Squadron
UNF	Unified Fine (screw thread type)
USAAF	United States Air Force
VHF	Very High Frequency
VIP	Very Important Person
VOR	Variable Omni Range
W/T	Wireless Telegraphy

Index

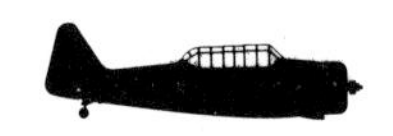